Communications in Computer and Information Science 1358

More information about this series at http://www.springer.com/series/7899

Nirmalya Kar · Ashim Saha ·
Suman Deb (Eds.)

Trends in Computational Intelligence, Security and Internet of Things

Third International Conference, ICCISIoT 2020
Tripura, India, December 29–30, 2020
Proceedings

 Springer

Editors
Nirmalya Kar ⓘ
National Institute of Technology Agartala
Jirania, Tripura, India

Ashim Saha ⓘ
National Institute of Technology Agartala
Jirania, Tripura, India

Suman Deb ⓘ
National Institute of Technology Agartala
Jirania, Tripura, India

ISSN 1865-0929   ISSN 1865-0937   (electronic)
Communications in Computer and Information Science
ISBN 978-3-030-66762-7   ISBN 978-3-030-66763-4   (eBook)
https://doi.org/10.1007/978-3-030-66763-4

This Springer imprint is published by the registered company Springer Nature Switzerland AG
The registered company address is: Gewerbestrasse 11, 6330 Cham, Switzerland

Preface

It is an immense pleasure and a matter of great privilege to present this preface for the proceedings of the Third International Conference on Computational Intelligence, Security & IoT (ICCISIoT 2020), which was organized by the Computer Science & Engineering department of National Institute of Technology Agartala, India during December 29–30, 2020. This distinct technical event covered the major aspects of computational intelligence, Security, and Internet of Things where the scope was not confined only to engineering disciplines such as computer science and electronics engineering but also included researchers from allied communities working in Bioinformatics, Computational Intelligence, Artificial Intelligence and Cognitive Science, Modelling and Simulation etc. This conference series was introduced in order to bring together researchers, academics, scientists and industry around the globe to share thoughts and promote research activities to derive benefits from the advances of next-generation computing technologies in the listed areas. It was our endeavour that the people participating in the conference would find common ground on which they could learn from each other, and that the conference would stimulate imminent scientific activities. Such collaborative ventures are necessary for the development of the cutting-edge solutions embodied within our society and their pragmatic application.

The Program Committee of ICCISIoT 2020 is extremely grateful to the authors, who showed an overwhelming response to the call for papers by submitting over 113 papers in three tracks. The entire review team (Technical Program Committee members along with external experts as reviewers) expended tremendous effort to ensure fairness and consistency in the selection process so that the best-quality papers were selected for presentation and publication. It was ensured that every paper received at least three, and in most cases four, reviews. Checking of similarities and overlaps was also done based on international norms and standards. We are very thankful to our reviewers for their efforts in finalizing the high-quality papers and finally, based on the recommendations, 27 papers were accepted for publication. The proceedings of the conference are published in this volume of Communications in Computer and Information Science (CCIS), Springer, indexed by ISI Proceedings, DBLP, Ulrich's, EI-Compendex, SCOPUS, Zentralblatt Math, MetaPress and Springerlink. We, in our capacity as volume editors, convey our sincere gratitude to Springer for providing the opportunity to publish the proceedings of ICCISIoT 2020 in their esteemed CCIS series.

The conference program was enriched by a series of keynote presentations, and the keynote address by eminent researchers like Prof. K. M. Deb, Professor & Koenig Endowed Chair, Electrical and Computer Engineering, Michigan State University, USA. We are grateful to the keynote presenters for sharing their insights on their latest research with us.

The Organizing Committee of ICCISIoT 2020 is indebted to Prof. H. K. Sharma, Director, National Institute of Technology Agartala, and Honorary Chair for the confidence that he bestowed on us in organizing this international conference. We would also like to take this opportunity to extend our heartfelt thanks to the General Chairs of this conference, Prof. K. M. Deb, Michigan State University, USA and Prof. Tokunbo Ogunfunmi, Santa Clara University, USA, for their active involvement from the very beginning until the end of the conference; without their support, this conference could never have assumed such a successful shape. We gratefully acknowledge the active support received from the General Co-Chairs of the conference, Prof. Ardhendu Saha and Prof. Debashish Bhattacharya of National Institute of Technology Agartala, India. Special thanks to EasyChair for the paper submission platform, which we used to organize reviews and collate the files for these proceedings.

Special words of appreciation are expressed to note the enthusiasm of all the faculty, staff and students of the Computer Science and Engineering department of NIT Agartala who organized the conference in virtual mode in a most befitting manner even under the constrained situation of the COVID-19 global pandemic. The involvement of faculty coordinators and student volunteers is particularly praiseworthy in this regard. It is needless to mention the role of the contributors. The editors take this opportunity to thank the authors of all the papers submitted for their hard work, the more so because all of them considered the conference as a viable platform to showcase some of their latest findings, not to mention their adherence to the deadlines and patience with the tedious review process. The quality of a refereed volume primarily depends on the expertise and dedication of the reviewers who volunteer with a smiling face. The editors are further indebted to the Technical Program Committee members and external reviewers who not only produced excellent reviews but also did these in short time frames, in spite of their very busy schedule. Because of their quality work, it has been possible to maintain the high academic standard of the proceedings. We also wish to express our thanks to Amin Mobasheri, Editor–CCIS Supervisor, Computer Science Editorial, Springer-Verlag GmbH, Dr. Guido Zosimo-Landolfo, Editorial Director, Springer Nature Switzerland AG and Alla Serikova, Computer Science Editorial, Springer Nature for their timely help and complete cooperation.

Last but not the least, the editors gracefully thank all who directly or indirectly helped the organisers in making ICCISIoT 2020 a grand success and helped the conference to achieve its technical purpose and strong academic objective. Happy Reading!

December 2020

Nirmalya Kar
Ashim Saha
Suman Deb

Organization

Honorary Chair

H. K. Sharma   NIT Agartala, India

General Chairs

Tokunbo Ogunfunmi   Santa Clara University, USA
K. M. Deb   Michigan State University, USA

General Co-chairs

Ardhendu Saha   NIT Agartala, India
Debashish Bhattacharya   NIT Agartala, India

Organizing Chairs

Nirmalya Kar   NIT Agartala, India
Ashim Saha   NIT Agartala, India
Suman Deb   NIT Agartala, India

Technical Committee Members

Ahcene Bounceur   Université de Bretagne Occidentale, France
Alok Ranjan Prusty   MSDE, Government of India, India
Anish Kr. Saha   NIT Silchar, India
Anupam Jamatia   NIT Agartala, India
Ardhendu Saha   NIT Agartala, India
B. Subramaniam   NIT Warangal, India
Banani Saha   University of Calcutta, India
Bidyut Bhattacharya   Georgia Institute of Technology, USA
Dhiman Saha   IIT Bhilai, India
Dipankar Debnath   IIT Kharagpur, India
Diptendu Bhattacharya   NIT Agartala, India
Dwijen Rudrapal   NIT Agartala, India
Eric Gamess   Jacksonville State University, USA
Farid Farahmand   Sonoma State University, USA
Kaoru Sakatani   Nihon University, Japan
Kunal Chakma   NIT Agartala, India
Lov Kumar   BITS Pilani, India
Mahalinga V. Mandi   Dr. Ambedkar Institute of Technology, India
Mahendra Pratap Singh   NIT Karnataka, India

Meryem Elmoulat	Mohammed V University, Morocco
Miltos Alamaniotis	The University of Texas at San Antonio, USA
Mridu Sahu	NIT Raipur, India
Mrinal Kanti Debbarma	NIT Agartala, India
Nikhil Debbarma	NIT Agartala, India
Pakize Erdoğmuş	Düzce University, Turkey
Partha Pakrey	NIT Silchar, India
Sutanu Chakraborti	IIT Madras, India
R. P. Sharma	NIT Agartala, India
Rupa G. Meheta	SVNIT Surat, India
S. N. Pradhan	NIT Agartala, India
Sadhan Gope	Mizoram University, India
Samir S. Sahasrabudhe	IIT Mumbai, India
Sergi Trilles Oliver	Universitat Jaume I, Spain
Sharmistha Roy	Usha Martin University, India
Shital Raut	VNIT Nagpur, India
Shivakumar Mathapathi	California Polytechnic State University, USA
Shovan Bhoumik	IIT Patna, India
Smita Das	NIT Agartala, India
Sujay Deb	IIIT Delhi, India
Swapan Debbarma	NIT Agartala, India
Tanmoy Roy Choudhury	KIIT, Bhubaneswar, India
Tribid Debbarma	NIT Agartala, India

Additional Reviewers

A. Kertesz
A. Vidhya
Abdalraouf Alarbi
Abdelkader Ouda
Abdulmohsin Hammood Dalal
Abhilash Das
Abhishek Pal
Abu Mitul
Abu Wasif
Achmad Basuki
Ahmed Ahmim
Akhilesh Sharma
Akib Jayed Islam
Akram Reza
Alak Roy
Alka
Amitabha Nath

Ammar Odeh
Ana Paula G. Lopes
Angga Rahagiyanto
Aniket Patel
Anindya Iqbal
Anish Kumar Saha
Anjali Singh
Ankit Kumar Jain
Ankush B. Pawar
Annapurani Panaiyappan K.
Arnab Kumar Maji
Arpita Biswas
Asha Sohal
Ashok Kumar Das
Bhaskar Bhuyan
Bhumica Verma
Bijoy Kumar Mandal

Biman Debbarma
Bipasha Mahato
Braja Gopal Patra
Chen Feng
Chinmoy Ghosh
Chuan Zhou
Cuiling Li
D. Sathya
Daheng Dong
Debraj Chatterjee
Deepali Jain
Deepsubhra Guha Roy
Devki Nandan Jha
Dhinakaran K.
Diana Teresa Parra
DiazMartinez Jorge Luis
Fei Chao
Filippo Menczer
Francisco Solís
G. Abirami
G. Kanagaraj
G. Manoj Sai
G. Sangeetha
Gouranga Mandal
Goutam Pal
Guang Gong
Gueltoum Bendiab
Haitham Assiri
Hassan N. Noura
Hongbin Zhao
Hoshang Kolivand
Iman I. M. Abu Sulayman
Ioannis Koufos
Ismail Keshta
James Jones
Jatin Patel
Jia Wu
Jianjun Zhang
Jonathan Todd
Jose L. Flores C.
Jun Zhao
Junling Qiu
Jyoti Kaubiyal
Kamalika Bhattacharya
Kannan Srinathan
Kaushal Bhardwaj

Kaustubh Choudhary
Kazi Masum Sadique
Kewei Sha
Konstantinos Panagiotis Grammatikakis
Koushik Bhattacharyya
Krishnajyothi Nath
Kriti Sharma
Leandro Y. Mano
Leandros A. Maglaras
Lianyong Qi
Longzhi Yang
Luis Fernando A. Roman
M. Nivetha
M. Sai Sarath
Maha Sabir
Malek Al Zewairi
Manikandan K.
Manju Khari
Mardiana Binti Mohamad Noor
Maroun Chamoun
Mayank Srivastava
Md. Monirul Islam
Md. Shamsuzzoha Bayzid
Md. Tareq Mahmood
Merrill Warkentin
Mohammad Hammoudeh
Mohammad Nikravan
Mohammed El Hajj
Mohammed Eunus Ali
Mohmmad Haseeb Haider
Mohsen Sayyadiharikandeh
Muhammad Abdullah Adnan
Muhammad Masroor Ali
Muhammad Shahzad
Musa G. Samaila
N. Poornima
N. Shanthi
Neelima K.
Nikolas Schmidt
Nilay R. Mistry
Nilesh Kumar
Noe Elisa
O. R. Deepa
Pankaj Sharma
Paulo R. L. Gondim
Pedro H. Gomes

Poonam Godhwani
Prajoy Podder
Preeti Sharma
Priyadarsi Nanda
Priyanka Ahlawat
R. C. Suganthe
Radha Mahendrabhai Raval
Raghav H. Venkatnarayan
Raj Shree
Rezwana Reaz
Ryan Pipetti
S. Benila
S. Narayanan
S. Shanthi
S. Suma
S. Venkatesh
Sadia Sharmin
Sadman Shahriar Alam
Safa Otoum
Saikat Basu
Sanchali Das
Sang Jin Lee
Sanjib Kumar Deka
Sanjit Kumar
Sanjoy Kumar Mukherjee
Sarada Musala
Sefer Kurnaz
Shakti Kundu
Shariq Aziz Butt
Shashikant Ghumbre
Shatrunjay Rawat
Shaveta Khepra
Sherali Zeadally
Shereen Saleh
Shishir Kumar Shandilya
Shivendu Mishra
Shubham Agrawal
Shuoshuo Xu

Siddhartha Bhattacharyya
Sneha K. Patel
Sonia Chhabra
Subhankar Shome
Subhrajyoti Deb
Sudhir Kumar
Sudipta Majumder
Sujata Ghatak
Sujata Sinha
Sujay Deb
Sujoy Mistry
Sukhpreet Kaur
Suliman Mohamed Fati
Supratim Bhattacharya
Sushanta Karmakar
Swagata Paul
Syafeeza Ahmad Radzi
T. Subbarao
Tahreem Haque
Tanusree Chatterjee
Tanzima Hashem
Thays A. Oliveira
Thongpan Pariwat
Tushar Mehrotra
U. Thiruvaazhi
Vinay Chamola Chamola
Vipul Negi
Walter Sebron
Wisam Gwad
Xiaolong Xu
Xiong Li
Xulei Yang
Yahya Atwady
Yuchen Yang
Zakaria El Mrabet
Zarana Kanani
Zeena N. AlKateeb

Contents

Computational Intelligence

The Sudoku Puzzle Generator Using DNA Computing

V. Sudha$^{(\boxtimes)}$(iD) and R. Kalaiselvi

Kumaraguru College of Technology, Coimbatore, TN, India
{sudha.v.cse,kalaiselvi.r.cse}@kct.ac.in

Abstract. Sudoku is a Japanese logical puzzle solved using brain power. In this puzzle, the player places a digit among 1 to n in such a way that no cell in the same row, grid and column have the same value. In an n × n grid, there exists n possibilities of placing a value in a cell. This puzzle is available at different difficulty level. Generating a Sudoku puzzle with a specific difficulty level is a challenging task. Though there are various algorithms exist in the literature for generating the brainteaser, all of them either uses Backtracking technique or patterns for problem generation. This leads to exponential time complexity. Hence, there is a need for a polynomial-time solution that takes care of all possible cases. In this paper, we propose a polynomial time algorithm for generating the Sudoku puzzle in DNA computing using the Adleman-Lipton model. The puzzle is initially represented as a graph, later graph colouring algorithm is applied to it. From the obtained solution, randomly few cells are removed to obtain the puzzle with required difficulty level.

Keywords: Sudoku puzzle · DNA computing · Graph coloring · Adleman-lipton model

1 Introduction

The Sudoku, a famous brain teaser is not only very interesting to solve but also finds its applications in various fields such as Stenography [1], Information Security [2], Artificial intelligence, etc., Due to its wide application, it is been studied by several researchers and applied in different domains. Usually, the research in puzzle is focused on the following manner: puzzle generator, solver and difficulty rating. Few peoples do not view generator and solver separately, as problems can be generated from the solutions. In literature, various algorithms are proposed for all these types. Though there are various strategies exists for puzzle generation, production with the inverse method [3] is the predominant one. In this strategy, initially a random Sudoku puzzle is taken and solved. Then few values are removed from the solution to generate the necessary puzzle. In the remaining strategies, the cells in the given dimensions are randomly filled and then verified whether these filled values lead to a valid solution. The above process is repeated until a solvable puzzle is obtained. In this case, it is required

© Springer Nature Switzerland AG 2020
N. Kar et al. (Eds.): ICCISIoT 2020, CCIS 1358, pp. 3–14, 2020.
https://doi.org/10.1007/978-3-030-66763-4_1

to generate all possible solutions. This issue leads to exponential time complexity. Hence, there is a need for a polynomial time algorithm to generate a Sudoku puzzle with different difficulty levels. Like puzzle generation, various strategies such as the only choice rule, single possibility rule, only square rule, two out of three rule, sub-group exclusion rule, Hien twin exclusion rule, backtracking exist for solving a Sudoku puzzle problem. All these strategies except backtracking cannot be generalized. To solve a problem using the backtracking, usually the technique is applied to each cell present in the grid until the required solution is obtained. Some of these strategies are discussed in this article.

Generally, pencil-and-paper method is used for solving Sudoku problems [4]. This algorithm is applicable especially for the problems classified as diabolical. Backtracking is applied on a mini grid instead of the individual cell thereby reducing the number of operations [5]. Few researchers compared the brute-force with pencil-and-paper algorithm to find their efficiency in solving a problem [6]. Brute force method guarantees a solution to the problem as it tries all possibilities. Also, this method can solve a Sudoku problem with any level of difficulty.

From the discussion, it is concluded that the pencil-and-paper method along with backtracking performs better than the brute-force method. Patterns such as Naked Singles, Hidden Singles, Naked Pairs, Hidden Pairs, and Locked Candidates are identified to speed up the process of solving this brainteaser [7]. Genetic algorithms [8], cultural learning [9], ant colony optimization [10] and heuristics [11] are also used for generating and solving Sudoku puzzle. Gauge system [13] and Meta heuristics [14] are also developed for solving this teaser. Few optimized encoding are also proposed for this puzzle [15]. Sudoku puzzle belongs to the NP-complete problem [12]. From this it is inferred that this problem does not have polynomial algorithm. In this paper, a polynomial time solution is proposed for generating Sudoku problem using DNA (Deoxyribo Nucleic Acid) Computing.

DNA computing is a molecular computing exploiting the parallelism of the DNA. It was invented by Leonard Adleman. He initiated DNA computing by solving an instance of the Hamiltonian Path Problem (HPP). He solved the problem using the operations such as Ligation, Amplification (using PCR), Separation by length (using gel electrophoresis) and Separation (using Affinity Purification). Followed by it, various models are proposed in the literature by Sudha et al. [16]. Among them, the Sudoku puzzle generation in this paper uses the Adleman-Lipton model.

In this paper, an algorithm for the Sudoku puzzle generation is proposed. To solve the Sudoku problem, the puzzle is represented as a graph. Any problem in DNA computing is solved by encoding it using DNA bases. Hence, the generated Sudoku graph is encoded using the DNA base. After changing the format, graph colouring algorithm described in [17] is applied to the Sudoku graph. From the obtained solution, randomly remove few colours to get the puzzle with required difficulty level. When generating puzzles, the optimization methods have to be adopted to balance the resource utilization [18].

2   Proposed System

The Sudoku is a logical puzzle played using n × n board. Though various sizes of boards available, the puzzle with grid size 9 × 9 is more famous. This lattice contains 81 cells partitioned into 4 sub-lattice each of size 3 × 3. The puzzle begins by some numbers (clues) assigned already to the cells. The minimum number of clues that a Sudoku puzzle must have is 17. Each Sudoku puzzle has a unique solution. To solve the given Sudoku puzzle, a player must place the digits between 1 and 9 in a 3 × 3 grids in such a way that each row/column in the 9 × 9 board contains exactly one occurrence of a digit. There are various type of Sudoku puzzle available depending upon their difficulty level. They are easy, medium, hard, and evil. The difficulty level depends upon the position of the empty cells in the grid. Any algorithm used for the Sudoku puzzle generation must satisfy the following properties.

1. Every problem must have a unique solution
2. Grading of the puzzle must be done carefully
3. The puzzle must contain a minimum number of clues so that there is only one solution to the problem

The flow of the proposed algorithm is described as shown in Fig. 1. To apply Graph colouring algorithm over the puzzle, first the Sudoku puzzle is converted to a graph. After conversion, vertices of the Sudoku graph are coloured with 9 colours using Graph Colouring algorithm. Finally, from the coloured graph, problem is reconstructed. The proposed algorithm generates the Sudoku puzzle with a grid size 9 × 9. This proposed procedure can also be extended to n values as shown in Fig. 1. The subsequent sections in the paper gives the detailed explanation for each of the component in the proposed system.

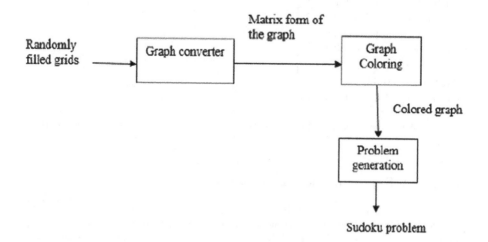

Fig. 1. Colored graph.

2.1   Graph Converter

Graph colouring is a special case of graph labelling where the vertices are coloured in such a way that no two adjacent vertices in the graph have same colours. This algorithm cannot be applied directly over the Sudoku puzzle. Hence, Graph Converter is used to create graph for Sudoku problem. To represent the puzzle as a graph, the Graph Converter initially labels the cells of the grid starting from integer 1. Thus, the maximum label value of the cell is 81. The procedure followed for creating a graph described as follows.

1. Create a vertex/node for each cell in the 9×9 grids
2. Name each vertex of the graph by numbers starting from 1 up to 81
3. Include an edge between two vertices in the above-constructed graph if the two vertices corresponding to the two cells are in the same column, row or within the 3×3 sub-grids

Thus, the Sudoku graph for the given puzzle is constructed. The matrix representation (graph) of a 4×4 Sudoku puzzles is given below.

$$
\begin{bmatrix}
0 1 1 1 1 1 0 0 1 0 0 0 1 0 0 0 \\
1 0 1 1 1 1 0 0 0 1 0 0 0 1 0 0 \\
1 1 0 1 0 0 1 1 0 0 1 0 0 0 1 0 \\
1 1 1 0 0 0 1 1 0 0 0 1 0 0 0 1 \\
1 1 0 0 1 1 1 1 0 0 0 1 0 0 0 \\
1 1 0 0 1 0 1 1 0 1 0 0 0 1 0 0 \\
0 0 1 1 1 1 0 1 0 0 1 0 0 0 1 0 \\
0 0 1 1 1 1 1 0 0 0 0 1 0 0 0 1 \\
1 0 0 0 1 0 0 0 0 1 1 1 1 1 0 0 \\
0 1 0 0 0 1 0 0 1 0 1 1 1 1 0 0 \\
0 0 1 0 0 0 1 0 1 1 0 1 0 0 1 1 \\
0 0 0 1 0 0 0 1 1 1 1 0 0 0 1 1 \\
1 0 0 0 1 0 0 0 1 1 0 0 0 1 1 1 \\
0 1 0 0 0 1 0 0 1 1 0 0 1 0 1 1 \\
0 0 1 0 0 0 1 0 0 0 1 1 1 1 0 1 \\
0 0 0 1 0 0 0 1 0 0 1 1 1 1 1 0
\end{bmatrix}
$$

The cells of the grid are numbered from 1 starting at the leftmost upper end of the grid.

2.2   Graph Representation in DNA Computing

To solve a problem in DNA computing, the problem must be represented using DNA bases. There are four different types of DNA bases namely: Adenine (A), Guanine (G), Cytosine (C) and Thymine (T). To represent a graph in DNA computing, the vertices and edges of the graph must be encoded using the DNA base. A string made up of these bases represent a DNA strand. There are two types of DNA strands: single-stranded DNA (ssDNA) and double-stranded DNA (dsDNA). Among these two types, experiments mostly makes use of dsDNA. In this paper, we make use of ssDNA for convenience. Biological operations are applied on ssDNA strands to perform the necessary task. Two ssDNA0s bond each other using Watson-Crick complementary resulting in dsDNA. Thus, the operation's applied on ssDNA can be extended for dsDNA also.

In this paper, the graph is encoded as DNA bases using the encoding method proposed by Adleman in solving an instance of the Hamiltonian path problem [18]. The method is repeated below for reference. Let $G(V, E)$ be a graph with V vertices and E edges. Each vertex in V of the graph is given unique encoding and the edges in E is encoded by taking complementary of half of the sequences from each vertex that it connects. Edges uses complementary DNA strands to get necessary graph structure through their bonding process. Consider the vertices v_1 and v_2 whose DNA encoding are given below, v_1: $ACGTGACT$ and v_2: $TAGCTTCC$ Then, the edge e_{12} connecting these two vertices is encoded as $CTCAATCG$. Note that in the edge encoding, the first four bases are the complement of the last four base values of v_1. Similarly, the last four bases in the encoding of the edge e_{12} is constituted from the complement of the first four bases in the encoding of vertex v_2. Thus, after hybridization- a biological operation, the sub-graph looks as shown below:

$ACGTGACTCTCAATCG$

$\qquad TAGCTTCC$

2.3 Graph Coloring

To the constructed Sudoku graph, graph colouring algorithm described in [17] is applied. To illustrate the proposed system, we have considered a Sudoku puzzle of size 9×9. As the cells in this brain teaser need to be filled with numbers between 1 and 9, the constructed graph is coloured using 9 colours. Let c_1, c_2, ..., c_9 be the 9 colours. Thus, a vertex $v_i \in V$ is assigned a color $c_j \in \{c_1, c_2, c_3, \ldots, c_9\}$ in such a way that no two adjacent vertices have the same color.

Algorithm for solving Sudoku problem using the Adleman-Lipton model is given in Algorithm 1.

Algorithm 1: Algorithm for solving Sudoku problem

Construct a graph $G(V, E)$ with $|V|=81$;
Let C be the set of colored vertices;
Let $|C| = \phi$;
while $G \neq empty$ **do**
  Select a vertex $v_i \in (V - C)$;
  Color v_i with the color $c_j \in \{c_1, c_2, c_3, \ldots c_9\}$ using the graph coloring algorithm
end
return G;

The coloured 4×4 Sudoku grids using the colours say c_1, c_2, c_3 and c_4 is shown in Fig. 2. The figure shows one possibility among the n possibility available for colouring the graph.

c_1	c_2	c_3	c_4
c_3	c_4	c_2	c_1
c_2	c_1	c_4	c_3
c_4	c_3	c_1	c_2

Fig. 2. Colored graph.

2.4 Problem Generation

The problem generation from the coloured Sudoku graph is the final step in the proposed model. This coloured graph represents a completely solved Sudoku problem. From this graph, few colours are randomly removed resulting in an unsolvable puzzle. As the difficulty level of a puzzle depends upon the number of values initially present in the grid, the number of colours to be removed from the coloured graph is determined by the puzzle to be generated. Thus, the Sudoku puzzle with required difficulty level is generated. As problem is generated from the solution, proposed method can also be used for solving and verifying a given Sudoku puzzle. The resulting puzzle after removing few random colours is shown in Fig. 3.

c_1		c_3	c_4
c_3		c_2	c_1
	c_1		c_3
c_4	c_3	c_1	

Fig. 3. Colored graph.

3 Complexity Analysis

The complexity of the proposed algorithm is the sum of the complexities of the following algorithm: graph representation of the problem, graph coloring and problem generation. In DNA computing, each of these operation is performed in parallel. Hence, the complexity of the proposed system is $O(1)$.

4 Results and Discussion

Various techniques such as pencil and paper method, Brute-force, backtracking, Genetic algorithms and simulated annealing are used in the existing system to solve the Sudoku puzzle. These techniques involve various strategies leading to different time complexities. Though Brute force is used for solving all the problems, it is not appropriate for brain teaser as it involves $O(n^2)$ time complexity. When Pencil-and-paper method is used to crack the classic puzzle, it required backtracking technique when the puzzle looks hard and evil. This leads to the time complexity $O(2^n)$. Generally, the complexity of the genetic algorithms is given as $O(g(nm))$ where g is the number of generations, n the population size and m the size of the individuals. When the fitness function used in the this algorithm is complex, then the complexity automatically increases. The above discussion is summarized in Table 1.

Table 1. Performance comparison.

Problem solving strategy	Complexity
Brute-force method	$O(n^2)$
Backtracking	$O(2^n)$
Pencil-and-paper method	$O(2^n)$ (Hard problems)
Genetic algorithms	$O(g(mn))$

From the above discussion it is inferred that all the techniques either directly or indirectly makes use of Backtracking to solve the problem. Thus, all the algorithms used for solving Sudoku puzzles are exponential in nature. In this paper, an algorithm using the DNA computing sticker-based model is proposed for solving, generating, and verifying the Sudoku puzzle. The proposed algorithm solves this brain teaser in constant time. This is achievable with the help of parallel nature of DNA computing. It generates the possible solution of the given problem and filters the necessary from it by applying predefined biological operations over all the strands at the same time. Since, plenty of DNA strands are available in nature, there is no restriction in the implementation of the proposed system. Here, the number of colours used for graph colouring depends on the size of the Sudoku puzzles. Some general concepts are proved by the following Lemma.

4.1   Implementation Details

All the algorithms in Table 1 are implemented using Java programming language. Since, it is difficult to experiment in DNA computing, we simulated the algorithm using the threads in Java. Various types of Sudoku problem are passed as input and time taken for the same is measured and tabulated in Table 2.

Table 2. Performance comparison.

Algorithms	Problem types			
	Easy	Medium	Hard	Evil
Brute-force method	10	12	60	80
Backtracking	14	50	100	130
Pencil-and-paper method	5	15	40	42
Proposed algorithm	5	5	5	5

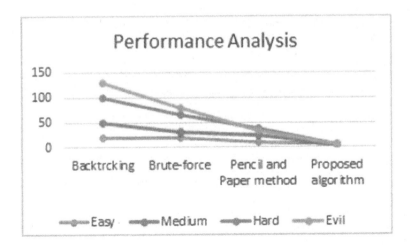

Fig. 4. Colored graph.

Figure 4 gives the performance of the algorithm for the various types of problems passed as input. Thus, from this is inferred that the proposed algorithm outperforms the other existing algorithms.

4.2   Optimizing the Performance Time Using Taguchi Method

Though there are several optimization techniques, Genichi Taguchi's [19] method can be used in finding the optimum level of process parameters that have an effect on the performance of the process. It can be performed with only a small number of tests to select the optimum level of parameters. Hence this method minimizes the experimental runs, time, and the cost. In this study, Taguchi and ANOVA methods are employed to analyse the effect of two process parameters such as Algorithm and puzzle level on the puzzle generating time. Ranking of the parameters and optimum levels of the parameters are determined in obtaining the desired output of the process using Taguchi method. Analysis of variance (ANOVA) is used to compute the percentage contribution of process parameters on the outcome of the process. Taguchi and ANOVA are performed using the software package MINITAB.

Here, smaller is better Signal to Noise (S/N) ratio is considered to find the optimum level of parameters because low puzzle generation time is desirable. Signal to Noise ratio is expressed in a decibel, calculated from the quadratic function. Signal indicates the mean value (desirable), and noise indicates the variance (undesirable) for the outcome of the process. The parameter which has maximum S/N ratio tells the desired quality. Mathematical equation of the S/N ratio for smaller is better can be represented as in Eq. (1).

$$S/N = -10Log(1/n\Sigma Y_i^2) \tag{1}$$

where Y_i and n are the observed data and the number of observations respectively. In the present investigation, parameters are analysed with L16 orthogonal array. Puzzle generation time is taken as output.

Accordingly, 16 tests are done, and each test is repeated 4 times to reduce the errors. Four different levels for each parameter are considered. The parameters and their corresponding levels are presented in Table 3.

Table 3. Parameters and their levels.

Code	Performance parameters	Levels		
		I	II	III
A	Algorithm (MB)	1	2	3
B	Puzzle level (GHz)	3.14	3.2	3.3

Experiments are conducted as per the Taguchi orthogonal array for analysing the fragmentation performance. 16 experiments are performed as per the run order given in Table 4. Fragmentation is executed for each run and the fragmentation time is noted. In addition, the experimental results are analysed using ANOVA to study the influence of the parameters on the fragmentation time. Measured values and the corresponding S/N ratios are given in Table 4.

Table 4. Measured values of puzzle generation time and S/N ratios.

Experiment no.	Performance parameters		Puzzle generation time (ms)	(S/N) ratio
	Algorithm (A)	Puzzle level (B)	Measured values	
1	1	1	10	−20.0000
2	1	2	12	−21.5836
3	1	3	60	−35.563
4	1	4	80	−38.0618
5	2	1	14	−22.9226
6	2	2	50	−33.9794
7	2	3	100	−40.0000
8	2	4	130	−42.2789
9	3	1	5	−13.9794
10	3	2	15	−23.5218
11	3	3	40	−32.0412
12	3	4	42	−32.4650
13	4	1	5	−13.9794
14	4	2	5	−13.9794

Table 5. Parameters and their ranks.

Level	Algorithm	Puzzle level
1	−28.80	−17.72
2	−34.80	−23.27
3	−25.50	−30.40
4	−13.98	−31.70
Delta	20.82	13.98
Rank	1	2

The performance parameters are ranked as given in Table 5. It can be observed from the response table, there is a delta value which is computed by averaging the difference between the highest and lowest characteristic $(S/N$ ratio) for a parameter. The factor with the largest delta value is given rank 1. Algorithm chosen for puzzle generation is the dominant factor as it has higher delta value of 4.1 followed by the puzzle level.

From the response diagram of S/N ratios (Fig. 3) it is found that the optimum level of parameters for algorithm and puzzle level are proposed algorithm and medium and respectively in obtaining lower puzzle generation time. When the level of puzzle is changed to evil; the puzzle generation time remains same but the memory space required gets increased to solve the problem. It is observed that as the threads are created for generating puzzle the time is less.

Lemma 1. *Prove that deg(v_i) in a Sudoku graph of n vertices is $3n - 2\sqrt{n} - 1$, $\forall v_i \in V$ where n is a perfect square number.*

Proof. It is known that in the Sudoku problem with grid size $n \times n$, a cell is connected to all the cells in the same row, column, and grid. Thus, in a row and column of a particular cell, $(n - 1)$ cells are be there. While considering all the cells in the grid, some of them may be already included in the row and column of a cell, then the degree for the remaining cells for which it will be connected is $n - (\sqrt{n} + (\sqrt{n} - 1))$. Thus, $\deg(v_i) = (n - 1) + (n - 1) + (n - (\sqrt{n} + (\sqrt{n} - 1)))$.
   Simplifying the above equation, we get $3n - 2\sqrt{n} - 1$. Thus proved.

Lemma 2. *Prove that the graph G constructed above requires 9 colours to color the vertices of the graph.*

Proof. To prove the above lemma, consider the most popular Sudoku puzzle that is of size 9×9. From the graph constructed for this puzzle, it is inferred that a vertex in the graph will be connected to 7 out of 9 vertices in the graph. But, among the 7 vertices, almost 5 vertices are intersecting with the other node's adjacent vertices. Thus, the graph requires 9 colours. The number of color cannot exceed 9 because a complete graph K_9 itself requires only maximum of 9 colours.

Lemma 3. *Proposed algorithm generates Sudoku puzzle of required complexity.*

Proof. From Lemma 2 it is inferred that the graph constructed for the Sudoku puzzle of size 9×9 requires 9 colors. We know that the each cell of the puzzle is a vertex in the constructed graph. Thus, after coloring the graph we get a solved Sudoku puzzle. By removing few colors randomly, we get a Sudoku puzzle of required complexity. Hence, proved.

5   Conclusion

In this paper, an algorithm proposed for generating Sudoku puzzle is with polynomial complexity. To generate puzzle of grid size $n \times n$, first the puzzle is represented as a graph consisting of n2 vertices. Then graph colouring algorithm is applied to color the vertices of the graph with n colours. Finally, the result is decoded to obtain the required result. The Adleman-Lipton model is used for solving the problem. The proposed system can be extended for generating Sudoku puzzle of size 255×255 as the maximum number available colours are 255. This system makes use of the parallel nature of the DNA computing. As biological operations can be applied in parallel on any number of DNA strands, we can generate all possible solutions of a given problem. Similarly, the valid solutions are also filtered in polynomial time.

References

1. Roshan Shetty, B.R., Rohith, J., Mukund, V., Rohan, H., Shanta R.: Steganography using Sudoku puzzle. In: 2009 International Conference on Advances in Recent Technologies in Communication and Computing, Kottayam, Kerala, pp. 623–626 (2009)

2. Okagbue, H.I., Omogbadegun, Z.O., Olajide, F.A., Opanuga, A.A.: On some suggested applications of Sudoku in information systems security. Asian J. Inf. Technol. **14**(4), 117–121 (2015)
3. Team #2306: Generating Sudoku Puzzles as an Inverse Problem (2008)
4. Crook, J.F.: A pencil-and-paper algorithm for solving Sudoku puzzles. Not. AMS **56**(4), 460–468 (2009)
5. Maji, A.K., Roy, S., Pal, R.K.: A Novel Algorithmic approach for solving Sudoku puzzle in guesses free manner. Eur. Acad. Res., 1052–1060 (2013)
6. Grados, F., Mohammadi, A.: A Report on The Sudoku Solver, Project Report (2013)
7. Iyer, R., Jhaveri, A., Parab, K.: A review of Sudoku solving using patterns. Int. J. Sci. Res. Publ. **3**(5), 1–4 (2013)
8. Mantere, T., Koljonen, J.: Solving, rating and generating Sudoku puzzles with GA with cultural learning. In: Proceedings of the 2007 IEEE Congress on Evolutionary Computation, pp. 1382–1389 (2007)
9. Mantere, T., Koljonen, J.: Solving and analyzing sudokus with cultural learning. In: Proceedings of the 2008 IEEE Congress on Evolutionary Computation, vol. 3, no. 2, pp. 4053–4060 (2008)
10. Pacurib, J.A., Seno, G.M.M., Yusiong, J.P.T.: Solving Sudoku puzzles using improved artificial bee colony algorithm. In: Proceedings of the Fourth International Conference on Innovative Computing, Information and Control (ICICIC 2009), pp. 885–888 (2009)
11. Pillay, N.: Finding solutions to Sudoku puzzles using human intuitive heuristics. S. Afr. Comput. J. **49**, 25–34 (2012)
12. Yato, T., Seta, T.: Complexity and completeness of finding another solution and its application to puzzles. IEICE Trans. Fundam. Electron. Commun. Comput. Sci. **E86-A**(5), 1052–1060 (2003)
13. Nicolau, M., Ryan, C.: Solving Sudoku with the GAuGE system. In: Collet, P., Tomassini, M., Ebner, M., Gustafson, S., Ekárt, A. (eds.) EuroGP 2006. LNCS, vol. 3905, pp. 213–224. Springer, Heidelberg (2006). https://doi.org/10.1007/11729976_19
14. Lewis, R.: Metaheuristics can solve Sudoku puzzles. J. Heuristics **13**, 387–401 (2007)
15. Kwon, G., Jain, H.: Optimized CNF encoding for Sudoku puzzles. In: Lecture Notes in Computer Science 's Instructions (2006)
16. Sudha, V., Easwarakumar, K.S.: A comprehensive study of insertion-deletion system in DNA computing. Int. J. Recent. Technol. Eng. **8**(1), 1211–1213 (2019)
17. Maazallahi, R., Niknafs, A.: A modified DNA computing approach to tackle the exponential solution space of the graph coloring problem. Int. J. Found. Comput. Sci. Technol. **3**(2), 1–7 (2013)
18. Adleman, L.: Molecular computation of solutions to combinatorial problems. Science **266**, 1021–1024 (1994)
19. Modi, V.K., Desai, D.A.: Review of Taguchi method, design of experiment (DOE) & analysis of variance (ANOVA) for quality improvements through optimization in foundry. Int. J. Emerg. Technol. Innov. Res. **5**(1), 184–194 (2018)

Intangible Learning Experience Using Leap Motion Controller for Distance Mapping

Tutan Nama[1(✉)] and Suman Deb[2]

[1] Indian Institute of Technology Kharagpur, Kharagpur, India
tutannama28@gmail.com
[2] National Institute of Technology Agartala, Agartala, India
sumandebcs@gmail.com

Abstract. Learning of classroom content with a teacher's monologue makes it droning over time. Due to affordable options of MOOCs, social media, open blogs, etc. paying attention to classroom content in the present scenario is an option only. This may limit the kindle of inspiring thought and natural apatite towards understanding classroom content. This work focuses on designing the interactions to explore the applications of Leap Motion for a better understanding of classroom content or simple things on the sense of game and logic. The brain-body coordination for distance mapping has introduced in this work. This work is established as an intangible learning interface where a user can learn elementary logic with an immersive experience. The derived outcome of the experiments shows the significant enhancement of learning and mind-body coordination of length and measure.

Keywords: Brain-body coordination · Leap motion · Gesture based learning · Logic learning · Interactive learning · Distance mapping

1 Introduction

Logic learning with pen and paper not always made student comfort. Some students are unable to get the teachers to monologue of teaching with chalk and talk. Students with a learning disorder are unable to pay the quality of attention whenever they try to learn logic [12,14]. There is a kind of student who did not put proper mind mapping about the distance calculation, color identification, or logical elementary operations, and they have the limitation of imagination, which directly cannot be mapped [1]. They need some special kind of learning concept, especially in logic learning [2].

Logic is a set of rules or a set of arguments based on which we make an idea about anything [12]. For example, if someone asked me that, what makes after multiplying 5 with 4, I used to start an analysis, search a data set stored in my mind about the multiplication table of 5 or 4, and examining the value for

N. Kar et al. (Eds.): ICCISIoT 2020, CCIS 1358, pp. 15–23, 2020.
https://doi.org/10.1007/978-3-030-66763-4_2

5 × 4 or 4 × 5. I may get the right or wrong result, but some logic is behind the searching. Let us consider another example. The Fig. 1 given below shows that the dog seems to taller than the elephant. It makes an illusion over our eyes because the dog is more near to us, and the elephant is far enough. The mental mapping of size at all is quite tricky for learning disabled people [13]. They need a realistic learning style and platform where learning is a pleasure. In this work, we considered only about the logic behind the mapping of distance in the term of brain-body coordination. By this work, we are trying to explore the applications of Leap Motion for a better understanding of simple things on the sense of the game. For the evaluating of the work, we are using leap motion. This work is an intangible learning interface where a user can learn elementary logic with an immersive experience. When someone asks about a particular length, our brain tries to map that distance. The mapping or guessing about the range is how accurate or perfect. This work can determine it. Students can evaluate the accuracy of their assumptions with this intangible interface. The collected results show the experience of learning and knowledge of a user and generate a report for that particular user.

Fig. 1. Knowledge over illusion

1.1 Leap Motion Controller and Visualizer

Leap motion controller is a small gesture acquisition device called which has various applications in the learning field, and we are trying to achieve and examine those. The API named as Leap Motion SDK is used to operate the leap motion controller after connecting it to a PC through an USB cable [3–8]. The leap motion controller used in this work as an input device that takes human hand gestures and passes to the program script for features extractions. Leap motion visualizer is diagnostic visualizer of the leap motion community setup that helps to setting up leap motion device [10]. It is mainly used to check the valid hand position over leap motion tracking zone (Fig. 2).

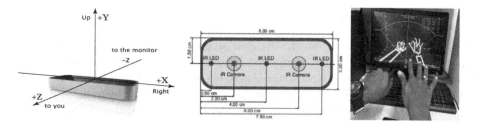

Fig. 2. Leap motion controller axis view (left), internal view (central), and leap motion visualizer (right)

2 Literature Survey and Related Works

Understanding logic and mental mapping of a practical thing not necessarily correct always. A different aspect of brain-body coordination needs different kinds of cognitive levels [16]. Those who have a lower cognitive level they need some particular type of learning treatment like interactive learning methods. Interactive learning is a real-world practical approach to education [15]. It reinvigorates the classroom for both students and faculty. Lectures are changed into discussions, and students and teachers become partners in the journey of knowledge acquisition. Interactive learning can take many different forms. Students strengthen their critical thinking and problem-solving skills using a much more holistic approach to learning. Interactive learning can take place across the curriculum with or without technology. Leap motion community provides a wide range of educational gaming concept over various platform [17]. By extracting features of leap motion controller there are various works done by researchers.

A Comparative Analysis Between the Mouse, Track-pad and the Leap Motion [18], in this work authors had done a comparative study about different input system with leap motion and describes the usage efficiency of leap motion.

Hand Gesture Recognition with Leap Motion [19], an ideal hand gesture recognition system with Leap Motion Controller has proposed in this work. A set of features are explored from Leap Motion tracking data. The learning concept adopt from this work is, how to pass gesture to the leap motion and how to identify the type of gesture.

Marker less Hand Gesture Interface Based on LEAP Motion Controller [20], in this work authors had designed a touch less interface for painting using leap motion. By simply moving fingers on leap motion tracking zone user can draw something with this interface. The concept adopt from this work is, how to use leap motion for marking on an tangible interface without any kind of physical contact.

Leap Motion Device Used to Control a Real Anthropomorphic Gripper [21], this work shows for the first time the use of the leap motion device to control an anthropomorphic gripper with five fingers. A description of the leap motion device is presented here by highlighting its main functional characteristics.

3   System Design

The Fig. 3 given below shows the detailed architectural view of this work. Leap motion takes hands data with extended index fingers then index fingers tip positions is extract through script. According to tip position distance is measures and store along with student id. After that a comparison is done between objective distance and mapped distance and display the accuracy of distance mapping.

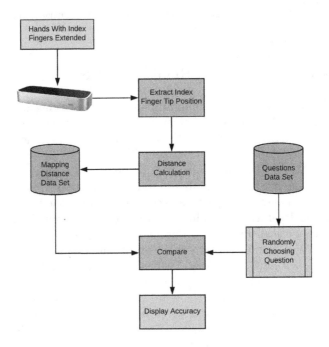

Fig. 3. System workflow

To model the intangible learning experience, we designed a Graphical User Interface (GUI) based on Visual C#, which provided a virtual interface for the leap motion used in our experiment. The objective of our model is to train subjects by which they can estimate a length using the index fingertips of both their hands. Subjects hand placed over the leap motion tracking zone is captured as frames and passes for feature extraction [22–24]. By placing the index finger of both hands in the tracking zone of the leap motion controller, students map the distance asking on the screen as objective. What we did here, we take the index fingertip position of both hands and perform a vector operation. The leap motion tracking zone has a three-dimensional area called interaction box. Hand gesture on this box considered a valid gesture. On the interaction-box X-axis represent the right-left movement of a hand, the Y-axis represents the upward-downward movement, and the Z-axis represents the backward and forward movement.

In this work, to identify the left hand or the right hand, we consider only the X-axis movement, −ve X value represents the leftmost hand, and +ve X value represents rightmost hand. After determining hands, we captured the extended index fingertip position and calculated the distance between the left-hand index fingertip and right-hand index fingertip.

Let, $V_1(X_1, Y_1, Z_1)$ is the vector position of left hand index fingertip and $V_2(X_2, Y_2, Z_2)$ is the vector position of right hand index finger tip.

Then the distance between two vector coordinates is,

$$D = |V_2 V_1| = \sqrt{(X_2 - X_1)^2 + (Y_2 - Y_1)^2 + (Z_2 - Z_1)^2} \tag{1}$$

4   Experiment Methodology

Ten (10) subjects volunteer to participate in our experiment. Each subject was asked to give an estimate measure of 10 different lengths using their index finger-tips and asked to draw the same on paper; this process considered as a pretest. The subjects were then asked to undergo a training process using the leap motion controller based on our interacting model for 100 random length trials. During this trial period, continuous feedback is provided through the GUI. This feed-back helps subjects to acquire knowledge about distance. The Fig. 4 shows the Graphical User Interface (GUI) of intangible learning experience model. Here one instance of learning through our model is shown with the system feedback about the accuracy of estimating length. The accuracy above 85% is taking as a correct attempt. After that, a post-test process conducted, where subjects were again asked to give an estimate measure of 10 different lengths, not necessarily similar to the pretest.

5   Result and Discussion

The number of correct attempt (CA) out of 10 and error making in pretest and post-test are noted in different tables given below (Table 1).

Table 1. Pretest results

Std. ID	std1	std2	std3	std4	std5	std6	std7	std8	std9	std10
CA	4	5	6	7	5	4	3	4	2	3
Errors (%)	60	50	40	30	50	60	70	60	80	70

All the correct estimation of post-test over pretest are shown below in detailed through graphs. The difference between the two estimates was used as a param-eter to evaluate the performance of our model (Table 2).

The chart given in Fig. 5 reflects the effectiveness of learning about distance through our proposed model over pretest. In our experiment we found that students were performing good after learning through our model.

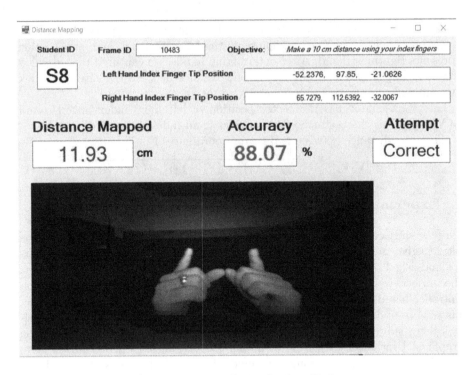

Fig. 4. An instance for Student ID-8

Table 2. Post-test results

Std. ID	std1	std2	std3	std4	std5	std6	std7	std8	std9	std10
CA	7	8	7	9	6	5	6	9	5	7
Errors (%)	30	20	30	10	40	50	40	10	50	70

Let us shown the results through a statistical analysis, in this case we performed the dependent sample t-test on the data.

$$H_0 : \mu_{pre} = \mu_{post} \tag{2}$$

$$H_1 : \mu_{pre} \neq \mu_{post} \tag{3}$$

Equation 1 and 2 shows the null and alternative hypothesis. Let us assume the Alpha $\alpha = 0.05$.

Since there are ten numbers of students in the examining period hence the degree of freedom for the dependent sample t-test.

$$df = N - 1 = 10 - 1 = 9 \tag{4}$$

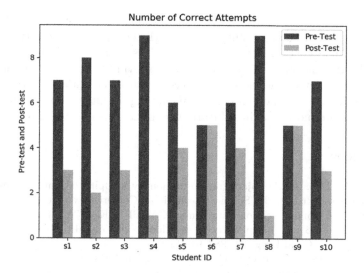

Fig. 5. Correct attempts in pretest and post-test

Here N is the number of students. With degree of freedom ($df = 9$) and $\alpha = 0.05$ we got critical value 2.2622 from the t-table and the range -2.2622 to 2.2622 define the decision state. If test statistic(t) is less than -2.2622 or greater than 2.2622 reject the null hypothesis. Here the difference in error for 10 different students are,

$X_D = 3$ for std1, 3 for std2, 1 for std3, 2 for std4, 1 for std5, 1 for std6, 3 for std7, 5 for std8, 3 for std9, 4 for std10.

The Mean value of differences is,

$$\bar{X}_D = \frac{3+3+1+2+1+1+3+5+3+4}{10} = 2.6 \tag{5}$$

The Standard Deviation is,

$$\sigma = \sqrt{\frac{\sum(X_D - \bar{X}_D)^2}{N}} = \sqrt{\frac{16.4}{10}} = 1.64 \tag{6}$$

Now the test statistic is,

$$t = \frac{\bar{X}_D}{\frac{\sigma}{\sqrt{N}}} = \frac{2.6}{\frac{1.64}{\sqrt{10}}} = \frac{2.6}{0.52} = 5 \tag{7}$$

Since $t(= 4) > 2.2622$ hence this eliminates null hypothesis (H_0) and follows H_1 hypothesis $\mu_{pre} \neq \mu_{post}$.

6   Conclusion

Designing an intangible application with size, shape and transitive application through which a coordinated expression of hand estimation is identified by computer is a learning "waao factor". Pleasurable logical estimation of length and size measure have successful achieved with the developed prototypes. Leap motion as a non contact interaction device gives an enhanced level of natural gesture. Formal modeling of interaction in improving the perception and effect analysis of the system has successfully accomplished the initial hypothesis. The findings as positive effect of domain specific intangible interaction can further be transformed into more meaningful learning experience and interaction sequence.

References

1. Nama, T., Deb, S.: 2D object transformation by mapping of hand gesture using leap motion controller. In: Second International Conference on Advanced Computational and Communication Paradigms (ICACCP). IEEE (2019)
2. MacWhinney, B.: A multiple process solution to the logical problem of language acquisition. J. Child Lang. **31**, 883–914 (2004)
3. White, T., Fraser, G., Brown, G.J.: Modelling hand gestures to test leap motion controlled applications. In: IEEE International Conference on Software Testing, Verification and Validation Workshops (ICSTW) (2018)
4. Ergonomic Quadcopter Control Using The Leap Motion Controller. Pazmany Peter Catholic University, Faculty of Information Technology and Bionics, Budapest, Hungary (2018)
5. Chan, A., Halevi, T., Memon, N.: Leap motion controller for authentication via hand geometry and gestures. In: Tryfonas, T., Askoxylakis, I. (eds.) HAS 2015. LNCS, vol. 9190, pp. 13–22. Springer, Cham (2015). https://doi.org/10.1007/978-3-319-20376-8_2
6. Guna, J., Jakus, G., Pogacnik, M., Tomazic, S., Sodnik, J.: Analysis of the precision and reliability of the leap motion sensor and its suitability for static and dynamic tracking. Sensors **14**, 3702–3720 (2014)
7. Xie, Q., Chao, J.: The application of leap motion in astronaut virtual training. In: IOP Conference Series: Materials Science and Engineering (2017)
8. Nifal, M.N.M., Logine, T., Sopitha, S., Kiruthika, P.: Space mouse - hand movement and gesture recognition using leap motion controller. Int. J. Sci. Res. Publ. **7**(12) (2017)
9. Mohandes, M., Deriche, M., Oladimeji, S.: Arabic sign language recognition using the leap motion controller. In: IEEE International Symposium on Industrial Electronics. https://doi.org/10.1109/ISIE.2014.6864742
10. Weichert, F., Bachmann, D., Rudak, B., Fisseler, D.: Analysis of the accuracy and robustness of the leap motion controller. Sensors **13**, 6380–6393 (2013)
11. Nama, T., Deb, S., Saha, S.: Designing a tangible user interface (TUI) using leap motion for elementary math learning. SSRN Int. J. Comput. Intell. IoT **2**(4) (2018)
12. Weng, J.-F., Tseng, S.-S., Lee, T.-J.: Teaching boolean logic through game rule tuning. IEEE Trans. Learn. Technol. **3**(4), 319–328 (2010)
13. Nama, T., Deb, S.: Interactive boolean logic learning using leap motion. In: IEEE Ninth International Conference on Technology for Education, vol. 1, pp. 220–222 (2018). https://doi.org/10.1109/T4E.2018.00060
14. Herman, G.L., Loui, M.C., Kaczmarxzyk, L., Zilles, C.: Describing the what and why of students' difficulties in Boolean logic, University of Illinois at Urbana Champaign. In: ACM International Computing Education Conference (2012)

15. Sinha, M., Deb, S.: An interactive elementary tutoring system for oral health education using an augmented approach. In: Proceedings of the 16th IFIP TC 13 International Conference Mumbai, India, Part II, September 25–29 2017

16. Khademi, M., et al.: Free-hand interaction with leap motion controller for stroke rehabilitation. In: CHI '14 Extended Abstracts on Human Factors in Computing Systems, pp. 1663–1668 (2014)

17. Vikram, S., Li, L., Russell, S.: Writing and sketching in the air, recognizing and controlling on the fly. In: CHI '13 Extended Abstracts on Human Factors in Computing Systems, pp. 1179–1184 (2013)

18. General, A., Da Silva, B., Esteves, D., Halleran, M., Liut, M.: A comparative analysis between the mouse, trackpad and the leap motion. In: CHI Conference 2016 (2016)

19. Naidu, C., Ghotkar, A.: Hand gesture recognition using leap motion controller. Int. J. Sci. Res. (IJSR) (2016)

20. Avola, D., Petracca, A., Cinque, L.: Markerless hand gesture interface based on LEAP motion controller

21. Staretu, I., Moldovan, C.: Leap motion device used to control a real anthropomorphic gripper. Int. J. Adv. Robot. Syst. **13**, 113 (2016)

22. Filho, I.A.S., Chen, E.N., da Silva Junior, J.M., da Silva Barboza, R.: Gesture recognition using leap motion: a comparison between machine learning algorithms. In: SIGGRAPH '18 ACM SIGGRAPH: Posters, Vancouver, BC, Canada, p. 2018 (2018)

23. Sharma, J.K., Gupta, R., Pathak, V.K.: Numeral gesture recognition using leap motion sensor. In: International Conference on Computational Intelligence and Communication Networks. IEEE (2015)

24. Shao, L.: Hand movement and gesture recognition using Leap Motion Controller. Int. J. Sci. Res. (IJSR) (2016)

25. SwipeGesture — Leap Motion Python SDK v3.2 Beta documentation "Swipegesture — Leap Motion Python SDK V3.2 Beta Documentation". Developer-archive.leapmotion.com. N. p., 2019. Web, 20 March 2019

A Novel Salp Swarm Algorithm
for Controller Placement Problem

Sanjai Pathak[1]($\boxtimes$), Ashish Mani[1]($\boxtimes$), Mayank Sharma[1],
and Amlan Chatterjee[2]

[1] Amity University, Noida, Uttar Pradesh, India
pathak.sanjai@gmail.com, {amani,msharma22}@amity.edu
[2] California State University Dominguez Hills, Carson, CA, USA
achatterjee@csudh.edu

Abstract. Self-adaptive control parameters and reverse learning mechanism are introduced in this paper to boost the performance of Salp Swarm Algorithm (SSA), through finding an optimal trade-off between exploitation and exploration for a class of benchmark problems. The proposed approach increases SSA's global search ability and decreases the probability of entrapment in local optima. The Self-Adaptive Salp Swarm Algorithm relies on an integrated approach where each individual has to maintain diversity using the introduced reverse learning strategy. The obtained simulation results of the modified SSA shows, that the proposed strategy and algorithm is promising. Also, we introduced a single objective SASSA approach to the controller placement problem that minimizes propagation latency between the controller and its associated forwarding elements in a given network topology. Internet2 OS3E network topology is simulated for the placement of controllers, that includes finding position along with the selection of controllers in SDN for optimum performance. The results of implementing the modified SSA algorithm for a class of benchmark problems and the controller placement problem in SDN confirmed the effectiveness of this novel approach.

Keywords: Computational intelligence · SSA · Swarm intelligence · SDN · The controller placement problem

1 Introduction

Metaheuristic algorithms are popular nowadays in the field of optimization, and is used to solve the complex optimization problems in many disciplines of science and engineering. Optimization is an intelligent process to search for the best solution among all available ones for a particular problem [1]. The traditional optimization algorithms such as gradient-based algorithm and many others are being used to solve the global optimization problems but due to the associated predefined assumptions in these algorithms, makes them inefficient in solving today's complex optimization problems such as problems in non-linear, non-differential, and multimodal. Metaheuristic algorithm approach is proposed to

© Springer Nature Switzerland AG 2020
N. Kar et al. (Eds.): ICCISIoT 2020, CCIS 1358, pp. 24–36, 2020.
https://doi.org/10.1007/978-3-030-66763-4_3

overcome the restrictions of the traditional optimization approach. The meta-heuristic optimization approach carried the advantage of being flexible and easy to deal with different types of optimization problems. Further, metaheuristic algorithm does not require gradient information and it comes with the bene-fits of intrinsic propensities, exploration and exploitation which decreases the probability of entrapment in a local optimum.

Inspired through nature behaviors, animal behaviors or physical phenom-ena, the metaheuristic algorithms are classified into three categories: Swarm-based, Evolution-based and Physics-based algorithms. Evolution based algo-rithms mimic the natural evolution process while physics-based algorithms imi-tate the rules of physics applied in the universe [2]. The swam-based algorithms simulate the foraging behavior of animals in a group such as bird flocking and fish schooling. Although metaheuristic approach efficiently solve optimization problems, its performance gets affected based on the nature of algorithm and introduced parameters. Thus, setting-up an appropriate parameter for a candi-date problem is a difficult task, and some time the computational cost increases and algorithm returns local solution when these parameters are not set appro-priately.

There are several approaches proposed and developed over the years into the domain of standard evolutionary algorithms to ameliorate traditional propen-sities of EAs i.e. exploration and exploitation, that also includes maintaining diversity, adaptive method, and self-adaptive parameters. Similarly, there are approaches to enhance the performance of SSA, that includes Chaotic Salp Swarm Algorithm for SDN multi-controller network, global optimization and feature selection [6,9], binary approach to the feature selection, Binary Salp Swarm Algorithm [13].

Salp swarm optimization algorithm (SSA) is a nature-inspired population-based metaheuristic optimization method that mimics the swarming behavior of salps in deep oceans by creating a salp chain, Mirjalili et al. [5] introduced it in 2017. SSA is similar to the other evolutionary algorithms in many aspects, it works efficiently for many real-world optimization problems. The SSA swarming behavior can avoid convergence for each solution into a local optimum up-to some extent due to its salp chain [6]. However, there are real-world optimization problems where it is difficult for the standard SSA to optimize. The controller placement problem is another domain of such kind, where global best is highly dependent on many factors of real-world scenarios such as latency, load balanc-ing, fault tolerance and cost of deployment. SSA lacks in improving the global best solution obtained so far, to achieve the expected global optima in the search space. The difficulty lies for SSA mainly because of entrapment in local minima and loss of population diversity.

In SSA, parameters are used to specify how a candidate solution will be used to generate a new solution along with other parameters of EAs such as population size, maximum generation etc. [11]. Choosing the right parameter values is a tedious task and requires previous years of experience of a user. The exploration and exploitation parameter's value in standard SSA does not change or adapt according to the changes in the environment and makes it weak in establishing a better balance between exploration and exploitation in the controller placement problem.

The literature shows an increasing interest for applying SSA in various stationary problems such as in hydrology for river flow forecasting [12], binary SSA and a novel chaotic SSA for feature selection problems in [9,13] respectively, and chaotic SSA for SDN multi-controller placement problems [6]. Faris et al. [13] presented a work to deal with feature selection task in machine learning, they considered a binary version of SSA (BSSA) and proposed two wrapper feature selection approaches. In the first approach, they used eight transfer functions for transforming the continuous version of SSA into binary and in another approach, the average operator is replaced by a crossover operator for deepening the exploration propensities of the digital algorithm. The proposed method of feature selection evaluated on the datasets of 22 benchmark problems and compared its result with another approach of feature selection for its effectiveness. Ismael et al. [14] used the original version of SSA to choose the best conductor in a real-world application of radial distribution system in Egypt. Ekinci et al. [15] applied the SSA to tune the stabilizer, that is an important task of a multi-machine power system to deliver the constant voltage regardless of changes in the input voltage of the power system. The result of the experiment shown its effectiveness and confirmed that SSA outperformed than other intelligent techniques.

All these works can demonstrate that SSA is flexible and capable of managing the exploration and exploitation propensities of nature-inspired algorithms. That is especially for the feature selection task in machine learning, the method can show satisfactory trends for the optimization problems and flexibility in detecting near-optimal solutions.

Placement of multiple SDN controllers in a large-sized network is a complex task and allude to choose an optimal number of controllers and its position in the network to meet a defined objective. There are many network performance metrics proposed to solve the Controller Placement Problem (CPP) by the researchers in literature. At first, Heller et al. [7] discussed the placement of the controller in Wide Area Network (WAN) considering the reaction time requirements to minimize latency between each switch and its associated controller. For this research work, we used propagation latency between switches and controller to be minimized as objective. Finding the location of controllers is an NP-hard problem and alike to facility location problem. To design an algorithm to generate the best solution for the controller placement is time-consuming and a full-scale task. The search space for an optimization algorithm includes the number of agents with assumed constraints, in case of CPP for controller k in n forwarding elements networks, all possible combination $\left(n_{C_k}\right)$ where $k < n$. As an illustration, to find an optimum location of 5 network controllers in a network of 50 forwarding elements, the solution is derived after performing a search from a total **211, 8760** possible placements. An evolutionary algorithm is an alternative for such scenarios, which explores a small subset of the entire search space, to provide close to an optimal solution [8].

In this study, the proposed SASSA is applied to solve the controller placement problem. To address the key issues of SSA, this article proposed a novel approach in SSA to make control parameters self-adaptive and use reverse learning strategy to improve population diversity during the optimization process. Further, this article investigates the performance of self-adaptive SSA and evaluates a class of benchmark problems. It should be mentioned that there is little consideration in the literature to boost SSA's performance [9]. As far as we know, a self-adaptive approach with reverse learning strategy to boost the performance of SSA is introduced first-time. The main contributions of this article are as follows:

- Based on self-adaptive and reverse learning strategy a novel approach to boost the overall performance of original SSA is introduced.
- The performance of the proposed approach for SSA is evaluated on a class of benchmark problems.
- An improved version of original SSA is evaluated for the controller placement problem where an attempt is made to minimize the propagation latency between the controllers and its associated forwarding elements.
- The performance of SASSA is compared with the original SSA on a class of benchmark problems for the global optimization problem.

The rest of the article is organized as follows: Sect. 2 presents the self-adaptive SSA algorithm with techniques to apply for a class of benchmark problems and the placement of controllers in SDN. The simulation results and discussion are presented in Sect. 3. Finally, Sect. 4 includes the conclusion and future work.

2   The Novel Self-Adaptive SSA Algorithm

An adequate exploration and exploitation proclivity of SSA algorithm on many real-world problems makes it appealing for the controller placement problem. There is a unique advantage of SSA that cannot be obtained using some other standard optimizer such as Particle Swarm Optimization [16,19], Grey Wolf Optimizer [18] and Whale Optimization Algorithm [17] techniques. The SSA is capable, simple, flexible, easy to understand, and can apply in the complex real-world applications to solve the optimization problems. Moreover, the single adaptable decreasing control parameter mechanism in SSA makes it more suitable to the optimization problems with a better balance between exploration and exploitation propensities.

Self-adaptive control parameter techniques with reverse learning strategy is an efficient approach for the controller placement problem, where the control parameters of an algorithm are adapting itself according to the progress of optimization process and the reverse learning strategy helps to increase the search-ability to achieve the global best [4]. An approach to modify the original SSA with self-adaptive control parameter techniques and reverse learning strategy could be a promising solution for a class of benchmark problems and the controller placement problem. In general, the self-adaptive SSA algorithm works as shown in Algorithm 1.

In SASSA, the positions of the population are calculated using Eq. (1) and (2) respectively during the optimization process.

$$X_j^i = \begin{cases} F_j + C_{1,\,j}\left((ub_j - lb_j)C_{2,\,j} + lb_j\right) \\ F_j - C_{1,\,j}\left((ub_j - lb_j)C_{2,\,j} + lb_j\right) \end{cases} \quad \dots 1$$

$$C_{1,\,j} = k_1 \cdot c_1$$

$$C_{2,\,j} = sin\left(\frac{C_{1,\,j}}{w_j}\right)$$

$$X_j^i = u \cdot (ub_j - lb_j) - X_j^i \quad \dots 2$$

where $C_{1,\,j}$, $C_{2,\,j}$ are self-adaptive and X_j^i indicates the position of the ith salp in j^{th} dimension and F_j reveals the position vector of food source in the search space as salp swarm's target in j^{th} dimension, w_j is based on the chaotic map, k_1 is a uniformly generated random values in the range $[0, 1]$. In the first iteration algorithm build a salp chain using the equations of standard SSA and in the subsequent iterations (1) and (2) continue updating the position of salps adaptively to increase the searchability of the algorithm, and decreases the probability of entrapment in local optima by applying reverse learning strategy.

There are some ideas proposed to improve the SSA in the literatures but we used the original version of SSA and applied an opposition-based learning strategy with self-adaptive control parameter techniques as described in [3, 4] to improve the global best solution. The self-adaptive control parameters $C_{1,\,j}$, $C_{2,\,j}$ in SASSA, maintains the expected explorative and exploitative ability of the salp chain during the optimization process. Further, we used the reverse learning strategy to allow some of the salps of the population to maintain diversity in the current population. This approach helps to maintain the diversity of individuals and prevent re-initialization of the population that introduces a severe loss of information. Flowchart of the self-adaptive SSA is proposed in this article, as shown in Fig. 1.

Software-defined network (SDN) decouples the control plane from forwarding elements and introduces the controller placement problem. In this article, the proposed SASSA algorithm is applied to solve the controller placement problem that includes finding the location of the controller in the network topology to minimize propagation latency between controller and forwarding elements. While minimizing the latency between each forwarding element and its associated SDN controller, which is one of the crucial aspects of the controller placement problem. There are other competing objectives also required consideration such as load balancing, inter-controller latency, and forwarding elements or link failure. Figure 2 illustrates a basic architecture of the SDN network.

In this paper, the network metric propagation latency has been used as an objective for the controller placement problem. The first and most important step in the placement of a controller using SSA is the problem formulation. In other words, the problem should be formulated in a way that is suitable for an

---

Algorithm 1. SASSA

1: **procedure** SELFADAPTIVESSA($Max_I teration, Iteration, lb, ub, dim, fObj$)
2:     **Initialization:** Population, Parameters, Best Solution, Fitness
3:     **while** $Iteration \leq Max_I teration$ **do**   ▷ Main Loop
4:         **if** $Iteration \geq 1$ **then**
5:             Update the positions
6:             Calculate self-adaptive control parameter
7:             Update position () using SASSA
8:             Followers update () with reverse learning
9:             Calculate Fitness
10:         **else**
11:             Build salp chain using standard SSA
12:     Best Solution   ▷ Returns the Best Solution

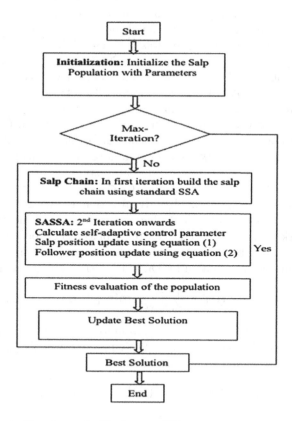

Fig. 1. Flowchart of self-adaptive SSA optimization algorithm.

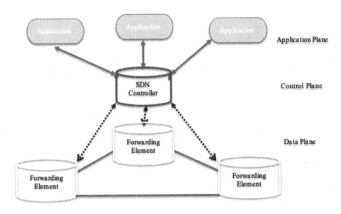

Fig. 2. Basic architecture of SDN.

optimizer. Indicated network in this work present $G = (V, E)$, where V is set of nodes or switches and E is a set of physical links among the switches. The set of nodes V consists of a set of forwarding elements S and set of controllers C . The set of controllers can be expressed as $C = \{C_1, C_2, C_3, C_4 \ldots C_m\}$ and the switches set $S = \{S_1, S_2, S_3, S_4 \ldots S_n\}$, where m indicate the total number of controllers and n indicates a total number of forwarding elements (or routers) i.e. $V = S \cup C$. Hence C_i present i^{th} controller and S_i present i^{th} forwarding element or router. To represent shortest path latencies among each pair of forwarding elements and controllers, a distance matrix d (s, c) entailed.

The given number of controllers k to be placed for a particular placement can be represented as $|C_i| = k$. For maintaining the simplicity, let's consider $C = \{C_1, C_2, C_3, C_4 \ldots C_m\}$ represents all possible locations of controllers. To find out the location of the controller $C_i \in C$ i.e. i^{th} controller present as an optimization problem in which objective function as a metric should be optimized. The latency between the controller and forwarding elements is the most common network metrics, used to the controller placement problem. It is denoted as the average distance between the switches (or routers) and its associated controller. The computation equation for calculating the average latency:

$$\Pi^{\text{Average Latency}}(C) = \frac{1}{|V|} \sum_{v \in V} \min_{c \in C_i} d(s, c) \quad \ldots 3$$

where $d(s, c)$ represent the shortest path from forwarding element s to its associated controller $c \in C_i$. The objective of solving the controller placement using SASSA is to achieve minimum average latency.

$$\text{Min} \left(\Pi^{\text{Average Latency}}(C) \right) \quad \ldots 4$$

3 Simulation Results and Computational Analysis

In this section, performance of the proposed algorithm SASSA is evaluated. There are two experiments conducted in this paper to assess modified SSA. Section 3.2 presents the first experiment that focus to assess the performance of SASSA to solve the global optimization problems and compared its performance with standard SSA. In this section, a class of unimodal and multimodal benchmark functions (F) are considered. Table 1 provides detail of the benchmark functions: De Jong's function, Rastrigin function, and Ackley's function with mathematics expressions, dimension, initial range and expected minimum (f_{min}) value. The second experiment presents in Sect. 3.3, aims to solve the controller placement problem in SDN, to find a position of controllers in given network topology, i.e. to minimize the average propagation latency between controllers and its associated forwarding elements.

3.1 Setup of the Experimental Environment

The computer experimental environment is based on Intel® Core™i7-3520M CPU @ 2.90 GHz, 16 GB of RAM, and the macOS v.10.15.5. The source code of self-adaptive SSA is implemented in MATLAB R2017b.

3.2 SASSA for the Global Optimization Problems

The performance of SASSA is evaluated on a class of benchmark problems. The adapted benchmark problems in this article are divided into two class: Unimodal and Multimodal. The unimodal problem has only one global optimum and there are no local optima. This function is used to benchmarked the convergence rate with exploitation capability of SASSA as the entire search space prefer the global optimum. Similarly, the performance of SASSA regarding the exploration capability and ability to avoid entrapment in local optimum is benchmarked using the adapted multimodal problems as it has many local optima. Also, the multimodal functions are considered more challenging for an algorithm than the unimodal functions.

The mean values and standard deviations of three benchmark functions De Jong's, Rastrigin, and Ackley's are recorded in Table 2, Table 3 and Table 4. The recorded values in all the experiments are the result of 50 independent runs, where the population size is set to 50 and the maximum iteration is set to 1000. Moreover, to have a fair comparison with original SSA, the initial position is initialized using the same interface and the same objective function were used for fitness evaluation. The numerical results show that SASSA with reverse learning strategy works better on all the benchmark functions as compared to the original SSA. Thus, the proposed strategy to modify SSA can significantly explore the most promising area in the search space and can find a better balance between exploration and exploitation propensities of EAs.

Table 1. Benchmark functions.

Function Name	Function	Dim	Rang	f_{min}
De Jong s Function (Unimodal)	$F_1(x) = \sum\limits_{i=1}^{n} ix_i^4 + random\,(0,1)$	10	[-1.28, 1.28]	0
Ackley's Function (Multimodal)	$F_2(x) = -20exp\left(-0.2\sqrt{\dfrac{1}{n}\sum\limits_{i=1}^{n} x_i^2}\right)$ $- exp\left(\dfrac{1}{n}\sum\limits_{i=1}^{n} cos(2\pi x_i)\right)$ $+ 20 + e$	10	[-32, 32]	0
Rastrigin Function (Multimodal)	$F_3(x) = \sum\limits_{i=1}^{n} [x_i^2 - 10cos(2\pi x_i) + 10]$	10	[-5.12, 5.12]	0

Table 2. F1- De Jong's function (Unimodal).

	Popsize (N)	Dimension (d)	Max-Iteration (L)	SSA	SASSA
Avg. Best	50	10	1000	1.29E-04	4.79E-07
Avg. Worst	50	10	1000	2.02E-02	4.90E-04
Avg. Mean	50	10	1000	4.91E-03	1.67E-04
STD.	50	10	1000	4.12E-03	1.23E-04

Table 3. F2- Rastrigin function (Multimodal).

	Popsize (N)	Dimension (d)	Max-Iteration (L)	SSA	SASSA
Avg. Best	50	10	1000	4.97E+00	1.90E-11
Avg. Worst	50	10	1000	2.98E+01	1.19E-10
Avg. Mean	50	10	1000	1.49E+01	5.91E-11
STD.	50	10	1000	5.99E+00	2.35E-11

Table 4. F3- Ackley's function (Multimodal).

	Popsize (N)	Dimension (d)	Max-Iteration (L)	SSA	SASSA
Avg. Best	50	10	1000	7.31E-06	2.44E-06
Avg. Worst	50	10	1000	2.81E+00	5.69E-06
Avg.Mean	50	10	1000	6.14E-01	4.33E-06
STD.	50	10	1000	8.75E-01	8.46E-07

3.3 SASSA for the Controller Placement Problem

To evaluate the performance of SASSA on the controller placement problem in SDN, we select the Internet2 OS3E topology with a number of 34 nodes and k as a given number of controllers to be placed. The objective of placements in this paper is to find a placement of controller k in the network topology to minimize the propagation latency between the controller and its associated forwarding elements. It has practical implications while designing the software, whether the controller can counter to events in real-time or the required actions to be pushed in advance to the forwarding elements [7].

Evaluation of all possible controller placements for a predefined number of controllers, that is to be placed in the network topology in respect of an objective function to find the optimal set of position in the network, is a time-consuming and exhaustive process. In many cases, it runs with, out of resources in the used machine such as the capacity of RAM exceeded [21]. In this case, the entire search space includes the combination of controllers k with network nodes n , where we seek for the best position of k controllers, which comes with all possible number of placements using Eq. (5).

$$\binom{n}{k} = \frac{n!}{k!(n-k)!} \quad \binom{n}{k} = \frac{n!}{k!\,(n-k)!} \cdots 5$$

Therefore, for the relatively small network nodes (n), the number rises exceedingly along with an increment in the number of controllers k. For instance, the network topology of **34** network nodes and **2** controllers, the total number of placements presents as $\binom{34}{2} = 561$ $\binom{34}{2} = 561$ and moving to $\binom{34}{5} = 27,82,56$ $\binom{34}{5} = 27,82,56$ placements. This increase in the number of possible placements, required an exhaustive evaluation with high computational effort and abounding of time. However, an efficient search strategy as defined in this paper to explore for the best solution is promising to the controller placement problem in terms of computational effort and time due to its stochastic nature of computation.

Table 5. Possible placements of (k=4) controllers.

Run #	Possible Placement Nodes	Latency (Best case)
1	[12 16 30 18]	0.2449
2	[18 11 17 29]	0.083536
3	[5 33 28 6]	0.13032
4	[9 11 30 13]	0.093734
5	[25 2 19 5]	0.094256
6	[8 34 15 3]	0.096316
7	[26 3 25 22]	0.16259
8	[28 12 21 23]	0.11234
9	[10 26 30 13]	0.17758
10	[2 12 22 5]	0.095963
11	[24 4 13 10]	0.17525
12	[10 16 27 15]	0.0785
13	[19 25 12 10]	0.16094
14	[3 30 34 1]	0.12703
15	[21 8 24 12]	0.091496
16	[28 32 31 34]	0.08738
17	[15 3 2 8]	0.092661
18	[28 3 7 31]	0.13955
19	[1 26 23 17]	0.089306
20	[26 17 15 32]	0.1007
21	[16 23 33 13]	0.078515
22	[13 26 25 24]	0.15203
23	[1 23 9 15]	0.36264
24	[34 1 33 17]	0.086439
25	[30 3 22 14]	0.11735
26	[31 26 29 28]	0.092625
27	[31 27 7 30]	0.15043
28	**[29 22 27 12]**	**0.078348**
29	[9 6 13 23]	0.12456
30	[13 31 5 19]	0.10181

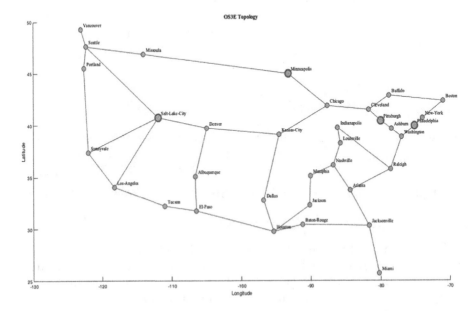

Fig. 3. Position of controllers (k = 4) in OS3E network topology [20].

SASSA algorithm applied to evaluate all the possible placements for network topology Internet2 OS3E with several nodes $n = 34$ for the number of controllers $k = 4$ as shown in Table 5, from an average latency of 30 independent runs. The best placement found in 28th iteration is highlighted in the table with underlined bold and indicated the position of controllers as Salt-Lake City, Minneapolis, Pittsburgh and Philadelphia as shown in Fig. 3.

4   Conclusion

This article introduces a novel approach based on SSA and self-adaptive parameters with opposition-based learning strategy, where the control parameters of the algorithms are adapting itself according to the progress of optimization process. In SASSA, after creating the salp chain the position of salps is modified according to the proposed equations based on self-adapting and reverse learning mechanism to obtain a good balance between exploitation and exploration. The proposed approach is employed to solve a class of benchmark problems in the category of unimodal and multimodal functions for the global optimization and the controller placement problem in SDN. The experimental results showed that embedding self-adaptive with reverse learning strategy in the original SSA significantly boost the overall performance of SSA while balancing the exploitative and explorative propensities of SSA. Also, the results on benchmark functions showed that the proposed SASSA is distinctly superior to original SSA in terms of mean value and standard deviation.

Since the decision-making capability has been moved into the controller, it makes essential to develop a method to find the optimal placement of controllers in a software-defined network. This research work is based on the existing formulation of the controller placement problem and the primary objective is to place the controllers in such a way so that latency between the controllers and forwarding elements should be minimized.

For future studies, the proposed SASSA will be employed to solve other real-world optimization problems.

References

1. Yang, X.: Review of meta-heuristics and generalized evolutionary walk algorithm. Int. J. Bio Inspired Comput. **3**(2), 77–84 (2011)
2. Gogna, A., Tayal, A.: Metaheuristics: review and application. J. Exp. Theor. Artif. Intell. **25**(4), 503–526 (2013)
3. Brest, J., Zamuda, A., Boskovic, B., Maucec, M.S., Zumer, V.: Dynamic optimization using self-adaptive differential evolution. In: 2009 IEEE Congress on Evolutionary Computation, Trondheim, pp. 415–422 (2009)
4. Tizhoosh, H.R.: Opposition-based learning: a new scheme for machine intelligence. In: Proceedings of the International Conference on Computational Intelligence for Modelling, Control and Automation and International Conference on Intelligent Agents, Web Technologies and Internet Commerce (CIMCA-IAWTIC), vol. 1, pp. 695–701, November 2005

5. Mirjalili, S., Gandomi, A.H., Mirjalili, S.Z., Saremi, S., Faris, H., Mirjalili, S.M.: Salp swarm algorithm: a bio-inspired optimizer for engineering design problems. Adv. Eng. Softw. **114**, 163–191 (2017)

6. Ateya, A.A., et al.: Chaotic salp swarm algorithm for SDN multi-controller networks. Eng. Sci. Technol. Int. J. **22**(4), 1001–1012 (2019)

7. Heller, B., Sherwood, R., McKeown, N.: The controller placement problem. In: Proceedings of the First Workshop on Hot Topics in Software Defined Networks. ACM, July 2012

8. Bouvry, P., Ruiz, P., Danoy, G., Dorronsoro, B., Pigné, Y.: Evolutionary Algorithms for Mobile Ad Hoc Networks. Wiley, Hoboken (2014)

9. Sayed, G.I., Khoriba, G., Haggag, M.H.: A novel chaotic salp swarm algorithm for global optimization and feature selection. Appl. Intell. **48**(10), 3462–3481 (2018). https://doi.org/10.1007/s10489-018-1158-6

10. Anderson, P.A., Bone, Q.: Communication between individuals in salp chains II. Physiology. Proc. R. Soc. Lond. B **210**, 559–574 (1980)

11. Andersen, V., Nival, P.: A model of the population dynamics of salps in coastal waters of the Ligurian Sea. J. Plankton Res. **8**, 1091–110 (1986)

12. Yaseen, Z.M., Sulaiman, S.O., Deo, R.C., Chau, K.-W.: An enhanced extreme learning machine model for river flow forecasting: state-of-the-art, practical applications in water resource engineering area and future research direction. J. Hydrol. **569**, 387–408 (2019)

13. Faris, H., et al.: An efficient binary salp swarm algorithm with crossover scheme for feature selection problems. Knowl. Based Syst. **154**, 43–67 (2018)

14. Ismael, S., Aleem, S., Abdelaziz, A., Zobaa, A.: Practical considerations for optimal conductor reinforcement and hosting capacity enhancement in radial distribution systems. IEEE Access **6**, 27268–27277 (2018)

15. Ekinci, S., Hekimoglu, B.: Parameter optimization of power system stabilizer via salp swarm algorithm. In: 2018 5th IEEE International Conference on Electrical and Electronic Engineering (ICEEE), pp. 143–147 (2018)

16. Du, K.L., Swamy, M.N.S.: Particle swarm optimization. In: Search and Optimization by Metaheuristics, pp. 153–173. Birkhäuser, Cham (2016). https://doi.org/10.1007/978-3-319-41192-7_9

17. Biyanto, T.R., et al.: Killer whale algorithm: an algorithm inspired by the life of killer whale. Procedia Comput. Sci. **124**, 151–157 (2017)

18. Mirjalili, S., Mirjalili, S.M., Lewis, A.: Grey wolf optimizer. Adv. Eng. Softw. **69**, 46–61 (2014)

19. Eberhart, R.C., Kennedy, J.: A new optimizer using particle swarm theory. In: Proceedings of the 6th International Symposium on Micro Machine and Human Science, pp. 39–43 (1995)

20. Mamushiane, L., Mwangama, J., Lysko, A.A.: Given a SDN topology, how many controllers are needed and where should they go? In: 2018 IEEE Conference on Network Function Virtualization and Software Defined Networks (NFV-SDN), Verona, Italy, pp. 1–6 (2018). https://doi.org/10.1109/NFV-SDN.2018.8725710

21. Lange, S., et al.: Heuristic approaches to the controller placement problem in large scale SDN networks. IEEE Trans. Netw. Serv. Manage. **12**(1), 4–17 (2015). https://doi.org/10.1109/TNSM.2015.2402432

Earthquake Magnitude Prediction Using Machine Learning Technique

Amirul Hoque[1(✉)], Jyoti Raj[1], Ashim Saha[1], and Paritosh Bhattacharya[2]

[1] CSE Department, NIT Agartala, Agartala, Tripura, India
amirul.csc@gmail.com
[2] Department of Mathematics, NIT Agartala, Agartala, Tripura, India

Abstract. The prophecy of an earthquake is a very complicated task which has been resolved in different ways. However, there is a need for an elementary definition along with adequate catalogues. These areas have been marked with widely used geological parameters. Total characteristics of study are based on not only the training and testing data sets but also qualitative data about earthquake prediction. The machine learning technique is applied on Japan, Turkey, Greece and Indian Subcontinent regions. The model show relationship be-tween calculated seismic data and future earthquake occurrences. It is the setup which has been fixed to provide the forecasts for earthquakes of a magnitude of 5.0 and its above for Japan, 4.5 and greater for Indian Subcontinent region, 3.7 and greater for Turkey region, 3.2 and greater for Greece region, before fifteen days to the earthquakes. A noticeable improvement has been produced by the model in earthquake predictions and compared to previous prediction studies. The studies bestowed during this work analysing the performance of the prediction across the earthquake magnitude statistics of the target seismogenic zones which will help in the further development and improvement of the system.

Keywords: Machine learning · Earthquake prediction · Artificial neural networks · Time series

1 Introduction

The definition for the forecast of an earthquake is to access the probability for the risk of earthquake hazard over an area, which includes the magnitude and frequency of it over a decade (Adeli and Panakkat [14]). Till date there is no reliable method to predict earthquakes, many have tried for it but none of the methods opted by them has been proven successful. After an effort of a decade seismology community to are unable to provide or develop any method for earthquake prediction. Earthquake prediction is still an unachievable task as the technology available is not feeble enough to measure stress temperature and pressure changes to higher accuracy beneath the earth's crust through scientific instruments, that's why extensive seismic data is always scarce. Lack of interdisciplinary effort between the department of seismology and computer science to

© Springer Nature Switzerland AG 2020
N. Kar et al. (Eds.): ICCISIoT 2020, CCIS 1358, pp. 37–53, 2020.
https://doi.org/10.1007/978-3-030-66763-4_4

accurately predict and measure the events of earthquakes has let the earthquake prediction as an unachievable task till date (Panakkat and Adeli [14]).

Higher occurrence of earthquakes during the full moon periods, changes occurring in fluids and gases before the earthquake, variation in level of oil & water in wells, movement of gravitational field around the earth, anomalous behavior of animals (Grant et al. 2015), radon & electromagnetic irregularities (Pulinets and Ouzounov 2011), an unusual formation of clouds are the few anomalies which are related to the prediction of earthquake. With the help of time-stamped sequences of past earth-quake, the seismic index is computed and recorded in earthquake catalogue which is fed to algorithms with enough computational intelligence for earthquake predictions & with the help of Seismic index upcoming earthquakes can be predicted (Graves et al. 2013).

Occurrences of an earthquake are treated to be an extremely nonlinear or random phenomenon. Till now no such model is existing to predicts exact locations, magnitude and time of an earthquake. According to some scientist's earthquake is difficult to predict prior to happening. While others are suggesting that it is a predictable phenomenon.

1.1   Tectonics of Japan Region

The Japan is the most seismic region in the world basically for seismic events occurring at intermediate depth of 70 km to 300 km (Pavlis and Das 2000). That seismic region is geologically formed by the collision of the Pacific, North American, Eurasian and Filipino plates during Eocene (Farah et al. 1984). Japan is affected frequently by volcanic disasters and earthquakes. The seismic and volcanic activities are monitored operationally by JMA throughout the whole country and the issues relevant warnings and informations to mitigate the damage caused by the disasters related to the earthquakes, volcanic eruptions and tsunamis. The stretching of the Ring of Fire of Japan is where the Philippine, Eurasian, Pacific and North American plates come together. Northern Japan sits mostly on the top of the western tip of the North American plate. Southern Japan is largely top of the Eurasian plate. Averagely, the Pacific Plate which is moving west almost 8.9 centimeters per year. And the movement has created major earthquakes in the past of magnitude 7 or above since 1973 [36].

1.2   Tectonics of Turkey Region

Turkey is the most seismic and volcanic region in the world, Turkey sits on or near the boundary of four tectonic plates: The Anatolian Plate or the continental tectonic plate is a Turkish Plate, Arabian Plate, Eurasian Plate and African Plate. Research indicates that the Anatolian Plate is rotating counter clockwise as it is being pushed west by the Arabian Plate, impeded from any northerly movement by the Eurasian Plate [31]. The representation is filtered on basis of magnitude which ranges from '3.0' to '10'. The country exists between two big tectonic plates, Eurasia and Arabia or Africa, which are inexorably overlapping into each another, north to south. The most of the landmass of Turkey lies on the Anatolian plate, squeezing westwards towards the Aegean Sea. Periodic movements occur mainly along two faults, the North and East Anatolian fault [32].

1.3 Tectonics of Indian Subcontinent Region

Indian subcontinent is the most seismically active region and the large-scale faulting which produces huge earthquakes striking, is complicated. The Indian tectonic plate lies in the north-east hemisphere. Geologically, the Indian subcontinent is related to the landmass which rifted from Gondwanaland, merged along with the Eurasian plate almost 5.5 crore years earlier. Geographically, it is the peninsular seismic region in south central Asia, marked by the Hindu Kush, Himalayas and Arakanese in the west, north and east respectively. Politically, the Indian subcontinent includes India, Bangladesh, Bhutan, Maldives, Pakistan, Sri Lanka and Nepal [33]. It is formed by four big tectonic plates, Australian, African, Arabian and Eurasian plates, to the south east, south west, west and North of the Indian plate respectively. India gets separated from Madagascar and drifted north eastward with the velocity of about 0.2 m per year. Nowadays, still India is propagating in the similar direction but with a very small velocity of about 0.04 m per year, because of the resistance of Eurasian plate [33].

1.4 Tectonics of Greece Region

Greece is the most seismically active region and the large-scale faulting which produces huge earthquakes striking, is complicated. Greece is a lots of source of seismic activity because of the several interactions in between three major plates: Aegean Sea, African and Eurasia Plates. Nowadays, The Aegean Sea Plate is moving at approximately 3 cm in a South-western direction against the Eurasia Plate. This action generates seismic activity occurring in central and Northern Greece. When this causes such earthquakes along with other seismic activities, interactions in between the African and Eurasian plates cause more fascinating phenomenon called as the Hellenic Volcanic Arc. [35].

2 Related Work on Earthquake Forecasting

Works related to earthquake forecasting has been shown in this section, although there is a vast literature on earthquake prediction but it is still considered a complex problem. There is no particular methodology for earthquake forecasting. Some researchers suggested that prediction of an earthquake is an unachievable task (Geller et al. [26]). Although it has been concluded by some scientists that it can be predicted (Braile and Brehm 1998; Knopoff [21]; Kirschvink [22]; Ellsworth et al. [20]). And also short-term earthquake prediction model using seismic electric signals is given by Varostos and Alexopoulos in the year 1984, further Greek scientists Kossobokov and Latoussakis [9] have pro-posed the algorithm named M8 for the forecast of earthquake using the intermediate terms. VAN method has been proposed by Varotsos et al. (1988, 1989) for forecasting earthquake experimentally, neural networks model using single multi layer perception has been proposed by Wang which gave the earthquake estimate in Mainland China in 2001 [11].

Three layered neural networks as proposed by Negarestani et al. (2002) in Thailand, to analyze the correlation of environmental parameters with the concentration of radon and its variation gives the better prediction for an earthquake. The approach using Chaotic analysis to a time series which is consisted of seismic activity took place, is used by Tzanaki and Plagianakos [12] in Greece. Multilayer constriction data deployed for electromagnetic signal detection & wave observation is proposed by Itai et al. [13]. Detecting earthquake's possibility using precursory electric field patterns of Neural networks is proposed by Ozerdem et al. [16]. Ozerdem et al. [16] have proposed neural networks based upon Self-organized maps for possible earthquake pioneering electric field pattern detection. Jusoh et al. [17] have proposed earthquake forecasting derived from GPS dual frequency system in the equatorial area.

3   Earthquake Catalogue

The obtained dataset for all four regions, is separated into training sets and testing sets. For validation and training purposes, 70% of the obtained dataset is selected, while the rest of 30% dataset is performed as testing purpose. The final results given in Section six (6) are the predicted results taken on the testing dataset for all four regions, separately. The setups and configurations are arranged in the purpose to train a model is kept similar for all four region's datasets. How-ever, trainings have been performed separately for each all region. The region having different properties and classifications tectonically of different categories cause separate training, such as strike-slip tectonics, thrusting tectonics and so on. Therefore, each type of all region possesses separate relations and behaviors to the earthquakes. Thus different training for each region is meant for learning and modeling of the relationship in between seismic features and earthquakes of that particular regions. Herein proposed methodology contains the use of two steps feature extraction or selection process. The features are selected after per-forming redundancy and relevancy checks, to be sure that specifically useful features are involved for earthquake forecasting. The magnitudes of Earthquake and frequency occurrence for every region are plotted as shown in Fig. 1.

In the above curve exponentially decreasing behavior is found assuring that every catalogue is fulfilled to its respective cut off magnitude. The catalogues of the said seismic regions are calculated for cut off magnitude. Cut off magnitude means to the lower magnitude and below which the earthquake catalogue is considered incomplete. Some numerous techniques are present to evaluate the cut off magnitude for the catalogue, whereas by studying it is obtained by using the statistical analysis of Gutenberg Richter curve. When Earth-quake frequency

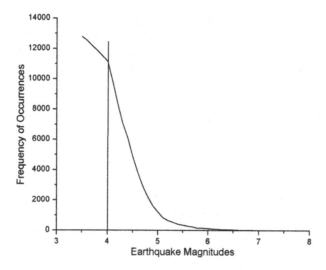

Fig. 1. Inverse log relationship plots between the magnitudes of Earthquake and frequency occurrence (K.M. Asim et al. [6]).

of occurrence is high then Earthquake magnitudes is very low. And frequency of occurrence is low at the time Earthquake magnitudes is very large or high. That is Inverse log relationship plot between the magnitudes of Earthquake and frequency occurrence as shown in Fig. 1.

4   Proposed Methodology

Our proposed methodology which includes the use of artificial neural network. Datasets obtained for each the four region, is separated into testing and training sets. For validation and training purposes, 70% of the dataset is considered, while the rest of 30% dataset is performed as testing purpose. The final results given in Section six (6) are the predicted results taken on the testing dataset for all four regions, separately. The setups and configurations are arranged in the purpose to train a model is kept similar for all four region's datasets.

4.1   Artificial Neural Network

Neural networks are made to work as nervous system of human. The network containing sensory units called as neuron, are interconnected by the weighted connections. The ability of neural networks is modeled highly nonlinear relationships. After training, network is given inputs which are unseen, without specifying the outputs, so on the basis of training, outcomes which are predicted by the network are calculated for checking the power of the network. The trained methodology which is used for training of neural network is LMBP (Levenberg Mar-quardt Backpropagation) (Bishop 1995). It's used in combination with an optimized technique like gradient descent. LMBP algorithm is much faster than other algorithms which reaches confluence everywhere between 10 to 100 times faster than the standard Backpropagation algorithm, but it needs large memory (Bishop 1995). There are two hidden-layers, first hidden-layer has 64 neurons and the second has 34 neurons as given in Fig. 2. This is considered manually depending on the experimentation for getting the best outcomes. The activation function which is used for the layer one is tansigmoid as shown in Eq. 1 and layer two is relu.

$$T_1(n) = tanh(cn) = \frac{e^{cn} - e^{-cn}}{e^{cn} + e^{-cn}} \tag{1}$$

The total synaptic connections which are evaluated using Eq. 2, where H1 represents the hidden number of neuron in layer 1 and H2 represents the hidden number of neuron in layer 2, while the number of inputs and outputs are indicated by I and O.

$$W = (I + 1)H1 + (H1 + 1)H2 + (H2 + 1)O \tag{2}$$

For our model this neural network densely connected or fully connected which means that each nodes connected to all the nodes in the previous layer and also all the nodes in the next layer. For activation functions are used "relu" which is rectified linear unit, this is commonly activation unit in the hidden layer. We have 6 variables as input layer for Japan zone and Indian subcontinent, 5 variables as input layer for Turkey and 4 variables as input layer for Greece. Input layer connects into first hidden layer and first hidden layer connects into second hidden layer, then the connection into the next layer which is called output layer (output layer with 1 neuron) for output layer we are not going to specify activation functions, here using default activation function is linear activation function.

Next phase is compiled the model because our y variable is numeric and we are dealing with regression problem so 'mse (mean square Error)' are used, while optimiser will be used 'rmsprop' which is default for matrix, we can specify 'mae'. Next phase my proposed model connects to fit here and we are going to use independent data and dependent data from test sets, 100 number of epochs and batch size is 32.

4.2   Data Set Description

The data should be accumulated from reliable sources. Many private and public organizations are present which provides database and earthquake catalogue for the earthquakes over all the world. These sources are available in Internet which provide advance search abilities such as ANSS (Advanced National Seismic System), NEIC (National Earthquake Information Center), NCEDC (the Northern California Earthquake Data Center), and others [3]. Here, the past seismicity which is available as a catalogue, which is openly available from the USGS (United States Geological Survey) [27]. The catalogue is treated for this

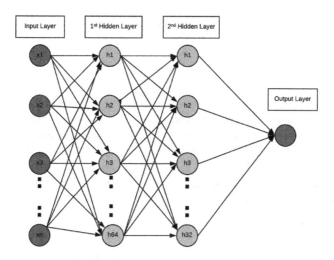

Fig. 2. Diagram of ANN for the earthquake prediction.

research, is obtained from duration of 1st January 2001 to 31st December 2018 for Japan region, December 1901 to July 2017 for Turkey, January 2000 to December 2017 for Indian Subcontinent and January 1901 to December 2018. Thus, the number of instances available for The Japan are 14093, Turkey are 24008, Greece are 256656, Indian subcontinent are 14699. For instance, we can have Earthquake dataset in Japan with time, latitude, longitude, depth, gap, mag, magType, dmin, rms, net, id, updated, place, type, horizontal, depthError, magError, magNst, status, location Source, magSource etc. For instance, we can have Earthquake dataset in Turkey with id, date, time, lat, long, depth, md, xm, country, city, area, direction, dist, Richter etc. For instance, we can have Earthquake dataset in Greece with Year, Month, Date, Hours, Minutes, Latitude, Longitude, Magnitude etc. For instance, we can have Earthquake dataset in Indian subcontinent with date, time, Latitude, Longitude, mag Type, Depth, nst, gap, Depth Error, place, Magnitude Type, Magnitude Error, source, Location, status, Horizontal Distance, magnitude, Magnitude Error, etc. The collection of data set for the Earthquake are in the form of csv files. In this research the proposed model is as a binary classification task with aim for generating forecasting for earthquakes of magnitude 5.0 and above for Japan region, 4.5 and greater for Indian Subcontinent region, 3.7 and greater for Turkey region, 3.2 and greater for Greece region 15 day's durations to the earthquake. The datasets are divided into two parts, validations and training purposes, 70% of the dataset is considered and testing purposes in the ratio of 30%, for the all regions respectively, its training and testing. It is a binary classification problem. Label '1' shows the occurrence of the earthquake magnitude 5 or above for Japan, 4.5 and greater for Indian Subcontinent region, 3.7 and greater for Turkey region, 3.2 and greater for Greece region. While the absence of seismic activity is shown either label '0'. Training of all four regions is per-formed almost 70% of the obtained dataset.

Evaluation or predicting is performed on the remaining datasets which is almost 30% of the obtained dataset.

4.3   Workflow

The earthquake forecasting models which are proposed in literature, where prediction model is suggested to machine learning. This is a combination of different machine learning techniques along with each technique complementing to the other through the knowledge gained during learning. Thus, in this model every step is further adding improvements into the toughness, therefore, which results a final upgraded version of prediction model. The flowchart of overall proposed model is shown in Fig. 3.

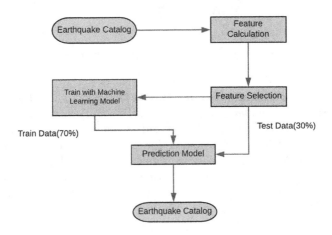

Fig. 3. Flowchart of model

Figure 3 is shown the overall flowchart of the Research Work. In this process the earthquake catalogue is the beginning point, therefore, catalogue quality precisely influences the prediction outcomes. Further involved processes are feature selection, calculation, trained model, and in conclusions, predictions are gained on the dataset unseen part. In the end performance of prediction model, outcome is calculated and then comparison is drawn.

4.4   Evaluation Parameters

This research is performed by the use of eight earthquake seismic indicators, which basically mean to refer the earthquake seismic state and capability of the earth. This section provides the summery of all parameters along with their calculations. We have the parameter of the Time T, which represents the complete duration of time over the end n number of seismic events and in our case n is 100 and then t indicates the time of the earthquake occurrences.

$$T = t_n - t_1 \tag{3}$$

Time T indicates the foreshocks frequency under consideration before the month. Measurement of distinct performance subsist due to binary classification problems. The performance of earthquake prediction is evaluated as expressed by the following measures:

1. **True Positives (TP):** Actually an earthquake was occurred and it is predicted by the algorithm.
2. **True Negative (TN):** No earthquake was actually occurred and there no alarm was in actual.
3. **False Positive (FP):** Actually no earthquake was occurred but it was wrongly predicted by algorithm.
4. **False Negative (FN):** actually an earthquake was occurred but algorithm was not able to predict.

Some other calculations criteria are educed from the aforesaid four measures. There are two types of most common statistical measures, Specificity and Sensitivity. Here Sensitivity Sn indicates to the rate of real positives predictions, whereas specificity Sp indicates to the rate of real negatives predictions.

$$S_n = \frac{TP}{TP + FN} \tag{4}$$

$$S_p = \frac{TN}{TN + FP} \tag{5}$$

Two other calculations criteria exclusively useful to predict earthquake which are P1 Precision or positive value of predictions and P0 or negative value of predictions. P1 Precision is indicated as the percentage of true positives within whole positive predictions of the classifier as given by Eq. 6. Whereas P0 is indicated as the percentage of true negative within whole negative predictions of classifier as given in Eq. 7.

$$P_1 = \frac{TP}{TP + FP} \tag{6}$$

$$P_0 = \frac{TN}{TN + FN} \tag{7}$$

Similarly, accuracy indicates another criterion which measures the percentage of total number of actual predictions out of whole predictions which the classifiers produce, irrespective of negative or positive predictions. It is evaluated as follows:

$$Accuracy = \frac{TP + TN}{TP + FP + TN + FN} \tag{8}$$

All these calculations criterion are evaluated from four elements of fortuitous table, i.e., False Negative, True Negative, False Positives and True Positives. The certain types of accomplishment of the classifier are highlighted by every criterion, for which the purpose of appointing all these criterion is to refer every types of classifier's accomplishment.

5   Result and Discussions

5.1   Prediction for Japan Zone

The data set on Japan zone has 14092 observations as rows and 7 variables as column, in which 6 column has numeric value and one column has binary value as factor variable. First thing is that we convert factor variable to numeric because neural network takes input as numeric variable. If more than one variable is factor variable, then all variable need to be converted at once in numeric. Our dataset consists of 7 attribute in which 6 of them are independent and 1 ('actual') is a dependent attribute. For neural network we have used four different layers which consist of one input layer, one output layer and two hidden layers. The 1st hidden layer has 64 neurons and 2nd hidden layer has 32 neurons. The input layer has 6 neurons, one neuron each for the independent variable and output layer has one node.

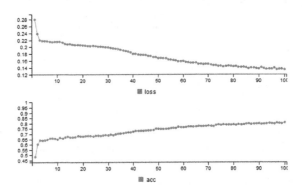

Fig. 4. The plot represents accuracy and loss of our proposed model for Japan earthquake zone

For the Japan zone out of 14092 observations we have 9864 observations for training and 4228 for testing purpose. The least results have been shown by NN based proposed model for the Japan zone with accuracy of 83.57%. Figure 4 represents the result for Japan Earthquake zone.

5.2   Prediction for Indian Subcontinent Zone

The data set on Indian Subcontinent zone has 14698 observations as rows and 9 variables as column, in which 8 column has numeric value and one column has binary value as factor variable. First thing is to convert factor variable to numeric because neural network needs numeric variable. In case more than one variable which are factor variable then all variable need to be converted to numeric at once. Our dataset consists of 8 attribute in which 7 of them are independent and 1 attribute ('actual') is dependent attribute. For neural network we have used four different layers which consist of one input layer, one output layer and two hidden layers. The 1st hidden layer has 64 neurons and 2nd hidden layer has 32 neurons. The input layer has 6 neurons, one neuron each for the independent variable and output layer has one node. For the Indian Subcontinent zone out of 14698 observations we have 10288 observations for training and 4410 for testing purpose. The least results have been shown by NN based proposed model for the Indian Sub-continent zone with accuracy of 87.14%. Figure 5 represents the result for Indian Subcontinent Earthquake zone.

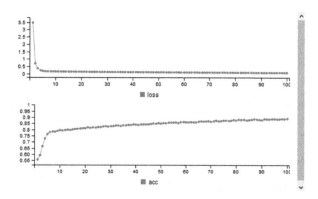

Fig. 5. The plot shows accuracy and loss of our proposed model for Indian subcontinent earth-quake zone

5.3 Prediction for Turkey Zone

The data set on Turkey zone has 24007 observations as rows and 6 variables as column, in which 5 column has numeric value and one column has binary value as factor variable. First thing is that we convert factor variable to numeric because neural network takes input as numeric variable. If more than one variable is factor variable, then all variable need to be converted at once in numeric. Our dataset consists of 6 attribute in which 5 of them are independent and 1 ('actual') is dependent attribute.

For neural network we have used four different layers which consist of one input layer, one output layer and two hidden layers. The 1st hidden layer has 64 neurons and 2nd hidden layer has 32 neurons. The input layer has 5 neurons, one neuron each for the independent variable and output layer has one node. For the Turkey zone out of 24007 observations, we have 16804 observations for training and 7203 for testing purpose. The least results have been shown by NN based proposed model for the Turkey zone with accuracy of 87.65%. Figure 6 represents the result for Turkey Earthquake zone.

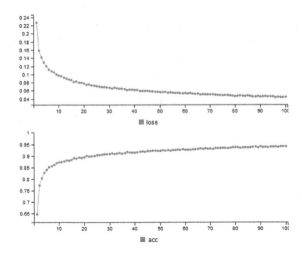

Fig. 6. The plot shows accuracy and loss of our proposed model for Turkey earthquake zone

5.4 Prediction for Greece Zone

The data set on Greece zone has 256655 observations as rows and 9 variables as column, in which 8 column has numeric value and one column has binary value as factor variable. First thing is that we convert factor variable to numeric because neural network takes input as numeric variable. If more than one variable is factor variable then all variables are to be converted at once in numeric. Our dataset consists of 9 attribute in which 8 of them are independent and 1 ('actual') is dependent attribute.

For neural network we have used four different layers which consist of one input layer, one output layer and two hidden layers. The 1st hidden layer has 64 neurons and 2nd hidden layer has 32 neurons. The input layer has 8 neurons, one neuron each for the independent variable and output layer has one node. For the Greece zone out of 256655 observations we have 179658 observations for training and 76997 for testing purpose. The least results have been shown by NN based proposed model for the Greece zone with accuracy of 78.36%. Figure 7 represents the result for Greece Earthquake zone.

We will normalize independent variables by subtracting mean for each value and dividing them by standard derivations i.e.

$$NormalizeValue = \frac{value - mean}{sd} \tag{9}$$

This neural network is densely connected or fully connected which means that each node is connected to every node in the previous layer and also to all the nodes in the next layer. For activation functions we use "relu" which is rectified linear unit this is the commonly used activations unit in the hidden layer. We have 6 variables as input layer for Japan zone and Indian Subcontinent,

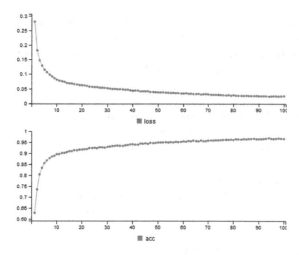

Fig. 7. The plot shows accuracy and loss of our proposed model for Greece earthquake zone

5 variables as input layer for Turkey and 4 variables as input layer for Greece. Input layer connects into first hidden layer and first hidden layer connects into second hidden layer, then connects into the next layer which is called output layer (output layer with 1 neuron). For output layer we are not going to specify activation function because by default it uses linear activation function.

Next phase is to compile the model because our y(dependent) variable is numeric and we are dealing with regression problem, so we are using mean square Error (mse) to calculate loss. While for optimizer we are using "rmsprop" and by default it takes "mae". In next phase model connects to 'fit' in which we are using independent and dependent attribute for training purpose. We are using epoch as 100 and batch size as 32. After training the model we are using our test data to predict the whether earthquake is present or absent in the particular zone.

Table 1. Prediction results for binary classification problem of proposed model based on Neural Network.

Performance evaluations (in %)	Japan	Turkey	Greece	Indian subcontinent
Sensitivity (S_n)	83.25	76.16	82.62	82.52
Specificity (S_p)	78.36	92.45	76.69	91.44
Positive Predictive (P_1)	97.13	87.54	91.10	92.63
Negative Predictive (P_0)	36.21	78.15	67.46	71.44
Accuracy	83.57	87.65	78.36	87.14

The performance of the proposed model for all four regions is summarized in Table 1. The proposed model exhibits remarkable performance for all four regions, particularly in terms of low false alarms generation. The Positive Predictive Value/Precision(P1) value of 97.13%, 87.54%, 91.10% and 92.63% for Japan, Turkey, Greece and Indian Subcontinent respectively. This Implies that the ratio of false alarms is considerably low. The model also shows remarkable performance in terms of Negative Predictive (P0) value of 36.21%, 78.15%, 67.46% and 71.44% for Japan, Turkey, Greece and Indian Subcontinent, respectively. The model represents prediction results in terms of accuracy value of 83.57%, 87.65%, 78.36% and 87.14% for the earthquake region Japan, Turkey, Greece and Indian Subcontinent respectively. Inter-regional comparison of results obtained through proposed methodology expresses that Indian Subcontinent takes lead followed by Turkey followed by Japan and then Greece.

5.5   Comparison to Existing Work

The developing seismic indicators based on neural network is to draw a comparison with previous results obtained for Indian Subcontinent regions. The Positive Predictive Value/Precision (P1) by [5] is 75.4 which has been improved to 92.63 in this study, thus showing notable improvement in the prediction results. Furthermore, the current methodology has also shown improved results for other criteria as well. Accuracy has improved from 82.7% to 87.4%. The only increased performance is P0, which is affordable, in comparison to all other recorded performance measure. The prediction results for Indian Subcontinent has improved using the proposed methodology in terms of all the used performance measures.

Table 2. Earthquake prediction results for Indian subcontinent region.

Performance evaluations (in %)	K. M. Asim et al. [5]	Proposed methodology
Sensitivity (S_n)	69.6	82.52
Specificity (S_p)	89.1	91.44
Positive predictive (P_1)	75.4	92.63
Negative predictive (P_0)	85.9	71.44
Accuracy	82.7	87.14

Different seismic indicator based predictions have already been performed for Indian Subcontinent regions by using machine learning technique. Thus, for the proof of the supremacy of the proposed methodology based on earthquake seismic indicators computation, the comparison has been drawn with previously pro-posed methodologies through said calculation measures. It is obvious from Table 2 that the predictions gained by the proposed methodology have outsailed the previously gained prediction results due to the respective zones. The Sensitivity (Sn) improved from 69.6 to 82.52. The prediction model with Specificity

(Sp) of 89.1% is preferable over other prediction model. In the proposed model Specificity improved from 89.1% to 91.44%, while a noteworthy enhancement has been also noticed in all the accomplishment measures without P0. However, the obtained results represent that the proposed model has outsailed the previously obtained results for the Indian Subcontinent zone.

6   Conclusions

In the field of seismology earthquake forecasting is a challenging problem which has received a great deal of attention over a couple of years. The machine learning technique has been performed so that we can predict earthquakes in the four different earthquake zone (Japan, Turkey, Greece and Indian Subcontinent), which are the most active seismic zone in the world. NN based prediction model has been trained and tested for the Japan, Turkey, Greece and Indian subcontinent regions. Application of ANN, has resulted to raise earthquake forecasting performance 15 day's duration's of an earthquake. Thus ANN based model is trained and tested effectively implement with encouraged and improved results for every region. The study represents, although an earthquake occurrence is supposed to become decidedly random and appears to be highly non-linear phenomenon, yet which can be modelled depending upon the geophysical event of the earthquake seismic zone with greatly sophisticated modelling and learning procedures of machine learning.

References

1. Asim, K.M., Idris, A., Iqbal, T., Martınez-A-lvarez, F.: Seismic indicators based earthquake predictor system using genetic programming and AdaBoost classification. Soil Dyn. Earthq. Eng. **111**, 1–7 (2018)
2. Asencio-Cortes, G., Scitovski, S., Scitovski, R., Martınez-A-lvarez, F.: Temporal analysis of Croatian seismogenic zones to improve earthquake magnitude prediction. Earth Sci. Inf. **10**(3), 303–320 (2017)
3. Alarifi, A.S., Alarifi, N.S., Al-Humidan, S.: Earthquakes magnitude predication using artificial neural network in northern Red Sea area. J. King Saud Univ. Sci. **24**(4), 301–313 (2012)
4. Reyes, J., Morales-Esteban, A., Martınez-A-lvarez, F.: Neural networks to predict earthquakes in Chile. Appl. Soft Comput. **13**(2), 1314–1328 (2013)
5. Asim, K.M., Idris, A., Iqbal, T., Martınez-A-lvarez, F.: Earthquake prediction model using support vector regressor and hybrid neural networks. PloS One **13**(7), e0199004 (2018)
6. Asim, K.M., Martınez-A-lvarez, F., Basit, A., Iqbal, T.: Earthquake magnitude prediction in Hindukush region using machine learning techniques. Nat. Hazards **85**(1), 471–486 (2017)
7. Varotsos, P., Alexopoulos, K.: Physical properties of the variations of the electric field of the earth preceding earthquakes. I. Tectonophysics **110**(1–2), 73–98 (1984)
8. Lighthill, M.J.: A Critical Review of VAN: Earthquake Prediction from Seismic Electrical Signals. World Scientific, Singapore (1996)

9. Latoussakis, J., Kossobokov, V.G.: Intermediate term earthquake prediction in the area of Greece: application of the algorithm M8. Pure Appl. Geophy. **134**(2), 261–282 (1990)

10. Hoque, A., Raj, J., Saha, A., Dr.: Approaches of earthquake magnitude prediction using machine learning techniques. In: International Conference on Computational Intelligence & IoT (ICCIIoT) (2018)

11. Wang, W., Cao, X., Song, X.: Estimation of the earthquakes in Chinese main-land by using artificial neural networks. Chin. J. Earthq. **3**(21), 10–14 (2001)

12. Plagianakos, V.P., Tzanaki, E.: Chaotic analysis of seismic time series and short term forecasting using neural networks, In: Proceedings of the International Joint Conference on Neural Networks 2001, IJCNN 2001, vol. 3, pp. 1598–1602. IEEE (2001)

13. Itai, A., Yasukawa, H., Takumi, I., Hata, M.: Multi-layer neural network for precursor signal detection in electromagnetic wave observation applied to great earthquake prediction. In: Nonlinear Signal and Image Processing, 2005, NSIP 2005. Abstracts. IEE-EEurasip, p. 31. IEEE (2005)

14. Panakkat, A., Adeli, H.: Neural network models for earthquake magnitude prediction using multiple seismicity indicators. Int. J. Neural Syst. **17**(01), 13–33 (2007)

15. Lakshmi, S.S., Tiwari, R.K.: Model dissection from earthquake time series: a comparative analysis using modern non-linear forecasting and artificial neural network approaches. Comput. Geosci. **35**(2), 191–204 (2009)

16. Ozerdem, M.S., Ustundag, B., Demirer, R.M.: Self-organized maps based neural networks for detection of possible earthquake precursory electric field patterns. Adv. Eng. Softw. **37**(4), 207–217 (2006)

17. Jusoh, M.H., Ya'Acob, N., Saad, H., Sulaiman, A.A., Baba, N.H., Khan, Z.I.: Earthquake prediction technique based on GPS dual frequency system in equatorial region, In: IEEE International Conference on RF and Microwave, RFM 2008, December 2008, pp. 372–376. IEEE (2008)

18. Varotsos, P., Lazaridou, M., Eftaxias, K., Antonopoulos, G., Makris, J., Kopanas, J.: Short term earthquake prediction in Greece by seismic electric signals. In: A Critical Review of VAN: Earthquake Prediction from Seismic Electrical Signals, pp. 29–76 (1996)

19. Dahmen, K., Ertas, D., Ben-Zion, Y.: Gutenberg-Richter and characteristic earthquake behavior in simple mean-field models of heterogeneous faults. Phys. Rev. E **58**(2), 1494 (1998)

20. Ellsworth, W.L., Matthews, M.V., Nadeau, R.M., Nishenko, S.P., Reasenberg, P.A., Simpson, R.W.: A physically-based earthquake recurrence model for estimation of longterm earthquake probabilities. US Geol. Surv. Open-File Rep. **99**(522), 23 (1999)

21. Knopoff, L.: The magnitude distribution of declustered earthquakes in Southern California. Proc. Natl. Acad. Sci. **97**(22), 11880–11884 (2000)

22. Kirschvink, J.L.: Earthquake prediction by animals: evolution and sensory perception. Bull. Seismol. Soc. Am. **90**(2), 312–323 (2000)

23. McCann, W.R., Nishenko, S.P., Sykes, L.R., Krause, J.: Seismic gaps and plate tectonics: seismic potential for major boundaries. In: Earthquake Prediction and Seismicity Patterns, pp. 1082–1147. Birkhauser, Basel (1979)

24. Nikulins, V.: Seismicity of the east baltic region and application-oriented methods. In: The Conditions of Low Seismicity (2017)

25. Gill, J.B.: Orogenic Andesites and Plate Tectonics, vol. 16. Springer, Heidelberg (2012). https://doi.org/10.1007/978-3-642-68012-0

26. Geller, R.J., Jackson, D.D., Kagan, Y.Y., Mulargia, F.: Earthquakes cannot be predicted. Science **275**(5306), 1616 (1997)
27. http://earthquake.usgs.gov/earthquakes/eqarchives/epic/
28. Gokkaya, K.: Geographic analysis of earthquake damage in Turkey between 1900 and 2012. Geomatics Nat. Hazards Risk **7**, 1948–1961 (2016). https://doi.org/10. 1080/19475705.2016.1171259
29. Makropoulos, K.C., Burton, P.W.: Greek tectonics and seismicity. Tectonophysics **106**(3–4), 275–304 (1984)
30. Marder, J., Marder, J.: Japan's Earthquake And Tsunami: How They Happened. In: PBS News Hour. N. Web, p. 2011, 24 April 2019
31. Anatolian Plate: En.wikipedia.org. N. p. 2019. Web, 24 Apr 2019
32. BBC News - Why Turkey Suffers Earthquake Misery : News (2019). http://bbc. co.uk/. http://news.bbc.co.uk/2/hi/europe/2992311.stm. Accessed 24 Apr 2019
33. Indian Plate : Eurasian Tectonics (2019). Accessed 24 Apr 2019.http:// eurasiatectonics.weebly.com/indian-plate.html
34. Increasing Seismic Activities in Aegean Sea, Greece (With Tectonic Summary. The Watchers - Daily News Service - Watchers NEWS (2012). Accessed 24 Apr 2019
35. https://watchers.news/2012/01/28/increasing-seismic-activities-in-aegean-sea-greecewith-tectonic-summary/
36. Aegean Sea Plate: En.Wikipedia.Org. Accessed 24 Apr 2019 (2019). https://en. wikipedia.org/wiki/AegeanSeaPlate
37. Science, L., Earth, P.: Japan's explosive geology explained. Live Science (2011). https://www.livescience.com/30226-japan-tectonics-explosivegeology-ring-of-fire-110314.html. Accessed 7 May 2019
38. Kaggle.com.: Earthquakes in Greece (1901–2018) (2019). https://www.kaggle. com/astefopoulos/earthquakes-in-greece-19012018. Accessed 8 May 2019
39. R-project.org.: R: What is R? (2019). https://www.rproject.org/about.html. Accessed 8 May 2019
40. Python.org.: Python Releases for Windows (2019). https://www.python.org/ downloads/windows/. Accessed 8 May 2019
41. Anaconda: Home - Anaconda (2019). https://www.anaconda.com/. Accessed 8 May 2019

Real-Time Vision-Based Vehicle-to-Vehicle Distance Estimation on Two-Lane Single Carriageway Using a Low-Cost 2D Camera at Night

Gouranga Mandal$^{(\boxtimes)}$ (ID), Diptendu Bhattacharya, and Parthasarathi De

National Institute of Technology Agartala, Agartala, Tripura, India
gourangamandal@yahoo.com

Abstract. Estimation of distance with great accuracy, especially at night where vehicles are not visible is really a challenging research area. This article presents a pleasant vision-based real-time assistance system on any two-lane single carriageway at night. In this paper, a complex traffic scenario is considered where both ongoing vehicles and oncoming vehicles run on a two-lane single carriageway. As the environmental condition is very dark at night, hence only headlights and taillights of vehicles are visible. The proposed assistance system can estimate the vehicle-to-vehicle distance of ongoing or oncoming vehicles with respect to the test vehicle at night. The distance of the slower vehicles in the front along with the oncoming vehicles are estimated by observing only the position of taillights and headlights respectively. Sensitive vision-based parameters of headlights and taillights are used to estimate the exact distance between vehicles. Numerous real-time experiments reveal that the estimation accomplishes greater accuracy over the state-of-the-art techniques using a low-cost 2D camera.

Keywords: Distance estimation · Two-lane single carriageway · Headlights and taillights · Low-cost 2D camera

1 Introduction

Driving assistance is very crucial during real-time driving at night. Due to lack of light drivers are unable to view the road properly and even unable to locate the position of other vehicles properly. Only headlights and taillights are visible at night. Therefore, it is very difficult for drivers to estimate the exact distance of other vehicles on the road. In the case of an autonomous vehicle also, the estimation of the exact distance of other vehicles is very difficult at night.

Due to road fatalities, almost 1.35 million people lost their valuable lives every year in the world. Statistics say that 3,287 people die per day in the world due to road fatalities. In addition, 20 to 50 million people get injured yearly in road crashes. It is also projected that road crashes cause the death of one person every

N. Kar et al. (Eds.): ICCISIoT 2020, CCIS 1358, pp. 54–65, 2020.
https://doi.org/10.1007/978-3-030-66763-4_5

23 s in the world. It is observed that, out of all road-accidental deaths, 44% are due to rash driving, which is likely due to over speed, overtaking, and driver's wrong prediction about other vehicles [1]. A vast percentage of road accident occurs due to the absence of light at night in dark condition. According to a report, almost 50% of traffic deaths happen at night. In India, the maximum number of road accidents (18.6%) recorded between 6:00 pm and 9:00 pm [2].

Fig. 1. Vehicles are not visible properly at night, only headlights and taillights are visible.

Few scholars attempted to estimate the distance of other vehicles on the road in real-time. But, most of these attempts are made in the daytime. Only a few attempts are made during night-time. Most of the scholars used high-cost sensors for real-time distance estimation. The sensors are in a fixed position on the road while other vehicles are moving in the existing approaches. However, real-time vehicle-to-vehicle distance estimation from another moving vehicle is really difficult, especially at night. The estimation becomes more difficult during complex traffic scenarios when a slower vehicle is in the front and another oncoming vehicle is coming from the reverse direction. This type of scenario is very common, but it makes a driver confused. If the driver is unable to realize the actual distance of the other vehicles, then it causes a pitiful road fatality in maximum cases. The distance of the front vehicle that is nearby can be guessed. Whereas, it is very hard to estimate the distance of oncoming (opposite direction) vehicle from a far distance in such dark condition. In this situation, objects and vehicles are not visible properly due to the absence of sunlight. Only taillights and headlights are visible (see Fig. 1). This situation is very dangerous because by watching only the headlights of an oncoming vehicle, it is not possible to estimate the driving trajectories properly for safe driving. However, assistance to estimate the position and the distance the other vehicles at night is sometimes very much essential. The primary contributions of this paper are summarized as follows:

- The proposed method can estimate the vehicle-to-vehicle distance between the ongoing/oncoming vehicles and the moving test vehicle at night.

- The vision-based estimation is made by observing only the position of tail-lights and headlights.
- No high-cost sensors are used for estimation like state-of-the-art techniques. A low-cost 2D camera is used in the proposed method.
- Sensitive vision-based parameters of headlights and taillights are used to estimate the exact distance between vehicles.
- The proposed approach aims to provide assistance in minimum processing time.

The rest of the entire article is systematized as follows. Section 2 designates some research work in literature which are closely associated with the proposed approach. Section 3 presents an explanation of the proposed approach. Section 4 represents an assessment of real-time experiential performance. Lastly, Sect. 5 defines the conclusion and describes future research.

2   Literature Survey

There are some existing approaches, which are used to estimate the distance of other vehicles on the road in real-time. But, most of the existing attempts are applicable for the daytime. Only a few attempts are made during the night-time. Most of the scholars used high-cost sensors for real-time distance estimation. The sensors are in a fixed position on the road while other vehicles are moving in the existing approaches. However, few existing approaches are stated below.

Mahdi et al. [3] developed a collision warning method of detecting all vehicles ahead and estimating safety distances for subconscious drivers, to prevent forthcoming crashes. Adaptive global Haar-like features are introduced for vehicle detection, taillight extraction, virtual regularity detection, and the inter-vehicle distance estimation. An effective single-sensor, multi-feature fusion method is also introduced to improve the robustness and accuracy of this method. The method can detect vehicles ahead at both day or night and also for short- and long-range distances. L-C Liu et al. [4] proposed a distance approximation technique to build the forward collision avoidance assist system (FCAAS). First, the RANSAC process is used to extract the lanes, which were collected from a reverse perspective mapping filtered by the steerable filters. Then, the extracted lines are tracked by using the Kalman filter accurately and efficiently. Second, a vehicle tracking method implemented a multiple-vehicle tracking system using the particle filter that detects the vehicles using the AdaBoost classifier. A modified particle filtering is used to forecast the succeeding movement of any vehicle. Then, spread the elements to the projected position of the vehicle, not to the current location of the vehicle. Finally, a distance approximation technique is derived to evaluate the distance of the front vehicle from the ego vehicle. The distance approximation process is tested by setting numerous standard points of the frame, whose positions can be estimated according to the regulations of the lane markings. Y. Weber et al. [5] analyzed and discussed the influence of the road anomalies and the vehicle suspension for tracking and distance estimation of vehicles. J. Kim et al. [6] estimated the distance of a vehicle driving in front by extracting the aggregated channel features of frames using a single black-box camera. Mateus et al. [7] and D. Bell et al. [8] used Convolutional Neural Networks (CNNs) and the "You Only Look Once" (YOLO) algorithm to detect vehicles with their distances and speeds. J. Liu et al. [9] introduced a lightweight network to amend the feature extraction layer of YOLOv3 to esti-mate the distance of vehicles. E. Vakili et al. [10] and A. Ali et al. [11] presented a single view geometry-based relative distance and speed estimation algorithm using a camera and the geometric information of the camera system. A. Zaarane et al. [12] introduced an inter-vehicle distance estimation method for self-driving completely based on the image processing technique. The system used one stereo camera (made with two cameras) which is installed behind the rearview mirror of the host vehicle to measure the distance based on camera view field angle.

3   Proposed Approach

In this article, a novel approach is proposed for distance estimation of other ongo-ing and oncoming vehicles from a running test vehicle at night. The proposed approach is completely vision-based and depends on the analysis of visual param-eters of headlights and taillights. The overall proposed framework is revealed in Fig. 2.

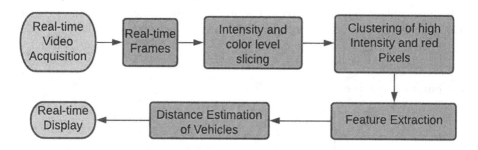

Fig. 2. The overall framework of the proposed system.

3.1   Intensity and Colour Level Slicing

A real-time frame at night may be considered as the vision of a driver at night. A night-time frame of a busy two-lane single carriageway consists of several head-lights and taillights. To extract headlights and taillights from frames, intensity, and colour level slicing is applied. Colour level slicing, segments area with a defined colour in a frame. Intensity level slicing, segments a defined range of the light intensities in a frame [13,14].

The graphical illustration of intensity level slicing is exposed in Fig. 3.

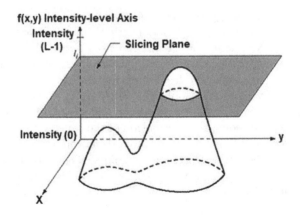

Fig. 3. Intensity level slicing to display lights with high-intensity range by a slicing plane.

For perfect detection of headlights, a threshold of intensity $T(\text{int}) = 220$ is used. Similarly, for taillights a threshold amount of red in RGB frame $T(red) = 200$ is provided. The threshold values which give the best output for all frames are finalized after many real-time experiments. The luminosity technique is applied to evaluate the intensity of a pixel because it expresses a weighted average for human perception. The green colour has given a higher priority than the red and blue colour. The luminosity (intensity of a pixel) is calculated as follows:

$$I(x,y) = Int(x,y) = 0.21R + 0.72G + 0.07B \tag{1}$$

The output frame is calculated as follows:

$$(x,y) = \begin{cases} I(x,y) & \text{for} Int(x,y) >= T(\text{int}) = 220 \text{ or} \\ & R(x,y) >= T(red) = 200 \\ 0 & otherwise \end{cases} \tag{2}$$

Hence, the frame is transformed into a new frame that comprises only high-intensity lights (headlights) and red-coloured lights (taillights) after the intensity and colour level slicing.

3.2   Clustering of High Intensity and Red Pixels

After finding the bright and red-coloured pixels, clustering is applied. The primary objective of the clustering is to extract the exact position of headlights and taillight with their corresponding centroid. Here, a traditional clustering method like K-Means is not applicable because the occurrence of headlights is unknown. Consequently, the cluster's quantity is also undefined. Therefore, the DBSCAN [15] (Conditional density-based spatial-clustering of the application with noise), an operative density-based clustering procedure is chosen. To avoid ambiguity of false headlight (which are not headlights, e.g.- street lights), the entire frame is divided into two zones through the skyline. All the lights above the skyline are considered false light and the lights below the skyline are either taillight or headlight. In the region below the skyline of the frame, the DBSCAN is applied to the following conditions.

1. The minimum radius of a cluster = 4 pixels.
2. The minimum area of a cluster = 8 pixels (considered a headlight holds at least eight pixels).

After clustering is done, three components are ready for use, viz: a) set of clusters for all headlights (S1) b) set of clusters of all taillights (S2) and c) centroid of all clusters. Two-lane single-carriageway in India (driving style: "drive on the left") are selected for real-time trials. Hence, it can be assumed that all the ongoing vehicles are on the left lane and all the oncoming vehicles are on the right lane of a road. Thus, to extract features from headlights and taillights, the focus needs to be given on the right half portion and left portion of the frame respectively.

3.3 Feature Extraction

Few significant features are extracted from the clusters of headlights and taillight with their corresponding centroid. A pair of lights can be confirmed as either headlights or taillights when the movement of two lights of a vehicle is identical (i.e.: two lights should be nearly in a horizontal line and the direction movements of two lights should be the same). A maximum difference of vertical movement of two centroids = 10 pixels and maximum horizontal distance changes of two centroids = 5 pixels are considered to extract best output by trial and error process. All pairs of lights are checked. If the horizontal distance changes <10 pixels and vertical distance changes <5 pixels between two light's centroids then the movement is called identical. Hence, the pair of lights is considered either a pair of headlights or taillights.

Now, a pair of lights can be identified explicitly as headlights by the following criteria:

1. The intensity of the lights should be very high (I >= T1, Where T1 = 220 is used as a Threshold value) Likewise, a pair of lights can be identified explicitly as taillights by the following criteria:
2. The colour of light should be reddish (R in RGB >=T2, Where T2 = 200 is used as a Threshold value).

After distinguishing the headlights and taillights, the following three features are calculated as follows.

1. The horizontal distance (Euclidean distance between two centroids) between every pair of headlights and taillights: Euclidean distance between two centroids is calculated as:

$$dist(a, b) = \sqrt{(ba - ax)^2 + (by - ay)^2} \qquad (3)$$

Where a = (ax, ay) and b = (bx, by) are two centroids. The Euclidean distance indicates a straight-line measure between two centroids. The greater the distance indicates closer the vehicle.

2. The height of every pair of headlights and taillights from the baseline is calculated as follows.

$$height = r\_\max - r\_centroid \tag{4}$$

Where baseline indicates a ground line (maximum y coordinate) of an image in the fourth quadrant. The r_max represents the maximum row number of the frame and r_centroid represents the row value of the centroid of the headlight. Less height indicates closer to the vehicle.

3. Area of all the headlights and taillights: A counter variable is used to calculate the area of light. The counter counts the quantity of high-intensity pixels within a headlight cluster. A larger count of pixels indicates the light occupied a bigger area in the frame which signifies the vehicle is close by. Three sets of rules are defined to calculate the stated features of headlights and taillights. The definition for estimating the distance of any vehicle that is coming from the opposite way using headlight position is shown in Fig. 4.

3.4 Distance Estimation of Vehicles

After calculating the above important features, the distance of an oncoming vehicle can be estimated using the defined set of rules. The following three different ways are defined to estimate the vehicle-to-vehicle distance. Viz.

1. The horizontal distance between a pair of headlights.
2. The vertical height of headlights from the baseline.
3. The area of a headlight.

The estimated distance may not be the same in all the procedures. Therefore, normalization is done from the three estimations according to the pseudocode 1.

Pseudocode 1: Vehicle-to-Vehicle Distance Estimation Algorithm: A Normalization approach

Input: d1 = estimated distance from way1 (i.e.: from horizontal distance between the two headlights)
d2 = estimated distance from way2 (i.e.: from heights of two headlights from baseline)
d3 = estimated distance from way3 (i.e.: from the area of the headlight)
Output: final_distance

Begin
find the closest pair among d1, d2 and d3.
calculate the average of the closest pair = avg_pair
define as "single" which is not in closest pair.
final_distance = (3*(avg_pair) + single) / 4
return final_distance
End

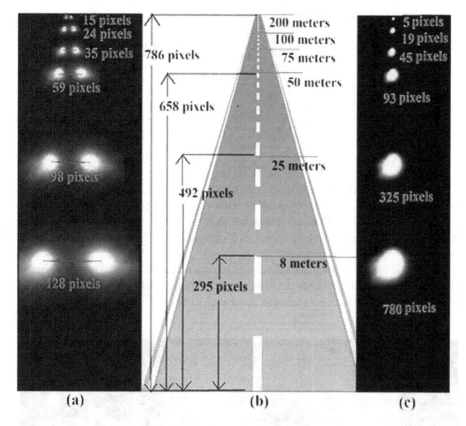

Fig. 4. Three defined rules for vehicle distance estimation in a frame with 1280786 resolution; (a) Horizontal distance (centroid's Euclidean distance) between the two headlights; (b) Heights of two headlights in a frame and their equivalent distance from the baseline of the road; (c) Area of a headlight (i.e.- number of high-intensity pixels available).

4   Real-Time Empirical Performance Evaluation

The proposed approach is tested in real-time during the night on two-lane single-carriageway roads. Two lanes have no separation and vehicles run in both directions. Empirical tests are conducted in complex traffic situations where cars are running in both directions on the two lane single carriageway. The accuracy in terms of errors of and distance estimation are shown in Table 1.

Table 1. Accuracy of the proposed distance estimation method.

Vehicles	Estimates value	Ground truth from GPS	Error	Mean error
1	32 m	32 m	0 m	**1.1 m**
2	95 m	94 m	−1 m	
3	126 m	128.5 m	+ 2.5 m	
4	51 m	50 m	−1 m	
5	76 m	77 m	+1 m	

There are no existing methods available, which can estimate the real-time distance any vehicle accurately at night. However, a compression among the proposed method and state-of-the-art techniques for distance estimation (in terms of the error and accuracy in percentage) of vehicles in real-time is revealed in Table 2.

A sample frame during a real-time experiment in a complex traffic scenario where the distances of both ongoing and oncoming vehicles are estimated is revealed in Fig. 5 with two different modes of view.

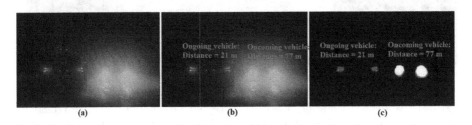

Fig. 5. a) A real-time input frame b) Original mode of distance estimation c) Special mode with processed frame

4.1 Analysis of Computation Time

The computation time is the most decisive factor in the case of driving. Numerous real-time experiments reveal that the computation time is amazingly less so that the drivers can see the distances of other vehicles in real-time without any time delay. The processing time is exposed in Fig. 6.

Table 2. Compression of the proposed method with state-of-the-art techniques for the distance estimation.

vehicles	Error (in %) of various distance estimation methods						
	Y. Weber et al. [5]	J. Kim et al. [6]	J. Liu et al. [9]	E. Vakili et al. [10]	A. Ali et al. [11]	A. Zaarane et al. [12]	Proposed Method
1	3.02	3.15	2.87	2.55	2.01	1.01	1.02
2	3.24	3.47	2.68	2.68	2.03	1.68	1.00
3	3.33	3.26	2.92	2.39	1.98	1.33	0.85
4	4.10	4.02	3.18	3.52	3.11	2.59	1.84
5	3.69	3.95	2.68	2.05	1.19	2.01	1.22
6	3.58	3.11	2.31	2.37	2.51	1.22	1.28
7	3.67	3.22	2.67	2.94	2.36	1.85	1.08
8	2.96	3.47	2.92	2.85	2.88	1.89	0.93
9	3.08	2.96	2.33	2.44	2.41	1.76	1.06
10	3.88	3.65	2.57	2.81	2.27	1.82	1.14
Avg. Error in %	3.455	3.426	2.713	2.66	2.275	1.716	1.142
Accuracy in %	96.55	96.57	97.29	97.34	97.73	98.28	98.86

In Fig. 6, it is observed that in the case of higher frame resolution the processing time is a little higher. However, many real-time experiments prove that this much time delay is petty and will not affect the real-time vision, even if we use a 1280 × 720 frame resolution.

A comparison of processing time (in millisecond) for frame size 1280 × 720 among various existing distance estimation methods is shown in Table 3.

Table 3. Comparison of processing time (in millisecond) for frame size 1280 × 720 among various existing distance estimation methods and the proposed method.

Methods	Y. Weber et al. [5]	J. Kim et al. [6]	J. Liu et al. [9]	E. Vakili et al. [10]	A. Ali et al. [11]	A. Zaarane et al. [12]	Proposed Method
Time (ms)	1820	232	171	500	236	185	37.15

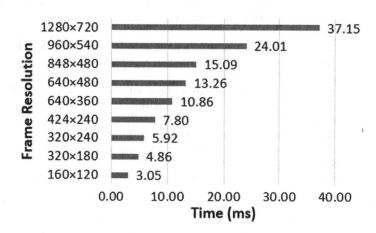

Fig. 6. Processing time observation (CPU configuration: Intel(R) Core (TM) i7-10510U @ 2133 MHz, 8 GB RAM, and 500 GB SSD)

5   Conclusion and Future Work

The night-time roads are really dangerous for driving because drivers are unable to notice objects, including other vehicles on the road. Only taillights and headlights are visible for ongoing and oncoming vehicles respectively. Making a perfect estimation of the distance of any vehicle is very tough. The proposed system presents a novel vision-based fast and accurate distance estimation system at night. The proposed system can assist drivers by showing the direction of vehicle with their distance of all the ongoing and oncoming vehicles in real-time complex traffic scenarios at night. A complex traffic scenario is considered where a slower vehicle is present in the front in the same lane. Besides, an oncoming vehicle may also come from the reverse direction in the adjacent lane at night. The proposed system will be very helpful for any driver for safe driving on bidirectional two-lane roads during driving at night. Drivers come to know the distance of other vehicles so that they can drive accordingly.

As future work, more complex scenarios can be considered, such as additional traffic travelling in different directions on multiple lanes, or having various traffic participants in addition to vehicles (e.g..- bikes). Further, the vehicle-tracking process at night needs to be extended to address the dark vehicle (vehicles which are in parking mode) without any headlights or taillights. More parameters can be estimated besides distance to assist drivers at night.

References

1. World Health Organization: Violence and Injury Prevention and World Health Organization: Global Status Report on Road Safety 2018: Supporting a Decade of Action, Geneve (2018)
2. Transport Research Wing, Ministry of Road Transport and Highways: Government of India, Road Accidents in India - 2017. New Delhi (2017)
3. Rezaei, M., Terauchi, M., Klette, R.: Robust vehicle detection and distance estimation under challenging lighting conditions. IEEE Trans. Intell. Transp. Syst. **16**(5), 2723–2743 (2015)
4. Liu, L., Fang, C., Chen, S.: A novel distance estimation method leading a forward collision avoidance assist system for vehicles on highways. IEEE Trans. Intell. Transp. Syst. **18**(4), 937–949 (2017)
5. Weber, Y., Kanarachos, S.: The correlation between vehicle vertical dynamics and deep learning-based visual target state estimation: a sensitivity study. Sensors **19**(22), 1–28 (2019)
6. Kim, J.B.: Efficient vehicle detection and distance estimation based on aggregated channel features and inverse perspective mapping from a single camera. Symmetry **11**(10), 1–20 (2019)
7. da Silva Bastos, M.E., Freitas, V.Y.F., de Menezes, R.S.T., Maia, H.: Vehicle speed detection and safety distance estimation using aerial images of brazilian highways. In: SEMINÁRIO INTEGRADO DE SOFTWARE E HARDWARE (SEMISH) 47, Cuiabá. Anais da XLVII edição do Seminário Integrado de Software e Hardware. Sociedade Brasileira de Computação, Porto Alegre, pp. 258–268 (2020)

8. Bell, D., Xiao, W., James, P.: Accurate vehicle speed estimation from monocular camera footage. ISPRS Ann. Photogram. Rem. Sens. Spat. Inf. Sci. **5**(2), 419–426 (2020)
9. Liu, J., Zhang, R.: Vehicle detection and ranging using two different focal length cameras. J. Sens. **2020**, 1–14 (2020)
10. Vakili, E., Shoaran, M., Sarmadi, M.R.: Single-camera vehicle speed measurement using the geometry of the imaging system. Multimedia Tools Appl. **79**, 19307–19327 (2020)
11. Ali, A., Hassan, A., Ali, A.R., Ullah Khan, H., Kazmi, W., Zaheer, A.: Real-time vehicle distance estimation using single view geometry. In: IEEE Winter Conference on Applications of Computer Vision (WACV) - Snowmass Village, CO, USA (2020)
12. Zaarane, A., Slimani, I., Okaishi, W.A., Atouf, I., Hamdoun, A.: Distance measurement system for autonomous vehicles using stereo camera. Array **5**, 1–7 (2020)
13. Gaba, G.S., Singh, P., Singh, G.: Implementation of image enhancement techniques. IOSR J. Electron. Commun. Eng. (IOSRJECE). **1**(2), 20–23 (2012)
14. Jayaraman, S., Esakkirajan, S., Veerakumar, T.: Digital Image Processing. New Delhi, McGraw Hill Education (2009)
15. Ester, M., Kriegel, H. P., Sander, J., Xu, X.: A density-based algorithm for discovering clusters in large spatial databases with noise. In: Proceedings of the 2nd International Conference on Knowledge Discovery Data Mining (KDD 1996), Portland, Oregon, pp. 226–231 (1996)

Distributed Telemetry System with High Speed Avionics Bus for Multi Stage Aerospace Vehicles

Sudarsana Reddy Karnati[1]([✉]), Lakshmi Bopanna[2], and D. R. Jahagirdar[3]

[1] Directorate of Flight Instrumentation, Research Centre Imarat, Vignyanakancha, Hyderabad, Telangana, India
karnati.sudha448@gmail.com
[2] Department of Electronics and Communication Engineering, National Institution of Technology, Warangal, Telangana, India
[3] Directorate of RF Seekers, Research Centre Imarat, Vignyanakancha, Hyderabad, Telangana, India

Abstract. The Telemetry system is being used during the development phase of an aerospace vehicle to monitor various parameters like shock, vibration, pressure, voltage and bus data. This data is captured by an Air-borne telemetry system and transmits to the ground telemetry station for evaluating the vehicle performance. In general, multi stage vehicle has huge measurement plan, distributed throughout the vehicle and also high bandwidth sources of data. The conventional telemetry system in multi stage vehicle increases complexity of cable harness, require more interface connectors etc. This problem is addressed in this paper by proposing a distributed telemetry system configuration for multi stage vehicles to reduce the complexity of vehicle integration. Here, a dedicated Data Acquisition Unit (DAU) is proposed to be deployed in each stage of the vehicle so that the local DAU transmits locally acquired data to the master data acquisition system which is deployed in the final stage (Payload). In this paper, it also proposed to achieve high data transfer rates of 2 to 8 Mbps between local DAUs and master DAU employing the Avionics Full Duplex bus (AFDX). The DAU functionality is implemented by modelling all the building blocks such as analog data acquisition, multiplexing, framing as per IRIG 106 and encoding using VHDL targeting ZYNQ XC 7Z020 FPGA. In addition, the high speed avionics bus AFDX IP core has been integrated on programmable logic of XC 7Z020 FPGA. The IP core initialisation and data acquisition is done by Processing system of ZYNQ SOC via AXI bus. The functionality and Hardware implementation of DAU with high speed bus is highlighted and presented here.

Keywords: Telemetry · AFDX · IIR seeker · DAU · End system · ZYNQ SOC

© Springer Nature Switzerland AG 2020
N. Kar et al. (Eds.): ICCISIoT 2020, CCIS 1358, pp. 66–72, 2020.
https://doi.org/10.1007/978-3-030-66763-4_6

1 Introduction

Telemetry is the process by which the characteristics of objects are measured and the results transmitted to a distant station where they are displayed, recorded and analysed. The transmission media is free space for aerospace applications. Pulse Code Modulation (PCM) Telemetry is a way of acquiring data, converting the data samples to digital words, encoding the data in a serial digital format and transmitting it on a carrier to another location for decoding and analysis. PCM systems are less susceptible to noise than analog systems and the digital data is easier to transmit record and analyse (Fig. 1).

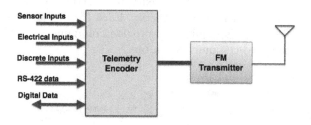

Fig. 1. Block diagram of the conventional telemetry system

Telemetry Encoder comprises of sensor interface modules and PCM Encoder with Pre-modulation Filter. PCM Encoder for Onboard Telemetry applications acquires data from various interfaces as mentioned in Table 1. PCM Encoder encodes the data acquired from the above sources as per IRIG-106 Compliant [4] PCM frame format. A pre-modulation filter limits the RF bandwidth and provides data for transmission. The data stream is transmitted through the S-Band transmitter and the antenna. Telemetry system at the ground station captures the data and de-multiplexes into individual sensor data as presented in Table 1.

Table 1. Typical measurement plan

S. no	Input	Band width	Quantity	Samples per sec
1	Shock	8000 Hz	03	32000
2	Vibration	2000 Hz	06	8000
3	Pressure	200 Hz	20	800
4	Temperature	25 Hz	12	100
5	Strain	25 Hz	10	100
6	Events	25 Hz	16	100
7	RS-422	921.6 Kbps	2 Node	200 bytes per sec
8	MIL-1553	1 Mbps	2 Node	2000 bytes per sec
9	Seeker data	8 Mbps	1 Node	8000 bytes per sec

2   Proposed Distributed Telemetry System

For multi stage aerospace vehicles, dense measurement plan is used and the sensors are distributed throughout the missile. For such type of vehicles, distributed telemetry configuration shown in Fig. 2 is proposed, which involves the deployment of a local data acquisitions systems (DAU) at each stage with the communication among DAUs over a digital bus. The local data acquisition system acquires data from the sensors located nearby and transmits to the master DAU. The Master DAU collects data from the slave DAUs, multiplexes and generates data to transmitter. Distributed telemetry configuration reduces cable harness between multiple stages, complexity in electrical integration, Weight, and Cost while enhancing the signal integrity. Each DAU is an integrated PCM Encoder with SCP and it is required to provide communication between local DAUs using a high speed communication bus.

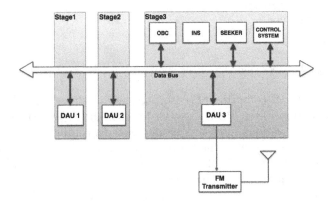

Fig. 2. Distributed telemetry configuration

The requirement of high speed communication bus arises from the mission requirements of Imaging Infrared Seeker (IIR), Integrated Avionics module (IAM), Dual Redundant Embedded Avionics Module (DREAM) etc. These systems handle huge data rates (upto 8 Mbps) and post the data to telemetry system for down streaming to ground stations. i.e. Bandwidth of information exchange between DAUs is more. The present data buses used in aerospace vehicles are MIL-Std-1553B and RS422, which cannot support the required high data rates. In this work, we propose to use Avionics full duplex (AFDX) bus as alternative to Mil-STD 1553B bus in the distributed telemetry configuration, which may be clear from the comparison of specifications of different buses presented in Table 2.

The DAU consists of Analog Interface Circuits (AIC), Bus interface circuits and Transmitter interface circuits. Analog interface circuit consists of bridge circuits, Programmable gain amplifiers, Excitation circuits, Anti-aliasing filters,

Table 2. Comparison of data buses

S. no	Parameter	MILSTD1553	AFDX
1	Data rate	1 Mbps	10/100 Mbps
2	Overhead	20%	6–7%
3	Packet length	32 Words	1500 Bytes
4	No. of systems on bus	Limited to 31 RTs and 1 BC	No limitation as per system design
5	Cost	High	Medium

ADC etc. Bus interface circuit consists of transformers, transceivers to interface Mil-Std-1553, UART, AFDX buses. Transmitter interface consists of pre-modulation filter and output amplitude adjustment circuits. The hardware of DAU has been implemented using discrete components and ZYNQ customized system on chip (SOC) as shown in Fig. 3. The inputs from Analog Interface Circuit and Bus interface circuits are time division multiplexed in IRIG106 standard format. The PCM Encoding functionality is implemented on ZYNQ FPGA. Finally, one of the DAU output is connected to the transmitter for RF signal transmission.

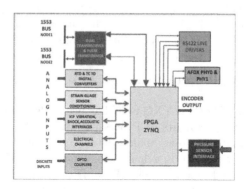

Fig. 3. Hardware implementation of DAU

3   High Speed Avionics Bus (ARINC 664 (AFDX))

Avionics Full-Duplex Switched Ethernet (AFDX) is a data network, patented by international aircraft manufacturer Airbus, for safety-critical applications that utilises dedicated bandwidth while providing deterministic quality of service (QoS). The AFDX data network is a specific [2] implementation of ARINCSpecification 664 Part 7, a profiled version of an IEEE 802.3 network per parts 1 and 2, which defines how commercial off-the-shelf networking components will be used for future generation Aircraft Data Networks (ADN). The six primary aspects of an AFDX data network includefull duplex, redundancy, determinism, high speed performance, switched and profiled network.

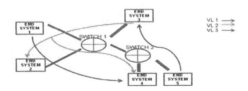

Fig. 4. AFDX netwrok configuration

In a traditional Ethernet switch operating at 10 Mbps, incoming Ethernet frames are routed to output links based on the Ethernet destination address. In AFDX, a 16-bit value called a Virtual Link ID is used to route Ethernet frames in an AFDX network. The switches in an AFDX network are "configured" to route an incoming Ethernet frame to one or more outgoing links. An important property of an AFDX network [1] is that Ethernet frames associated with a particular Virtual Link ID must originate at one, and only one, End System. In terminology each sub system treated as End system. In AFDX network end systems and switches connected as shown in Fig. 4. The AFDX switches are configured to deliver frames with the same Virtual Link ID between different End systems.

4   Hardware Implementation

In the design process of DAU, ZYNQ SOC has been selected for hardware realisation. The ZYNQ SOC consists of Processing system [3] and programmable logic. The DAU functionality like analog data acquisition, multiplexing, framing as per IRIG 106 and encoding has been done on programmable logic. In addition, the high speed avionics bus AFDX IP core has been integrated on programmable logic. This IP core initialisation and data acquisition is done by Processing system of ZYNQ SOC via AXI bus as shown in Fig. 5.

Two trans-receivers and two isolation transformers have been used for dual redundant bus interface. The prototype unit of DAU is shown in Fig. 5. The DAU packetizes the information and send to master DAU via AFDX bus. The data will be available on both the buses. The AFDX IP core prioritizes and validates the input data and then provides data to another DAU as shown in Fig. 6.

The hardware has been tested for both 10 Mbps and 100 Mbps data transfer between DAU1 and DAU2. The DAU data is generated 1000 bytes for every 10 msec and the same has been transmitted from one DAU to another DAU system. The received DAU data is stored in BRAM of FPGA and then for every 10 msec these bytes are merged with telemetry data and send to transmitter. The

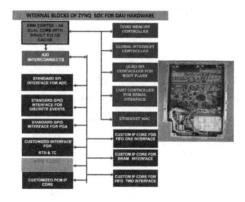

Fig. 5. AFDX IP core integration of ZYNQ SOC FPGA

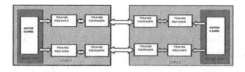

Fig. 6. Hardware modules of DAU to DAU communication via AFDX

storage capacity of DAU for receiving data is allocated of 4K bytes on FPGA. The same DAU hardware would be used for distributed telemetry with external AFDX switch.

The resources utilisation ZYNQ XC 7Z020 FPGA for hardware realisation of AFDX IP core are presented in Table 3. The AFDX IP core takes 23.65 % logical resources on ZYNQ XC 7Z020 FPGA and more number of memory resources for 16 VLID implementations on ZYNQ FPGA. The number of VLIDs depends on application of subsystem functionality. The resources utilisation of ZYNQ XC 7Z020 FPGA after integrating AFDX core with DAU system are presented in Table 4.

Table 3. AFDX IP core resource utilisation on ZYNQ SOC

Logical resources	Used	Available	Utilisation %
Slice LUTs	12582	53200	23.65
LUT as logic	12512	53200	23.51
Slice registers	7352	106400	6.90
Register as flip flop	7352	106400	6.90
Block RAM Tile	89	140	63.57
RAMB36/FIFO	84	140	60.00
RAMB18	10	280	3.57

Table 4. AFDX IP core with DAU system on ZYNQ SOC

Logical resources	Used	Available	Utilisation %
Slice LUTs	17378	53200	32.66
LUT as logic	17282	53200	32.48
Slice registers	11304	106400	10.62
Register as flip flop	11292	106400	10.61
Block RAM Tile	97	140	69.28
RAMB36/FIFO	92	140	65.71
RAMB18	10	280	3.57

5   Conclusion

In this paper, the distributed telemetry system is proposed for the multi stage
vehicles. This configuration provides modularity in the telemetry system design
which reduces the complexity of cable harness, hardware integration and testing.
It also reduces weight and power requirements of the vehicle. Data exchange
between DAUs of distributed telemetry configuration is established through
AFDX to achieve more bandwidth requirements in contrast to the present data
buses MIL-Std-1553B used in missiles. The DAU hardware has been implemented with AFDX IP core and tested for DAU to DAU communication with
10/100 Mbps data transmission. The same AFDX hardware can be extended for
other sub systems with more band width requirements so that DAU and other
sub systems communicate via AFDX Bus. Hence, AFDX will be a better choice
for futuristic avionic systems integration to handle high update rates.

Acknowledgement. The authors would like to acknowledge Smt K.V. Sujata, Technology Director of DOFI, RCI, Hyderabad, Shri U. Naresh Kumar, Group Head, DOFI,
RCI, Hyderabad for providing valuable suggestions and for granting permission to
publish innovative research work for an Airborne Telemetry applications. We are also
thankful to Mr G. Sanjeev Reddy, Scientist, DOFI, RCI for his continuous support to
make this innovative research work as a journal document.

References

1. Stock, M.: Fly by Wire for Experimental Aircraft, Stock Flight Systems (2009)
2. AFDX/ARINC 664 tutorial, AFDXprotocol Condor engineering, Inc (2005)
3. Zynq Soc System Architecture https://www.xlinix.com/ZynqSoc
4. IRIG standard106 -17, Telemetry Standards, RCC standards 106–17, Chapter 4,
   July 2017

Recognition of Indian Classical Dance Single-Hand Gestures Using Moment Invariant Features

Mampi Devi[1] and Alak Roy[2(✉)]

[1] Department of Computer Science and Engineering, Tripura University,
Suryamaninagar, India
drmampidevi@gmail.com
[2] Department of Information Technology, Tripura University, Suryamaninagar, India
alakroy@tripurauniv.in

Abstract. Recognition of single-hand gestures of classical dance is a challenging task due to its variation of age group of dancer. It is also a difficult task to find out the invariant features specially when same images are captured from different angle of view. The main objective of this paper is to recognize single-hand gestures of Indian Classical dance using $Hu\acute{s}$ invariant features. In this paper, three different types of image dataset namely boundary image, gray image and binary image dataset used. The seven $Hu\acute{s}$ invariant features were extracted from all the three image dataset. This paper also presents performance of accuracy for twenty eight different classes of hand gesture based on the extracted features set.

Keywords: $Hu\acute{s}$ moment feature · Hand gesture recognition · Mudra · Indian Classical dance

1 Introduction

Automated research on dance gesture is a very young field in computer science, but within this short period it has grown very rapidly. Among different dances, Indian Classical Dance gain more popularity throughout the world. It was observed during literature review that hand gesture is the foremost important part to learn any kind of Classical Dance. In Indian Classical dance form, the hand gestures are known as Mudra. In general a hand gesture recognition can be defined as hand image expression which convey meaning during natural conversation [1]. Recognition of hand gestures from a dancer is a very challenging task for any pattern recognition problem due to its different age group of people. Again, to find out the invariant features is a difficult task when images are captured from different angle of view. Each hand gestures represent different meaning artistically along with drama during performance. Generally, two types of Mudras Asamyukta Mudra (single hand gesture) and Samyukta Mudra (double

© Springer Nature Switzerland AG 2020
N. Kar et al. (Eds.): ICCISIoT 2020, CCIS 1358, pp. 73–80, 2020.
https://doi.org/10.1007/978-3-030-66763-4_7

hand gesture) are used. There are almost total 28 Asamyukta mudras are available in Indian Classical dance. The Samyukta mudras are depend on ASamyukta mudra so this paper focus on the 28 Asamyukta mudras only. In the first part of this paper Huś seven invariant features were extracted from three different types of single hand gestures dataset such as gray image dataset, binary image dataset and boundary image dataset. And, in the lateral part these extracted features are analyzed using four popular machine learning classifier-namely, K-NN, Bayesian network, naïve Bayes, decision tree. The evaluated results are demonstrates for performance analysis of the dataset. The rest of the paper can be organized as proposed method including dataset creation, feature extraction and classification are explained in Sect. 2. The experimental results are discussed in Sect. 3. Finally, the chapter is concluded with future direction in Sect. 4.

2   Proposed Methods

The proposed method for recognition of Indian Classical dance single-hand gestures (Asamyukta hasta) using Moment invariant features is discussed in the following subsection.

2.1   Dataset Creation

A dataset used in this experiment consists of a total of 1120 images from four volunteer dancers for twenty eight single-hand gestures, which are captured using a digital camera of 12 megapixel. The dataset sample of twenty eight single-hand gestures are shown in Fig. 1. The 280 images are captured from each of four dancers. So, 1120 (28 types × 10 variation × 4 individuals) with different angle variation are used for this experiment.

A number of steps are been performed to preprocess the single hand gestures dataset. In first step, background of hand images were subtracted using Gaussian Mixture Model (GMM). Then, background subtracted images were resized to 400 × 400 pixels for experiment. The resized images are converted into gray image dataset, binary image dataset and boundary image dataset [2]. The sample of each dataset has shown in Fig. 2.

After preprocessing step the images are converted to MAT images [3] and proceed to the next subsection.

2.2   Feature Extraction

Feature extraction is the transformation of features into a lower dimensional space. It is the special form of dimensionality reduction. In image processing, feature describes the pattern of an image. The mapping from pattern to feature is one: one but from feature to pattern is one: many. That means one pattern can describe one feature but a single feature never describe a pattern.

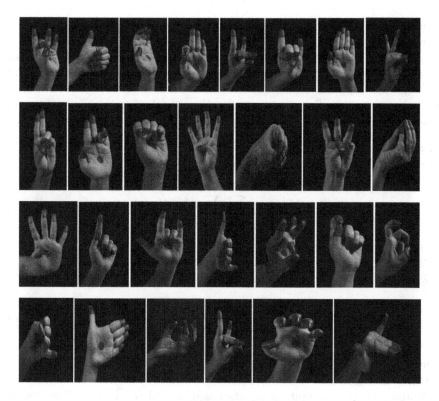

Fig. 1. Sample of expert mudra

Gray Image   Binary Iamge   Boundary detected Image

Fig. 2. Sample of dataset

One single pattern can have many features or set of features. It is not possible to consider all the features or feature set for analysis purpose otherwise the computational time will very high. It is necessary to reduce the feature set and to select the relevant feature by removing the unnecessary information. Hu introduced seven invariant moments depending on normalized central moments. Here, this invariants moments are extracted from three types of dataset: gray image dataset, binary image dataset and boundary extracted dataset. These seven invariant moments are not only independent of position, size and orientation but also parallel projection. To compute the Hu's moments [6], the following steps are carried out The fundamental problem of gesture recognition or classification is to find numerical attribute feature from images. Hu's invariant features are seven extracted features from the images which address the invariant property with respect to scale, rotation and translation. In 1962 M. K Hu introduced these seven nonlinear features function based on geometric and central moment [4].

1. Preprocess the input images.
2. Compute the geometric moment

$$Mm_{pq} = \sum_{x=0}^{M-1} \sum_{y=0}^{M-1} x^p y^q f(x,y) \tag{1}$$

where p,q=0,1,2... and centroid of this moment (x_0, y_0)
3. Calculate central moment upto 3rd order. When moment $f(x,y)$ is translated by an amount (x', y') then central moment can be written as

$$\mu_{pq} = \sum_{x=0}^{M-1} \sum_{y=0}^{M-1} (x - x')^p (y - y')^q f(x,y) \tag{2}$$

here (x', y') represent the Centroid of the image can be defined as x' = Mm_{10}/Mm_{00} and y' = Mm_{01}/Mm_{00}
4. Compute seven invariants moments based on 3rd order normalized central moments. Equations of this seven invariant moments are as follows:

$$\phi_1 = \mu_{20} + \mu_{20} \tag{3}$$

$$\phi_2 = (\mu_{20} - \mu_{20})^2 + 4\mu_{11} \tag{4}$$

$$\phi_3 = (\mu_{30} - 3\mu_{12})^2 + 3(\mu_{21} - \mu_{03})^2 \tag{5}$$

$$\phi_4 = (\mu_{30} + \mu_{12})^2 + (\mu_{21} + \mu_{03})^2 \tag{6}$$

$$\phi_5 = (\mu_{30} - 3\mu_{12})(\mu_{30} + \mu_{12})[(\mu_{30} + \mu_{12})^2 - 3(\mu_{21} + \mu_{03})^2]$$
$$+ 3(\mu_{21} - \mu_{03})(\mu_{21} + \mu_{03})[3(\mu_{30} + \mu_{12})^2 - (\mu_{21} + \mu_{03})^2] \tag{7}$$

$$\phi_6 = (\mu_{20} - \mu_{02})[(\mu_{30} + \mu_{12})^2 - (\mu_{21}$$
$$+ \mu_{03})^2] - 4\mu_{11}(\mu_{30} + \mu_{12})(\mu_{21} + \mu_{03}) \tag{9}$$

$$\phi_7 = (3\mu_{21} - \mu_{03})(\mu_{30} + \mu_{12})[(\mu_{30} + \mu_{12})^2 - 3(\mu_{21} + \mu_{03})^2]$$
$$- (\mu_{30} + 3\mu_{12})(\mu_{21} + \mu_{03})[3(\mu_{30} + \mu_{12})^2 - (\mu_{21} + \mu_{03})^2] \tag{10}$$

2.3   Classification

Classification means to classify the hand images into one of its twenty eight classes. Here, the twenty eight classes represent the twenty eight mudra of Indian classical dance. In this experiment, total 1120 images from four individual's dancers of different age group are used. The moment invariants feature were computed on these three type datasets. For each dataset, 70% of the data are used for training set and remaining 30% are used validate the result.

3   Experimental Results

The experimental description and the obtained outcome for the proposed method on single-hand gestures of dancers are discussed in the following sub-sections.

3.1   Experimental Setup

The experiment is carried out in a machine with configurations: Windows10 OS(64 bits), 4 GB RAM, 500 GB Hard-disk and MATLAB 2015. Additionally, we use the open source machine learning tool 'Weka-3-6-13' to test the classification accuracy.

3.2   Result Discussion

In this paper, the experiment had been done for classified the dataset images into individual classes based on the twenty eight type of Asamyukta Mudra. Each type of Asamyukta Mudra represent one individual class. The term Classification means mapping the images into predefined classes i.e., it is the function from input image feature to the output class. A class consists of a group of features that are found in the training phase. Our work for classification consists of two stages: training and testing. Different existing machine learning classifiers are used to find out the accuracy of the feature set. For each classifier, 70% of data are used as training set and remaining 30% are used to validate the results. The Hu's invariant feature set are analysed using four famous machine learning classifiers- namely, K-NN, Bayesian network, naïve Bayes, decision tree. The evaluated results are demonstrates in Table 1.

It can be seen from the above table, lowest level of performance 20%. And highest is 80%. Confusion matrix of highest accuracy classifier for gray image, binary image and boundary image dataset are shown as Fig. 3, 4 and 5 respectively. This confusion matrix described the performance of classifier on test dataset where diagonal element of each row gives the actual class performance and others column shows occurrence of mismatches. From our experiment, we can conclude that only seven Hu's invariant features are not sufficient for dance hand gesture recognition.

Table 1. Performance evaluation of Hu's invariant feature

Dataset	Classifier	Correctly classified	Average rate
Gray-image	K-nn(n = 5)	773	69.01
	Bayesian network	704	62.8571
	Naïve Bayes	570	50.8928
	Decision Tree	819	73.125
Boundary-image	K-nn(n = 4)	867	77.4107
	Bayesian network	696	62.1428
	Naïve Bayes	905	80.8880
	Decision tree	900	80.3571
Binary-image	K-nn (n = 5)	802	71.6071
	Bayesian network	813	72.5892
	Naïve Bayes	794	70.8928
	Decision tree	902	80.5357

Fig. 3. Confusion matrix of gray image dataset

Fig. 4. Confusion matrix of binary image dataset

```
 a  b  c  d  e  f  g  h  i  j  k  l  m  n  o  p  q  r  s  t  u  v  w  x  y  z aa ab   <-- classified as
34  0  0  0  0  0  0  0  0  0  0  0  0  0  0  0  0  0  0  0  1  0  0  0  0  0  0  0   | a = 1
 0 28  0  0  0  0  0  0  0  0  3  0  0  1  0  0  0  0  1  0  0  0  0  0  1  0  1      | b = 2
 2  0 33  0  0  0  0  0  0  0  0  0  0  0  0  0  0  0  0  0  0  0  0  0  0  0  0      | c = 3
 0  1  0 26  1  0  0  0  0  0  1  0  1  0  0  0  0  0  1  0  0  0  0  0  0  0  2      | d = 4
 0  1  0  0 24  0  0  0  0  0  3  0  0  3  0  0  0  0  2  2  0  0  0  0  0  0  1      | e = 5
 2  0  0  0  0 29  0  0  0  0  0  0  0  0  0  0  0  0  3  0  0  0  0  0  0  0  0      | f = 6
 0  1  0  0  2  2 24  2  0  0  1  0  0  0  0  0  0  0  1  1  0  0  1  0  0  0  0      | g = 7
 0  0  1  0  2  2  2 24  0  0  0  0  0  0  0  0  0  0  0  2  1  1  0  0  0  0  0      | h = 8
 0  0  0  0  1  0  0  0 28  0  1  1  0  0  0  0  1  0  0  0  1  0  0  0  1  0      | i = 9
 0  1  1  0  0  0  1  0  0 29  0  2  0  0  0  0  0  1  0  0  0  0  0  0  0  0      | j = 10
 0  2  0  2  0  0  0  1  0  0 26  0  1  0  0  0  0  0  0  0  0  0  0  0  0  0      | k = 11
 0  1  0  1  0  0  0  1  0  0  0 28  0  2  0  0  0  0  2  0  0  0  1  0  0  0      | l = 12
 0  0  1  1  1  1  1  1  0  0  0  0 26  0  0  1  0  0  0  1  0  0  0  0  0  2      | m = 13
 0  1  0  1  1  1  0  0  0  0  4  1  1 21  2  0  0  0  0  1  0  0  0  0  0  2      | n = 14
 0  1  1  1  0  0  0  0  2  0  0  0  0  0 27  0  0  0  0  0  0  0  0  0  0  0      | o = 15
 0  0  0  0  0  0  0  1  0  0  0  0  0  0  0 32  0  2  0  0  0  0  0  0  0  0      | p = 16
 0  0  0  0  0  0  0  0  0  0  0  0  0  0  0  0 35  0  0  0  0  0  0  0  0  0      | q = 17
 0  0  0  0  0  0  0  1  0  0  0  0  0  0  0  0  0 34  0  0  0  0  0  0  1  0      | r = 18
 0  1  0  1  0  0  0  0  1  0  1  4  1  0  1  0  0  0 19  0  0  0  0  0  1  1  2   | s = 19
 0  1  1  1  0  2  1  0  0  0  0  1  1  0  0  0  0  0  0 19  0  1  0  0  1  0  2   | t = 20
 0  1  0  3  0  1  0  0  0  0  1  1  2  0  0  0  0  0  0  0 23  0  1  0  1  0  1   | u = 21
 0  0  0  0  2  0  1  1  0  0  0  0  1  2  0  0  0  0  2  0  0 24  0  1  0  0  2   | v = 22
 1  0  0  0  0  1  0  0  0  2  1  1  1  2  0  0  0  0  0  1 23  0  1  1  0  0   | w = 23
 0  0  1  0  1  0  1  0  2  1  0  0  0  1  0  0  0  0  0  1  0  1 22  1  4  0  0   | x = 24
 0  3  1  0  2  0  0  1  0  3  0  0  0  1  0  0  0  0  0  0  2  0  1 22  1  0  0   | y = 25
 0  3  1  0  0  1  0  3  0  0  1  1  0  0  0  0  0  0  2  1  0  0  0  0 25  0  1   | z = 26
 0  2  0  5  1  0  1  0  2  0  1  2  0  1  0  0  0  0  0  1  0  0  0  0  0 17  1   | aa = 27
 0  0  0  1  2  0  4  0  0  1  2  1  1  0  1  0  0  0  0  3  0  0  0  0  1  0 18   | ab = 28
```

Fig. 5. Confusion matrix of boundary image dataset

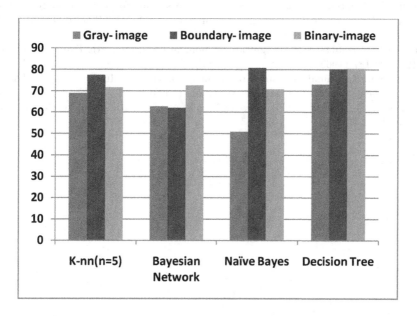

Fig. 6. Comparision analysis of Hu's moments featureset

4 Conclusion and Future Direction

In this paper, a single hand gesture dataset of Indian Classical dance which includes 1120 images, are used. To extract the feature, Hu's seven invariant moments feature extraction method is used on this dataset. Also, four machine learning classifiers namely K-nearest neighbour, Bayesian network, naive Bayes, decision tree are used to analyze the single hand gestures recognition of Indian classical dance has been used. In this experiment, the result indicates that decision tree classifier shows a better performance compared to other classifiers for all variation of dataset, and could achieve an accuracy of 80.88%. A major disadvantage of Hu's feature is that it only focuses on global feature rather than local feature. For the future, we will consider the local features of the single hand gestures of dancer.

References

1. Devi, M., Saharia, S., Bhattacharyya, D.K.: Dance gesture recognition: a survey. Int. J. Comput. Appl. **122**(5), 19–26 (2015)
2. Devi, M., Saharia, S., Bhattacharyya, D.K.: A dataset of single-hand gestures of Sattriya dance. In: Chanda, B., Chaudhuri, S., Chaudhury, S. (eds.) Heritage Preservation, pp. 293–310. Springer, Singapore (2018). https://doi.org/10.1007/978-981-10-7221-5_14
3. Devi, M., Saharia, S.: A two-level classification scheme for single-hand gestures of Sattriya dance. In: 2016 International Conference on Accessibility to Digital World (ICADW), 16 December 2016, pp. 193–196. IEEE (2016)
4. Hu, M.-K.: Visual pattern recognition by moment invariants. IRE Trans. Inf. Theory **8**(2), 179–187 (1962)
5. Mukundan, R., Ramakrishnan, K.R.: Moment Functions in Image Analysis: Theory and Applications. World Scientific, Singapore (1998)
6. Clowes, M.B., Parks, J.R.: A new technique in automatic character recognition. Comput. J. **4**(2), 121–128 (1961)

Comparison of GEP and ANN Method with Experimental Data to Forecast the Laminar Fluid Stream and Heat Transmission Characteristics Through a Tube with Spiral Ribs and Twisted Tapes

Sagnik Pal⊙, Sameer S. Gajghate$^{(\boxtimes)}$⊙, and Swapan Bhaumik⊙

Mechanical Engineering Department, National Institute of Technology Agartala,
Tripura 799046, India
mtech_sameer@yahoo.in

Abstract. The Two extensively used prediction methods, Artificial Neural Network and Gene Expression Programming have been utilized in the current study to forecast the laminar fluid stream and heat transmission nature through a duct with spiral ribs and twisted tapes. The fluid stream and heat transmission characteristics were collected from the experimental data [1]. The fluid stream properties are signified by friction factor and Reynolds Number as 'fxRe' and the heat transmission property is signified by average Nusselt Number 'Nu_{avg}'. Further, these two prediction tools were compared with the existing correlations and observed that the both Artificial Neural Network and Gene Expression Programming models were better than the correlations. The value of Adj.R^2 of the Artificial Neural Network model for 'fxRe' and 'Nu_{avg}' is 0.99588 and 0.99870 and the Gene Expression Programming model is having 0.99222 and 0.97674. It is found that the Gene Expression Programming model is not as good as the Artificial Neural Network model and correlation.

Keywords: Spiral rib · Twisted tape · Heat transfer · ANN · GEP

1 Introduction

Heat transfer enhancements by the passive techniques are more popular than the active techniques because they offer a low-cost solution to the heat transfer problem. Thus, the number of research projects and studies have been increasing constantly embark on the subject. The advances in the enhancement techniques [2–4] have been periodically reported by many authors. Namely, there are three different approaches available for the augmentation of duct-side convective heat

National Institute of Technology Agartala.

N. Kar et al. (Eds.): ICCISIoT 2020, CCIS 1358, pp. 81–95, 2020.
https://doi.org/10.1007/978-3-030-66763-4_8

transfer and they are external inserts, inner fins, and the internal surface roughness. Twisted tapes are most extensively used among all other types of insert, particularly in laminar flow devices for the heat transfer enhancement [1]. Garcia et al. [5] experimentally tested the behavior of wire-coil insert for different pitch and wire diameters in laminar, transition and turbulent regions inside a horizontal pipe. It was found that the wire-coil insert shows the higher performance in transition region with the drop in pressure and increased in heat transfer up to eight times in compared to the plain tube. Garcia et al. [6] conducted comparative works on thermal-hydraulic performance of corrugated pipes, pipes with dimpled and wire-coils using their previous experimental works [7–10] in all the fluid flow regimes. Researcher reported that the shape of the artificial roughness had greater effect on the pressure drop features compared to the heat transfer. Also, recommended the range of Re and the corresponding suitable surface roughness to be adopted. Bergels [11] considered compound techniques as fourth generation heat transfer technology, where combined multiple techniques may be employed concurrently to boost in the enhancement, which is higher than the specific enhancement techniques functional independently. Zimparov [12] proposed a mathematical model for spirally corrugated tube to predict the heat transfer coefficients. Saha et al. [13] studied the combined effect of wire-coil and twisted-tape inserts in circular tube. Author realized from their published work [14,15] related to twisted tapes and wire coils that the above stated combination may lead to better thermo-hydraulic performance. Also observed that, the influence of wire coil inserts was much prominent on Nusselt number compared to the friction factor. It is due to larger effects on thermal boundary layer than the hydrodynamic layer. Thianpong et al. [16] examined experimentally the influence of compounding twisted tape and dimpled tube, under fully established turbulent flow condition $(12{,}000 < \text{Re} < 44{,}000)$. It was found that the Nusselt number is higher for the combined twisted tape inserts on dimpled tube by 15 to 56% and 66 to 303%, respectively, compared to individual dimpled and plain tube. Also, the friction factor 2.12 times and 5.58 times higher than the each normal tube. Bharadwaj et al. [17] examined the influence of twisted tape insert in spirally grooved tube at constant heat flux condition and found that the trend of twist (clockwise or anticlockwise) have great effect on thermal-hydraulic performance and shows the augmentation in heat transfer by 400% and 140%, respectively, in laminar and turbulent flow.

Now a days, forecast of dissimilar features of heat transmission are becoming a region of investigation in numerous engineering uses because of its fewer time over whelming technique. Artificial Neural Network (ANN) and Gene Expression Programming (GEP) are the most applying techniques. ANN has massive uses in several engineering regions such as ventilating, refrigerator, heating and air conditioning, heating, and solar steam generators etc., [18]. Another vast applied forecasting tool is GEP that can estimate extra compound utility to develop a relation between input and output [19]. A comparison between the most applied prediction tools have been accomplished by the various researchers and found that the sometimes ANN is superior to GEP and sometimes GEP is superior to ANN [20–23].

Thus, it is relevant to make a conclusion that there is no prior investigation of application of ANN and GEP in the prediction of heat transmission characteristics through a pipe with passive techniques of heat transfer augmentation. Hence, the current research aims to investigate the proficiency of the ANN and GEP in the prediction of the laminar fluid stream and heat transmission features through a pipe with twisted tapes and spiral ribs and further these two methods are compared with a published correlation. Also, the effect of the different parameters of the ANN and GEP models have been investigated.

2   Experimental and Computing Investigations

2.1   A Experimental Set-Up and Data Reduction

In a 2 m long made stainless steel duct of circular shape and having 19 mm inner dia. and 0.5 mm thickness, the experiments were accomplished. Figure 1 depicts the graphical representation of the experimental setup. For providing the constant surface heat ux on the test section, nichrome heater is used. And, the thickness of the duct was made quite significant for assurance of constant heat flux flow and also the conductivity of the channel material was great enough. Asbestos rope and glass fleece protected the warmth exchange test segment after the warmer wire. At long last the test segment was secured with jute sack for further warm protection. Winding crease harshness for warmth exchange tests was made of metal. Servo-therm medium oil, which has Prandtl number reach to 152–549 is accomplished for utilized as operational liquid. Curved tape additions were set at the focal point of the conduit cross-segment by SS carries. Rota meters and vertical mercury manometer are used for the measurement of Oil mass ow and Strain drops. The mixing of boundary layer thickness at the downstream of the ribs the heat transfer augmentation gently scatters. As a consequence, ribs pitch and heights were selected nearby the heat switch coefficient. Therefore, Using K-type thermocouples and digital multi-meter outside wall temperatures at seven axial locations (each locations have 4 (four) K-type thermocouples at ninety degree separately alongside the duct periphery) have been measured in heat switch experiment portion. Customarily, at four axial places 3–3.7% of higher wall temperature were noted and also same results were obtained for Prandtl and Reynolds number. The difference wall temperature along the duct periphery were observed due to change in ribs pitch and heights, buoyancy and swirl induced in the insert tape. Nevertheless, the results don't seem to be terribly sturdy. Thermocouples were hooked up on the tube outside surface by using brazing. Thermocouples are placed at 5 and 50 cm, 1.00, 1.25, 1.5, 1.75 and 1.95 m, respectively, from the beginning of heating tube at downstream till the end of the tube at upstream direction. Using, one dimensional heat conduction equation wall temperatures was assessed by calculating the drop in wall temperature in the tube.

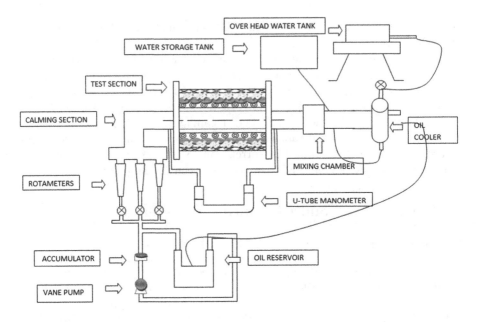

Fig. 1. Graphical representation of the experimental setup.

2.2 Uncertainty Analysis

All the amounts that are dignified to assess the Nusselt number and the friction factor are conditional on particular uncertainties because of errors in the experimental procedures and its measurement. Therefore, an inclusive measurement uncertainty exploration was accomplished to recognise and enumerate the inaccuracy connected with the experimental procedures, instrumentation, standardisation of these and observation accuracy. Kline and McClintock [24] uncertainty method was adopted, to evaluate the specific uncertainties and its collective consequence are depicted in this paragraph. The overall description of the uncertainty analysis are shown in Eqs. 1–13 and the accuracy of measured quantity is shown in Table 1. Friction factor:

$$f = 1/2((\Delta P/L_p)((\rho D^3)/(Re^2 \mu^2))) \tag{1}$$

$$\frac{\Delta f}{f} = \frac{1}{f}\left[\left\{\frac{\partial f}{\partial(\Delta P)}\Delta(\Delta P)\right\}^2 + \left\{\frac{\partial f}{\partial L_p}\Delta L_p\right\}^2 + \left\{\frac{\partial f}{\partial D}\Delta D\right\}^2 + \left\{\frac{\partial f}{\partial(Re)}\Delta(Re)\right\}^2\right]^{0.5} \tag{2}$$

$$\frac{\Delta f}{f} = \left[\left\{\frac{\Delta(\Delta P)}{\partial(\Delta P)}\right\}^2 + \left\{\frac{\Delta L_p}{L_p}\right\}^2 + \left\{\frac{3\Delta D}{D}\right\}^2 + \left\{\frac{2\Delta Re}{Re}\right\}^2\right]^{0.5} \tag{3}$$

$$\Delta P \propto h \tag{4}$$

$$(\Delta(\Delta P))/\Delta P = \Delta h/h \tag{5}$$

$$Re = 4\dot{m}/\pi D\mu \tag{6}$$

$$\frac{\Delta Re}{Re} = \left[\frac{\Delta \dot{m}}{\dot{m}} + \left\{\frac{\Delta D}{D}\right\}^2\right]^{0.5} \tag{7}$$

From the above equations uncertainty of friction factor has been calculated. Nusselt Number:

$$Nu = hD/K \tag{8}$$

$$(\Delta Nu/Nu) = [(\Delta h/h)^2 + (\Delta D/D)^2]^0.5 \tag{9}$$

$$h = q''/(T_{wi} - T_b) \tag{10}$$

$$(\Delta h/h) = [((\partial q''/q'')^2) + ((\Delta T_{wi})/(T_{wi} - T_b))^2 + ((T_b)/(T_{wi} - T_b))^2]^{0.5} \tag{11}$$

$$q'' = (0.5/(\pi D L_h)[(V^2/R) + \dot{m}C_p(T_{bo} - T_{bi})] \tag{12}$$

$$\frac{\Delta q''}{q''} = \frac{1}{q''}\left[\left\{\frac{\partial}{\partial R}\Delta R\left(q''\right)\right\}^2 + \left\{\frac{\partial}{\partial v}\left(q''\right)\Delta V\right\}^2 + \left\{\frac{\partial}{\partial \dot{m}}\Delta \dot{m}\left(q''\right)\right\}^2 + \left\{\frac{\partial}{\partial T_{bo}}\Delta T_{bo}\left(q''\right)\right\}^2\right.$$
$$\left. + \left\{\frac{\partial}{\partial T_{bi}}\left(q''\right)\Delta T_{bi}\right\}^2 + \left\{\frac{\partial}{\partial D}\Delta D\left(q''\right)\right\}^2 + \left\{\frac{\partial}{\partial L_h}\Delta L_h\left(q''\right)\right\}^2\right]^{0.5}$$

$$\frac{\Delta q''}{q''} = \left[\frac{1}{(1 + \dot{m}C_p R\Delta T_b/V^2)^2}\left(\frac{\Delta R}{R}\right)^2 + \frac{4}{(1 + \dot{m}C_p R\Delta T_b/V^2)^2}\left(\frac{\Delta V}{V}\right)^2 + \frac{1}{\left(1 + \frac{V^2}{R\dot{m}C_p\Delta T_b}\right)^2}\left(\frac{\Delta \dot{m}}{\dot{m}}\right)^2\right.$$
$$\left. + \frac{1}{\left(1 + \frac{V^2}{R\dot{m}C_p\Delta T_b}\right)^2}\left(\frac{\Delta T_{bo}}{T_b}\right)^2 + \frac{1}{\left(1 + \frac{V^2}{R\dot{m}C_p\Delta T_b}\right)^2}\left(\frac{\Delta T_{bi}}{\dot{m}}\right)^2 + \left(\frac{\Delta L_h}{L_h}\right)^2 + \left(\frac{\Delta D}{D}\right)^2\right]^{0.5} \tag{13}$$

where, $\Delta T_b = (T_{bo} - T_{bi})$. From the above equations uncertainty of Nusselt number has been calculated.

Table 1. Accuracy details of the measured quantities.

Quantity	Accuracy
ΔD_h	0.00002 m
$\Delta \dot{m}$	1.667 E-5 kg/s
ΔT	0.025°C
ΔR	0.00001 Ω
ΔL	0.001 m
Δh	0.001 m
ΔV	0.1 V

2.3   Experimental Outcomes

There are various input parameters that involved in the experiments for evaluating the 'Nusselt Number' and 'friction factor'. The ranges of that input parameters are shown here.

Twist ratio, y = 2.5, 5.0;
Twisted-tape tooth horizontal length, $t^*_{hl} = 1, 1.5$, and 2 mm;
Twisted-tape tooth angle, $\theta = 30^0$, 45^0 and 60^0;
Rib height, $h_{r^*} = 1, 1.5$, and 2 mm;
Rib helix angle $(\alpha) = 30^0$, 45^0 and 60^0.

As per the experimental published data [1], it was concluded that the reduction in the 't_{hl}' [where 'hl' is subscript], 'θ' and rib height and increment in the rib pitch reduces the friction factor and as well as the Nusselt number.

It was also concluded that, the combination of two techniques i.e. twisted-tape with oblique teeth and rough integral spiral rib perform superior than the singular technique of enhancement. The heat transfer improvement were found around 122–348% at constant pumping power and the same time for constant heat duty 2–72% reduction was found in pumping power, which was depends on the values of different parameters. It was also observed that the 'f' and 'Nu' both were inversely proportional to the rib pitch and directly proportional to the rib height. The inertia force because of swirl movement engendered by the twisted-tape augments the periodic physical phenomenon partition and re-affix with temperature and rate profiles similarly blandish, caused by the rough integral spiral rib and therefore the improvement occurred. Where, in compound techniques, hydrodynamic layers were much disturbed than the thermal boundary layers due to the roughness of the helical ribs present in the duct. The profile of temperature was superior to the velocity as asymmetric profiles was more, which shows the loss in momentum due to fluid involvement. Moreover, the quicker drop in thermal layer than hydrodynamic boundary layer. Hence, the increment of heat transfer is higher compared to pressure drop increment.

2.4   Artificial Neural Network

Artificial neural network is a soft computing scheme that simply works as a biological neural structure (especially the brain). In any ANN model, number of modest neurons are well settled. These are all reasonably joined with each other to pass the distinct weights and also to convey the signals. This overall enterprise of the connections of the neurons into diverse stages is termed as network architecture. The output is being developed by the input neurons that are organized with the numbers of hidden layer neuron [25]. The most general numeric expression of a particular artificial neuron can be stated as:

$$y(x) = f(\sum_{i=0}^{n} w_i x_i + b) \tag{14}$$

where, 'x' is an input neuron having corresponding weight 'w' and 'b' indicating the bias [26]. Here, 'f' is the activation function used to decide the values of 'w' to develop the output by the help of input and hidden layers and this 'f' can be expressed as [26].

$$f(x) = 1/(1 + e^{-x}) \tag{15}$$

In the present analysis, a feed forward ANN structure is utilized which comprise multi stages with different neurons. Three layers (i.e. input, hidden and output) of this multi stages are used in the present optimization study. The consider model has been proficiently employed in several heat transfer investigation in combining with experimental data [27–29].

Training ANN: Different training algorithm is available in which widely utilized algorithm is Levenberg–Marquardt algorithm [21, 22, 30]. This algorithm has been ap-plied for training the current made-up network for estimating the 'fxRe' and 'Nu_{avg}'. A back propagation error algorithm has been employed such that, at first error be-tween the predicted data and the expected data was calculated and then passed back through network for minimizing the error by modifying the corresponding weights. In any ANN model, primarily it is required to develop the network (known as training) from some collected data. A best network is trained by adjusting the values of weights and bias. In the current study, 70% of the overall data that were collected from [1], have been employed in the training set. The left over data were designated for testing and validation of the trained network. Some restrictions are being provided by the 'sigmoid function' in the ANN tool in MATLAB, because of which the input and output values are constrained between 0.1 and 0.9. Consequently, the values are normalized by the succeeding equation:

$$x_i = ((x_i - x_{min})/(x_{max} - x_{min})) \tag{16}$$

where, x_i = Real input/output;
x_n = Normalized data;
x_{min} = Minimum value of inputs/outputs;

x_{max} = Maximum value of inputs/outputs.

Optimal Network Model: For progressing an ANN tool, the amount of neurons in the input, hidden and output layers have to select faultlessly. Right thing assortment also denotes an essential individual in the awareness of the ANN gadget that is hired in the current study. Concern to the precision requisite, the wide variety of layers like hidden and the hidden neurons range may fluctuate. After a tribulation and blunders method, it got observed that a hidden layer of 12 neurons fits the precision that prerequisite in forecast the friction factor traits and 10 neurons for the Nusselt Number values. The optimal values of Adj.R^2 for different neurons are tabulated in Table 2. The designed optimal neural network structure 6-12-1 (6, 12 and 1 neurons in input, hidden and output layer, respectively.) for 'friction factor' and 7-10-1 for "Nusselt Number" of the present study are shown in Fig. 2 (Table 3 and Table 4).

Table 2. Optimal network table of ANN model having 70% data as training.

Sl. No	No. of neurons in hidden layer	Adj. R^2 of 'fxRe'	Sl. No	No. of neurons in hidden layer	Adj. R^2 of 'Nu_{avg}'
1	5	0.98561	1	5	0.98529
2	10	0.99489	2	8	0.99071
3	15	0.99264	3	10	0.99870
4	12	0.99588	4	15	0.99750
5	13	0.99515	5	20	0.98957

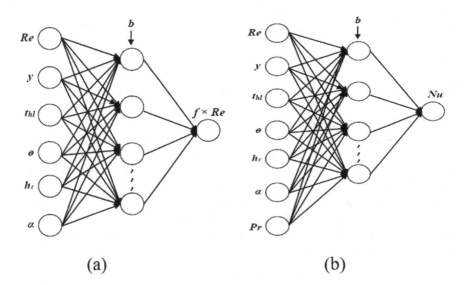

(a)   (b)

Fig. 2. ANN model of the current study for (a) 'fxRe', and (b) 'Nu_{avg}'

Table 3. Bias and weight information of the optimized ANN model of the 'fx Re.'

Bias and weights								
Input layer to hidden layers							Hidden layer to output layer	Output layer
Weights					Bias	Weight		Bias
1.037	0.65	0.286	−0.586	−0.005	1.991	−2.514	−2.514	
−0.047	0.385	−0.236	−2.21	0.007	2.644	2.096	2.096	
0.491	1.32	1.71	−0.505	0.202	−1.166	−1.367	−1.367	
−1.988	0.442	−0.482	−2.771	0.194	−1.746	0.982	0.982	
0.656	−1.101	−0.65	−0.349	1.198	−0.825	−0.382	−0.382	
0.582	1.477	0.901	0.051	−0.571	−1.451	−0.397	−0.397	−0.382
−0.009	1.844	2.32	−0.32	1.117	−0.712	−1.894	−1.894	
0.392	1.881	−0.395	0.519	2.279	−0.32	−0.032	−0.032	
0.364	−2.248	0.594	−0.36	0.7	−0.676	2.001	2.001	
−0.843	1.738	0.754	−0.046	0.083	−0.404	−1.163	−1.163	
−1.395	−0.548	0.503	−1.066	2.021	0.269	−1.932	−1.932	
−1.815	1.008	−0.846	−1.506	0.323	−0.793	−0.989	−0.989	

Table 4. Bias and weight information of the optimized ANN model of the 'Nu_{avg}.'

Bias and weights									
Input layer to hidden layers							Hidden layer to output layer		Output layer
Weights						Bias	Weight		Bias
−0.405	0.624	−0.528	1.071	0.888	0.435	−0.944	−1.972	−0.5284	
0.973	1.269	0.075	0.667	0.887	0.04	−0.197	−2.265	0.3942	
1.054	−1.614	−0.653	−0.317	−0.361	−0.934	0.712	−0.702	0.0093	
−0.396	−1.53	−0.939	0.622	−0.694	−0.85	−0.294	1.068	−0.3737	
0.773	0.836	0.863	1.314	−1.042	0.277	0.329	0.053	0.2252	−1.415
−0.858	1.717	−0.914	0.895	−0.767	0.029	−0.724	−0.098	−1.1155	
0.025	−0.62	0.524	−0.647	1.318	0.82	0.523	−0.843	−1.1566	
0.942	−1.232	−0.014	−2.146	−0.892	−1.224	0.04	−0.511	−0.8319	
0.624	0.924	−1.183	0.693	0.753	−0.833	−1.017	0.565	0.6617	
0.084	0.282	−0.48	−0.269	−0.623	1.546	0.017	−2.222	−0.9778	

2.5   Gene Expression Programming

GEP is a gadget of rising capabilities thru populace primarily based biological process technique combining the leads of genetic algorithm rule (GA) and genetic programming (GP), planned via Ferreira [19]. It's associate in nursing extension of GA during which easy or linear chromosomes area unit encoded to the people, afterward reworked into associate in using expression dissect tree (ET) fully separating the genotype and com-position that makes GEP a lot of quicker (100–10,000 times) than the GP [19,31]. As an instance, an ET of an arithmetical expression (Eq. 17).

$$(x + y)(y - z) \tag{17}$$

In GEP, there are compound sequences during a body and many subprograms are en-coded with every gene. Thus, any program is encoded for economical progress the results by the unique arrangements of the genes within the GEP formula [19]. The whole possible section of the matter is employed by the unique structure of the genes within the GEP to own well-ordered genetic operators searching for the results. In GEP, additional complicated logical and technical programs is evaluated with the assistance of linear chromosomes and ET. Every linear body is influenced heritably, i.e. replication, recombination and amp, mutation, and transposition [19]. The fitness worth of ETs is that the choice criteria for the presence within the system. For accomplishment the best result, trees having the poorest fitness worth square measure terminated. When dismissing the poorest fitness valued trees, left over population embraces of continuous trees depend upon distinguishing choice technique.

GEP Model of Present Input and Output Data: The GEP is expressed for the relation between the input and output data. In every GEP equations the k-fold strategy has been retain. The data was distributed in three sub category such as training, testing, and validation. Where, for training 70% was selected and remaining kept for testing and validation. Thereafter, code was modelled 3 times and to find the Adj.R^2 the predicted values were averaged.

The MATLAB software was used to assessed the input and output data with advance the empirical correlations. Diverse signs from perform set and Terminal set are employed in scientific expressions. Several scientific functions and mathematics operators out there in utility set are employed in this investigation (as depicted in the Table 4) to get the relation among input and output by progressing the system. The quantities of plans within the every linear body are set by the populace size i.e. range of chromosomes. The higher the populace size creates the repetition time lengthier. The program is taken into ac-count as converged once there aren't any respectable changes within the performance of the system and also the repetition is then clogged. In the current study, the fore-most objective of application of the GEP is to forecast and develop an explicit precise equation of the laminar fluid stream and heat transmission characteristics through a tube with spiral ribs and twisted tapes. The ET of the corresponding expression of 'fxRe' and 'Nu_{avg}' is depicted in Eqs. 18 and 19, respectively.

$$f_x Re = 7154.68898 \times e^{(-35.298 \times x_3 \times x_4 \times x_5)} - (35.9779 \times \sin(e^{x_1}))$$
$$- (35.9779 \times x_2) - 1032.8597 \times x_6^4 + 860908.6562 \times x_4^2 \times x_6^4 \times$$
$$\sin(x_5^2) - 130415.9632 \times x_4 \times x_5^2 \times x_6^2 \times \sin(x_2 \times x_4) + (0.3193 \times x_3 \times$$
$$\sin(x_4 \times x_6) \times e^{(x_2 \times x_1 - 11.2605)} - 6.3971e + 03 \qquad (18)$$

$$Nu_{avg} = (2.0882 \times x_1) + (94.1265 \times e^{(\sin(x_1) \times (x_5 - x_6))}) - (27.5604 \times$$
$$\sin(2x_2 + 2x_3 + x_6)) - (21.5576 \times \cos(x_7)^2) - (29.7471 \times \cos(2x_1 + x_2) \times e^{(x_5 - x_6)})$$
$$- (21.5576 \times 3^{\frac{1}{2}} \times x_1^{\frac{1}{2}}) + (4.1765 \times \sin(x_1 + 2x_2 + x_4)) + 115.9083 \qquad (19)$$

The efficiency of the GEP to predict the heat transfer coefficient is measured by Adjusted R-Square (Adj. R^2) and expressed as:

$$R^2 = 1 - (\sum_i (N_i - P_i)^2 / (\sum_i (P_i^2)) \qquad (20)$$

where, Ni= Actual Value, Pi=Predicted Value and Root Mean Squared Error (RMSE) is used to measure the error between the actual and predicted data and defined as:

$$RMSE = \sqrt{(1/n \sum_i (N_i - P_i)^2)} \qquad (21)$$

where, n = total number of data.

3   Results and Discussions

In the current study, two soft computing tools, GEP and ANN have been used to pre-dict the laminar fluid stream and heat transmission characteristics through a tube with spiral ribs and twisted tapes. The models were developed by the experimental data collected from [1]. The different input parameters were Twist ratio (y), Twisted-tape tooth horizontal length (t_{hl}), Twisted-tape tooth angle (θ), Rib height (h_r) and Rib helix angle (α) and the output factors are friction factor (f) and Nusselt Number (Nu). Further, the both models have been compared with each other and also with the cor-relation developed by [1].

The experimental data that found by a series of combinations of the inputs are predicted by the GEP and ANN. In between of them, GEP is capable to deliver an implicit relation among the inputs and outputs but ANN is not capable to develop that kind of relation. The predicted outputs are 'fxRe' and 'Nu_{avg}'. The discrepancy of the predicted results by ANN, GEP and correlation [1] with the experimental results are depicted in the Fig. 3 and 4, respectively. These figures delivers the information about the essential sensitivity and sturdiness of the models in its ability to make the fluid stream and heat transmission outcomes

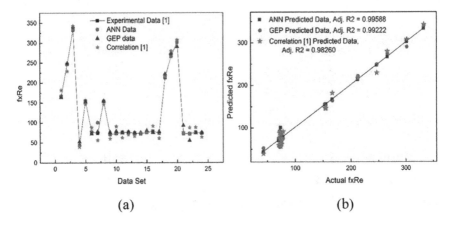

Fig. 3. (a) Prediction of 'fxRe' data by ANN, GEP and correlation, and (b) linear fit of predicted results with experimental results.

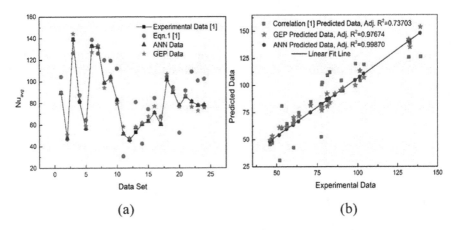

Fig. 4. (a) Prediction of 'Nu_{avg}' data by ANN, GEP and correlation, and (b) linear fit of predicted results with experimental results.

concurrently with exceptional precision. From the experimental 'fxRe' data that are predicted by the GEP having the Adj.R^2 as 0.9922, RMSE as 1.1233 and MAPE as 1.0584. The ANN predicted 'fxRe; results is having Adj.R^2 as 0.9959, RMSE as 0.5345 and MAPE as 0.1492.

The motive behind the present study is to generate a relationship between the in-puts and the outputs so that the model can predict the experimental data very efficiently. A correlation has been already developed by the one of the authors in [1] and found that the predicted data has ± 9.11% error and having Adj.R^2 as 0.9826, RMSE as 1.3699 and MAPE as 1.0703 for 'fxRe' data and Adj.R^2 as 0.7370, RMSE as 1.3913 and MAPE as 0.2061 for 'Nu_{avg}' data. The GEP and ANN model predicted 'Nu_{avg}' data are having Adj.R^2 as 0.9767,

RMSE as 0.7376 and MAPE as 0.0489 and Adj.R^2 as 0.9987, RMSE as 0.4601 and MAPE as 0.0066 respectively. Further, the models are compared with each other (summarized in Table 5) and found that the ANN model is much efficient than the GEP model and also than the correlation. The ANN model has highest regression coefficient value and lowest statistical error value. The same amount of data were utilized in training, testing and validation for both the models i.e. ANN and GEP. But, comparatively very large amount of data were used in the previous article [1] to develop the correlation. Thus, an ANN model with optimized number of neurons can have the utmost potentiality to forecast the friction factor and Nusselt Number characteristics through a tube with spiral ribs and twisted tapes.

Table 5. Discrepancy of predicted data between ANN, GEP and Correlation.'

Method	ANN			GEP			Correlation [1]		
Data	Adj.R^2	RMSE	MAPE	Adj.R^2	RMSE	MAPE	Adj.R^2	RMSE	MAPE
'fxRe'	0.9959	0.5345	0.1492	0.9922	1.1233	1.0584	0.9826	1.3699	1.0703
'Nu_{avg}'	0.9987	0.4601	0.0066	0.9767	0.7376	0.0489	0.737	1.3913	0.2061

4   Conclusion

Two different prediction methods. ANN and GEP have been employed to forecast the friction factor and Nusselt Number characteristics through a duct with spiral ribs and twisted tapes. Both the models were trained by the experimental data collected from one of the authors published article [1]. The predicted outcomes are 'friction factor' and 'Nusselt Number' that associated with numbers of input parameters. By the amalgamations of the input factors, a set a data has been collected and then the models have been developed. The two prediction methods further then compared with a correlation which is already published in an article. After the current investigation, the following conclusions can be made:

1. Both the ANN and GEP are efficiently capable to estimate the fluid stream and heat transmission characteristics.
2. Both the ANN and GEP are efficiently capable to estimate the fluid stream and heat transmission characteristics.
3. The proficiency of the GEP model is lying on the critical values of 'No. of Chromosomes', 'Head Size' etc.
4. The ANN and GEP models both are much proficient than the correlation developed in [1] but ANN is superior to all of the models by having very little error with the new outcomes/results.

Thus, the present ANN model can be applied in further fluid stream and heat trans-mission through different tubes in laminar and turbulent flow regime with various working conditions for predicting the mentioned consequences.

References

1. Pal, S., Saha, S.K.: Laminar fluid flow and heat transfer through a circular tube having spiral ribs and twisted tapes. Exp. Thermal Fluid Sci. **60**, 173–181 (2015)
2. Bergles, A.E., Techniques to augment heat transfer. Handbook of heat transfer (A 74–17085 05–33), pp. 1–10. McGraw-Hill Book Co., New York (1973)
3. Dewan, A., et al.: Review of passive heat transfer augmentation techniques. Proc. Inst. Mech. Eng. Part A J. Power Energy **218**(7), 509–527 (2004)
4. Dalkilic, A., Wongwises, S.: Intensive literature review of condensation inside smooth and enhanced tubes. Int. J. Heat Mass Transf. **52**(15), 3409–3426 (2009)
5. Garcia, A., et al.: The influence of artificial roughness shape on heat transfer enhancement: corrugated tubes, dimpled tubes and wire coils. Appl. Therm. Eng. **35**, 196–201 (2012)
6. Vicente, P.G., Garcia, A., Viedma, A.: Experimental study of mixed convection and pressure drop in helically dimpled tubes for laminar and transition flow. Int. J. Heat Mass Transf. **45**(26), 5091–5105 (2002)
7. Vicente, P., Garcia, A., Viedma, A.: Mixed convection heat transfer and isothermal pressure drop in corrugated tubes for laminar and transition flow. Int. Commun. Heat Mass Transf. **31**(5), 651–662 (2004)
8. Vicente, P.G., Garcia, A., Viedma, A.: Experimental investigation on heat transfer and frictional characteristics of spirally corrugated tubes in turbulent flow at different Prandtl numbers. Int. J. Heat Mass Transf. **47**(4), 671–681 (2004)
9. Vicente, P.G., Garcia, A., Viedma, A.: Heat transfer and pressure drop for low Reynolds turbulent flow in helically dimpled tubes. Int. J. Heat Mass Transf. **45**(3), 543–553 (2002)
10. Garcia, A., Vicente, P.G., Viedma, A.: Experimental study of heat transfer enhancement with wire coil inserts in laminar-transition-turbulent regimes at different Prandtl numbers. Int. J. Heat Mass Transf. **48**(21), 4640–4651 (2005)
11. Bergles, A.E.: ExHFT for fourth generation heat transfer technology. Exp. Thermal Fluid Sci. **26**(2), 335–344 (2002)
12. Zimparov, V.: Prediction of friction factors and heat transfer coefficients for turbulent flow in corrugated tubes combined with twisted tape inserts. Part 2: heat transfer coefficients. Int. J. Heat Mass Transf. **47**(2), 385–393 (2004)
13. Saha, S.K., Barman, B.K., Banerjee, S.: Heat transfer enhancement of laminar flow through a circular tube having wire coil inserts and fitted with center-cleared twisted tape. J. Therm. Sci. Eng. Appl. **4**(3), 031003 (2012)
14. Pramanik, D., Saha, S.K.: Thermohydraulics of laminar flow through rectangular and square ducts with transverse ribs and twisted tapes. J. Heat Transf. **128**(10), 1070–1080 (2006)
15. Saha, S.K.: Thermal and friction characteristics of laminar flow through rectangular and square ducts with transverse ribs and wire coil inserts. Exp. Thermal Fluid Sci. **34**(1), 63–72 (2010)
16. Thianpong, C., et al.: Compound heat transfer enhancement of a dimpled tube with a twisted tape swirl generator. Int. Commun. Heat Mass Transf. **36**(7), 698–704 (2009)
17. Bharadwaj, P., Khondge, A., Date, A.: Heat transfer and pressure drop in a spirally grooved tube with twisted tape insert. Int. J. Heat Mass Transf. **52**(7), 1938–1944 (2009)
18. Kalogirou, S.A.: Applications of artificial neural-networks for energy systems. Appl. Energy **67**(1), 17–35 (2000)

19. Ferreira, C.: Gene expression programming: a new adaptive algorithm for solving problems. Complex Syst. **13**, 87–129 (2001)
20. Dey, P., Sarkar, A., Das, A.K.: Prediction of unsteady mixed convection over circular cylinder in the presence of nanofluid - a comparative study of ANN and GEP. J. Naval Archit. Mar. Eng. **12**(1), 57–71 (2015)
21. Dey, P., Sarkar, A., Das, A.K.: Development of GEP and ANN model to predict the unsteady forced convection over a cylinder. Neural Comput. Appl. **27**(8), 2537–2549 (2015). https://doi.org/10.1007/s00521-015-2023-8
22. Dey, P., Sarkar, A., Das, A.K.: Capability to predict the steady and unsteady reduced aerodynamic forces on a square cylinder by ANN and GEP. Neural Comput. Appl. **28**, 1933–1945 (2016). https://doi.org/10.1007/s00521-016-2186-y
23. Martí, P., et al.: Artificial neural networks vs. gene expression programming for estimating outlet dissolved oxygen in micro-irrigation sand filters fed with effluents. Comput. Electron. Agric. **99**, 176–185 (2013)
24. Kline, S.J., McClintock, F.: Describing uncertainties in single-sample experiments. Mech. Eng. **75**(1), 3–8 (1953)
25. Sreekanth, S., et al.: A neural network approach for evaluation of surface heat transfer coefficient. J. Food Process. Preserv. **23**(4), 329–348 (1999)
26. Kurtulus, D.F.: Ability to forecast unsteady aerodynamic forces of flapping airfoils by artificial neural network. Neural Comput. Appl. **18**(4), 359–368 (2009). https://doi.org/10.1007/s00521-008-0186-2
27. Kamble, L.V., Pangavhane, D.R., Singh, T.P.: Artificial neural network based prediction of heat transfer from horizontal tube bundles immersed in gas-solid fluidized bed of large particles. J. Heat Transf. **137**(1), 012901–012909 (2015)
28. Ricardo, R.-M., et al.: Use of artificial neural networks for prediction of convective heat transfer in evaporative units. Ingeniería, Investigación y Tecnología **15**(1), 93–101 (2014)
29. Zdaniuk, G.J., Chamra, L.M., Walters, D.K.: Correlating heat transfer and friction in helically-finned tubes using artificial neural networks. Int. J. Heat Mass Transf. **50**(23–24), 4713–4723 (2007)
30. Das, A.K., Dey, P.: Prediction of unsteady forced convection over square cylinder in the presence of nanofluid by using ANN. Int. J. Mech. Aerosp. Ind. Mechatron. Manuf. Eng. **102**, 899–904 (2015)
31. Ferreira, C.: Gene expression programming in problem solving. In: Roy, R., Koppen, M., Ovaska, S., Furuhashi, T., Hoffmann, F. (eds.) Soft Computing and Industry, pp. 635–653. Springer, London (2002). https://doi.org/10.1007/978-1-4471-0123-9_54

Analysing Social Media Responses in Natural Disaster

Tanu Satija[(✉)] and Nirmalya Kar[iD]

Computer Science and Engineering Department, NIT, Agartala, India
tanu0994@gmail.com, nirmalya@nita.ac.in

Abstract. Natural disasters are the wrath of nature from which Earth has never been immune. Natural disasters like hurricanes, cyclones, earthquakes, mudslides, floods, wildfires, volcanic eruptions and weather events like extreme droughts and monsoons have struck human civilization for years. But due to Global warming and climate change due to human activities their frequency is likely to increase. These events disrupt the normal functioning of mankind, resulting in deaths of thousands and damage to infrastructure. In the wake of natural disaster all the ways of communication goes down and there is no way left to communicate with people who are stuck there and are in need of help. But with the advancement of technology and increasing use of social media in today's era, we can somehow solve this problem. Today people are very much active on social media. Sites like Facebook and Twitter can be very much useful when a natural disaster strikes. In this paper, it is being explored how these social media sites can be useful during and after natural disaster in India. Twitter mining has been used to find out how people are using twitter in wake of a disaster like Kerala floods 2018 and Amphan Cyclone 2020 to communicate and help the people who are stuck in disaster stuck area and raise donations for them.

Keywords: Social media · Twitter mining · Kerala floods 2018 · Machine learning · Amphan cyclone 2020

1 Introduction

Due to Global Warming and all other reasons, in recent years a series of Natural Disaster has hit various parts of world. According to the National Oceanic and Atmospheric Administration (NOAA): Average surface temperatures rose a total of 1.71 degrees Fahrenheit (0.95 degrees Celsius) between 1880 and 2016 [1]. Therefore, due to increasing temperature, all the natural disasters from tornadoes to droughts will occur with higher intensity and will cause an increase in the economic effects. Natural disasters have devastating impacts on our society. From the death of thousands of people to the destruction of buildings and to the spread of disease, natural disasters can devastate entire countries overnight. For example: In June 2013, devastating floods and landslides in North Indian state of Uttarakhand. Natural Disaster like earthquakes, floods etc. results in

© Springer Nature Switzerland AG 2020
N. Kar et al. (Eds.): ICCISIoT 2020, CCIS 1358, pp. 96–107, 2020.
https://doi.org/10.1007/978-3-030-66763-4_9

death of thousands of humans. One of the most immediate and economically devastating effects is the damage to both public and private infrastructure. In the wake of a disaster, people can end up losing their entire asset. Almost every means of communication in disaster affected areas is lost. It becomes difficult to know about people who are struck in disaster affected areas. No help can be provided to them until the disaster passes and communication is somehow restored. Also billions of dollars are required in the process of post-disaster clean-up and rebuilding and not all countries have that much fund with them.

In recent years, communication through social media has increased exponentially. Now-a- days, people are very much active on Social Sites like Facebook and Twitter. Social media has given a platform to connect globally. It can help you connect before, during and after networking events, a conference or a meeting. Data from Global Web Index shows that the average social media user spends 2 h and 19 min using social platforms each day. In 2018, there were 250 million active users on social media in India [2]. Social media has changed the way we communicate today making it instant and fast. It offers rapid connectivity, global responses on issues and quick information flow. It helps in discovering the updates and news almost instantly. You can immediately check the news feed and update your knowledge with the current happenings in the world. Because of such qualities it can act as a very useful tool for communication when the disaster strikes and can help in fund generation and providing help to people stuck in disaster affected areas.

This paper presents case studies of two natural disaster that have hit India namely, Kerala floods of 2018 and Amphan Cyclcone of 2020 and shows analysis of tweets related to the same and how people used Twitter during and after the disasters. This paper is using Twitter social media site to analyse how social media can help during and after the natural disaster because Twitter is less restrictive and it is easy to attain large scale data as compared to other social media sites like Facebook.

2   Background

There has been a lot of work done in the field of data mining, specially Twitter mining. Researchers are continuously trying to identify different areas where data mining can be used in order to achieve better accuracy. One such application is movie recommender system [3]. It can be used to identify the people's choice on any matter be it political, social etc. [4]. This paper is trying to identify the usage of social media in the wake of any disaster using Twitter mining. Following are some previous works where twitter mining has been used in studies related to natural disasters and its effects. Oliver Gruebner et al. in [5] used twitter data to study the emotions of people during and after Superstorm Sandy in 2012. The authors have negative tweets from Twitter and what kind of discomforts people faced during and after the storm and its variations geographically. C Yates et al. in [6] have analysed how the citizens of Australia used social media during a natural disaster. In this paper, the authors have given an insight how the common people respond to such circumstances. Alisa Kongthon et al. have anaylsed the role of social media in wake of a natural disaster using the case study of Thai floods 2011. [7] The authors have included multiple analysis methods like content analysis of Twitter messages, trend analysis of different message categories, and influential Twitter users analysis. Yury Kryvasheyeu et al. in [8] have discussed how social media data can be useful in disaster response and damage assessment. The authors have analysed how social media improves situational awareness, facilitates dissemination of emergency information, enables early warning systems, and helps coordinate relief efforts. Paige Maas et al. in [9] have used a large scale survey using Facebook related to 2019 Australia Bushfires to measure demographic responses to natural disaster.

3   Methodology

This paper focuses to find out how social media sites like Twitter is used for communication and other purposes in the wake of a natural disaster like Kerala Floods 2018 and Amphan cyclone 2020. Twitter has been preferred in this paper over Facebook even when Facebook is more famous among masses and have more active users because of data availability issues. Twitter is wonderful for research related work. It is public by default and the platform is happy to share data with users for research purposes. Also Twitter has an API which is used for getting data. Whereas Facebook is the largest social network but some of its gestures like 'friending' are noted for their disposable vapidity. Researchers are usually locked out of Facebook and it is very difficult to get Facebook data for research purpose [10] (Fig.1).

The method proposed is divided into following main steps:

1. Creating Twitter API [11,12].
2. Establish the connection with Twitter (handshake) using Access Token Secret, Access token, Consumer key and Consumer Secret key in Rstudio [13].
3. Collecting the tweets using keywords.
4. Cleaning the tweets obtained to convert them in a format on which we can operate.
5. Analysis of the Tweets.

The proposed method is same for both the case studies: Case study 1: Kerala Flood 2018; Case study 2: Amphan Cyclone 2020.

Keywords For Case Study 1: Kerala Flood 2018
Some famous hashtags have been chosen as keywords that were used with the tweets related to Kerala 2018 floods. The Twitter API is queried using these keywords and tweets are extracted and further analysed. Query keywords used in the API are space sensitive but not case sensitive. Table1 contains the keywords that we have used:

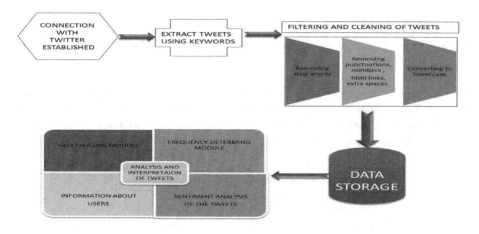

Fig. 1. Workflow of proposed methodology

Table 1. List of keywords for Case Study 1

"#OpMadad"	"#keralaflood"	#PolicaInKeralaFloods"
"#keralafloods2018"	"#Ke"	"#KeralaDonationChallenge"
"#rebuildkerala"	"#keralaFloodRelief"	"#Donate"
"#keralafloods"		

Keywords For Case Study 2: Amphan Cyclone 2020

Some famous hashtags have been chosen as keywords that were used with the tweets related to Amphan Cyclone 2020. The Twitter API is queried using these keywords and tweets are extracted and further analysed.

Table 2. List of Keywords for Case Study 1

"#AmphanCyclone"	"#Cyclone_Amphan"	"#COVID19"
"#CycloneAmphanUpdate"	"#PrayForWestBengal"	"#Amphan2020"
"#COVID_19 "	"#Ampha_Alert"	"#kolkatacyclone"
"#SuperCyclone"		

Tweets for both the case studies are being extracted in English language because English is the most frequently learned and spoken languages all over the world and many researchers have used English tweets in their research work before.

3.1   Data Set Details

Data sets for both the case studies are collected from Twitter using Twitter mining in R language. For that an API, called as Twitter API is created. Twitter provides programmatic access to Twitter data through their APIs (application programming interfaces). Twitter API allows downloading near real-time Tweets. Table 2 contains the details of data set. The data set contains tweets and details related to the account which tweeted the tweets like id, name, description, verified field, location etc. (Table 3).

Table 3. Data set details for both case studies

Data set details	Case study 1(D1)	Case study 2(D2)
Number of Tweets	2000	2000
Size of data set	2.5 MB	3 MB

4   Social Media Usages in Disaster Situation

Social media sites like Twitter and Facebook can play a very vital role in disaster situations. Facebook has now- a-days added a new feature called Crisis Response. When an incident such as an earthquake, hurricane, occurs where people might be in danger, Facebook will activate Safety Check. People who are in the affected area will receive a notification from Facebook to mark themselves safe. In this way people can tell their friends that they are safe. This feature played a very crucial role during the Terrorist Attacks in Paris in November 2015. [14] In Twitter people can tweet about their safety as well as reach out and help other people around them who are also struck in disaster even if they don't follow each other as Twitter is public. These social media sites help them to stay connected and a feeling of oneness help them to survive and be patient in disaster situations. Communication is critical in moments like these, both for people struck in disaster and for their friends and families anxious for news.

In this paper we mined Twitter and extracted tweets related to Kerala Floods which occurred in 2018 and Amphan Cyclone 2020. After analysing the data, following different types of tweets were found:

1. Eyewitness tweets: These tweets were of individual who were present in and around areas (like Kerala, Kolkata, Odisha) where the disaster struck at the time of disaster. Also there were some tweets from News portals too who sent some of their correspondents to ground zero location.
2. Rescue tweets: Some of these tweets were regarding the rescue operation that was ongoing in that area while others were request for help.
3. News portal tweets: These tweets were from different news portal giving all information about Kerala floods and Amphan Cyclone respectively and creating awareness about the disaster.

4. Individual tweets: These tweets were from people from all over the world who were expressing their grief about the disaster and wanted to help in any way.
5. Donation tweets: Some tweets were highlighting the donations that Kerala, Kolkata and other surrounding areas received to help those who were struck by disaster. These tweets also included request to raise funds for helping the people of Kerala and kolkata in respective cases.

Tweets were categorised on the basis of the location from where they were tweeted in order to find out how much National and Global attention was given to such Natural disaster. Information about the users were also extracted – their screen name and whether they are verified because people who are verified by twitter are usually some famous personalities and their follower count is usually high. So the information about the disaster will reach more number of people. And if they encourage people for donation, more people will actively participate. Also with that, other different hashtags were extracted from the tweets which were used with the tweets and words which were frequently appearing in the tweets to understand the sentiments of the person who tweeted it and therefore doing a sentiment analysis of the tweets.

5   Implementation and Discussion

This section highlights the implementation details and related results and discussions for both the case studies. R language has been used to extract tweets from Twitter and to obtain the analysis results.

5.1   Analysis of Twitter Data for Case Study 1: Kerala Flood 2018

In all there were 2000 tweets were extracted from Twitter with the help of Twitter API using the 10 keywords hashtags mentioned in Table 1. The 10 selected keywords were divided in 2 Groups and tweets were extracted (Table 4). The keywords were divided in two groups based on with which kind of tweets these keywords were used. For example group 1 hashtags like "#rebuildkerala", "#keralaFloodRelief", "#KeralaDonationChallenge", "#Donate" were in tweets were people were talking about helping Kerala People and for fund raising for them. Hashtag "#OpMaDad" was related to 'Operation Madad'. It was the rescue operation which was carried by Indian Army in Kerala whereas group 2 hashtags were related to all tweets which were giving information about the Kerala floods.

Table 4. Keywords of Case study 1 divided in groups

Group 1	"#rebuildkerala", "#keralaFloodRelief", "#KeralaDonationChallenge", "#Donate", "#OpMadad"
Group 2	"#Keralafloods", "#Keralafloods2018", "#Ke", "#Keralaflood", "#PolicaInKeralaFloods"

Further in this section the results of extracted tweets is shown group wise. To analyse the tweets extracted, word clouds were created on the basis of the

frequency of the words that appeared in the tweets for different groups (Fig. 3).
Figure 4 shows the most frequent words for different groups. These words show
the sentiments of the people which they were trying to reflect through these
tweets. Words like support, pleasehelp, pleasesuppot, help, family shows the
sympathy of the people from all over the world towards the people who were
struck with disaster in Kerala. It indicates that some tweets that we extracted
may be of people who were eyewitness to this disaster. Also there are some words
of different languages which indicate that this disaster was given global attention
and people from all over the world were praying for the welfare of the people of
Kerala (Fig. 2).

(a) Group 1   (b) Group 2

Fig. 2. Word cloud of hashtags (Case study 1)

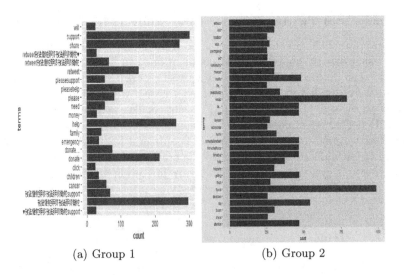

(a) Group 1   (b) Group 2

Fig. 3. Most frequent words in hashtag tweets (Case study 1)

Figure 5 shows top locations of the tweets for different groups. Users like
gulf_news, globalmedicdmgf also tweeted about Kerala using these hashtags

which means Kerala floods had global attention (Fig. 6). Also Indian news channels like financial express etc. were too tweeting about it. Verified users were separated because usually they are having more followers that the rest. Therefore when they will tweet about something it will reach out to more number of people and more people will come to know about it.

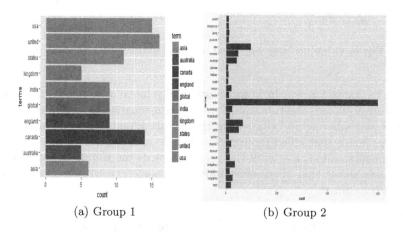

(a) Group 1   (b) Group 2

Fig. 4. Location of the tweets (Case study 1)

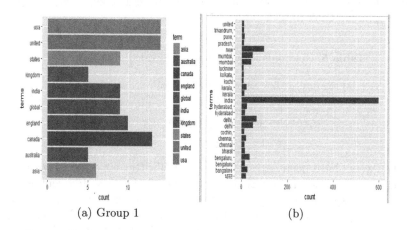

(a) Group 1   (b)

Fig. 5. List of verified users were concerned about Kerala floods (Case study 1)

Figure 7 shows the other hashtags which were used in tweets which were having Group 1 and 2 hashtags in them. In the year 2018 Neelakurinji were supposed to bloom after 12 years in Munnar which attracted thousands of tourist

(a) Group 1   (b) Group 2

Fig. 6. Other hashtags appeared in tweets extracted (Case study 1)

but due to floods tourism in Munnar was badly hit and therefore the hashtag #neelakurinji. Words like Himachal Pradesh, Himachal floods indicate that people were remembering and comparing the Kerala Floods with one of the most dangerous floods that killed thousands of people in India. Words like help show the sentiments and sympathy of the people towards the Kerala disaster. Words like witness shows that there must have been some eye witness tweets which used these hashtags.

5.2   Analysis of Twitter Data for Case Study 2: Amphan Cyclone 2020

Cyclone Amphan had badly hit the eastern part of India during may 2020 when India was already trying to cope with COVID19. Therefore the keywords chosen for this case study include few related to COVID19. The keywords are divided into two groups (Table 5):

Table 5. Keywords for Case Study 2 divided in two groups

Group 1	"#CycloneAmphan", "#Cyclone_Amphan", "#COVID19" "#CycloneAmphanUpdate", "#Amphan2020"
Group 2	"#PrayForWestBengal", "#COVID__19", "#Ampha_Alert", "#kolkatacyclone", "#SuperCyclone"

2000 Tweets have been extracted from the Twitter for different groups and analysis is further shown in this section. Figure 8 the most frequent words in the tweets of respective groups. Keywords of group are giving basic information about the Amphan cyclone. Also in Fig. 8(a) words like national, international, attention shows that this natural disaster had attain the attention of people from India as well as from other parts of the world. In Fig. 8(b), words like aid, Khalsa aid, love, humanity shows the sympathy of people towards the people who were living in disaster struck areas. Also it highlights the aids and helps that were being given by the Government and from sources like Khalsa aid NGO. Figure 9 shows the top states of India from where maximum people tweeted about this disaster on Twitter.

(a) Group 1   (b) Group 2

Fig. 7. Word clouds of most frequent words in Tweets (Case study 2)

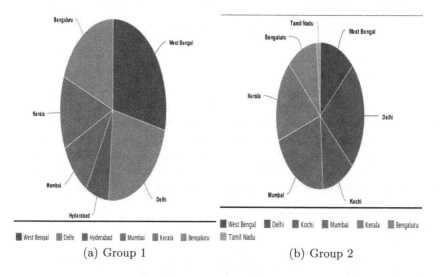

(a) Group 1   (b) Group 2

Fig. 8. Location analysis of Tweets (Case study 2)

During May 2020, India was already trying to tackle with the pandemic COVID19 when Amphan Cyclone hit India. Figure 9 shows the sentiment analysis of the tweets extracted for different groups. In this paper, all the tweets have been categorised in main 3 emotions: positive, negative and neutral. Figure 9(a) shows sentiment analysis for Group 1. Group 1 contains keywords which provide updates related to cyclone therefore, tweets show more negative emotions. Whereas group 2 contains keywords which discuss the help or aid that was given, or about raising donation for disaster hit areas, therefore, it has tweets show more positive emotions.

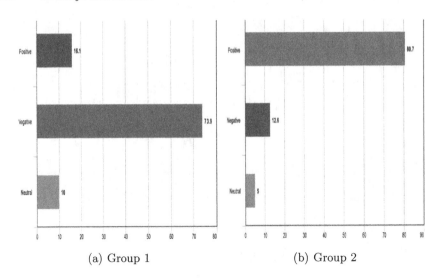

(a) Group 1   (b) Group 2

Fig. 9. Sentiment analysis of Tweets (Case study 2)

6 Conclusion

From the tweets extracted for two natural disaster that struck India, it can be observed that social media sites like Facebook, Twitter and Instagram etc. can play a very crucial and vital role in wake of disaster. They can act as our medium to talk to people who are struck in disaster area and also they can help in fund collection. These sites can bring global attention to an issue and therefore handling the issue becomes easy and faster.

References

1. Livescience.com. https://www.livescience.com/37003-global-warming.html
2. Wearesocial.com. https://digitalreport.wearesocial.com/
3. Das, D., Chidananda, H.T., Sahoo, L.: Personalized movie recommendation system using Twitter data. In: Pattnaik, P.K., Rautaray, S.S., Das, H., Nayak, J. (eds.) Progress in Computing, Analytics and Networking. AISC, vol. 710, pp. 339–347. Springer, Singapore (2018). https://doi.org/10.1007/978-981-10-7871-2_33
4. Meduru, M., Mahimkar, A., Subramanian, K., Padiya, P.Y., Gunjgur, P.N.: Opinion mining using twitter feeds for political analysis. Int. J. Comput. **25**(1), 116–123 (2017)
5. Gruebner, O., Lowe, S.R., Sykora, M., Shankardass, K., Subramanian, S.V., Galea, S.: Spatio-temporal distribution of negative emotions in New York City after a natural disaster as seen in social media. Int. J. Environ. Res. Publ. Health **15**(10), 2275 (2018)
6. Yates, C., Partridge, H.: Citizens and social media in times of natural disaster: exploring information experience. Inf. Res. **20**(1) (2015)

7. Kongthon, A., Haruechaiyasak, C., Pailai, J., Kongyoung, S.: The role of social media during a natural disaster: a case study of the 2011 Thai flood. Int. J. Innov. Technol. Manage. **11**(03), 1440012 (2014)

8. Kryvasheyeu, Y., et al.: Rapid assessment of disaster damage using social media activity. Sci. Adv. **2**(3), e1500779 (2016)

9. Maas, P., Almquist, Z., Giraudy, E., Schneider, J.W.: Using social media to measure demographic responses to natural disaster: insights from a large-scale Facebook survey following the 2019 Australia Bushfires. arXiv preprint. arXiv:2008.03665 (2020)

10. Towardsdatascience.com. https://towardsdatascience.com/social-network-data-twitter-vs-fb-vs-google-vs-everyone-else-830ea0291c86

11. Trupthi, M., Suresh, P., Narasimha, G.: Sentiment analysis on twitter using streaming API. In: 2017 IEEE 7th International Advance Computing Conference (IACC), pp. 915–919. IEEE (2017)

12. Hino, A., Fahey, R.A.: Representing the Twittersphere: archiving a representative sample of Twitter data under resource constraints. Int. J. Inf. Manage. **48**, 175–184 (2019)

13. Khanna, P., Kumar, S., Mishra, S., Sinha, A.: Sentiment analysis: an approach to opinion mining from Twitter data using R. Int. J. Adv. Res. Comput. Sci. **8**(8), 1–5 (2017)

14. Time.com. http://time.com/4112882/facebook-safety-check-paris/

Machine Learning Approaches for Rapid Pothole Detection from 2D Images

Chandrika Acharjee$^{(\boxtimes)}$, Somya Singhal, and Suman Deb📀

Department of Computer Science and Engineering, Natioan Institute of Technology
Agartala, Jirania, India
acharjeechandrika372@gmail.com, soumy.asinghalsomya14@gmail.com,
sumandeb.cse@nita.ac.in

Abstract. Roads are inevitable parts of human civilisation, and construction of roads are considered under a Civil Engineering problem; but periodically these roads require maintenance and assessment, which is highly dependent on adequate and timely pavement condition data. Howbeit, in some cases, it has been found that the manual practice of collecting and analysing such data often leads to delay in reporting about the issues and fixing them on time. Also, repairing potholes is time consuming, and locating these manually is a huge task. We want to find out some mechanism which can identify the construction conditions as well as any kind of deformities on the road from the dashboard camera fitted into a car, and at the same time, can analyse the conditions of road surface and formation of potholes on the road. Optimization of manual pothole detection through automation has been a part of scientific research since long. Pothole identification has significantly been adapted in different screening and maintenance systems. But in our country, owing to the large number of road networks and wide variations in the nature of rural and urban road conditions, it is very difficult to identify potholes through an automated system. In this paper, we have looked into several methods of Computer Vision, like image processing techniques and object detection method so as to identify potholes from the video input stream to the system. But these techniques have been found to have different challenges like lighting conditions, interference in the line of vision on waterlogged roads, and inefficiency at night vision. Hence, furthermore, we have explored the viability of Deep Learning method for identifying the potholes from the processing of input video streams, and have also analysed the Convolutional Neural Networks approach of Deep Learning through a self-built CNN model. In this paper, the expediency of all the methods as well as their drawbacks have been discussed.

Keywords: Automated system · Computer vision · Image processing · Optimization · CNN

1 Introduction

Regardless of the dimension, potholes can be more than an annoyance, and can cause severe injuries and damages to people and vehicles. Overloaded vehicles,

© Springer Nature Switzerland AG 2020
N. Kar et al. (Eds.): ICCISIoT 2020, CCIS 1358, pp. 108–119, 2020.
https://doi.org/10.1007/978-3-030-66763-4_10

climate change, and heavy rainfall are major factors that further worsen the condition of roads with potholes. It becomes difficult to recognize potholes during rainy nights; sometimes, the bright light of the sun and the shadow of the trees also make it less visible. From the record of injuries it has been found that in several states, due to bad road conditions the large number of accidents occur. In this case, a prior detection of potholes on daily basis is a necessity for prolonging the useful life and reducing the mortality rates caused by deaths due to potholes.

Methods like Statistical analysis based on usage intensity of a road segment, and manual image analysis based on photos gathered and uploaded to a central server, have for long been under consideration as profound approaches to detect road damage. However, these approaches were found to have required a strong user interaction and engagement. Other existing techniques for pothole detection involves approaches like vibration-based system, sensor system, and stereo vision techniques [1]. The vibration based system can give incorrect outcomes, such as in cases that the vehicle did not pass over any pothole, or that the normal cracks and irregularities on the road get identified as potholes, and the actual potholes remains undetected. The sensor-based approach is troubled with unfavourable error rates in the outcome, and is still under research. The stereo-vision techniques sometimes fail to derive results in real time. This process depends highly on the computational performance and also requires that the cameras being used for screening the road surface, are well aligned. This requirement is found difficult to be met in case of moving vehicles. Hence, a computerized approach for real-time pothole detection with no manual engagement of any kind is more favourable and efficacious in terms of cost and time.

An effective solution towards solving this issue of pothole detection may potentially be in developing a device connected to our vehicle, that would be able to do a continuous screening of the road surface. For this, a dashboard camera is attached at a certain angle to properly scan the upcoming road surface. Then it extracts the road surface and uses the algorithmic approach to identify the region of interest. Thus, whenever a pothole is recognised, the device would help the driver get al.erted eventually, so that a mishap of any form may be avoided.

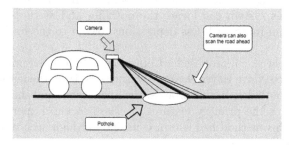

Fig. 1. A schematic of the proposed model of scanning road surface via the car's dashboard camera

This paper discusses the methods for detecting potholes. As these approaches are vision based, it is perceptible that the outcome would rely upon conditions like lightning, weather, and traffic, i.e., factors that can visually diminish the proficiency of the system to perceive a pothole. In the next section, the implementation of these methodologies, along with their preliminary outcomes has been demonstrated and a comprehensible conclusion on their efficacy has been drawn.

2   Related Works

Automation of the pothole detection and localization methods has been under research works since long. Numerous approaches to solving this issue have also been proposed by various researchers till now. Detailed deliberation on these various methods can be found in Kim [1]. Mednis A, Strazdins G et al. [2] proposed a real time road irregularity identification model using android sensors, with accelerometers incorporated in them. This methodology depends on internet availability, appropriate databases and API for storing data and timely monitoring of information. Murthy, Sachin Bhardwaj Sundra et al. [3] proposed a vision-based approach of processing 2D images for pothole detection. Data in form of images were collected using a camera mounted over the vehicle, and the MATLAB software was used to aid the processing of these images.
This method does not show preferable results under every possible lightning conditions and is limited to only the recognition and restructuring of the potholes.

Harish V. Mekali et al. [4] proposed the method of building a robot vehicle proficient at detecting potholes and notifying about the same to the vehicles within its reach.
This method, is however, limited to issuing warnings about the road condition only after the process of detection, and thus, cannot provide early assistance in avoiding the potholes or any other severe depressions while driving.

Venkatesh, Abhiram et al. [5] proposed a model that uses laser scanner and sensors for detecting potholes and determining their depths. Besides, it uses several algorithms such as road damage prediction algorithm for creating reports on the level of damages on the roads ahead, and routing algorithms for avoiding the potholes. This system can locate the potholes and at the same time, can suggest an optimal route with less depressions, owing to the routing algorithm applied.

Kanza Azhar et al. [6] proposed a Computer Vision based pothole detection approach, in which Naive Bayes classifier was used to train the features and label the images with potholes. In this process, the appearance and shapes of potholes were considered as the primary features of classification. Experimental results premised upon this method had shown considerably high accuracy in detection and localization of potholes.

In our study, we have focused on the visionbased methods for pothole detection, as their results were found to be more accurate in real time as compared to the other methods discussed in this section.

3   Pothole Detection Techniques

3.1   Image Processing Method

Image processing is a subset of Computer Vision. It is the technique of processing on raw input images and enhancing them by tuning many parameter and features of the images. Rapid progression of image processing techniques in terms of speed, time and cost in the past few years, has led into various methods of automated locating of potholes [7]. The appearance of potholes are observably different from the background of the surface in terms of shape, coarseness, surface texture and fineness, and this specific property significantly contributes to the feasibility of the image processing technique discussed here. The method we have discussed here involves contour detection and canny edge filter algorithms for detecting potholes [8].

Counter Detection and Canny Edge Detection. In this approach, for detecting potholes and analysing their shape and size, contour detection was performed on the source image. Each of the discrete contours are identified in the form of Numpy arrays that store the coordinates along the extremity line of an object. The contour retrieval mode has been applied to extract the outer contours in an image. Next, since we have the boundary points, contours were drawn using cv.drawContours() function. This function takes into account the source image, the contours as a Python list, index of contours and the color and thickness of the contours to be drawn. For prior pothole detection, we need all the boundary points on the contours to represent the potholes. That's why cv.CHAIN_APPROX_NONE has been passed as it would store all the boundary points [9].

Applying Smoothing and Noise Reduction Techniques. This segment looks into the several image smoothing and noise reduction operations. In the proposed image processing method, the blurring functions used are namely Gaussian Blur and Median Blur. Each of these functions uses a kernel to scan the image and produces a smoothed image as output [10]. Further, the morphological operations namely erosion and dilation were applied that use a kernel convoluted with the input image to produce the output. These operations mainly remove the residual noise created when edge detection is implemented [11].

Fig. 2. Algorithmic Block Diagram for pothole detection on an image

Experimental Results. The image processing method discussed here is suitable for rough estimation of potholes. Also, this method does not require any training stage and so it has low computational cost as compared to other supervised methods. But this method is highly influenced by the characteristic intensity values of the considered pixels. Therefore, the performance of this method has turned out to be better for bright images as compared to the dark images. It may also detect normal patches and shadows as suspected potholes. The correctness of the proposed method thus highly depends on the frame condition. The results produced on applying the various filters on the selected input image, and the final output image generated by this method have been shown in Fig. 6c and 6d.

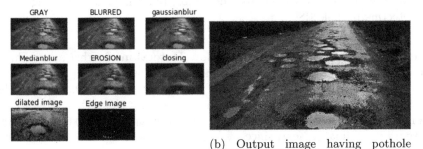

(b) Output image having pothole boundary contours marked

(a) Output image obtained after applying different image processing filters

Fig. 3. Edge Detection and Image Processing filters applied on the pothole image

3.2 Object Detection Method

Object Detection is a technique mainly associated with computer vision, and has already produced excellent results. It can handle operations like detecting, locating and even counting instances of a target object in an images or video. Pothole detection can clearly be included under the various practical uses served by the Object detection method. Fortunately, object detection can address this pothole detection using haar cascade. It is an effective way for object detection which is a machine learning based approach where a lot of positive and negative images are used to train the classifier. After the classifier is trained, it can be applied to a region of interest in an input image [12].

Algorithm Working. The proposed method begins by having the input road segment image converted to a grey-scale version, which is then applied with a Gaussian filter so as to reduce noise within the image and to produce an image which is even in terms of pixel intensity difference. At this point, it has been

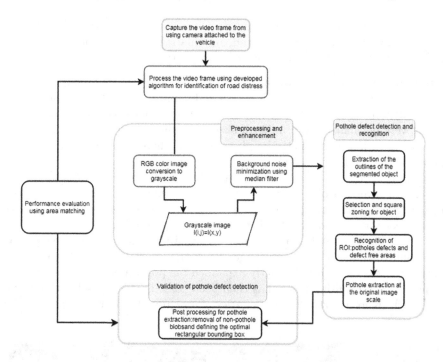

Fig. 4. Process flow for pothole detection using Object Detection methodology

found out that filters tend to blur the edges; but as we want our model to effectively detect potholes, so preserving the edges becomes an important task. For this purpose, bilateral filter, followed by the median blur operation has been applied. Next, in order to produce an image with distinctly detected edges, a canny edge detection operation has been carried out on the extracted road surface image. This operation results into an image in which edges were detected by white lines against the rest of the setting. The dark segments detected within a pothole are normally insignificant in terms of size, and in most of the cases, a single pothole generates numerous unconnected smaller outlines instead of a single edge. One more issue experienced was that, sometimes, the input road surface visuals had intense unrelated and undesirable components along its extremities [13]. This problem occurred as a result of applying the convex hull algorithm, which could not differentiate the unwanted components alongside the road and perceived these as part of the road section, and hence, this approximate shape of the road resulted into false positives. Geared towards resolving this issue, the undesirable edges close to the extremities were determined to be removed by dilating the output obtained on applying the canny-edge filter. This operation of dilation lead into an increase in the area with lighter pixels. Consequently, on performing dilation on the image, the undesirable edges got merged into the outer boundaries, leaving only the outline contours perceptible [14]. A further expediency of this approach lies in the fact that, it can be applied to aid the removal of other vehicles within the frame. Close to the extremities of the frame, a number of vehicles are normally found, and dilation by a sufficient degree would mean that these too are merged into the extremity.

Implementation and Results. This experiment collected 89 images of damaged road at different angles, with cracks and depressions of different sizes, and under different conditions from online downloads. Due to variable sizes, the images were normalized to a uniform size, discarding the undesirable segments [15]. In Fig. 5, it can distinctly be observed that there are plenty of irrelevant particulars, which are not needed while detecting potholes. Outputs of the algorithm have been demonstrated below in stages. The first image is that of a grey-scale conversion of the extracted road. This method of scaling down the image pixels to values ranging between 0 and 1 makes the data managing easier and reduces the need for any further complicated processing.

Then, a gaussian and bilateral filter, followed by a canny edge detector has been applied to obtain the next image. Next, the image has been applied with dilation process which has distinctly expanded the portion under white pixels in the image. The resulting image has then been passed, and applied with erosion process which erodes away the boundaries of foreground object [16]. Finally, the

Fig. 5. Left:Original image, Middle: Grayscale image, Right: blur image

(a) Canny image Left: without using filters,Right: with filters

(b) Dilated Image Left:without using filters, Right: with filters

(c) Eroded image Left: without using filters,Right: with filters

(d) Contoured Image

Fig. 6. Systematic application of filters and identifying the pothole.

contours were detected within the eroded image. In the output, the contours detected within definite size constraints have been categorized as potholes.

3.3 The Deep Learning Approach

Automated pothole detection through road images is still a challenging issue among computer-vision community. It faces several challenges like inefficiency at night vision, dependency on lighting and frame conditions, and falsely deeming any shape of contour as potholes. Rapid advancement in the field of deep learning in the past few years, has enabled researchers to come up with efficacious tools for analyzing pothole images with remarkable accuracies. Considering the disadvantages of the image processing techniques, in this section, we have reviewed our preceding studies, in which a labeled pothole dataset was presented as the first step towards a more robust, easy-to-deploy pothole detection system [17]. We have developed a new, large-scale road damage dataset, and then trained and evaluated a pothole detection model that is based on Convolutional Neural Network (CNN) method. The Deep Learning method here focuses on detecting pothole images using Keras and Tensorflow and training the model on the labelled image dataset [18].

Methodology. This section discusses the methodology premised upon the Deep Learning approach:
1) Building a CNN model for Pothole detection.
2) Analysing and evaluating the self built CNN model for pothole identification In order to evaluate the viability of Deep Learning techniques in this regard, we have chosen to apply Convolutional Neural Network(CNN) for image classification on a labelled image dataset. Therefore, collecting data comprising of road images with and without potholes, and creating the dataset has been our first step. *Data Acquisition and Preprocessing*

For creating own image dataset for pothole identification,a suitable amount of various road condition images were collected and two classes of road status-'normal' and 'potholes' were considered. The image dataset had 329 pothole images and 352 normal images. The variable sized and shaped images were resized and each category labelled with numerical index values and appended to the training data [19].

After data acquisition, the images were pre-processed to remove the temperature scales and other marks and were normalized to same dimensions. Following this, different techniques were applied to augment the collected data to prevent overfitting of the model, to help the model in training and to expand the number of image samples in the dataset. Eventually, classification using the Convolutional Neural Networks (CNN) model was performed and the feasibility of this method was evaluated [20]. The workflow of the proposed work using CNN is shown below: **Implementation and Results** The architecture of the self-built CNN model is as follows:

- A sequential model has been developed, in which layers are sequentially connected to each other. Before feeding the data through neural network, the data was normalized in order to avoid negative impacts that may be caused by input data with pixel values too wide in a range. Since an imagary dataset is used here, the max rgb value of 255 is used for scaling the data.
- After being normalized, the input is moved through a series of 2-D convolutional layers with 3×3 filter and ReLU activations, each of which were followed by an activation layer and a maxpooling layer to perform feature extraction, and to further diminish the dimensions of the input. Maxpooling layer reduces the size of the output of preceding layers by filtering it with only the high intensity pixel values. The ReLU layer was applied so as to maintain the dimensionality of the data.
- The output after a 2×64 layer convolutional neural network is again normalized, this time using Batch normalization to make sure that the network creates activations with the same distribution.
- The output is next propagated to the global average pooling layers which compute the average value for each output, and further diminishes the scope of overfitting.
- The output layer is then passed to a dense layer with one neuron that uses sigmoid activation for classifying the input.
- The model uses binary cross entropy as the loss function which is a logarithmic loss function, and as optimizer, adam optimizer with accuracy as its parameter has been used.
- The model thus trained gives a training accuracy of 80.5% and validation accuracy of 82.5% at the last epoch [21].

Observations. A total of 786 image frames were extracted from an input video clip for experiment. Upon feeding the trained model on some randomly chosen image frames, the model accurately predicts if the input images belongs to the 'normal' or the 'pothole' category for most of the pothole images. But, for experiments by close-up conditions and brightness conditions, it was found that the proposed model detects pothole more accurately in close-up images and in dark images. Now, on examining the efficiency of the trained model, the following results were obtained:

Using this self-built CNN model, we attained an average training accuracy of 68.19%, and an average validation accuracy of 65.147%.

The validation and training losses on this model are 39.4% and 29.4%, which are quite high. Figure 8 shows the graphical representations of the results of this experiment:

We saw that accuracy achieved from the self-built CNN model was not good enough and also losses were high. Hence, this work has to be extended to be trained on some pre-trained CNN based models for better accuracy and satisfactory results as part of future work. Nevertheless, we confirmed that a pothole detection system based on CNN model can potentially be used for automatic pothole management.

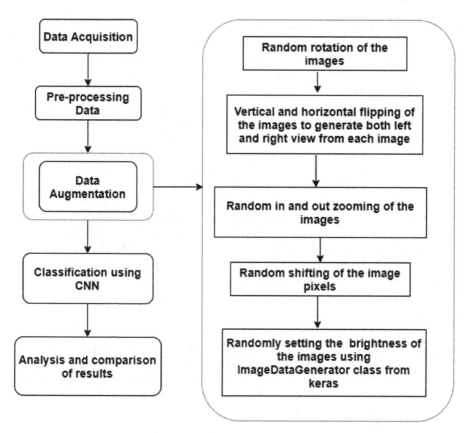

Fig. 7. Workflow for Self-built CNN model for pothole identification.

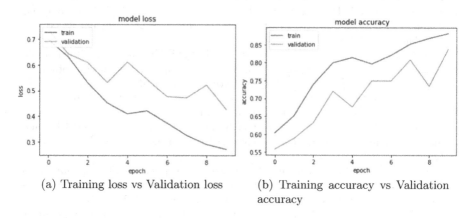

(a) Training loss vs Validation loss

(b) Training accuracy vs Validation accuracy

Fig. 8. Loss and accuracy of the model.

4   Summary and Conclusion

This review paper describes the implementation as well as robustness of the various existing methods of 2D image based pothole detection. However, there are some limitations in all the proposed methods. The image processing method using contour detection and canny edge filter may falsely recognize even a shadow as a pothole. In the object detection method using computer vision, for a slight change in lightning conditions, it will make major impacts, and the change in location will also affect the performance. Further, to accurately detect potholes, images of different size, severity, origin and conditions were collected, and the proposed deep learning model premised upon training these different images reaches an overall accuracy of 65.147%. However, on being experimented with some pre-trained models on a more diverse data, this model can deliver a more efficacious performance. Therefore, future work for lessening the pothole detection time, and improving the performance of the discussed methods is required for enabling the pothole detection system to be applied to a real time pothole identification, localization and notification service.

References

1. Kim, T., Ryu, S.-K.: Review and analysis of pothole detection methods. J. Emerging Trends Comput. Inf. Sci. **5**(8), 603–608 (2014)
2. Mednis, A., Strazdins, G., Zviedris, R., Kanonirs, G., Selavo, L.: Real time pothole detection using android smartphones with accelerometers. In: 2011 International Conference on Distributed Computing in Sensor Systems and Workshops (DCOSS), pp. 1–6. IEEE (2011)
3. Murthy, S.B.S., Varaprasad, G.: Detection of potholes in autonomous vehicle. IET Intel. Transport Syst. **8**(6), 543–549 (2014)
4. Hegde, S., Mekali, H.V., Varaprasad, G.: Pothole detection and inter vehicular communication. In: 2014 IEEE International Conference on Vehicular Electronics and Safety, pp. 84–87. IEEE (2014)
5. Venkatesh, S., Abhiram, E., Rajarajeswari, S., Sunil Kumar, K.M., Balakuntala, S., Jagadish, N.: An intelligent system to detect, avoid and maintain potholes: a graph theoretic approach. In: 2014 Seventh International Conference on Mobile Computing and Ubiquitous Networking (ICMU), pp. 80–80. IEEE (2014)
6. Azhar, K., Murtaza, F., Yousaf, M.H., Habib, H.A.: Computer vision based detection and localization of potholes in asphalt pavement images. In: 2016 IEEE Canadian Conference on Electrical and Computer Engineering (CCECE), pp. 1–5. IEEE (2016)
7. Tiwari, S., Bhandari, R., Raman, B.: Roadcare: a deep-learning based approach to quantifying road surface quality. In: Proceedings of the 3rd ACM SIGCAS Conference on Computing and Sustainable Societies, pp. 231–242 (2020)
8. Nienaber, S., Booysen, M.J., Kroon, R.S.: Detecting potholes using simple image processing techniques and real-world footage (2015)
9. Bello-Salau, H., Aibinu, A.M., Onwuka, E.N., Dukiya, J.J., Onumanyi, A.J.: Image processing techniques for automated road defect detection: a survey. In: 2014 11th International Conference on Electronics, Computer and Computation (ICECCO), pp. 1–4. IEEE (2014)

10. Xie, G., Wen, L.: Image edge detection based on opencv. Int. J. Electron. Electrical Eng. **1**(2), 104–6 (2013)
11. Buza, E., Omanovic, S., Huseinovic, A.: Pothole detection with image processing and spectral clustering. In: Proceedings of the 2nd International Conference on Information Technology and Computer Networks, vol. 810, pp. 4853 (2013)
12. Amit, Y.: 2D Object Detection and Recognition: Models, Algorithms, and Networks. MIT Press (2002)
13. Viola, P., Jones, M., et al.: Robust real-time object detection. Int. J. Comput. Vision **4**(34–47), 4 (2001)
14. Topal, C., Akınlar, C., Genç, Y.: Edge drawing: a heuristic approach to robust real-time edge detection. In: 2010 20th International Conference on Pattern Recognition, pp. 2424–2427. IEEE (2010)
15. Ravi, V., Rajendra Prasad, Ch., Sanjay Kumar, S., Ramchandar Rao, P.: Image enhancement on opencv based on the tools: Python 2.7
16. Lee, S.W., Kim, S., Han, J., An, K.E., Ryu, S.-K., Seo, D.: Experiment of image processing algorithm for efficient pothole detection. In: 2019 IEEE International Conference on Consumer Electronics (ICCE), pp. 1–2. IEEE (2019)
17. Pereira, V., Tamura, S., Hayamizu, S., Fukai, H.: A deep learning-based approach for road pothole detection in timor leste. In: 2018 IEEE International Conference on Service Operations and Logistics, and Informatics (SOLI), pp. 279–284. IEEE (2018)
18. Munoz-Organero, M., Ruiz-Blaquez, R., Sánchez-Fernández, L.: Automatic detection of traffic lights, street crossings and urban roundabouts combining outlier detection and deep learning classification techniques based on GPS traces while driving. Comput. Environ. Urban Syst. **68**, 1–8 (2018)
19. Chandan, G., Jain, A., Jain, H., et al.: Real time object detection and tracking using deep learning and opencv. In 2018 International Conference on Inventive Research in Computing Applications (ICIRCA), pp. 1305–1308. IEEE (2018)
20. Lim Kuoy Suong and Jangwoo Kwon: Detection of potholes using a deep convolutional neural network. J. UCS **24**(9), 1244–1257 (2018)
21. Chen, H., Yao, M., Gu, Q.: Pothole detection using location-aware convolutional neural networks. Int. J. Mach. Learn. Cybernet. **11**(4), 899–911 (2020). https://doi.org/10.1007/s13042-020-01078-7

Computing Exact Solutions of Evolutionary Rescue Equations of Spatial Population Dynamics

Subin P. Joseph$^{(\boxtimes)}$ (iD)

Government Engineering College, Wayanad, Kerala, India
subinpj@gecwyd.ac.in

Abstract. The theory of natural evolution and computations has contributed many advancement in science and engineering. In this paper, the equation which explicitly investigate evolutionary rescue in the case of spatial invasions is studied. The exact solutions for such equations are required to analyze the real situations in a better way and also such solutions can be utilized to verify the accuracy of any approximate solutions that are derived using any of the evolutionary algorithms and computations which may depend on several random parameters. Such solutions will give more insight to the behaviour of biological evolution also. We have derived several exact solutions to the general evolution equation which represents the evolutionary rescue from biological invasion. Since the evolution equation considered here is highly nonlinear, the solutions are computed using an algorithm that is implemented with the help of computer algebra system.

Keywords: Evolution equation · Evolutionary rescue · Biological invasion · Exact solutions

1 Introduction

The theory investigating evolutionary rescue has mainly focused on well-mixed populations that are declining due to an environmental shift [2,12,13,16–18]. Recently, the theory which explicitly investigate evolutionary rescue in the case of spatial invasions is presented in [19]. Evolutionary rescue is considered to be the prevention of population extinction by adaptation [3,4,9]. In the case where the invader has a frequency-independent fitness advantage of σ, the rate of change in relative invader frequency $u(x,t)$ under local selection and spatial diffusion is given by

$$\frac{\partial u(x,t)}{\partial t} - \eta \frac{\partial^2 u(x,t)}{\partial x^2} = \sigma u(x,t)(1 - u(x,t)) \tag{1}$$

Partially supported by TEQIP-II Four funds, Government Engineering College, Wayanad.

N. Kar et al. (Eds.): ICCISIoT 2020, CCIS 1358, pp. 120–130, 2020.
https://doi.org/10.1007/978-3-030-66763-4_11

where η is the species diffusion constant, which is same for both the resident and invader. In the second case where the fitness of the resident decreases linearly with the frequency of invader, the rate of change in relative invader frequency $u(x,t)$ is given by

$$\frac{\partial u(x,t)}{\partial t} - \eta \frac{\partial^2 u(x,t)}{\partial x^2} = \sigma u(x,t)^2 (1 - u(x,t)) \tag{2}$$

Analysis of these evolutionary equations can lead to the comparison of effectiveness of evolutionary rescue in preventing extinction in both the cases.

In this paper we consider the evolutionary equation which generalizes both the above equations, given by

$$\frac{\partial u(x,t)}{\partial t} - \eta \frac{\partial^2 u(x,t)}{\partial x^2} = \alpha_1 u(x,t) + \alpha_2 u(x,t)^2 + \alpha_3 u(x,t)^3 \tag{3}$$

where α_i's are real parameters. Putting $\alpha_1 = \sigma, \alpha_2 = -\sigma$ and $\alpha_3 = 0$ in this equation we can recover Eq. (1). Similarly Eq. (2) can be obtained from Eq. (3) by putting $\alpha_1 = 0, \alpha_2 = \sigma$ and $\alpha_3 = -\sigma$. The evolutionary Eq. (3) also generalizes the Nagumo Eq. [14,15]

$$\frac{\partial u(x,t)}{\partial t} - \frac{\partial^2 u(x,t)}{\partial x^2} = u(x,t)(1 - u(x,t))(u(x,t) - \rho) \tag{4}$$

All the above evolutionary equations are finding increasing applications in natural computation and other areas [1,5–8,10,11]. But the available exact solutions are very less for these nonlinear partial differential equation, which affect its application in these fields. We apply an algorithm to find new travelling wave exact solutions to the general evolution Eq. (3). Exact solutions are closed form solutions obtained in terms of elementary functions or special functions. A powerful computer algebra system is needed to implement the algorithm. Several new exact solutions are derived for this equation in this paper. The algorithm used here is explained in the next section. In the third section, this algorithm is applied to obtain the exact solutions. The paper is concluded in the last section.

2   The Algorithm

To find the travelling wave exact solutions to the given evolution Eq. (3), we apply the following algorithm.

STEP 1: Convert the given equation in to an ordinary evolution equation by means of the traveling wave transformation $u(x,t) = v(\zeta)$, where $\zeta = dx + ct$ and d and c are travelling wave parameters.

STEP 2: Assume the existence of exact solutions for the ordinary evolution equation in the form

$$v(\zeta) = a_0 + \frac{a_1 + a_2 g(\zeta) + a_3 h(\zeta)}{b_1 + b_2 g(\zeta) + b_3 h(\zeta)} \tag{5}$$

where g and h are trial functions to be applied and a_i's and b_i's are parameters to be determined.

STEP 3: Substitute $v(\zeta)$ given by Eq. (5) in to the derived ordinary evolution equation and then compute the value of the parameters so that the resulting equations are satisfied identically.

STEP 4: Use the parametric values obtained in the previous step to derive the required exact solutions to the original evolution Eq. (3).

In the next section we derive exact solutions to the evolution equation using the above algorithm. In this algorithm, most crucial steps are two and three. Step three is to be implemented separately in any of the computer algebra system to find and solve resulting algebraic equations.

3   Derived Solutions

Applying the above algorithm, we derive several exact travelling wave solutions to the general evolution Eq. (3). The algorithm is implemented in any of the computational algebra system in deriving the exact solutions. As per first step of the algorithm, we apply the traveling wave transformation $u(x,t) = v(\zeta)$ and convert the evolution equation to the ordinary differential equation given by

$$d^2\eta v''(\zeta) - cv'(\zeta) + \alpha_1 v(\zeta) + \alpha_2 v(\zeta)^2 + \alpha_3 v(\zeta)^3 = 0. \tag{6}$$

In step two, we take the trial functions as $g(\zeta) = \tanh(\zeta)$ and $h(\zeta) = \coth(\zeta)$. Some other trial functions can also be used to derive exact solutions. But we use these two function only in this paper in deriving the required exact solutions. Then Eq. (5) becomes

$$v(\zeta) = a_0 + \frac{a_1 + a_2 \tanh(\zeta) + a_3 \coth(\zeta)}{b_1 + b_2 \tanh(\zeta) + b_3 \coth(\zeta)}. \tag{7}$$

Now, we need to substitute this value of $v(\zeta)$ in the derived ordinary differential Eq. (6). Then performing certain amount of computational procedure in any of the computational algebra system, it can be shown that (7) is a solution to the differential equation if a system of nonlinear algebraic equations are satisfied. This system of nonlinear equations are given in appendix. We need to solve this system of equations simultaneously to obtain the value of the parameters, so that $v(\zeta)$ given by Eq. (7) is a solution to the ordinary differential Eq. (6). It is possible to obtain several solutions and we will discuss the following general set of solutions here.

SET 1: The first set of solutions to the system of nonlinear algebraic equations is given by

$$a_0 = 0, a_1 = 1, a_2 = 0, a_3 = 0, b_3 = 0$$

$$c = \pm\frac{\alpha_2\sqrt{\alpha_2^2 - 4\alpha_1\alpha_3}}{4\alpha_3}, \quad d = -\frac{\sqrt{4\alpha_1\alpha_3 - \alpha_2^2}}{2\sqrt{2}\sqrt{\alpha_3}\sqrt{\eta}}, \tag{8}$$

$$b_1 = -\frac{\alpha_2}{2\alpha_1}, \quad b_2 = \mp\frac{\sqrt{\alpha_2^2 - 4\alpha_1\alpha_3}}{2\alpha_1}.$$

Then the corresponding exact solutions to the original evolution Eq. (3) are given by

$$u(x,t) = \frac{-2\alpha_1}{\alpha_2 \pm \sqrt{\alpha_2^2 - 4\alpha_1\alpha_3} \tanh(\zeta)} \tag{9}$$

where

$$\zeta = \frac{\pm\alpha_2\sqrt{\alpha_2^2 - 4\alpha_1\alpha_3}\,t - \frac{\sqrt{2}\sqrt{\alpha_3}\sqrt{4\alpha_1\alpha_3 - \alpha_2^2}\,x}{\sqrt{\eta}}}{4\alpha_3} \tag{10}$$

A graphical representation of first of these solutions is given in Fig. 1.

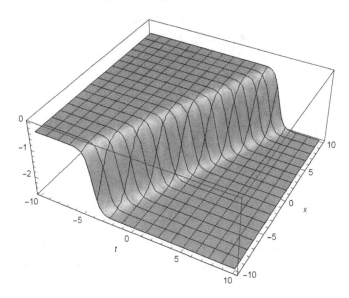

Fig. 1. Graphical representation of the first solution in (9), where $\eta = 1, \alpha_1 = -1, \alpha_2 = -3, \alpha_3 = -1$

SET 2: The second set of solutions to the system of nonlinear algebraic equations is given by

$$a_0 = 0, a_1 = 1, a_2 = 0, a_3 = 0, b_2 = 0$$

$$c = \pm\frac{\alpha_2\sqrt{\alpha_2^2 - 4\alpha_1\alpha_3}}{4\alpha_3}, \quad d = -\frac{\sqrt{4\alpha_1\alpha_3 - \alpha_2^2}}{2\sqrt{2}\sqrt{\alpha_3}\sqrt{\eta}}, \tag{11}$$

$$b_1 = -\frac{\alpha_2}{2\alpha_1}, \quad b_3 = \mp\frac{\sqrt{\alpha_2^2 - 4\alpha_1\alpha_3}}{2\alpha_1}.$$

Then the corresponding exact solutions to the original evolution Eq. (3) are given by

$$u(x,t) = \frac{-2\alpha_1}{\alpha_2 \pm \sqrt{\alpha_2^2 - 4\alpha_1\alpha_3} \coth(\zeta)} \tag{12}$$

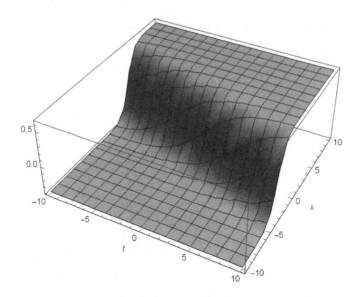

Fig. 2. Graphical representation of the first solution in (12), where $\eta = 1, \alpha_1 = 1, \alpha_2 = 1, \alpha_3 = -4$

where

$$\zeta = \frac{\pm\alpha_2\sqrt{\alpha_2^2 - 4\alpha_1\alpha_3}\,t - \dfrac{\sqrt{2}\sqrt{\alpha_3}\sqrt{4\alpha_1\alpha_3 - \alpha_2^2}\,x}{\sqrt{\eta}}}{4\alpha_3} \tag{13}$$

A graphical representation of first of these solutions is given in Fig. 2.

    SET 3: The third set of solutions to the system of nonlinear algebraic equations is given by

$$a_0 = 0, \quad a_1 = 1, \quad a_2 = 1, \quad a_3 = 0,$$

$$c = \frac{\alpha_2\sqrt{\alpha_1^2\left(\alpha_2^2 - 4\alpha_1\alpha_3\right)}}{8\alpha_1\alpha_3}, \quad d = -\frac{\sqrt{4\alpha_1\alpha_3 - \alpha_2^2}}{4\sqrt{2}\sqrt{\alpha_3}\sqrt{\eta}},$$

$$b_1 = -\frac{2\sqrt{\alpha_1^2\left(\alpha_2^2 - 4\alpha_1\alpha_3\right)} + \alpha_1\alpha_2}{2\alpha_1^2}, \quad b_2 = -\frac{\sqrt{\alpha_1^2\left(\alpha_2^2 - 4\alpha_1\alpha_3\right)} + 2\alpha_1\alpha_2}{4\alpha_1^2},$$

$$b_3 = -\frac{\sqrt{\alpha_1^2\left(\alpha_2^2 - 4\alpha_1\alpha_3\right)} + 2\alpha_1\alpha_2}{4\alpha_1^2}.$$

$$\tag{14}$$

and

$$a_0 = 0, \quad a_1 = 1, \quad a_2 = 1, \quad a_3 = 0,$$

$$c = -\frac{\alpha_2\sqrt{\alpha_1^2\left(\alpha_2^2 - 4\alpha_1\alpha_3\right)}}{8\alpha_1\alpha_3}, \quad d = -\frac{\sqrt{4\alpha_1\alpha_3 - \alpha_2^2}}{4\sqrt{2}\sqrt{\alpha_3}\sqrt{\eta}},$$

$$b_1 = \frac{2\sqrt{\alpha_1^2\left(\alpha_2^2 - 4\alpha_1\alpha_3\right)} - \alpha_1\alpha_2}{2\alpha_1^2}, \quad b_2 = \frac{\sqrt{\alpha_1^2\left(\alpha_2^2 - 4\alpha_1\alpha_3\right)} - 2\alpha_1\alpha_2}{4\alpha_1^2}, \quad (15)$$

$$b_3 = \frac{\sqrt{\alpha_1^2\left(\alpha_2^2 - 4\alpha_1\alpha_3\right)} - 2\alpha_1\alpha_2}{4\alpha_1^2}.$$

Then the corresponding exact solutions to the original evolution Eq. (3), after simplification, are given by

$$u(x,t) = \frac{-2\alpha_1^2(\sinh(2\zeta) + 2\cosh(2\zeta))}{\sqrt{\alpha_1^2\left(\alpha_2^2 - 4\alpha_1\alpha_3\right)}(2\sinh(2\zeta) + \cosh(2\zeta)) + \alpha_1\alpha_2(\sinh(2\zeta) + 2\cosh(2\zeta))} \tag{16}$$

where

$$\zeta = \frac{\alpha_2\sqrt{\alpha_1^2\left(\alpha_2^2 - 4\alpha_1\alpha_3\right)}t - \frac{\sqrt{2}\alpha_1\sqrt{\alpha_3}\sqrt{4\alpha_1\alpha_3 - \alpha_2^2}x}{\sqrt{\eta}}}{8\alpha_1\alpha_3} \tag{17}$$

and

$$u(x,t) = \frac{4\alpha_1^2\sinh^2(\zeta)\left(\coth^2(\zeta) + \coth(\zeta) + 1\right)}{\sqrt{\alpha_1^2\left(\alpha_2^2 - 4\alpha_1\alpha_3\right)}(2\sinh(2\zeta) + \cosh(2\zeta)) - \alpha_1\alpha_2(\sinh(2\zeta) + 2\cosh(2\zeta))} \tag{18}$$

where

$$\zeta = -\frac{\sqrt{\alpha_1^2\left(\alpha_2^2 - 4\alpha_1\alpha_3\right)}\alpha_2 t + \frac{\sqrt{2}\sqrt{\alpha_3}\sqrt{4\alpha_1\alpha_3 - \alpha_2^2}\alpha_1 x}{\sqrt{\eta}}}{8\alpha_1\alpha_3}. \tag{19}$$

A graphical representation of the solutions (16) and (18) are given in Figs. 3 and 4 respectively.

SET 4: The fourth set of solutions to the system of nonlinear algebraic equations is given by

$$a_0 = 0, \quad a_1 = 1, \quad a_2 = 1, \quad c = \frac{\alpha_2 F\left(4\alpha_3\alpha_1^2 - \alpha_1\alpha_2^2 - A\right)}{8\sqrt{2}a_3\alpha_1\alpha_3\left(4\alpha_1\alpha_3 - \alpha_2^2\right)},$$

$$d = -\frac{\sqrt{4\alpha_1\alpha_3 - \alpha_2^2}}{2\sqrt{2}\sqrt{\alpha_3}\sqrt{\eta}}, \quad b_2 = -\frac{2\alpha_2 + \sqrt{2}F}{4\alpha_1},$$

$$b_1 = \frac{1}{8a_3\alpha_1^2\left(\alpha_2^2 - 4\alpha_1\alpha_3\right)}\left(a_3\left(\sqrt{2}AF - 4\alpha_3\alpha_1^2\left(4\alpha_2 + \sqrt{2}F\right)\right.\right. \tag{20}$$

$$\left.\left. +\alpha_2^2\alpha_1\left(4\alpha_2 + \sqrt{2}F\right)\right) + \sqrt{2}F\left(\alpha_1\left(\alpha_2^2 - 4\alpha_1\alpha_3\right) + A\right)\right),$$

$$b_3 = -\frac{1}{8a_3\alpha_1^2\left(\alpha_2^2 - 4\alpha_1\alpha_3\right)}\left(4\alpha_1\alpha_2\left(\alpha_2^2 - 4\alpha_1\alpha_3\right)a_3^2\right.$$

$$\left. + 2\sqrt{2}\alpha_1\left(4\alpha_1\alpha_3 - \alpha_2^2\right)a_3 F + \sqrt{2}F\left(\alpha_1\left(\alpha_2^2 - 4\alpha_1\alpha_3\right) + A\right)\right).$$

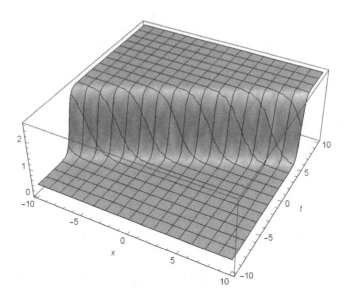

Fig. 3. Graphical representation of the solution (16) is given, where $\eta = 1, \alpha_1 = -1, \alpha_2 = 3, \alpha_3 = -1$

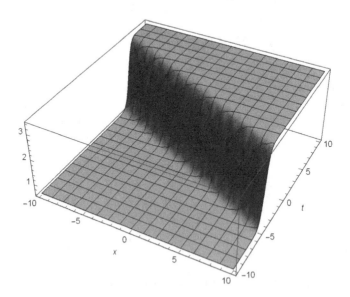

Fig. 4. Graphical representation of the solution (18) is given, where $\eta = 1, \alpha_1 = -1, \alpha_2 = 3, \alpha_3 = -1$

where

$$A = \sqrt{-(4a_3 - 1)\alpha_1^2 (\alpha_2^2 - 4\alpha_1\alpha_3)^2},$$

$$F = \sqrt{-(2a_3 - 1)(\alpha_2^2 - 4\alpha_1\alpha_3) - \frac{A}{\alpha_1}}. \tag{21}$$

Then the corresponding exact solution to the original evolution Eq. (3), after simplification, is given by

$$u(x,t) = \frac{\Gamma(\zeta)}{\Delta(\zeta)} \tag{22}$$

where

$$\Gamma(\zeta) = -8a_3\alpha_1^2 \left(4\alpha_1\alpha_3 - \alpha_2^2\right) \left(a_3 \coth^2(\zeta) + \coth(\zeta) + 1\right)$$

and

$$\Delta(\zeta) = -\sqrt{2}a_3 AB \coth(\zeta) + \alpha_1 \left(4\alpha_1\alpha_3 - \alpha_2^2\right) \left(4a_3\alpha_2 \left(a_3 \coth^2(\zeta)\right.\right.$$
$$\left. + \coth(\zeta) + 1\right) + \sqrt{2}B \left(a_3 \left(\coth(\zeta) - 2\csc h^2(\zeta)\right)\right.$$
$$\left.\left. + (\coth(\zeta) + 1)\coth(\zeta)\right)\right) - \sqrt{2}AB(\coth(\zeta) + 1)\coth(\zeta).$$

with

$$\zeta = -\frac{\alpha_2 Ft \left(\alpha_1 \left(\alpha_2^2 - 4\alpha_1\alpha_3\right) + A\right)}{8\sqrt{2}a_3\alpha_1\alpha_3 \left(4\alpha_1\alpha_3 - \alpha_2^2\right)} - \frac{\sqrt{4\alpha_1\alpha_3 - \alpha_2^2}x}{2\sqrt{2}\sqrt{\alpha_3}\sqrt{\eta}}$$

and

$$B = \sqrt{-\frac{4(1 - 2a_3)\alpha_3\alpha_1^2 + (2a_3 - 1)\alpha_2^2\alpha_1 + A}{\alpha_1}}$$

A graphical representation of the solution (22) is given in Fig. 5.

4   Conclusion

Several exact solutions to the nonlinear evolution Eq. (3), which represents the evolutionary rescue from biological invasion are derived in this paper. The available exact solutions for this equation are very less. But, such exact solutions are necessary to analyze and compare the approximate solutions obtained for real situations in a better way . They can also be used to verify the accuracy of any approximate solutions that are derived using evolutionary algorithms and computations which may depend on several random parameters.

Computation of the derived solutions is done using an algorithm and this algorithm can also be utilized to extract other exact solutions and exact solutions of similar evolution equations. The difficult steps in deriving these exact solutions are obtaining the large system of nonlinear algebraic equations and finding the nontrivial solutions which simultaneously satisfy this system of equations. This is performed by implementing an algorithm in a computational algebra system. Further exact solutions for evolution equation can also be derived by making suitable modifications in the given algorithm.

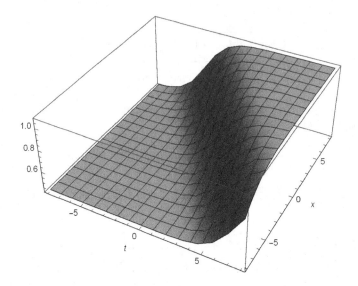

Fig. 5. Graphical representation of the solution (22) is given, where $\eta = 1, \alpha_1 = -10/11, \alpha_2 = 3, \alpha_3 = -2, a_3 = -2$

5 Appendix

The function $v(\zeta)$ given by Eq. (7) is a solution to the ordinary evolution Eq. (6), if the following system of nonlinear algebraic equations are satisfied.

$$b_3 \left(b_3 \left(2a_2 c - 3a_0 b_1 \left(a_0 \left(a_0 \alpha_3 + \alpha_2\right) + \alpha_1\right)\right)\right.$$
$$+ a_1 \left(b_3 \left(-2a_0 \alpha_2 - 3a_0^2 \alpha_3 - \alpha_1 + 2d^2 \eta\right) + b_1 c + 6b_2 d^2 \eta\right)\right)$$
$$- a_3 \left(3a_1 \alpha_3 \left(2a_0 b_3 + a_3\right) + b_1^2 c + 2b_3 \left(a_1 \alpha_2 + b_2 c\right) + b_1 \left(a_3 \left(3a_0 \alpha_3 + \alpha_2\right)\right.\right.$$
$$+ 2b_3 \left(2a_0 \alpha_2 + 3a_0^2 \alpha_3 + \alpha_1 + d^2 \eta\right) + 6b_2 d^2 \eta\right) = 0,$$

$$b_2 \left(a_1 \left(b_2 \left(-2a_0 \alpha_2 - 3a_0^2 \alpha_3 - \alpha_1 + 2d^2 \eta\right) + b_1 c + 6b_3 d^2 \eta\right)\right.$$
$$+ b_2 \left(2a_3 c - 3a_0 b_1 \left(a_0 \left(a_0 \alpha_3 + \alpha_2\right) + \alpha_1\right)\right)\right)$$
$$- a_2 \left(3a_1 a_2 \alpha_3 + 2b_2 \left(a_1 \left(3a_0 \alpha_3 + \alpha_2\right) + b_3 c\right) + b_1^2 c\right.$$
$$+ b_1 \left(a_2 \left(3a_0 \alpha_3 + \alpha_2\right) + 2b_2 \left(2a_0 \alpha_2 + 3a_0^2 \alpha_3 + \alpha_1 + d^2 \eta\right) + 6b_3 d^2 \eta\right) = 0,$$

$$b_2 \left(a_1 \left(b_2 c + 2b_1 d^2 \eta\right) - b_2 \left(a_0 b_2 \left(a_0 \left(a_0 \alpha_3 + \alpha_2\right) + \alpha_1\right) + 2a_3 d^2 \eta\right)\right)$$
$$- a_2 \left(\alpha_3 a_2^2 + b_2^2 \left(a_0 \left(3a_0 \alpha_3 + 2\alpha_2\right) + \alpha_1\right)\right.$$
$$+ b_2 \left(a_2 \left(3a_0 \alpha_3 + \alpha_2\right) - 2b_3 d^2 \eta\right) + b_1 b_2 c + 2b_1^2 d^2 \eta\right) = 0,$$

$$b_3\left(a_1\left(b_3c+2b_1d^2\eta\right)-b_3\left(a_0b_3\left(a_0\left(a_0\alpha_3+\alpha_2\right)+\alpha_1\right)+2a_2d^2\eta\right)\right)$$
$$-a_3\left(\alpha_3a_3^2+a_3b_3\left(3a_0\alpha_3+\alpha_2\right)+b_3\left(b_3\left(a_0\left(3a_0\alpha_3+2\alpha_2\right)+\alpha_1\right)\right.\right.$$
$$\left.\left.-2b_2d^2\eta\right)+b_1b_3c+2b_1^2d^2\eta\right)=0,$$

$$a_3\left(-2b_2\left(a_1\left(3a_0\alpha_3+\alpha_2\right)+b_2c-b_3c\right)\right.$$
$$+2b_1\left(b_2\left(-2a_0\alpha_2-3a_0^2\alpha_3-\alpha_1+3d^2\eta\right)+b_3d^2\eta\right)+b_1^2c\right)$$
$$+a_2\left(-6a_1\alpha_3\left(a_0b_3+a_3\right)-2b_3\left(a_1\alpha_2+b_2(-c)+b_3c\right)+b_1^2c\right.$$
$$\left.+2b_1\left(-a_3\left(3a_0\alpha_3+\alpha_2\right)+b_3\left(-2a_0\alpha_2-3a_0^2\alpha_3-\alpha_1+3d^2\eta\right)+b_2d^2\eta\right)\right)$$
$$-\left(\alpha_3a_1^3+a_1^2b_1\left(3a_0\alpha_3+\alpha_2\right)+a_0b_1\left(b_1^2+6b_2b_3\right)\left(a_0\left(a_0\alpha_3+\alpha_2\right)+\alpha_1\right)\right)$$
$$-a_1\left(b_1^2\left(a_0\left(3a_0\alpha_3+2\alpha_2\right)+\alpha_1\right)+2\left(b_3b_2\left(2a_0\alpha_2+3a_0^2\alpha_3+\alpha_1+6d^2\eta\right)\right.\right.$$
$$\left.\left.+b_2^2d^2\eta+b_3^2d^2\eta\right)+\left(b_2+b_3\right)b_1c\right)=0,$$

$$a_2^2\left(3\alpha_3\left(a_0b_3+a_3\right)+\alpha_2b_3\right)+b_2\left(a_1^2\left(3a_0\alpha_3+\alpha_2\right)\right.$$
$$+3a_0\left(b_1^2+b_2b_3\right)\left(a_0\left(a_0\alpha_3+\alpha_2\right)+\alpha_1\right)$$
$$a_3\left(b_2\left(2a_0\alpha_2+3a_0^2\alpha_3+\alpha_1-8d^2\eta\right)-3b_1c-6b_3d^2\eta\right)$$
$$\left.+a_1\left(2b_1\left(2a_0\alpha_2+3a_0^2\alpha_3+\alpha_1+d^2\eta\right)+b_2c\right)\right)$$
$$a_2\left(3\alpha_3a_1^2+b_1^2\left(2a_0\alpha_2+3a_0^2\alpha_3+\alpha_1-2d^2\eta\right)+6b_3^2d^2\eta\right.$$
$$+b_1\left(2a_1\left(3a_0\alpha_3+\alpha_2\right)+b_2(-c)+3b_3c\right)$$
$$\left.+2b_2\left(a_3\left(3a_0\alpha_3+\alpha_2\right)+b_3\left(2a_0\alpha_2+3a_0^2\alpha_3+\alpha_1+4d^2\eta\right)\right)\right)=0,$$

$$a_3^2\left(3\alpha_3\left(a_0b_2+a_2\right)+\alpha_2b_2\right)+a_3\left(3\alpha_3a_1^2+2a_2b_3\left(3a_0\alpha_3+\alpha_2\right)+6b_2^2d^2\eta\right.$$
$$+b_1^2\left(2a_0\alpha_2+3a_0^2\alpha_3+\alpha_1-2d^2\eta\right)+2b_2b_3\left(2a_0\alpha_2+3a_0^2\alpha_3+\alpha_1+4d^2\eta\right)$$
$$\left.+b_1\left(2a_1\left(3a_0\alpha_3+\alpha_2\right)+3b_2c-b_3c\right)\right)+b_3\left(a_1^2\left(3a_0\alpha_3+\alpha_2\right)\right.$$
$$+3a_0\left(b_1^2+b_2b_3\right)\left(a_0\left(a_0\alpha_3+\alpha_2\right)+\alpha_1\right)$$
$$+a_2\left(b_3\left(2a_0\alpha_2+3a_0^2\alpha_3+\alpha_1-8d^2\eta\right)-3b_1c-6b_2d^2\eta\right)$$
$$\left.+a_1\left(2b_1\left(2a_0\alpha_2+3a_0^2\alpha_3+\alpha_1+d^2\eta\right)+b_3c\right)\right)=0.$$

References

1. Banasiak, J., Mokhtar-Kharroubi, M. (eds.): Evolutionary Equations with Applications in Natural Sciences. LNM, vol. 2126. Springer, Cham (2015). https://doi.org/10.1007/978-3-319-11322-7
2. Bell, G.: Evolutionary rescue. Ann. Revi. Ecol. Evol. Syst. **48**, 605–27 (2017)
3. Barfield, M., Holt, R.D.: Evolutionary rescue in novel environments: towards improving predictability. Evol. Ecol. Res **17**, 771–786 (2016)
4. Carlson, S.M., Cunningham, C.J., Westley, P.A.H.: Evolutionary rescue in a changing world. Trends Ecol. Evol. **29**, 521–530 (2014)

5. FitzHugh, R.: Mathematical models of excitation and propagation in nerve. In: Schwann, H., (ed.) Biological Engineering, pp. 1–85. McGraw-Hill, New York (1969)
6. Foroutan, M., Manafian, J., Taghipour-Farshi, H.: Exact solutions for Fitzhugh-Nagumo model of nerve excitation via Kudryashov method. Opt. Quant. Electron. **49**, 352 (2017)
7. Gawlik, A., Vladimirov, V., Skurativskyi, S., Solitary wave dynamics governed by the modified fitzhugh-nagumo equation. J. Comput. Nonlinear Dynam. **15**(6), 061003 (2020)
8. Gawlik, A., Vladimirov, V., Skurativskyi, S.: Existence of the solitary wave solutions supported by the modified fitzhugh-nagumo system. Nonlinear Anal. Modell. Control **25**(3), 482–501 (2020)
9. Gonzalez, A., Ronce, O., Ferriere, R., Hochberg, m. E., Evolutionary rescue: an emerging focus at the intersection between ecology and evolution. Philosophical Transactions of the Royal Society B, 20120404 (2013)
10. Khan, Y.: A variational approach for novel solitary solutions of FitzHugh-Nagumo equation arising in the nonlinear reaction-diffusion equation. Int. J. Numer. Methods Heat Fluid Flow (2020). https://doi.org/10.1108/HFF-05-2020-0299
11. Kumar, D., Singh, J., Baleanu, D.: A new numerical algorithm for fractional Fitzhugh-Nagumo equation arising in transmission of nerve impulses. Nonlinear Dyn. **91**, 307–317 (2018)
12. Kovach-Orr, C., Fussmann, G.F.: Evolutionary and plastic rescue in multitrophic model communities. Philos. Trans. Royal Soc. B **368**, 20120084 (2013)
13. Lindsey, H.A., Gallie, J., Taylor, S., Kerr, B.: Evolutionary rescue from extinction is contingent on a lower rate of environmental change. Nature **494**, 463–467 (2013)
14. McKean Jr., H.: Nagumo's Equation. Adv. Math. **4**(3), 209–223 (1970)
15. Nagumo, J., Arimoto, S., Yoshizawa, S.: An active impulse transmission line simulating nerve axon. Proc. IRE **50**(10), 2061–2070 (1962)
16. Orr, H.A., Unckless, R.L.: The population genetics of evolutionary rescue. PLoS Genet. **10**, e1004551 (2014)
17. Samani, P., Bell, G.: The ghosts of selection past reduces the probability of plastic rescue but increases the likelihood of evolutionary rescue to novel stressors in experimental populations of wild yeast. Ecol. Lett. **19**, 289–298 (2016)
18. Tanaka, H., Stone, A., Nelson, D.R.: Spatial gene drives and pushed genetic waves. PNAS **114**(32), 8452–8457 (2017)
19. Van Dyken, J.D., Evolutionary rescue from a wave of biological invasion. Am. Naturalist **195**(1) (2020). https://doi.org/10.1086/706181

Security

Variants of Generative Adversarial Networks for Credit Card Fraud Detection

Leichombam Somorjit[1]([⊠]) and Mridula Verma[2]([⊠])

[1] University of Hyderabad, Hyderabad, India
leichombam38@gmail.com
[2] Institute for Development and Research in Banking Technology, Hyderabad, India
vmridula@idrbt.ac.in

Abstract. One of the major problems in the field of Banking, Financial Services and Insurance (BFSI) is detecting fraudulent transactions. It is a big challenge to accurately detect fraudulent transactions because of the huge variation in the number of fraudulent and non-fraudulent samples, called the class imbalance problem. Many approaches address this problem, such as over-sampling, under-sampling, cost-sensitive methods, etc. to name a few. In recent years, Generative Adversarial Network (GAN)-based approaches for oversampling have drawn attention from both industry and academia to overcome this problem. In this paper, we have explored and compared various state-of-the-art GAN based approaches such as Vanilla GAN, Conditional GAN (cGAN), Wasserstein GAN (WGAN), and Conditional WGAN (WcGAN) for the problem of credit card fraud detection. It is found that the recent techniques have been very sensitive to the hyperparameters. To solve this problem we introduced two new methods, WGAN with Gradient Penalty (WGAN-GP) and Conditional WGAN with Gradient Penalty (WcGAN-GP) for credit card fraud detection. It is found that these approaches not only generate more realistic data but also provide more stable results.

Keywords: Data imbalance · Deep learning · Fraud detection · Generative Adversarial Network

1 Introduction

In today's modern society cashless payment systems are on the rapid rise and credit card payment systems constitute a crucial component in Banking, Financial Services, and Insurance (BFSI). With the increase in popularity of this payment system, the chances of developing fraudulent methods are also on the rapid rise, thereby affecting all the directly involved parties including banks, merchants, and costumer. So, developing a system that can detect fraudulent transactions accurately is of utmost importance in order to reduce loss and boost the confidence of consumers in the banking system.

© Springer Nature Switzerland AG 2020
N. Kar et al. (Eds.): ICCISIoT 2020, CCIS 1358, pp. 133–143, 2020.
https://doi.org/10.1007/978-3-030-66763-4_12

Currently, the fraud detection system tries to identify the suspicious user from the transaction log by monitoring it, using a highly sophisticated analytical design. But, since the data is a mixture of both legit and illicit transaction, and a fraudulent transaction occurs rarely it suffers from a data imbalance problem, where one of the classes (the illicit transaction in our case) is of minimum instances in the data distribution and the other called the majority class has maximum instances [1]. Applying classification algorithms is difficult in imbalanced data sets as the minority class is under-represented and is often ignored as noise by the algorithms [2].

Primarily, there are three approaches to tackle the data imbalance problem [3]. The first one consists of modifying or creating a whole new algorithm [4] to make it bias towards the minority. The second approach consists of a cost-sensitive method in-order to reduce the cost [5]. And the final method which is also more commonly used is the approach where the data distribution is rebalanced using techniques such as under-sampling [6], over-sampling [1], or a hybrid of the two [7]. In under-sampling, data from the majority class is reduced so that the distribution is balanced and in the over-sampling, instances in the minority class are generated for the same effect in the data distribution.

This work is focused on the over-sampling method for binary imbalanced data, and the various techniques employed to synthesize the data in the minority class before the classification algorithm is applied. As the classification algorithm has no influence on the type of oversampling being used. And for a multi class data set, it can always be simplified using the One-Against-All idea [8] to a form of binary data set. There are two main approaches for over-sampling, the first one is the standard method called Synthetic Minority Oversampling Technique (SMOTE) [1] and its variants. The second approach is the recent development, which uses deep learning frameworks, specifically Generative Adversarial Network (GAN) [9], to solve this problem. In this paper, we not only present a comparative study of the traditional and GAN-based deep learning frameworks, we also propose two new *gradient penalty* based GAN frameworks, namely WGAN-gp and WGAN-GP, to solve the problem of credit card fraud detection.

Our main contributions are two-fold:

- Discuss and apply the latest *gradient penalty* based GAN architectures, namely, WGAN-GP and WcGAN-GP to the problem of class imbalance in credit card fraud detection.
- Perform a detailed comparative study of the traditional as well as GAN-based oversampling methods on the publicly available fraud detection data set and analyze if the problem of mode collapse and non-convergence improves empirically as it does in theory.

2 Background

In this section, we will be discussing in detail about the different oversampling methods which are already in existence, their working principle and the different advantages and shortcomings of each method. The traditional methods to solve the problem of class imbalance include Random oversampling, SMOTE [1], ADASYN [10] and Borderline-SMOTE [11]. In the past decade, GAN and its variants are being applied to solve this problem. Generative adversarial Network (GAN) [9] consists of two neural network layers- Generative and Discriminative. Both of them consist of deep neural networks where the output of one layer becomes the input of the next corresponding layer, higher the level in the network, higher is the abstraction of the real data. The Generative model G is defined as G: Z →X, where Z is noise samples and X is the data samples, so G takes random noise Z as input and transform it through a function to produce instances which are very close to the real data X, it tries to achieve this by learning to map the noise Z to a data distribution as close as possible to the real data.

The Discriminator model, defined as D : X → [0, 1], tries to estimate the probability whether the data sample X is from the real data distribution or the fake one i.e. the data generated by G, by penalizing the generator for producing artificial instances. These two models compete with each other in two players' min-max game and try to outperform each other, thereby making it possible for the generator network to produce more realistic data instances and the discriminator to easily recognize a fake instance from a real one until an equilibrium is obtained.

The objective of the generator G is to trick the discriminator D into identifying the fake data as the real one, to achieve this it tries to keep the differentiation between the real and fake to the minimum. And the discriminator D aims to classify real and fake data, and is trained by maximizing the differentiation between the two. The min-max game competition between the two models can be functionally represented as follows:

$$\min_{G} \max_{D} V(D, G) = \underset{x \sim P_{data}}{E} [\log D(x)] + \underset{z \sim P_z(z)}{E} [\log(1 - D(G(z)))]. \quad (1)$$

Here P_{data} is the real data distribution and P_z is the prior distribution for the random noise. Please note that the class labels are not considered while training the GAN architecture.

cGAN (Conditional GAN). The cGAN [12] is a simple extension of the GAN model by including an additional space y. So, the modified structure will become $G : Z \times y \to X$ and $D : X \times y \to [0, 1]$. The modified objective function will be:

$$\min_{G} \max_{D} V(D, G) = \underset{x \sim P_{data}}{E} [\log D(x/y)] + \underset{z \sim P_z(z)}{E} [\log(1 - D(G(z/y)))] \quad (2)$$

٠   Both the models GAN and cGAN suffer from mode collapse and unstable training mainly because both of them use *Jensen-Shannon* (JS) divergence to measure the difference in the distribution of real and the generated.

WGAN and WcGAN. In WGAN [13], the Earth-Mover distance is used to measure the difference between the real data and generated data distribution instead of JS divergence as in the case of GAN and cGAN. This gives superior smoothness in comparison; also theoretically it solves the gradient vanishing problem. The EM distance is given by,

$$W(P_r, P_g) = \inf_{\gamma \in \Pi(P_r, P_g)} E_{(x,y) \sim y}[\|x - y\|].$$ (3)

Here, $\Pi(P_r, P_g)$ represents the joint feasible distribution for both the real data distribution P_r and the generated data distribution, P_g. $W(P_r, P_g)$ is defined as the minimum cost of transportation for transforming P_r to P_g. But, this particular equation is highly intractable. So Kantorovich-Rubeinstein duality is used to reconstruct the equation as follow,

$$W(P_r, P_g) = \frac{1}{K} \sup_{\|f\|_L \leq K} E_{x \sim P_r}[f(x)] + E_{x \sim P_g}[f(x)],$$ (4)

where f is K-Lipschitz function and K is constant for the function. The objective function between the generator and the critic is

$$\min_G \max_D V(D, G) = E_{x \sim P_r}[D(x)] - E_{x \sim P_g}[D(x)]$$ (5)

WcGAN is very similar to cGAN where an additional space y is introduced which can be class label information or some other auxiliary information which provides the condition while training. Other training mechanism is very similar as in the WGAN, so the modified cost function is as,

$$\min_G \max_D V(D, G) = E_{x \sim P_r}[D(x/y)] - E_{x \sim P_g}[D(x/y)].$$ (6)

In WGAN clipping of weight is used to ensure that the Lipschitz continuity constraint is maintained. However, this clipping results in unstable model performance, since it becomes very sensitive to the hyperparameter K given in Eq. 4. As a result, optimizing the model becomes very difficult - a slight change in the value gives a drastic difference in the performance result. To handle this problem, the WGAN-GP and WcGAN-GP frameworks are introduced.

3   WGAN-GP and WcGAN-GP for Credit Card Fraud Detection

3.1   Gradient Penalty

K-Lipschitz requires that a differentiable function has its gradient norm with maximum value K throughout the distribution to maintain its continuity. The way of achieving this other than clipping of weight is to constrain the gradient norm of the critic's output with respect to the input [14], and we can achieve this by introducing a penalty term at the loss function.

$$gradient penalty = \lambda E_{\hat{x} \sim P_{\hat{x}}}[(\|\nabla_{\hat{x}} D(\hat{x})\|_2 - 1)^2]$$ (7)

where $P_{\hat{x}}$ is sampled uniformly along the straight line joining two points from the data distribution P_r and generated distribution P_g it is inspired by the fact that optimal critic has a straight line with gradient norm 1 connecting points between P_r and P_g. λ is gradient penalty coefficient and its value is set to 10. Our main contribution is to apply this penalty to the task of Credit card fraud detection using WGAN-GP and WcGAN-GP, which we will discuss in detail in the following subsection. Please note that the gradient penalty for WGAN-GP and WcGAN-GP are exactly the same the only difference is the conditional term added in WcGAN-GP.

3.2   WGAN-GP and WcGAN-GP

WGAN still has the problem of generating poor samples or failing to converge as found in the paper [5], but after the changes were made it was found that it gives better results with almost no parameter tuning; this approach was given the name WGAN-GP [14]. So, the new objective function is:

$$\min_{G} \max_{D} V(D, G) = E_{x \sim P_r}[D(x)] - E_{\tilde{x} \sim P_g}[D(\tilde{x})] - \lambda E_{\hat{x} \sim P_{\hat{x}}}[(\|\nabla_{\hat{x}} D(\hat{x})\|_2 - 1)^2]$$
(8)

In this technique, batch normalization is not used because it changes the problem of mapping single input to single output to a form of mapping batch input to batch output, so it is not applicable for our penalized training objective as it focuses on penalizing the norm of critic's gradient for individual input. In WcGAN-GP [15] a conditional auxiliary term y is concatenated along the real data x and random noise z in both the critic and generator. This term y can be any type of information, in our case we have used the class label as the additional information similar to the conditional version of GAN. The concatenated information y for the discriminator both in P_r and P_g and also for the generator $p(z)$ has the same representation. The objective function of the conditional version is

$$\min_{G} \max_{D} V(D, G) = E_{x \sim P_r}[D(x/y)] - E_{\tilde{x} \sim P_g}[D(\tilde{x}/y)] - \lambda E_{\hat{x} \sim P_{\hat{x}}}[(\|\nabla_{\hat{x}} D(\hat{x}/y)\|_2 - 1)^2],$$
(9)

where λ is the coefficient of gradient penalty, similar to that of WGAN-GP and $\hat{x}$ is sampled along the straight line joining points between the real data distribution and the generated data distribution.

The training algorithm we have employed for WcGAN-GP is given in Fig. 1 with time complexity O(nm) and space complexity O(m), where n is the number of iterations and m is data samples. Initially, we have to initialize the weights for the networks i.e ω for critic and θ for generator. The training of the model is continued for 5000 iterations and the critic model is trained 5 times more for each generator training. We sample real data x, noise z and a random number ϵ. x and z are concatenated with class label y. Now using the generator, new data $\tilde{x}$ is generated, next we find the data along the line joining real data x and generated data $\tilde{x}$ using ϵ and it is represented as $\hat{x}$, this term is used to constraint the norm of the gradient by introducing it in the loss function as a

---

Algorithm 1: Training procedure for WcGAN-GP. Hyperparameters value are λ=10, n_{critic} =5, Adam optimizer α=0.35, β_1=0.9, β_2=0.999

Require: initialization of parameters both for critic (ω_0) and generator (θ_0)
for 5000 iteration **do**
    for number of critic iteration **do**
        for i as number of data samples **do**
- Sample x from real distribution $\mathbb{p}_r$, z from latent distribution $p(z)$ and a random number $\epsilon \sim U[0, 1]$.
- Concatenate x and z with the class label y
- $\tilde{x} \leftarrow G_\theta(z/y)$
- $\hat{x} \leftarrow \epsilon(x/y) + (1-\epsilon)(\tilde{x}/y)$
- $L^{(i)} \leftarrow D_\omega(\tilde{x}/y) - D_\omega(x/y) + \lambda(|| \nabla_{\hat{x}} D_\omega(\hat{x}/y)||_2 - 1)^2$

        end for
        $\omega \leftarrow Adam(\nabla_\omega \frac{1}{m}\sum_{i=1}^m L^{(i)}, \omega, \alpha, \beta_1, \beta_2)$
    end for
    sample a batch of latent variables $z^{(i)} \sim p(z/y)$
    $\theta \leftarrow Adam(\nabla_\theta \frac{1}{m}\sum_{i=1}^m -D_\omega(G_\theta(z)), \theta, \alpha, \beta_1, \beta_2)$
end for

Fig. 1. Training algorithm for WcGAN-GP

penalty. Then we can calculate the loss L (with the added penalty) and using the gradient of this loss we can update the weights of both critic(ω) and the generator(θ). For optimization we have used adam optimizer, where α is the learning rate and β_1 and β_2 are decay rates for the optimizer. We can use the algorithm for WGAN-GP by removing the augmented class label y, others will remain unchanged.

4   Experiments

Our goal is to evaluate the performance of WGAN-GP and WcGAN-GP for solving the class imbalanced problem in fraud detection and present a comparative study of traditional as well as GAN frameworks for this problem. We have considered the traditional oversampling methods such as SMOTE, ADASYN, BORDERLINE and compared them with the GAN-based generative approaches. After oversampling, to evaluate the performance of these methods, we have used three classifiers: Linear Regression, Support Vector Machine (SVM) and Xgboost. We have used the popular credit card transaction dataset, which is publicly available in Kaggle. It consists of 284,807 data samples and from this 492 samples belong to the minority class i.e. the fraudulent transaction, so the dataset has a high imbalanced ratio of 1:0.00172. The dataset includes 31 features labeled as *time, amount, class,* and 28 other anonymous labels *v1, v2, v3,* $\cdots$ *v28.* The class label has two values *0* (for non-fraudulent transactions) and *1* (for fraudulent transactions). The dataset contains only numeric input variables which are the result of a PCA transformation. There is no missing value and 'NaN' value in the dataset. We have employed the imblearn package and Tensorflow, numpy, pandas, sklearn, Matplotlib, Xgboost libraries.

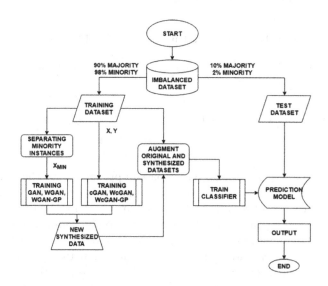

Fig. 2. Flow chart of the experimental design

The experimental setup for evaluating the performance of the oversampling methods discussed is shown in Fig. 2. This flowchart explains the process we employed to train the GAN-based frameworks. Consider X be the set carrying all the instances, Y be the set of corresponding labels, and X_{MIN} be the set of all the minority instances. It is depicted in the flowchart that to train the GAN, WGAN, and WGAN-GP only minority instances are needed, whereas to train the cGAN, WcGAN and WcGAN-GP models, both X and Y are required. The synthesized data may affect the testing values, to prevent this training data and testing data are isolated during pre-processing and the models are exposed only to the training data for oversampling. Using data-utils function in python the imbalanced data is separated as 90% of the majority and 98% of the minority in the training set and 10% of the majority and 2% of the minority in the testing set. The synthesized data and the training data are then combined such that it becomes balanced data and used it to train the classifier. The classifier is then evaluated using the testing dataset. To diminish the impact of randomness from the sampling of the data both in training and testing, the experiment is repeated ten times and the average is taken as the output.

The classical performance metrics such as accuracy is not a good measure to evaluate the performance in imbalanced data since it ignores the minority class. As an evaluation metric, we will be using F-measure, G-mean and receiver operating characteristics (ROC) area under the curve (AUC) as the performance metrics. The oversampling of the data is performed in two approaches, first one uses the traditional variant of SMOTE and the second uses the generative approach of the variants of GAN. The parameter setting for the traditional approach is listed in the Tables 1 and 2.

Table 1. Parameter setting for variants of SMOTE

Approaches	m-neighbours	n-neighbours	k-neighbours
SMOTE	10	None	5
Borderline	10	None	5
ADASYN	None	5	None

Most of the parameters for the GAN-based approaches are the same besides activation function and loss function. The number of layers for GAN, cGAN, WGAN, WCGAN, WGAN-GP, WCGAN-GP are three for the discriminator or critic and four for the generator. The noise is randomly sampled from a uniform distribution with dimensions ranging 8–64. No dropout or batch normalization is used both in the generator and the discriminator network. The number of hidden nodes for the discriminator is 24 and the generator is 104. The batch size is set in 16–128 and the number of epochs is 5000. Activation function for GAN and cGAN is the sigmoid function in the output of discriminator while for the others no activation function is used. In all the models, default parameters of Adam optimizer are used during training. The value of te gradient penalty 'λ' in WGAN-GP and WCGAN-GP is set to 10.

Table 2. Parameter setting for variants of GAN

Approaches	Batch-size	Learning-rate	Z-dimension
GAN	16	0.05	32
cGAN	128	0.2	28
WGAN	32	0.004	16
WcGAN	16	0.1	8
WGAN-GP	64	0.03	8
WcGAN-GP	32	0.35	16

In order to evaluate the different oversampling methods we use three different classifiers i.e. Linear Regression, Support Vector Machine (SVM) and Xgboost.

The first two are implemented using python library Scikit-Learn with the default parameter and the Xgboost classifier is from XGBClassifier also with default parameter settings.

4.1   Experimental Results

In this section, we give the experimental result of the different oversampling methods as given by the classifiers. A comparative study is performed with no sampling and various types of oversampling approaches. The results are shown in Table 3. It is found that for the f1-measure the oversampling of GAN and its variants give better results than the traditional SMOTE and its variants or the no sampling method in all the classifiers. But in the case of G-mean SMOTE and its variants give very high results. The value of ROC-AUC is comparatively similar in all the cases. In the SMOTE and its variants, they have very low f1-measure value and very high G-mean value while GAN and its variants have a comparatively average range in both the cases. In our ranking method to evaluate the performance, we have assigned the highest value as rank 1 and keep increasing the rank with a decrease in value. It is found that for the Logistic Regression and Support Vector Machine classifier WGAN-GP has the highest rank of 3.33 and 2.66 respectively and in the case of Xgboost classifier WcGAN has the highest rank of 3.

Table 3. Detailed results

Algorithm	LR				SVM				XGB			
Metrics	F1	G-m	AUC	Rank	F1	G-m	AUC	Rank	F1	G-m	AUC	Rank
Without	0.709	0.746	0.966	7	0.747	0.775	0.921	8.33	0.830	0.845	0.973	8.33
SMOTE	0.392	0.934	0.976	3.66	0.491	0.916	0.956	4	0.545	0.932	0.979	5.33
ADASYN	0.148	0.915	0.972	5	0.444	0.828	0.908	8.66	0.285	0.939	0.978	6
Borderline	0.605	0.929	0.953	4	0.752	0.910	0.956	3.66	0.825	0.934	0.971	6.33
GAN	0.751	0.794	0.962	6	0.874	0.890	0.966	3.33	0.872	0.887	0.980	3.66
cGAN	0.738	0.770	0.970	5.33	0.782	0.805	0.948	6	0.871	0.883	0.983	4.33
WGAN	0.761	0.802	0.924	6	0.838	0.859	0.924	5.66	0.841	0.860	0.967	8.33
WcGAN	0.727	0.764	0.966	7	0.738	0.779	0.937	7.66	0.876	0.886	0.981	**3**
WGAN-GP	0.779	0.807	0.966	**3.33**	0.878	0.890	0.954	**2.66**	0.868	0.885	0.979	5
WcGAN-GP	0.763	0.795	0.943	5.66	0.866	0.884	0.867	3	0.875	0.888	0.978	4

Figures 3, 4 and 5 show the box plot of the values achieved after repeating the experiment 10 times with the same configuration. The first row is for the LR classifier and the second, third for SVM and Xgboost respectively. The first column of figures is for F-measure metric, the second for G-mean and the third for ROC-AUC, here also it is visible the performance of generative networks is giving better results for F-measure but for other metrices, it is showing almost similar values.

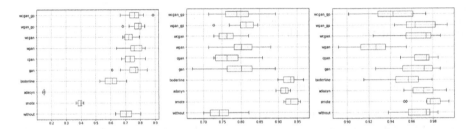

Fig. 3. Boxplot of F1, G-mean and AUC respectively for all the over-sampling methods after 10 iterations using logistic Regression

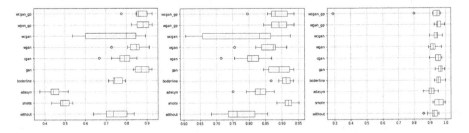

Fig. 4. Boxplot of F1, G-mean and AUC respectively for all the over-sampling methods after 10 iterations using SVM

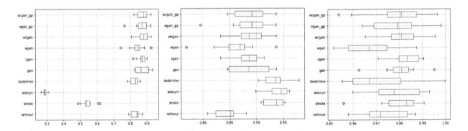

Fig. 5. Boxplot of F1, G-mean and AUC respectively for all the over-sampling methods after 10 iterations using Xgboost

5   Conclusion

In this research, we tried to deal with the class imbalance problem by using the over-sampling methods. Various over-sampling techniques have been discussed including the traditional methods and the newly developed deep neural network approach and comparative study has been performed and it is found that for the F1-measure metric the generative approach gives much better results but not as much in the case of G-mean. So, there seems to be no standard generalized metric which we can use for evaluating data imbalance problems, this is still one of the challenges encountered. If we consider the F1-measure WGAN-GP gives better and more consistent results but for the other metrics the results are not consistent.

References

1. Chawla, N.V., Bowyer, K.W., Hall, L.O., Kegelmeyer, W.P.: SMOTE: synthetic minority over-sampling technique. J. Artif. Intell. Res. **16**, 321–357 (2002)
2. Japkowicz, N., Stephen, S.: The class imbalance problem: a systematic study. Intell. Data Anal. **6**(5), 429–499 (2002)
3. Fernandez, A., Lopez, V., Galar, M., Jesus, M.J., Herrera, F.: Analysing the classification of imbalanced data-sets with multiple classes: binarization techniques and ad-hoc approaches. Knowl. Based Syst. **42**, 99–110 (2013)
4. Galar, M., Fernandez, A., Barrenechea, E., Bustince, H., Herrera, F.: A review on ensembles for the class imbalance problem: bagging boosting and hybrid based approaches. IEEE Trans. Syst. Man Cybern. Part C (Appl. Rev.) **42**(4), 463–484 (2012)
5. Zhou, Z.H., Liu, X.Y.: Training cost-sensitive neural networks with methods addressing the class imbalance problem. IEEE Trans. Knowl. Data Eng. **18**(1), 63–77 (2006)
6. Wu, J., Liu, X.Y., Zhou, Z.H.: Exploratory undersampling for class-imbalance learning. IEEE Trans. Syst. Man Cybern. Part B (Cybern.) **39**(2), 539–550 (2009)
7. Batista, G.E., Prati, R.C., Monard, M.C.: A study of the behaviour of several methods for balancing machine learning training data. ACM SIGKDD Explor. Newslett. **6**(1), 20–29 (2004)
8. Hsu, C.W., Lin, C.J.: A comparision of methods for multiclass support vector machines. IEEE Trans. Neural Netw. **13**(2), 415–425 (2002)
9. Goodfellow, I., Pouget-Abadie, J., Mirza, M.: Generative adversarial nets. In: Advances in Neural Information Processing Systems, pp. 2672–2680 (2014)
10. He, H., Bai, Y., Garcia, E.A., Li, S.: ADASYN: adaptive synthetic sampling approach for imbalanced learning. In: Proceedings of the International Joint Conference on Neural Networks, pp. 1322–1328 (2008)
11. Han, H., Wang, W.-Y., Mao, B.-H.: Borderline-SMOTE: a new over-sampling method in imbalanced data sets learning. In: Huang, D.-S., Zhang, X.-P., Huang, G.-B. (eds.) ICIC 2005. LNCS, vol. 3644, pp. 878–887. Springer, Heidelberg (2005). https://doi.org/10.1007/11538059_91
12. Mirza, M., Osindero, S.: Conditional generative adversarial nets. arXiv preprint arxiv:abs/1411.1784 (2014)
13. Arjovsky, M., Chintala, S., Bottou, L.: Wasserstein generative adversarial networks. In: Proceedings of the 34th International Conference on Machine Learning, vol. 70, pp. 214–223 (2017)
14. Gulrajani, I., Ahmed, F., Arjovsky, M.: Improved training of Wasserstein GANs. In: Advances in Neural Information Processing Systems, NIPS, vol. 30 (2017)
15. Zheng, M., Li, T., Zhu, R.: Conditional Wasserstein generative adversarial network-gradient penalty-based approach to alleviating imbalanced data classification. Inf. Sci. **512**, 1009–1023 (2020)

A Compact Network Intrusion Classifier Using Fuzzy Logic

Kanubhai K. Patel[(⊠)][iD]

Charotar University of Science and Technology, Changa, Gujarat, India
kkpatel7@gmail.com

Abstract. A method to construct compact fuzzy logic classifier is proposed for network intrusion detection (NID) problem. The proposed method attempts to deal with two major issues related to the network intrusion detection by fuzzy rule-based classifier modeling approach, viz., optimized fuzzy rule discovery, and membership functions tuning. For the determination of effective optimized fuzzy rules, genetics-based fuzzy rule discovery algorithm is proposed. For membership functions tuning, we have used genetics-based optimization method to calculate fitness of the rules. The method is experimentally evaluated with KDD Cup 1999 data set. Various experimental and comparative studies signify the effectiveness of the method. Our technique gives comparatively high detection rates than other machine-learning techniques.

Keywords: Fuzzy rule discovery · Network security · Intrusion detection · Genetics-based approach · Machine learning

1 Introduction

Hasty technological transformation has resulted in many facets of our lives, being connected and affected by digital communications. In today's global digital world, computer, smart devices, and Internet are being essential and vital components of our lives. Finding effective ways for safeguarding personal sensitive data, financial and other kinds of information, intellectual property, privacy and our reputation is a crucial part of our strategy. The increasing number of ransomware, malware, attacks, and phishing scams realized that much closer attention is required to detect intrusion in our computing environment. Many new kinds of security threats, in a large number, are enormously increasing and becoming more dangerous. It is mandatory to enhance the network intrusion detection systems (NIDS) [13]. Therefore, NIDS have concerned attention. NIDS distinguish normal and malicious activities in networks. A good number of researchers have proposed fuzzy rule based classifiers for NIDS [2–4,11,13,15,18,24,27]. Although, various these approaches having been proposed, potential of the techniques is still under-utilized for network intrusion detection problem. Following are two open challenges in fuzzy rule-based classifier for IDS:

– discovery of optimized fuzzy rules [10], and

© Springer Nature Switzerland AG 2020
N. Kar et al. (Eds.): ICCISIoT 2020, CCIS 1358, pp. 144–155, 2020.
https://doi.org/10.1007/978-3-030-66763-4_13

– tuning the membership functions,

Construction of a Rule Base (RB) is the most challenging problem in developing rule-based NIDS. [10]. In current rule-based NIDS, rules are crafted manually by domain experts. To automate the rule crafting process, rules are required to discovered. For the determination of effective optimized rules, genetics-based fuzzy rule discovery algorithm is proposed. For membership functions tuning, we have proposed adaptive genetics-based optimization method to consider accuracy, coverage, and simplicity of rules in calculating fitness of the rules. The effectiveness of the fuzzy rule based classifier is significantly influenced by the granularity level [8]. By combining genetics-based approach with fuzzy set theory, the proposed method can be used for i) data records that contain both nominal and continuous attributes, and ii) to address both anomaly (to some extend) and misuse detection in network intrusion detection problem. The method is verified and validated with KDD Cup 1999 data set. A comparative studies signify the effectiveness of the method. Experimental study proved that competitively high ID rates is given by the proposed method as compared to other machine learning techniques. We have got 98.87% detection rate to classify the network connections data. We have summarized the main contributions of this research paper as below:

– We aim to enhance the existing NIDS by having technique to craft the fuzzy rules with out domain experts.
– We aim at finding the number of fuzzy labels for each variable, specifically in NID problem. In order to do so, we have considered genetics-based optimization method approach.

The remaining paper is organized as follows. Section 2 reviews the related works. Section 3 describes the method used for generating fuzzy rules. Section 4 describes the procedure and planning of the experiment. Section 5 discusses the results of the experiment. Section 6 concludes our paper along with future directions.

2 Related Works

2.1 Fuzzy Classifier for NID

Intrusion Detection (ID) framework is proposed by Denning [9] in 1987. Since then many researchers have proposed IDS using various approaches including fuzzy logic and genetic algorithm [2–4,11,15,18]. Specifically a good number of researchers have used fuzzy logic classifier based approach for computer security [2,3,11,13,24]. Table 1 shows a list of various ML techniques used by various researchers for generating fuzzy logic classifier for NID (See Table 1):

Table 1. List of ML techniques used for NID.

Technique	Researchers
FL+GA	[2]
Complete Binary Tree	[13]
Genetic programming	[24]
Compact one-class GFRCS	[26]
Granulation-based adaptive clustering	[4]
Evolutionary optimization technique	[11]
Weighted Fuzzy C-Means clustering	[12]
Multilevel GP approach	[27]
Multi-Objective cooperative function	[5]
GA	[15]

2.2 Learning Fuzzy Classification Rules

Many researchers have proposed fuzzy rule based classification system and used various approach to discover fuzzy classification rules [2,6,7,10,14,19,19,21,25, 28]. Table 2 shows a list of techniques used by various researchers for NID (See Table 2):

Table 2. List of techniques used for learning fuzzy rules

Technique used	Researchers
Fuzzy-ARTMAP, Q-learning, and GA	[21]
Multi-objective GA	[14]
Parameterizable greedy-based learning method (Selection-Reduction)	[10]
Hybrid learning method	[28]
Fuzzy+GA	[2,25]
Tuning methods	[17]
IVTURS	[23]
Weighted fuzzy interpolative reasoning method	[7]
Complete binary tree structure	[13]
Genetic design of linguistic terms	[19]
Rule granulation and consolidation	[6]

3   Method

We have used fuzzy logic classifier evolved by genetic algorithm (GA) to solve the network intrusion detection problem efficiently. We combine genetics-based approach and fuzzy set theory to classify the data set into various attack types. We evolved Rule Base (RB) by using our learning technique from the labelled data examples. A fuzzy IF−THEN rule $R^k, k = 1, 2, 3, ..., n$, for such a classifier is represented as in Eq. (1).

$$R^k : IF x_1 is A_1^k and x_2 is A_2^k and ... and x_n is A_N^k THEN y is C^k with r^k \quad (1)$$

where $A_j^k, j = 1, 2, ..., N$ are fuzzy sets, j^{th} input feature variable, y is the class $C^k \in C$, and R^k is k^{th} rule. This kind of fuzzy classification rules is used by researchers frequently in FRCS [16]. Our fuzzy rule base model is constructed using supervised learning. We used labelled patterns $F = f^p = (x^p, c^p), p = 1, 2, ..., G$ to evolve the classifier by GA. The following steps are involved in developing an efficient fuzzy rule-based classifier that has higher accuracy and less false alarms:

3.1 Normalization and Partition of Data

We have used Min-max scaling method to normalize the data. For this, we have assigned the numerical values to the discrete features. First, we need to find out min and max of attribute data. Then we normalize the values by following formula:

$$Z_i = \frac{x_i - min(X)}{max(X) - min(X)} \quad (2)$$

KDD Cup 1999 data set [1] has 41 attributes. For each attribute, partitions are performed by following formula to get fuzzy set. We have used equal-length partition method.

$$ai = [Lb + (i - 1)\frac{Ub - Lb}{j}, Lb + i\frac{Ub - Lb}{j}] \quad (3)$$

here j is number of intervals, i is interval number, Lb is lower bound of U, Ub is upper bound of U. When j is 4, we get four partitions i.e. [0, 0.25], [0.25, 0.5], [0.5, 0.75], and [0.75, 1.0]. After finding partitions, fuzzy labels are assigned to the partitions. For ex. For Duration attribute, we assign Low, MediumLow, Medium, High, and VeryHigh fuzzy labels (See Fig. 1).

3.2 Fuzzy Intervals Optimization

After getting partitions of data, it is optimized by using genetics-based fuzzy intervals optimization algorithm (See Algorithm 1) to get highly accurate and interpretable fuzzy rules.

3.3 Membership Function to Create Fuzzy Sets

We have used trapezoid function to create fuzzy sets (See Fig. 1). Trapezoid function returns a fuzzy set whose membership grades represent a trapezoid defined by parameters a, b, c, and d. Universal space (max and min values) of each attribute is found out.

3.4   Genetics-Based Fuzzy Classification Rules Discovery Algorithm

After creating fuzzy set, we generate rule base by following proposed algorithm. Here each individual represents a fuzzy rule in the form as given in Eq. (1). We encoded the IF part of fuzzy classification rule in each individual. The THEN part of the fuzzy classification is not included in the individual. A large population of individuals is generated randomly in the beginning of the algorithm. Then new populations are generated from previous generations' populations. Every individual is the encoded in binary values. Fitness of every individual is then find out. We calculate confidence, simplicity, and coverage of the rule [20] to evaluate the performance of each individual in a population.

Algorithm 1 : Genetics-based fuzzy intervals optimization algorithm

Input: no-of-intervals, min-initial = 0; Output: fuzzy-sets

1. Finding Universe of Discourse (i.e. min and max values for each attributes).
2. Generate a population (using Michigan approach) where each individual of the population is membership functions for all the attributes. For example, for all attributes, define initial population with Min-initial, a, b, c, ..., value-no-of-intervals-2, max
3. Find the fitness value of each membership function (MF) in the current population i.e. to check fitness values for each individual (with respect to accuracy)
4. Add the best MF in the population to newly generated MF to form the next population.
5. Generate new MF by Genetic operators: selection, crossover, and mutation.
6. Go to Step 3 if the pre-specified ending condition is not satisfied.

Algorithm 2 : Genetics-based fuzzy classification algorithm

Input: $2D$ matrix of 41 features; minSuppThresshold; No-of-generations Output: Rule-base

1. Create initial population randomly (set of chromosomes), $Pop[0]$
2. $Gen \leftarrow 0$
3. Determine fitness of each individuals (in $Pop[0]$)
4. Selection of individuals as per fitness values (i.e. $Pop[Gen]$ from $Pop[Gen-1]$)
5. Crossover and Mutation operations are performed on selected individuals, creating new population
6. $Gen \leftarrow Gen + 1$
7. repeat 3,4,5,6 (for next generation, $Pop[Gen]$)
8. Selection of best rules for first type of consequent part (i.e. attack type)
9. Add into RuleBase
10. Repeat step 2 to 9 for next type of consequent part (i.e. attack type)
11. Return RuleBase

3.5   Genetic Operators

Following operators are set in GA,

- Selection: Tournament selection method is applied to select the individuals with tournament size of 5.
- Mutation Mutation is performed on a individual. We set 1% mutation probability.
- Crossover Inter-genes crossover is performed. We set 95% crossover probability.

3.6   Fitness Function

The rule (R) is in the form "IF Exprn THEN Class" where Exprn is antecedent and Class is the consequent. Fitness of rules are calculated by considering confidence, simplicity, and coverage of the rules as reported in [20].

4   Planning and Procedure for Experiment

We have designed two experimental studies to investigate the following:

- The validity of the fuzzy rule discovery approach for NID.
- The validity of the membership function (MF) tuning method for NID

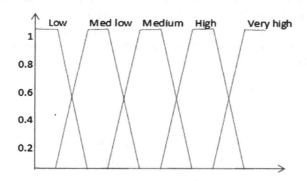

Fig. 1. Trapzoid fuzzy set

4.1   Experimental Apparatus

The proposed fuzzy rule-based classifier is evolved by using R package, frbs [22]. First, we have used KDD Cup 1999 data set [1] to generate rule base. Separate data sets were used for training and for testing phases. The experimental software was run on a desktop system with a 3.60 GHz Intel Core i3 processor, and 8 GB RAM. Network packets were captured through WinPcap 4.1.3 tool. We have tested our approach in Charotar University of Science and Technology (CHARUSAT) networks.

4.2 Research Instruments

Eight main instruments were developed to serve the study. From these, the last three instruments were developed for the collection of quantitative data. The research instruments were:

- The network: The network considered for the study is a network of CHARUSAT with 2 data servers, 1 web server, 3 file servers, and 3 OS servers.
- R Studio 1.0.1: R Studio enabled us to create FIS in R language. It is also used to perform the rule-discovery task.
- Snort: To capture network packets, we need to run snort in packet logger mode.
- Evaluation Schemes: It aimed at determining the degree and extent of (i) reliability and effectiveness of the method, and (ii) experimental parameters such as accuracy, sensitivity, specificity, Kappa, and detection rate, etc.
- Computer network log: the log enabled us to analyze the proposed approach in the network as regards to intrusion detection rate, FPR, FNR, and length (for interpretability) of rules are stored in database.
- Rule-discovery Task: It aimed at determining the fuzzy rules from KDD Cup Data Set and thereby to create Rule Base. Rule Base becomes one of the inputs to FIS.
- MF-tuning Task: It aimed at determining the number of fuzzy labels or terms for the attributes of KDD Cup Data Set. It would derive efficient rules and thereby it improves the performance of FRM approach for NID.
- Attack-detection Task: Attacks are imposed from one PC on network. Various attack imposed tools are used for the same. Our system creates log when attack is detected.

4.3 Data Set

KDD Cup Data Set [1] is used to generate rule base, which is created by Lincoln laboratory of MIT. Each record of KDD Cup 1999 data set has 41 features. In these features, there are 34 numeric and 7 discrete features.

4.4 Procedure

We have conducted two experimental studies. Procedure for the first study was designed to validate the effectiveness of our method through the prototypical implementation in R. It was expected that such a method would learn the rules effectively, and efficiently. Rule-discovery task is performed for five times in five tests. During each test, results of each performance variables are stored for evaluation. The task is carried out by setting the parameters viz., number of generation (as 1000), one-point cross over method and its probability (as 0.7), and mutation rate as 0.01. Next, we have tested our evolved classifier by using this RB and testing data set. We have conducted training and testing for five times and each times we evaluated our classifier based on performance parameters.

Procedure for the second study was designed to validate the membership function (MF) tuning method for NID through the prototypical implementation in R based on the algorithm as described in Sect. 3.2. It was expected that fine tuning of MF would improves the performance of our approach for NID. MF-tuning task is performed with various number of MF (i.e. 5, 6, 7, 9, *and* 11) for five times in five tests. During each test, results of each performance variables are stored for evaluation.

4.5 Design

In the first experimental study, we have measure the performance of the classifier in terms of thirteen performance variables viz.,(i) accuracy, (ii) sensitivity, (iii) specificity, (iv) positive prediction value, (v) negative prediction value, (vi) precision, (vii) recall, (viii) F1, (ix) prevalence, (x) detection rate, (xi) detection prevalence, (xii) balanced accuracy, and (xiii) Kappa. From the above mentioned performance variables, performance variables (ii) to (xii) provide class-wise performance values. While performance variables (i) and (xiii) provide overall performance of the FRM approach In the second experimental study, the independent variable is number of labels and the dependent variables are thirteen viz., (i) accuracy, (ii) sensitivity, (iii) specificity, (iv) pos pred value, (v) neg pred value, (vi) precision, (vii) recall, (viii) F1, (ix) prevalence, (x) detection rate, (xi) detection prevalence, (xii) balanced accuracy, and (xiii) Kappa. From the above mentioned dependent variables, from dependent variables (ii) to (xii) provide class-wise performance values. While dependent variables (i) and (xiii) provide overall performance of the FRM approach.

5 Results

We have tested our classifier using KDD Cup 1999 training and testing data sets. In training phase, we have derived 70 IF-THEN fuzzy rules during 1000 generations which takes more than eight minutes time. In the testing phase, we have obtained 98.87% detection rates for samples. FPR and FNR both are near to zero. Class-wise values of various performance parameters during first experimental study are shown as in Fig. 2. Here, class indicates various attack type i.e. decision attribute of KDD Cup Data Set. We have got confusion matrix table as shown in see Fig. 3. Total records in test data are 428. As shown in Fig. 3 some of records of class-2 and class-18 are misclassified, while records of other classes are correctly classified by our method. We have got accuracy value of 95.33% and Kappa value as 0.9501. We have compared the value of accuracy of our method with accuracy given by other machine learning techniques as shown in Table 3. We have also got Kappa value near to 1. Compare to other machine learning techniques, our method provides significantly higher accuracy in classifying the network packets. In second experimental study, we have got accuracy value and Kappa value as shown in Table 4. We have compared the values of accuracy of our approach tested with different number of intervals. We have also got Kappa value more near to 1 in case of fine-grained fuzzy labels.

Class	Parameters										
	Sensitivity (a)	Specificity (b)	Pos pred value (P*)	Neg pred value (N*)	Precision (p)	Recall (R)	F1 (f)	Prevalence (b)	Detection rate (d)	Detection Prevalence (e)	Balanced accuracy (A)
Class: 1	1.0000	1.0000	1.0000	1.0000	1.0000	1.0000	1.0000	0.0841	0.0841	0.0841	1.0000
Class: 2	0.7818	1.0000	1.0000	0.9688	1.0000	0.7818	0.8776	0.1285	0.1005	0.1005	0.8909
Class: 3	1.0000	1.0000	1.0000	1.0000	1.0000	1.0000	1.0000	0.0654	0.0654	0.0654	1.0000
Class: 4	1.0000	1.0000	1.0000	1.0000	1.0000	1.0000	1.0000	0.0491	0.0491	0.0491	1.0000
Class: 5	1.0000	1.0000	1.0000	1.0000	1.0000	1.0000	1.0000	0.0374	0.0374	0.0374	1.0000
Class: 6	1.0000	0.9698	0.7209	1.0000	0.7209	1.0000	0.8378	0.0724	0.0724	0.1005	0.9849
Class: 7	1.0000	1.0000	1.0000	1.0000	1.0000	1.0000	1.0000	0.0467	0.0467	0.0467	1.0000
Class: 8	1.0000	1.0000	1.0000	1.0000	1.0000	1.0000	1.0000	0.0561	0.0561	0.0561	1.0000
Class: 9	1.0000	1.0000	1.0000	1.0000	1.0000	1.0000	1.0000	0.0421	0.0421	0.0421	1.0000
Class 10	1.0000	1.0000	1.0000	1.0000	1.0000	1.0000	1.0000	0.0187	0.0187	0.0187	1.0000
Class 11	1.0000	1.0000	1.0000	1.0000	1.0000	1.0000	1.0000	0.0397	0.0397	0.0397	1.0000
Class: 12	1.0000	0.9902	0.8333	1.0000	0.8333	1.0000	0.9091	0.0467	0.0467	0.0561	0.9951
Class: 13	1.0000	1.0000	1.0000	1.0000	1.0000	1.0000	1.0000	0.0654	0.0654	0.0654	1.0000
Class: 14	1.0000	0.9903	0.8000	1.0000	0.8000	1.0000	0.8889	0.0374	0.0374	0.0467	0.9951
Class: 15	1.0000	1.0000	1.0000	1.0000	1.0000	1.0000	1.0000	0.0561	0.0561	0.0561	1.0000
Class: 16	1.0000	1.0000	1.0000	1.0000	1.0000	1.0000	1.0000	0.0374	0.0374	0.0374	1.0000
Class: 17	1.0000	1.0000	1.0000	1.0000	1.0000	1.0000	1.0000	0.0514	0.0514	0.0514	1.0000
Class: 18	0.7143	1.0000	1.0000	0.9804	1.0000	0.7143	0.8333	0.0654	0.0467	0.0467	0.8571

Fig. 2. Class-wise results of rule-discovery task

```
            Reference
Prediction  1  2  3  4  5  6  7  8  9 10 11 12 13 14 15 16 17 18
        1  36  0  0  0  0  0  0  0  0  0  0  0  0  0  0  0  0  0
        2   0 43  0  0  0  0  0  0  0  0  0  0  0  0  0  0  0  0
        3   0  0 28  0  0  0  0  0  0  0  0  0  0  0  0  0  0  0
        4   0  0  0 21  0  0  0  0  0  0  0  0  0  0  0  0  0  0
        5   0  0  0  0 16  0  0  0  0  0  0  0  0  0  0  0  0  0
        6   0 12  0  0  0 31  0  0  0  0  0  0  0  0  0  0  0  0
        7   0  0  0  0  0  0 20  0  0  0  0  0  0  0  0  0  0  0
        8   0  0  0  0  0  0  0 24  0  0  0  0  0  0  0  0  0  0
        9   0  0  0  0  0  0  0  0 18  0  0  0  0  0  0  0  0  0
       10   0  0  0  0  0  0  0  0  0  8  0  0  0  0  0  0  0  0
       11   0  0  0  0  0  0  0  0  0  0 17  0  0  0  0  0  0  0
       12   0  0  0  0  0  0  0  0  0  0  0 20  0  0  0  0  0  4
       13   0  0  0  0  0  0  0  0  0  0  0  0 28  0  0  0  0  0
       14   0  0  0  0  0  0  0  0  0  0  0  0  0 16  0  0  0  4
       15   0  0  0  0  0  0  0  0  0  0  0  0  0  0 24  0  0  0
       16   0  0  0  0  0  0  0  0  0  0  0  0  0  0  0 16  0  0
       17   0  0  0  0  0  0  0  0  0  0  0  0  0  0  0  0 22  0
       18   0  0  0  0  0  0  0  0  0  0  0  0  0  0  0  0  0 20
```

Fig. 3. Confusion matrix table

Table 3. Results obtained by other machine learning techniques.

Machine learning technique	Accuracy (%)
Support Vector Machine	95.50
C4.5	95.00
MLP	94.50
k-NN	92.00
LPM	94.00
RDA	92.00
C4.5+Hybrid ANN	93.28
γ-means clustering	65.00
k-means clustering	65.00
ANN+PCA	92.22
Genetic programming	91.00
C4.5+PCA	92.16
Y-means clustering	89.89
Hidden Markov Model (HMM)	79.00
Single leakage clustering	69.00

Table 4. Perfo. eval. for vari. fuzzy labels.

No. of lingui. terms per fuzzy variables	Accuracy (%)	Kappa value
5	95.33	0.9501
6	95.57	0.9503
7	95.89	0.9506
9	96.21	0.9602
11	96.45	0.9615

6   Conclusion

We have integrated the novel genetics-based approach with fuzzy logic to enable fuzzy rule learning and membership function tuning to overcome network intrusion detection (NID) problem efficiently. The motivation to use genetics-based approach was driven by its potential to search near-accurate solutions in the solution space. Results reveal that the fuzzy rules for classification are discovered through our method to get high accuracy, more converge and more comprehensibility. By results of experimental study-2 we can say that compare to less number of linguistics terms per fuzzy labels, fine grained fuzzy labels provide significantly higher accuracy in classifying the network packets. The experimental results have conclusively indicated that the method is very effective for less attended fuzzy rule learning and thereby enhancement of NID. Its simplicity of design makes it an effective method for rule discovery and thereby for NID. The results match with our expectations that our method would result in discovering complete fuzzy rules that considerably increase accuracy of NID with less human intervention in rule crafting.

References

1. KDD Cup 1999 KDD cup 1999 data set. kdd.ics.uci.edu/databases/kddcup99/kddcup99.html. Accessed 10 Aug 2019
2. Abadeh, M.S., Mohamadi, H., Habibi, J.: Design and analysis of genetic fuzzysystems for intrusion detection in computer networks. Expert Syst. Appl. **38**(6), 7067–7075 (2011). https://doi.org/10.1016/j.eswa.2010.12.006
3. Abdullah, B., Abd-alghafar, I., Salama, G.I., Abd-alhafez, A.: Performance evaluation of a genetic algorithm based approach to network intrusion detection system. In: Proceedings of ASAT-13, Kobry Elkobbah, Cairo, Egypt, pp. 1–17 (2009)
4. Al-Shammaa, M., Abbod, M.F.: Automatic generation of fuzzy classification rules using granulation-based adaptive clustering. In: 2015 Annual IEEE Systems Conference (SysCon) Proceedings, pp. 653–659, April 2015. https://doi.org/10.1109/SYSCON.2015.7116825
5. Amin, H., Radu, S.: On the optimality of cooperative intrusion detection for resource constrained wireless network. Comput. Secur. **34**, 16–35 (2013)
6. Andri, R., Jürgo-Sören, P.: Design of fuzzy rule-based classifiers through granulation and consolidation. J. Artif. Intell. Soft Comput. Res. **7**(2), 137–147 (2017). https://doi.org/10.1515/jaiscr-2017-0010

7. Chen, S.M., Chang, Y.C.: Weighted fuzzy rule interpolation based on ga-based weight-learning techniques. IEEE Trans. Fuzzy Syst. **19**(4), 729–744 (2011). https://doi.org/10.1109/TFUZZ.2011.2142314

8. Cordon, O., Herrera, F., Villar, P.: Generating the knowledge base of a fuzzy-based system by the genetic learning of the data base. IEEE Trans. Fuzzy Syst. **9**(4), 667–674 (2001)

9. Denning, D.E.: An intrusion-detection model. IEEE Trans. Softw. Eng. **13**(2), 222–232 (1987)

10. Dutu, L.C., Mauris, G., Bolon, P.: A fast and accurate rule-base generation method for Mamdani fuzzy systems. IEEE Trans. Fuzzy Syst. **PP**(99), 1 (2017). https://doi.org/10.1109/TFUZZ.2017.2688349

11. Fries, T.P.: Evolutionary optimization of a fuzzy rule-based network intrusion detection system. In: 2010 Annual Meeting of the North American Fuzzy Information Processing Society, pp. 1–6, July 2010. https://doi.org/10.1109/NAFIPS.2010.5548289

12. Ganapathy, S., Kulothungan, K., Yogesh, P., Kanna, A.: A novel weighted fuzzy c-means clustering based on immune genetic algorithm for intrusion detection. In: Proceedings of International Conference on Modeling Optimisation and Computing, pp. 1750–1757 (2012)

13. Gomez, J., Gill, C., Banos, R., Marquez, A.L., Montoya, F.G., Montoya, M.G.: A pareto-based multi-objective evolutionary algorithm for automatic rule generation in network intrusion detection systems. Soft Comput. **17**(2), 255–263 (2013)

14. Gorzałczany, M.B., Rudziński, F.: A multi-objective genetic optimization for fast, fuzzy rule-based credit classification with balanced accuracy and interpretability. Appl. Soft Comput. **40**, 206–220 (2016). https://doi.org/10.1016/j.asoc.2015.11.037. http://www.sciencedirect.com/science/article/pii/S1568494615007553

15. Hoque, M.S., Mukit, M.A., Bikas, A.N.M.: An implementation of intrusion detection system using genetic algorithm. Int. J. Netw. Secur. Appl. (IJNSA) **4**(2), 109–120 (2012)

16. Ishibuchi, H., Yamamoto, T.: Rule weight specification in fuzzy rule-based classification systems. IEEE Trans. Fuzzy Syst. **13**(4), 428–435 (2005). https://doi.org/10.1109/TFUZZ.2004.841738

17. Johanyák, Z.C., Ailer, P.: Rule base identification toolbox for fuzzy controllers. In: 2014 9th Iberian Conference on Information Systems and Technologies (CISTI), pp. 1–6, June 2014. https://doi.org/10.1109/CISTI.2014.6877094

18. Lin, C.C., Wang, M.S.: Genetic-clustering algorithm for intrusion detection system. Int. J. Inf. Comput. Secur. **2**(2), 218–234 (2008)

19. Nguyen, C.H., Pedrycz, W., Duong, T.L., Tran, T.S.: A genetic design of linguistic terms for fuzzy rule based classifiers. Int. J. Approx. Reason. **54**(1), 1 – 21 (2013). https://doi.org/10.1016/j.ijar.2012.07.007. http://www.sciencedirect.com/science/article/pii/S0888613X12001405

20. Patel, K., Buddhadev, B.: Predictive rule discovery for network intrusion detection. In: Buyya, R., Thampi, S.M. (eds.) Intelligent Distributed Computing. AISC, vol. 321, pp. 287–298. Springer, Cham (2015). https://doi.org/10.1007/978-3-319-11227-5_25

21. Pourpanah, F., Lim, C.P., Saleh, J.M.: A hybrid model of fuzzy ARTMAP and genetic algorithm for data classification and rule extraction. Expert Systems with Applications **49**, 74 – 85 (2016). https://doi.org/10.1016/j.eswa.2015.11.009. http://www.sciencedirect.com/science/article/pii/S0957417415007691

22. Riza, L., Bergmeir, C., Herrera, F., Benítez, J.: FRBS: fuzzy rule-based systems for classification and regression in r. J. Stat. Softw. **65**(1), 1–30 (2015). https://doi.org/10.18637/jss.v065.i06. https://www.jstatsoft.org/index.php/jss/article/view/v065i06

23. Sanz, J., Fernandez, A., Bustince, H., Herrera, F.: IVTURS: a linguistic fuzzy rule-based classification system based on a new interval-valued fuzzy reasoning method with tuning and rule selection. IEEE Trans. Fuzzy Syst. **21**(3), 399–411 (2013)

24. Sen, S., Clark, J.A.: Evolutionary computation techniques for intrusion detection in mobile ad hoc networks. Comput. Netw. **55**(15), 3441–3457 (2011)

25. Tan, C.H., Yap, K.S., Yap, H.J.: Application of genetic algorithm for fuzzy rules optimization on semi expert judgment automation using Pittsburg approach. Appl. Soft Comput. **12**(8), 2168–2177 (2012). https://doi.org/10.1016/j.asoc.2012.03.018

26. Villar, P., Krawczyk, B., Sanchez, A.M., Montes, R., Herrera, F.: Designing a compact genetic fuzzy rule-based system for one-class classification. In: 2014 IEEE International Conference on Fuzzy Systems (FUZZ-IEEE), pp. 2163–2170, July 2014. https://doi.org/10.1109/FUZZ-IEEE.2014.6891872

27. Wu, S.X., Banzhaf, W.: A hierarchical cooperative evolutionary algorithm. In: Pelikan, M., Branke, J. (eds.) Proceedings of 12th Genetic and Evolutionary Computation Conference (GECCO10), Portland, OR, USA, pp. 233–240 (2010)

28. Zhao, W., Niu, Q., Li, K., Irwin, G.W.: A hybrid learning method for constructing compact rule-based fuzzy models. IEEE Trans. Cybern. **43**(6), 1807–1821 (2013). https://doi.org/10.1109/TSMCB.2012.2231068

Tamper Detection and Correction of ELF Binaries by Remote Parties via Merkle Trees

Anish Sujanani[✉] and K. M. Manoj Vignesh

Independent Researcher, Bengaluru, Karnataka, India
ansujanani@gmail.com, kmmanoj1990@gmail.com

Abstract. Though the exponential growth of computational resources has led to increased software capability, it has also given rise to a wide array of security issues. The variability of on-system software is such that traditional run-time security measures by operating systems cannot provide generalized protection. This paper proposes a solution rooted in static analysis of ELF binaries that allows for integrity verification and correction, thereby defending against binary patching, padding injection, code addition and flow redirection. The solution is implemented as a software module on the client holding the executable. The verification server implemented by the provider of that executable performs a remote audit on that client using a depth-first binary merkle tree with pseudo-random parameters. The proposed protocol further details remote correction of the errors, avoiding the need for re-transmission of the entire executable and ensuring safe execution. The solution has been tested by varying parameters such as the executable size, merkle tree leaf size and corruption percentage. The time taken for the entire protocol and the time taken for tree construction on the client has been studied.

Keywords: Reverse engineering · System security · Integrity verification

1 Introduction

The rise in computing power, dedicated hardware, networked systems and programming paradigms has allowed for modern day software to reach levels of complexity that was previously unheard of. However, with a wider array of software and hardware components, integration and intelligent networked devices, comes increased security risk. The growth of software tampering for data collection, malicious code installation and piracy for 'extended' feature-sets has become too large a problem to be ignored. Though a multitude of signature-based and anomaly-based intrusion detection systems continue to be built and improved, there are certain vectors within core on-system software that have security vulnerabilities so specific, that developing heuristics and pattern-recognition is infeasible at scale. A solution based on integrity verification of static executables has been proposed, the preliminaries of which are explained in the following subsections.

© Springer Nature Switzerland AG 2020
N. Kar et al. (Eds.): ICCISIoT 2020, CCIS 1358, pp. 156–168, 2020.
https://doi.org/10.1007/978-3-030-66763-4_14

1.1   The ELF Binary Format

The Executable and Linkable File format [8] is among the most common representation of executable program files on Unix-like systems. This can be attributed to its compatibility across computer architecture, instruction sets and its self-contained nature. The contents of an ELF file can be analysed through two views; a linking view and an execution view. In terms of the linking view, the file primarily consists of an ELF header, section table, symbol table and the sections themselves. The ELF header provides information about underlying components such as operating system architecture, word size, kernel details and offsets to all other components of the file. The section header details memory offsets, size and flags for the sections of the program. Each section represents a chunk of opcodes and/or data for the program, such as the '.text' section which contains executable instructions, '.data' for static data defined during compilation, '.bss' for global data definitions and so on. The symbol table provides ASCII annotations for the elements within this file. In context of ELF binaries, the terms 'symbols' and 'debug-symbols' are often confused. Debug-symbols refer to mapping detailed variable and function labels from source code into the executable and needs to be specified during compilation. Though typically used for debugging during development, it is usually removed during the final build process. 'Symbols' refer to labels corresponding to internal procedure names within sections that are inserted during the compilation and assembly process. This is typically included by default, however, can be explicitly removed. Executables lacking both 'symbols' and 'debug-symbols' are known as stripped binaries, whereas those containing only internal compiler 'symbols' are known as un-stripped binaries.

When execution is invoked, the 'executable view' of the ELF file is interpreted. The in-memory view of the file consists of memory segments, each containing one or more sections from the 'linking view'. The program table of the ELF file dictates the mapping of sections to segments, segment permissions and paging details. The linker and loader also include null-byte padding between the segments to provide adequate space between them and to align the start addresses of these blocks depending on the system architecture. Also contained is a relocation table which is responsible for mapping dynamically linked symbols and procedures into run-time memory.

1.2   Attack Surface

Executable files such as ELF binaries are exposed to a wide attack surface that can broadly be classified into two categories; static analysis and dynamic analysis. Dynamic analysis often refers to tampering with dependencies, network communications, inter-process communications or the binary itself during run-time. Common methods include DLL-injection, stack overflows, heap overflows, inter-process memory corruption and network packet tampering. All of these take place while the process is running and can alter the state of the process in memory. State changes can lead to change of values in memory, overwriting of intended procedures, corruption of sibling processes among many other adverse effects [2].

Static analysis, commonly referred to as 'binary patching' involves analysing the ELF format, parsing out the headers and sections and tampering with the opcodes themselves. These methods are commonly used to bypass procedures in software and cause unintended execution flow. A bad-actor may alter opcodes to permanently change the variable values before they are loaded into memory or may redirect execution by changing the target of branch instructions such as 'jmp', 'jne', 'jge' and so on. While this poses a substantial risk to the integrity of the executable and the process it aims to accomplish, a bad actor may be able to add new functionality into the executable altogether. New functionality may be added to the software by injecting opcodes into a particular section. However, this is unreliable as the offset of all sections/segments located after the point of injection will have to be recalculated and patched throughout the file. A more common approach of adding new functionality is accomplished by overwriting the null-bytes present in the padding between segments. Due to the process of overwriting rather than appending, the size and offset of all sections/segments stays the same [4]. Combining this with the prior approach of redirecting execution, a bad-actor may achieve arbitrary code execution, remote code execution and further pivoting into the underlying system. This seemingly unchanged file may be distributed by the original provider or by a third-party, causing potentially large scale security impact.

1.3 Integrity Verification

Integrity of data is typically audited by taking a hash of the data and comparing the output (digest) to a digest taken at an earlier time when the data was known to be good. Hashing algorithms such as SHA-256, belonging to the SHA-2 algorithm family, are one-way functions that map variably-sized inputs to a unique and highly volatile fixed-size output that serves as a representation of integrity. Though the mismatch of hashes may indicate that the data was changed, it does not indicate the extent or region of change. A merkle tree [7], shown in Fig. 1 is a tree-based data structure that not only proves integrity of data but is also able to localize the areas that have been modified. This tree can be constructed as a n-ary tree, however, typically is constructed with two children per node, i.e. a binary tree. The data in question is split into chunks of typically equal sizes. Each chunk of data is put through a hashing algorithm and the digest value forms the value of the leaves. Assuming a binary implementation, pairs of nodes are taken and their values (hash digests) are appended as string values. If an odd number of leaves were present, a final 'balancing' node is added containing a null value or has the value of its sibling node. These appended hash-strings are then put through another round of hashing, providing the hash of leaf hashes, which forms the second-to-bottom layer of the tree. This process of concatenating pairs of node hashes, balancing odd nodes and hashing the strings to form a new level is repeated until the root of the tree is formed. This tree is now stored and can be used for verification of integrity in the future by re-building the tree in that moment and comparing it to the stored structure. The hash algorithm property of 'diffusion' states that even an incremental change in a value will cause substantial difference in its hash. This property applies to every node of this tree - if the newly constructed tree's root differs from the stored tree's root, it implies that at least one of the newly constructed tree's children have changed. If only the root's right child is different from what was recorded earlier, we can derive that the left sub-tree from the root has maintained integrity and the right sub-tree has been tampered with. The right sub-tree can then be traversed to arrive at the leaf nodes that have been changed, thereby localizing the point of corruption causing the original data to lose integrity.

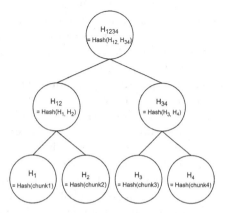

Fig. 1. General merkle tree structure

2 Prior Work

Binary tampering has been attempted by including check-sums of blocks of bytes in the executable itself, recalculating these values and comparing to the stored values during run-time. During execution, 'checker' procedures are invoked to iterate process space and recalculate check-sums of the memory map [1]. Recursive Neural network models have been proposed that generalize and compare features of legitimate software against patched software and have been tested with open source ELF binaries [3]. Attempts at making programs tamper-tolerant have been made by duplicating and re-arranging blocks of instructions within the executable. During execution, a control flow graph (CFG) is generated and random instances of duplicate blocks are selected for execution. Integrity is verified by comparing all instances of blocks for parity [5]. A multi-stage approach for detection of binary tampering has been proposed. The first stage involved augmenting the ELF file header with RSA-3072 generated keys and the SHA family of hashing algorithms. The second stage involved performance profiling during run-time. Deviations from operating system paging performance was used to signify loss of integrity of execution flow [6]. Prediction of run-time buffer overflow attacks has been attempted through analyzing vulnerable programming constructs and retrieving static attributes of localized source code to form templates. Further data mining into the source code based on these templates was performed to detect similar vulnerable patterns [9]. Automatic patching of software errors has been proposed through studying normal execution flow and noting deviations. Patches are generated to rectify the conditions that caused these variations. Each patch is tested and the sample that removes the deviation is applied to the executable [10]. Reactive attestation has been implemented by moving certain functionality of the executable off the client and onto the server. Client and server execution needs to reach a 'synchronization point' before control can be transferred back and forth. This approach is based on the fact that the application server is trusted and can ensure safe execution of code. If the client is unable to meet the synchronization point with certain conditions, the server can safely assume that integrity has been lost [11]. Anti-tampering measures have been introduced in the Android operating system by securely storing the hashes of cache files of a known-good application. This approach relies on the fact that once an application has been tampered with, it would produce different ART cache files whose hashes would differ from the stored samples, thereby proving compromise [12]. Software vulnerabilities have been detected through extensive control flow graph analysis, in-code feature recognition and feature embedding. Supervised and unsupervised learning models have been applied to these features including K-nearest neighbors, support vector machines, Bayesian classification, neural networks and rule mining among others [13]. Detection of publicly known security issues within the Android operating system has been proposed through heuristic matching strategies. Further, patching of these components has been implemented through complex dynamic memory modification [14].

Prior approaches have involved usage of machine learning, run-time taint analysis and modification of the ELF file itself. While they may provide adequate results in terms of detection, they rely on computationally heavy modelling, significant parsing efforts and complex graph analysis. Moreover, many of the approaches do so after the program has been loaded into memory, posing a significant risk due to the growing nature of self-replicating and polymorphic code. The proposed solution not only addresses tamper detection before execution by examining the opcodes of the file itself, but also details a protocol for correcting these errors to ensure safe execution.

3   Methodology

A client-server architecture is followed as described in the sections below. The verification server is implemented by the software provider and is contacted by the client system module. The module may be implemented within the client's operating system itself as a kernel module or as stand-alone software with elevated privileges. The attack vectors in scope include changes to existing instructions (binary patching) and insertion of new instructions by overwriting segment padding. An overview of the protocol is provided in Fig. 2.

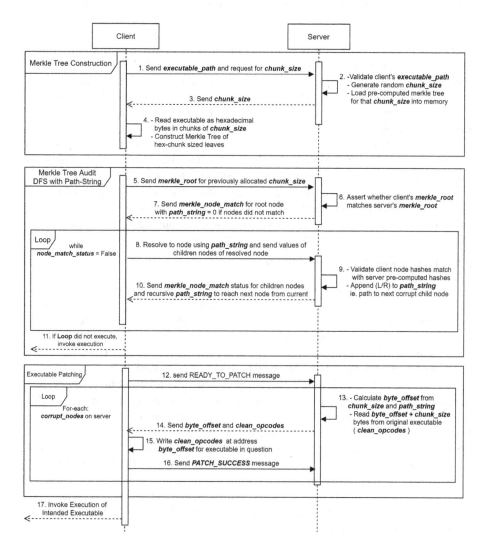

Fig. 2. Protocol overview for tamper detection and correction via merkle tree

3.1   Construction of the Merkle Tree

The proposed solution acts as an intermediate party between the host system and verification server by proving integrity of the executable and patching corrupted opcodes, if any. Upon invocation of an executable, the module forms a reliable connection over TCP sockets with the verification server. The module sends the first message containing the path to the executable and a request for a 'chunk size' which will later be used to build the merkle tree. The verification server contains a list of clients and the executable paths they can invoke that require verification and patching.

After verifying that the executable in question is registered for the audit process, the server selects a psuedo-random integer chunk size from the range [200..400]. This chunk size denotes the size of each leaf that the tree is to be built from. The server contains pre-computed trees for all combinations of known-good executables and chunk sizes - thereby serving as a source of truth. The client proceeds to read the hexadecimal notation of the executable's object code in increments of the newly received chunk size. A merkle tree is constructed from these chunks, now acting as leaves of the tree using SHA-256 as the hashing algorithm and the ASCII representation of the digest. Hashes from the second-lowest level upwards are formed by concatenating the ASCII hashes of children nodes and setting the node's value to the SHA-256 digest of that string. By virtue of binary merkle trees, each level needs to have an even number of nodes. A level containing an odd number of nodes is appended with a node containing a NULL value.

3.2   Detection of Corrupt Nodes

The module sends the root of the newly constructed merkle tree and the chunk size received previously to the verification server. The server is context-aware and verifies the client merkle root with its own merkle root for the tree of that chunk size. Equality of the roots implies that integrity of the executable has been maintained. The server sends back a message indicating that the audit was successful and that the client can continue execution. The module then passes control to the underlying operating system which loads the program into memory. However, if the roots did not match, then the virtue of the merkle tree proves that one or more client leaf nodes (chunks of instructions/opcodes) have been corrupted, thereby changing hashes across one or more sub-trees, up to the root hash. The client tree will need to be pruned to detect corrupt leaves. This is done by sending one node at a time over the TCP socket through a depth-first search algorithm and a server-controlled 'path-string' to maintain state during communication. This path-string represents the path that the client should traverse through its own tree before sending the children of the resulting node for audit and is constructed from the grammar shown in Eq. 1

$$S \rightarrow 0\alpha \tag{1a}$$
$$\alpha \rightarrow L \mid R \mid \alpha \mid \epsilon \tag{1b}$$

where 0 references the root, 'L' references the left child of the current node and 'R' references the right child of the current node. This is illustrated in Fig. 1 where a path string of '0R' would map to node H_{34}, '0LR' would map to node H_2 and so on. Each corrupt node's path-string is maintained on the server, as shown in Algorithm 1 and is used later for path-traversal and byte offset calculation during patching.

Algorithm 1: Server: Merkle Tree Verification with Path-String

---

Result: List of corrupt tree nodes
corrupt_nodes_path_strings = array();
if *client_merkle_root == server_merkle_root* **then**
   | **return** 'AUDIT_SUCCESS - Proceed to execution';
   | close_socket();
else
   | path_string = '0';
   | client_hashes = socket_request_children_for_path(path_string);
   | recursive_dfs(*path_string, client_hashes*)
end
Subroutine recursive_dfs(*path_string, client_hashes*)
   | ptr = server_merkle_root;
   | **for** *d in path_string* **do**
   | | **if** *d == 'L'* **then**
   | | | ptr = ptr.left_child;
   | | **else if** *d == 'R'* **then**
   | | | ptr = ptr.right_child;
   | **end**
   | **if** *ptr.children == NULL* **then**
   | | corrupt_nodes_path_strings.append(path_string);
   | | **return**;
   | **if** *ptr.left_child != client_hashes.left_child_hash* **then**
   | | t_path_string = path_string + 'L';
   | | t_client_hashes = socket_request_children_for_path(t_path_string);
   | | recursive_dfs(*t_path_string, t_client_hashes*);
   | **if** *ptr.right_child != client_hashes.right_child_hash* **then**
   | | t_path_string = path_string + 'R';
   | | t_client_hashes = socket_request_children_for_path(t_path_string);
   | | recursive_dfs(*t_path_string, t_client_hashes*);

3.3 Correction of Corrupt Nodes

After performing the recursive depth-first validation of the client tree, the verification server forms a list of path-strings. Each path string resolves to a node in the tree whose hash does not match with that of the server tree, implying opcode corruption. These opcodes are extracted from copies of the clean executable present on the verification server and are sent over the network to the client module, as shown in Algorithm 2. The offset of these instructions in the executable are efficiently calculated through the path-string itself. The server derives an 'index' value by encoding the path-string into a binary number and taking its integer representation. This index is multiplied by the chunk size resulting in the offset of the opcodes that are to be patched. For example, a path-string of '0LR' would map to binary 001, and further to integer 1. Given a chunk size of 200, the server performs $chunk\_size * index$, i.e. $200 * 1$, reaching the offset of 200 bytes and correctly locating the instructions corresponding to the second leaf of the tree. This calculation is performed for each path-string and messages are sent back to the client containing byte-offsets and clean opcodes. The module parses this message, opens the executable for writing and overwrites content starting at the byte-offset with the newly received opcodes, thereby correcting corrupt chunks. After all corrupt chunks have been patched, the server sends a message indicating that patching is complete and the module allows execution to begin.

Algorithm 2: Server: Offset Computation and Patching

Result: Child node transfer of the resulting node by path-string traversal

if *length(corrupt_nodes) > 0* **then**

    for *i in corrupt_nodes_path_strings* **do**

        i_encoded = i.replace("L", 0);

        i_encoded = i.replace("R", 1);

        index = binary_to_integer_base10(i_encoded);

        byte_offset = chunk_size * index;

        f = open(executable_name', O_RDONLY);

        f.seek(byte_offset);

        clean_opcodes = f.read(chunk_size);

        socket_send_patch_message(start_offset, clean_opcodes);

        socket_wait_for_client_patch_ack();

    end

    socket_send_patch_proc_complete();

---

4   Results and Analysis

Testing was carried out by iterating the protocol a minimum of three times for each combination of parameters - executable size, chunk size and corrupted nodes. Each executable was subjected to varying levels of tampering including combinations of binary patching, instruction addition through padding injection and code flow redirection by changing branch targets. Variation in corruption percentage (CP), average time taken by client to construct the tree and average time taken for entire protocol was studied. The number of corrupted nodes was varied to demonstrate corruption percentages ranging from 2% to 20%, shown in Table 1. Variation in average time taken for client tree construction and average time for the entire protocol execution with executable size, chunk size and corruption percentage is studied in Fig. 3. The client ran on an Intel i5-8250U CPU and a total 8 GB of memory. The server was an AWS EC2 instance in a different region running an Intel Xeon E5-2676 CPU and a total 16 GB of memory.

Despite an exponential increase in executable size, client construction time shows a linear trend, shown in Fig. 3a. Time taken for the entire protocol shows the same trend, increasing linearly with exponential increase in executable size, with a lower gradient, shown in Fig. 3b. The scale of chunk size is significantly inversely proportional to the time taken on the client for tree construction, as shown in Fig. 3c and has little effect on the time of execution of the entire protocol, shown in Fig. 3d. Figure 3e shows that as corruption percentage increases, time taken for the entire protocol increases. Figure 4 shows the programmatic output containing the difference of two trees.

Table 1. Experimental results

exec_size (byte)	chunk_size (byte)	CP	Time: client (average: second)	Time: protocol (average: second)
8168	200	4.89	0.001196225	0.482743979
		9.79	0.001172622	0.543742736
		19.58	0.001207431	0.93909359
	300	7.34	0.000979424	0.342224439
		11.01	0.001267672	0.438973983
		18.36	0.001696348	0.850053072
	400	4.89	0.00127395	0.42854921
		9.79	0.000831525	0.513786554
		19.58	0.001007716	0.581204017
16240	200	4.92	0.007605632	0.768957059
		9.85	0.006165107	1.16596969
		19.70	0.00898687	2.1384751
	300	5.54	0.005413135	0.6539886
		9.23	0.00555706	0.938573758
		19.47	0.003680627	1.51160423
	400	4.92	0.004830758	0.570374966
		9.85	0.004602114	0.678690592
		19.70	0.005227566	1.273030837
32256	200	2.48	0.012580713	0.912698666
		4.96	0.009965897	1.359845956
		10.54	0.013297876	2.209083319
	300	5.58	0.007583459	0.917192777
		10.23	0.008696953	2.107287963
		15.81	0.009582361	2.72522521
	400	4.96	0.008941491	0.722190221
		9.92	0.008925438	1.147878647
		19.84	0.006297429	1.985893647
64648	200	1.23	0.023341894	1.292353471
		2.47	0.01700743	1.196692387
		5.25	0.02303497	2.277854602
	300	2.78	0.01626118	2.438886563
		4.17	0.013587316	1.363871177
		7.88	0.013075193	2.464957635
	400	2.47	0.014056762	0.766752958
		5.56	0.010951757	1.437512159
		10.51	0.010887384	2.718632936

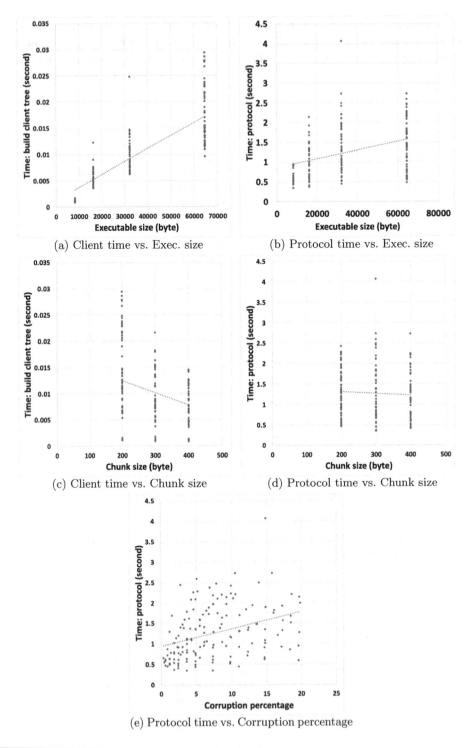

(a) Client time vs. Exec. size

(b) Protocol time vs. Exec. size

(c) Client time vs. Chunk size

(d) Protocol time vs. Chunk size

(e) Protocol time vs. Corruption percentage

Fig. 3. Graphical results

A small chunk size will lead to a higher degree of computation on the client, as more leaves will have to be hashed to create the merkle tree. Similarly, a higher corruption percentage will increase computation time of the entire protocol as the tree will have to be pruned deeper and more nodes will need to be corrected. The linear increase in client construction time and protocol time with the exponential increase in executable size is statistically significant compared to prior approaches taken towards this problem statement. A real-world implementation may choose to rely on large chunk sizes, regardless of executable size and degree of corruption if network bandwidth can be afforded.

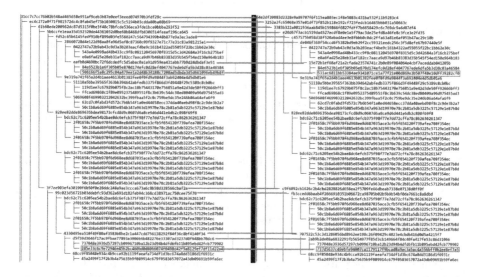

Fig. 4. Programmatic output showing difference in trees

5   Conclusion

Each strain of software is specific enough in its executable form for completely custom attack vectors to be used against it. This does not allow for generalization for detection systems as we know it. The bypass of certain in-code procedures, modification of instructions, addition of programming directives and redirection of execution flow are critical problems that pose risk to not only the provider, but also to the consumer's system and data safety. The proposed solution is novel in its virtue of being able to defend against all of the above vectors and correct errors in distributed software by means of static binary analysis. This approach provides an additional measure of security as it does not rely on loading the process into memory for complex analysis. The proposed client-server model for integrity verification and correction is comparatively more feasible than dynamic protection and can be generalized to a higher degree for the majority of software providers and system architectures.

References

1. Banescu, S., Ahmadvand, M., Pretschner, A., Shield, R., Hamilton, C.: Detecting patching of executables without system calls. In: Proceedings of the Seventh ACM on Conference on Data and Application Security and Privacy. CODASPY 2017, pp. 185–196. Association for Computing Machinery, New York (2017). https://doi.org/10.1145/3029806.3029835

2. Brooks, T.N.: Survey of automated vulnerability detection and exploit generation techniques in cyber reasoning systems. CoRR abs/1702.06162 (2017). http://arxiv.org/abs/1702.06162

3. Feng, Q., et al.: Learning binary representation for automatic patch detection. In: 2019 16th IEEE Annual Consumer Communications Networking Conference (CCNC), pp. 1–6 (2019)

4. Hosseinzadeh, S., et al.: Diversification and obfuscation techniques for software security: a systematic literature review. Inf. Softw. Technol. (2018). https://doi.org/10.1016/j.infsof.2018.07.007

5. Jakubowski, M., Saw, C., Venkatesan, R.: Tamper-tolerant software: modeling and implementation, pp. 125–139 (2009). https://doi.org/10.1007/978-3-642-04846-3_9

6. Liu, X.H., Ruan, K.l., Yang, C.: A hybrid multi-level mechanism for application integrity checking. DEStech Trans. Comput. Sci. Eng. (2017). https://doi.org/10.12783/dtcse/cnsce2017/8891

7. Merkle, R.C.: A digital signature based on a conventional encryption function. In: Pomerance, C. (ed.) Advances in Cryptology – CRYPTO 1987, pp. 369–378. Springer, Heidelberg (1988). https://doi.org/10.1007/3-540-48184-2_32

8. Matz, M., Jan Hubicka, A.J.: System V application binary interface. AMD64 architecture processor supplement. https://www.uclibc.org/docs/psABI-x86_64.pdf

9. Padmanabhuni, B.M., Tan, H.B.K.: Buffer overflow vulnerability prediction from x86 executables using static analysis and machine learning. In: 2015 IEEE 39th Annual Computer Software and Applications Conference, vol. 2, pp. 450–459 (2015)

10. Perkins, J.H., et al.: Automatically patching errors in deployed software. In: Proceedings of the ACM SIGOPS 22nd Symposium on Operating Systems Principles. SOSP 2009, pp. 87–102. Association for Computing Machinery, New York (2009). https://doi.org/10.1145/1629575.1629585

11. Viticchié, A., et al.: Reactive attestation: automatic detection and reaction to software tampering attacks (2016). https://doi.org/10.1145/2995306.2995315

12. Wan, J., Zulkernine, M., Eisen, P., Liem, C.: Defending application cache integrity of android runtime. In: Liu, J.K., Samarati, P. (eds.) ISPEC 2017. LNCS, vol. 10701, pp. 727–746. Springer, Cham (2017). https://doi.org/10.1007/978-3-319-72359-4_45

13. Xue, H., Sun, S., Venkataramani, G., Lan, T.: Machine learning-based analysis of program binaries: a comprehensive study. IEEE Access 7, 65889–65912 (2019)

14. Zhang, X., Zhang, Y., Li, J., Hu, Y., Li, H., Gu, D.: Embroidery: patching vulnerable binary code of fragmentized android devices. In: 2017 IEEE International Conference on Software Maintenance and Evolution (ICSME), pp. 47–57 (2017)

Device Independent Key Generation Using Decoy State

Supriyo Banerjee[1]($\boxtimes$) ⓘ, Biswajit Maiti[2] ⓘ, and Banani Saha[3] ⓘ

[1] Department of Computer Science and Engineering, Kalyani Government Engineering College, Kalyani, Nadia 741235, India
supriyo.cal@gmail.com
[2] Government Degree College, Kharagpur II, India
bmkgec@gmail.com
[3] Department of Computer Science and Engineering, University of Calcutta, Kolkata, India
bsaha_29@yahoo.com

Abstract. It is a common belief that the unavailability of perfect single-photon source and detector will limit the feasibility of Quantum key distribution (QKD). A perfect device independent protocol can overcome this limitation in a long distance secure communication. This paper proposes to minimize the detector dependency at receiver's end by introducing a device independent key generation protocol. Here, impurity is embedded in the data string using a decoy source. A one way function known to both Alice and Bob is guided to determine the subsequent basis for generating the key and the impurity. Since the basis of both key as well as impurity (decoy state) is fixed by this function, it provides self checking mechanism for both the legitimate users, thereby providing better results in key generation process by some imperfect devices at the receiver's end.

Keywords: Quantum key distribution protocol · Decoy state · Qutrit · Key extraction · Eavesdropping · Secrecy capacity · Mutual information gain

1 Introduction

Quantum key distribution (QKD) provides unconditional security between two legitimate users by employing the fundamental characteristics of quantum indistinguishability. Different phase shift operations on photons during encoding procedure in QKD have the advantages of long distance optical fibers or even free space transmission. In 1984, Bennett and Bassard in their seminal paper first introduced the BB84 protocol, practical realization of QKD [1]. Since then, the physicist and computer scientist conceived different QKD protocols by exploiting the quantum properties of uncertainty and entanglement [2–4]. Using privacy amplification the legitimate users can discard the intercepted bits so that the key

© Springer Nature Switzerland AG 2020
N. Kar et al. (Eds.): ICCISIoT 2020, CCIS 1358, pp. 169–177, 2020.
https://doi.org/10.1007/978-3-030-66763-4_15

extraction process becomes much more accurate. While in 1991 Ekert's protocol achieved better security using the entangled states, any kind of interception will be easily detected as both the photons are in a correlation [5]. Within a limited transmission range practical realization of this protocol has been achieved [6–8]. Though the scientist achieved secure QKD through optical fibers where secure communication can be achieved more than 302 Km, but due to this correlation between two entangled photons, key generation rate is less than 1 Mb/sec. Moreover, the Quantum Bit error rate (QBER) is less than 20% [9]. A research group from China are working on free space QKD and the ground-to-satellite QKD implementation has already been achieved in 2016 [10]. Even networked based QKD development is in progress [11]. The higher key generation rate and sufficient error tolerance are the key issues for this progress in secure communication using QKD [12,13].

When attenuated coherent light pulse at Alice's end is used due to the limitation of developing efficient source and detector at both ends, transmission losses will occur in the optical fiber and inefficient reliable single photon source will make it vulnerable to photon number splitting (PNS) attack. Several PNS tolerable protocols with higher tolerance limit like the differential phase shift protocol (DPS) have been developed [14]. Tamaki et al. [15] provided information theoretic security proof. Unfortunately, it suffers from very low tolerance (4%) to bit error rate. In 2005, Hk Lo et al. [16] had demonstrated the practical aspects of QKD protocol using decoy state. In this paper, the comparison between the key generation rate using two decoy states (One vacuum + one decoy), one decoy state have been sighted. But the protocol suffers due to inefficient basis selection and its agreement which leads to huge data loss. As a result, key rate is much less. To further increase the key rate, combining a biased basis with the decoy state is proposed [17–19] by the scientist but still it suffers from same kind of problems. Recently, a four-intensity decoy-state BB84 QKD [20] has been proposed but the security and feasibility of this protocol have still not been implemented in reality. Due to inefficient detector in the receiver's end data losses will be much more. This practical imperfect device suffers high data loss due to correlation in conventional entangled based protocol as a result the key generation rate is much less. Besides, the conventional scheme of QKD, we have thought of a scheme using one way function at both ends for basis selection purpose. In this protocol, after an agreement on the basis of the first bit, the subsequent bases will be determined by the one way function. Also, in this protocol a self checking mechanism for both ends can be introduced. On the other hand the onetime pad procedure can minimize the coherent attack.

The paper is organized as follows. In Sect. 2, the background of the proposed methodology of QKD using decoy state has been described. The three important parameters for analyzing the proposed protocol such as Quantum bit error rate (QBER) analysis, Gain Analysis and Key Generation rate has been evaluated in Sect. 3 and the paper ends with a conclusion mentioned in Sect. 4.

2   Proposed Algorithm

In this protocol, we have used phase encoding techniques for encoding the qutrit. After encoding, the data will be sent through free space or optical fiber communication which is considered to be an insecure communication channel. Three non orthogonal states from the selected basis have been employed to encode data for cryptographic key generation.

In the algorithm proposed here Alice prepares an encoding scheme using qutrit before sending it through quantum channel to Bob. Alice uses the qutrit to design a set of basis vectors in 3H Hilbert space and $|1\rangle$, $|2\rangle$, $|3\rangle$ which are taken as the prime quantum states of a qutrit. The complete set of four unbiased basis vectors can be encoded in the phase space as follows [21]

$$|u\rangle = |1\rangle$$
$$|v\rangle = |2\rangle$$
$$|w\rangle = |3\rangle$$

Or

$$|u\rangle = \frac{1}{\sqrt{3}}(|1\rangle + |2\rangle + |3\rangle)$$
$$|v\rangle = \frac{1}{\sqrt{3}}(|1\rangle + e^{\frac{2\pi i}{f(n)}}|2\rangle + e^{-\frac{2\pi i}{f(n)}}|3\rangle)$$
$$|w\rangle = \frac{1}{\sqrt{3}}(|1\rangle + e^{-\frac{2\pi i}{f(n)}}|2\rangle + e^{\frac{2\pi i}{f(n)}}|3\rangle)$$

Or

$$|u\rangle = \frac{1}{\sqrt{3}}(e^{\frac{2\pi i}{f(n)}}|1\rangle + |2\rangle + |3\rangle)$$
$$|v\rangle = \frac{1}{\sqrt{3}}(|1\rangle + e^{\frac{2\pi i}{f(n)}}|2\rangle + |3\rangle)$$
$$|w\rangle = \frac{1}{\sqrt{3}}(|1\rangle + |2\rangle + e^{\frac{2\pi i}{f(n)}}|3\rangle)$$

Or

$$|u\rangle = \frac{1}{\sqrt{3}}(e^{-\frac{2\pi i}{f(n)}}|1\rangle + |2\rangle + |3\rangle)$$
$$|v\rangle = \frac{1}{\sqrt{3}}(|1\rangle + e^{-\frac{2\pi i}{f(n)}}|2\rangle + |3\rangle)$$
$$|w\rangle = \frac{1}{\sqrt{3}}(|1\rangle + |2\rangle + e^{-\frac{2\pi i}{f(n)}}|3\rangle)$$

where, $0 \leq \frac{2\pi}{f(n)} \leq \frac{2\pi}{3}$ gives the pure states. Alice randomly chooses one basis out of these four mutually unbiased bases.

In this process, Alice using these three non orthogonal states prepares a qutrit for encoded data string is

$$|\psi\rangle = \sin(\phi)\cos(\gamma)|u\rangle + e^{\phi_{ij}}\sin(\phi)\sin(\gamma)|v\rangle + e^{\phi_{ik}}\cos(\phi)|w\rangle$$

where ϕ_{ij} and ϕ_{ik} are the relative phases between the qutrit states, ϕ, γ provides the relative orientation of the polarized states and the cipher data will be the mixed quantum states of $|u\rangle, |v\rangle$ and $|w\rangle$ prepared in randomly chosen bases.

The encoded data string is prepared by Alice and sent to Bob through an insecure quantum channel. The onetime pad encoding is applied, i.e., changing the length of the key and impurity in data string in successive communications will be different. For example, if we take data string of length $N = n + l$ where n as the number of $|u\rangle$ in the main data string and l as the number of $|v\rangle$ in impurity. In every successive communication the number n, l will go on changing depending on the agreed upon count of $|v\rangle$. Since the string length is changing every time where the key is located, it is difficult for a person who is unaware of the change to determine it, thereby, providing added security. In this scheme we are proposing a one time pad scheme in which the number of impurities as well as data will change in every session. As a result of this any kind of Eavesdropping on it will be much more difficult to segregate the actual data from impure one.

To initiate the protocol, the data string $|u\rangle$ will be generated by signal source S and $|v\rangle$, the impurity by decoy source S'. In this scheme the added advantage will be indistinguishable for data and impurity by a complete unaware person(Eve). On Eve's side the total number of photon will be the only available information. In this proposed method, to achieve better security, the same number or little less for both the data and impure state has been used. Alice never shares the bases of the photons, which provides added advantages over existing protocols of those share bases [22,23].

Upon agreement, Alice prepares the subsequent basis for both data and impurity for secure communications using a one way function known only to them. Thus, Bob can easily segregate the data string from impurity within a predefined sequence, whereas Eve has to guess in order to choose the correct basis. So, Eve's probability of getting both data as well as impurity in correct basis will surely be less. At this point, Bob can extract key from the entire string.

Since there are both the impurity and data string in a correlation which in known only by the legitimate sender Alice and receiver Bob, it is provided with a self-checking mechanism that provides the QBER rate which will be much less at the Bob's end. The loss due to imperfect device will be much less. The erroneous data can easily be detected and corrected by the receiver. As a result, this protocol will leads to a device independent secure communication protocol.

An important parameter yield, $Y_N = 1 - channel\ loss$, needs to be verified before every session begins. If the channel loss is within the threshold limit then the protocol will continue otherwise it will abort. The probability p_N of generation of multi-photon including decoy state and signal state due to imperfection of the source must be less than the yield Y_N i.e.

$$Y_N \rangle \ p_N$$

Alice prepares n, the number of photon with a probability $p_n(\mu) = \frac{e^{-\mu}\mu^n}{n!}$ with $\mu < 1$ for signal state and $\mu \geq 1$ for decoy state. $Y_S = \sum_n p_n(\mu)y_n$ and $Y_{S'} = \sum_n p_n(\mu')y_l$ will be the yield of the signal source and decoy source measured by Bob at the receiver's end respectively.

On the receiving side Bob uses the imperfect photon detector devices. The two following condition can arise due to non availability of perfect photon detector:

In case of ideal situation where no eavesdropping occurs (where n = 0) the corresponding yield will be Y_0 which is due to some background rate including dark count, stray light timing pulses.

In other cases (where $n \geq 1$) the corresponding yield Y_n for detection of signal photon from sources η_n with the background rate Y_0 will be [21]

$$Y_n = Y_0 + \eta_n - Y_0\eta_n$$
$$\simeq Y_0 + \eta_n$$

3 Analysis of Proposed Protocol

In this protocol, the first communication is a dummy set with the qutrit states will be in the first basis where the relative phase between the states is zero. If the discussion about the impurity count is settled, the basis set of the other two states, $|u\rangle$ and $|v\rangle$ are set one after the other using the one-way function taking feedback from the impurity count of the first communication. In the subsequent communications, the same is repeated until Alice and Bob reach an agreement on the impurity count. Since the basis of $|u\rangle$ and $|v\rangle$ has been set beforehand, after few runs they are sure to get it and then further communication is not needed. Now, Alice and Bob are able to generate the same key for encoding and decoding of the message.

The gain analysis, quantum bit error rate analysis and key generation rate are the three important parameters for analyzing the protocol. Using the self checking mechanics we can improve these three parameters as a result of which the performance of the overall system will improve.

(a) Gain Analysis: The gain can be defined as the product of the photon sent by Alice and the conditional probability of detection of that photon at Bob's end. The gain [24] of the nth photon will be

$$Q_n = Y_n p_n(\mu) = Y_n \frac{e^{-\mu}\mu^n}{n!}$$

In our proposed algorithm, the bases are fixed by one way function which is available to both the legitimate users Alice and Bob. Hence, the error rate other than transmission loss during the key extraction process from the received string will be minimized. In this proposed protocol any bit loss or any kind of reconciliation from the received yield is not required.

In this protocol, the channel loss will be much less as the generated strings are always guided by the one way function. So the error correction will be much higher than existing protocol. Hence, the yield will be

$$Y_n \rightarrow 1$$

Hence, the gain of our proposed protocol will be

$$Q_n \rightarrow \frac{e^{-\mu}\mu^n}{n!}$$

So from this we can conclude that besides the environmental loss, the rate at which Alice will prepare both data and decoy state will be received at the receiver's end.

(b) QBER Analysis: In the quantum key distribution, a cryptographic key is transmitted after proper encoding through insecure communication channel where a series of photons has been transmitted. At the receiver end, after measuring in selected basis, only those data which have compatible basis with the ancila preparation of the photon are considered for the key. Besides the environmental noises, Eve introduces errors due to choice of wrong basis. The percentage of error rate within the received key is known as Quantum bit Error rate (QBER) and is an important factor in determining the efficiency of the protocol.

The Quantum Bit Error rate (QBER) of the photon states is defined as [24]

$$e_n = \frac{e_0 Y_0 + e_{detector}\eta_n}{Y_n}$$

where $e_{detector}$ signifies the erroneous detection by Bob at the receiving end. The self checking mechanism fixed the bases for both the sender and receiver's end. The bases are predefined as a result the detector error, $e_{detector} \rightarrow 0$. As the Background rate is the physical phenomenon hence it is totally unpredictable and depends on the channel properties, the error and yield remain constant.

Hence we can say $e_n \propto \frac{e_{detector}\eta_n}{Y_n}$. We can conclude that $e_n \propto \frac{e_{detector}}{\frac{Y_n}{\eta_n}}$.

In our protocol, the detection of signal photon from sources η_n will be maximized hence $\frac{Y_n}{\eta_n}$ or $\frac{1}{\frac{Y_0}{\eta_n}+1} \rightarrow \epsilon$ where ϵ will be much less than 1. Both $e_{detector}$ and $\frac{Y_n}{\eta_n}$ will be much less. Hence, we can conclude that $e_n \rightarrow 0$.

(c) Analysis of Key Generation Rate: The concept of secret key generation rate for a system of two legitimate users Alice and Bob sharing common information is developed in [25]. In the existing QKD protocols at the receiving end, due to mismatch and privacy amplification, some data will be discarded as a result the resultant key will be much shortened but in our proposed method as basis are predefined, the privacy amplification is not required as a result the key will be much longer than previous existing schemes. Hence the key generation rate will be higher than others.

In the paper [24] Gottesman et al. have analysed the key generation rate for BB84 Protocol

$$R \geq q\{-Q_\mu f(E_\mu)H_2(E_\mu) + Q_1[1 - H_2(e_1)]\}$$

Where q, the probabilistic factor for detecting the correct value in Bob's End, E_μ, is the overall quantum bit error rate, H_1 and H_2, is binary entropy function, depends on the protocol design. In case of standard and efficient BB84 $q = \frac{1}{2}$ and $q = 1$ respectively. In the later case no bases mismatch occurs hence $q \to 1$.

In our proposed algorithm as the bases are bound by the one way function thus the later case will also be applicable for our case i.e, $q \to 1$.

$$E_n Q_n = \sum_{n=0}^{\infty} E_n Y_n p_n(\mu) = \sum_{n=0}^{\infty} E_n Y_n \frac{e^{-\mu}\mu^n}{n!} = e_0 Y_0 + e_{detector}(1 - e^{-n\mu})$$

In this protocol, the bases are predefined hence the error at the receiver's end, $e_{detector} \to 0$ and $e_0 Y_0$ remains constant. Hence the overall quantum bit error rate will be $E_\mu < 1$.

As the bases are fixed for our proposed method, the error rate of the single photon state will be $e_1 \to 0$. Hence $Q_1[1 - H_2(e_1)] \to Q_1$. It shows that we will get the entire gain for the single state photon as a result no loss other than channel loss will occur. Overall quantum bit error rate will be $E_\mu \to 0$ then $H_2(E_\mu) \to 0$.

Then overall key generation rate will be $R \geq \{-f(E_\mu) + Q_1\}$.

4   Conclusion

In the proposed protocol, limitation of imperfect device at the sender and receiver's end will be minimized. Existing standard QKD protocols have suffered huge data loss due to this physical limitation as a result device independence can be achieved to improve the overall system performance. The general principle of device independent QKD is developed here. This protocol can have widespread applications such as open-air QKD (from Ground to Ground and Ground to satellite both) or QKD with different photon sources [26]. One can overcome the data loss due to theses imperfect devices and can achieve almost all the benefits of our method with only one or two decoy states.

On the other hand, the key generation rate will be much higher as some of the data required in previous protocol probabilistic error for correct data recognizing will be much less at Bob's end. In case of BB84 protocol the probabilistic factor for detecting the correct data at Bob's end is $q = \frac{1}{2}$ but using this self checking mechanism results in greater accuracy. Hence, $q \to 1$. This will make a significant improvement in the key generation rate. In this proposed mechanism, the privacy amplification is required as both legitimate users are guided by one way function. The data required for testing the privacy will not be required. Hence, the key generation rate will increase.

The proposed protocol also provides better security in case of man-in-the-middle attack. Previous Quantum key distribution based protocols deal with the presence of Eve in case of man-in-the-middle attack through public discussion between Alice and Bob, two legitimate users. But in this case, self checking mechanism can reveal the presence of Eve before the public discussion made by the two legitimate users. This will provide added security.

References

1. Bennett, C.H., Bassard, G.: Proceedings of IEEE International Conference on Computers, Systems and Signal Processing, Bangalore, India, p. 175. IEEE, New York (1984)
2. Bennett, C.H.: Quantum cryptography using any two nonorthoganol states. Phys. Rev. Lett. **68**, 3121–3124 (1992)
3. Ekert, A.K., Rarity, J.G., Tapster, P.R., Palma, G.M.: Phys. Rev. Lett. **69**, 1293 (1992)
4. Bennett, C.H., Brassard, G., Mermin, N.D.: Quantum cryptography without Bell's theorem. Phys. Rev. Lett. **68**, 557–559 (1992)
5. Ekert, A.K.: Quantum cryptography based on Bell's theorem. Phys. Rev. Lett. **67**(6), 661 (1991)
6. Hughes, R.J., Luther, G.G., Morgan, G.L., Peterson, C.G., Simmons, C.: Quantum cryptography over underground optical fibers. In: Koblitz, N. (ed.) CRYPTO 1996. LNCS, vol. 1109, pp. 329–342. Springer, Heidelberg (1996). https://doi.org/10.1007/3-540-68697-5_25
7. Muller, A., Herzog, T., Huttner, B., Zbinden, H., Gisin, N.: Plug and play systems for quantum cryptography. Appl. Phys. Lett. **70**(7), 793–795 (1997)
8. Gisin, N., Ribordy, G., Tittle, W., Zbinden, H.: Quantum cryptography. Rev. Mod. Phys. **74**(1), 145–195 (2002)
9. Comandar, L.C., et al.: Quantum key distribution without detector vulnerabilities using optically seededlasers. Nat. Photonics **10**(5), 312–315 (2016)
10. Yin, J., et al.: Science **356**, 1140–1144 (2017)
11. Bedington, R., et al.: Progress in satellite quantum key distribution. Nature **3**, 30 (2017)
12. Wang, J., Yang, B., Liao, S., Zang, L., Shen, Q., Hu, X., et al.: Direct and full-scale experimental verifications towards ground-satellite quantum key distribution. Nat. Photonics **7**(5), 387–393 (2013)
13. Namekata, N., Fuji, G., Inoue, S., Honjoand, T., Takesue, H.: Differential phase shift quantum key distribution using single-photon detectors based on a sinusoidally gated InGaAs/InP avalanche photodiode. Appl. Phys. Lett. **91**, 011112 (2007)
14. Inoue, K., Waksand, E., Yamamoto, Y.: Differential-phase-shift quantum key distribution. Phys. Rev. Lett. **89**, 037902 (2002)
15. Tamaki, K., Koashi, M., Kato, G.: Unconditional security of coherent state based differential phase shift quantum key distribution protocol with block-wise phase randomization. arXiv preprint arXiv:1208.1995v1 (2012)

16. Ma, X.-F., Qi, B., Zhao, Y., Lo, H.-K.: Practical decoy state for quantum key distribution. Phys. Rev. A **72**, 012326 (2005)
17. Wei, Z., Wang, W., Zhang, Z., Gao, M., Ma, Z., Ma, X.: Sci. rep. **3**, 2453 (2013)
18. Jiang, H., Gao, M., Yan, B., Wang, W., Ma, Z.: Eur. Phys. J. D **70**, 78 (2016)
19. Mao, C.-C., Li, J., Zhu, J.-R., Zhang, C.-M., Wang, Q.: Quantum Inf. Process. **16**, 256 (2017)
20. Yu, Z.-W., Zhou, Y.-H., Wang, X.-B.: Phys. Rev. A **93**, 032307 (2016)
21. Bechmann-Pasquinucci, H., Peres, A.: Quantum cryptography with 3-state systems. Phys. Rev. Lett. **85**(15), 3313–3316 (2000)
22. Zhang, Y.S., Li, C.F., Guo, G.C.: Phys. Rev. A **64**, 024302 (2001)
23. Cerf, N.J.: Phys. Rev. Lett. **84**, 4497 (2000)
24. Gottesman, D., Lo, H.-K., Luetkenhaus, N., Preskill, J.: Quantum Inf. Comput. **4**, 325 (2004). Lo, H.-K., Ma, X., Chen, K.: Phys. Rev. Lett. **94**, 230504
25. Maurer, U.M.: Secret key agreement by public discussion from common information. IEEE Trans. Inf. Theory **39**(3), 733–742 (1993)
26. Variable Optical Attenuators (VOAs) at repetition rates as high as 100 GHz are commercially widely available. Those attenuators can be directly applied to fiber-optics based QKD systems

A Novel Cryptographic Approach to Implement Confidentiality Using Point Reflection Property

Tamar Das[1]($\boxtimes$) and Nirmalya Kar[2]

[1] Tripura Institute of Technology, Narsingarh, India
tamardasnit@gmail.com
[2] National Institute of Technology Agartala, Jirania, India
nirmalya@ieee.org

Abstract. Data Privacy is a prime concern in 21st century. To maintain secrecy of data, many cryptographic algorithms are available. Cryptography is the science or study of the techniques of secret writing, esp. code and also figures frameworks, techniques, and so forth. Cryptography is required so content can be kept secret. Here in our proposed work we have shown a simple point reflection based cryptographic technique for security of data. The user encoded the data using point reflection technique and the receiver can decode the data by applying the process in reverse direction. The encrypted message generated using the mechanism proposed here is quite sturdy and it becomes more difficult for a person to retrieve or predict the original message from the encrypted message. We used PRNG technique by which we can get the random number and also use the LFSR technique for robustness of this technique. Experimental result shows that our method gives a high security and the accuracy during the encoding and decoding process. We narrated the algorithms and explicit formulas to demonstrate that our reflection process support high practical security in cryptographic applications.

Keywords: PRNG · LFSR · Point reflection · Encryption · Cryptography

1 Introduction

Cryptography is the pair of process and study of the techniques used to correspond and/or store information or data privately and securely, without being intercepted by third parties. Data sharing process mainly depend on security, efficiency, and how much flexibility gets from the system when the data is to be shared with the other person. But in today's scenario various cryptanalysis techniques are available by which different attackes can be mounted in the system easily. In cryptography method, the cipher may be generated through substitution and/or transposition techniques. A substitution cipher is a method of encoding technique by which units of plaintext are replaced with cipher text,

© Springer Nature Switzerland AG 2020
N. Kar et al. (Eds.): ICCISIoT 2020, CCIS 1358, pp. 178–187, 2020.
https://doi.org/10.1007/978-3-030-66763-4_16

according to a fixed scheme; the "units" also may be single letters, pairs of letters, triplets of letters, mixtures of the above, and so forth. The receiver deciphers the text by performing the inverse substitution process [1]. Substitution cryptosystems divided into two categories. Mono-alphabetic substitution involves replacing each letter in the message with another letter of the alphabet. Poly-alphabetic substitution includes utilizing a progression of mono-alphabetic ciphers that are periodically reused. Homophonic substitution makes it possible to have each letter of the plaintext message correlate to a desirable group of other characters. Polygraphic substitution includes reinstatement a class of characters in the message with another class of characters [2,10]. Transposition cipher is a method of encryption by which the positions controlled by units of plaintext (which are generally characters or class of characters) are changed according to a regular system, so that the cipher text build a permutation of the plaintext message. That is, the order of the units is changed. Ceaser cipher is the example of substitution cipher. It is the simplest and basic known technique. Here an attacker knows or guesses that some sort of simple substitution cipher has been used. In this case attacker uses frequency analysis or pattern words technique. Another thing is that it (ceaser cipher) uses limited number of possible shifts (26 in English) [3].

In 2010 author Jayanta Kumar Pal and author J. K. Mandal proposed a substitution technique "A Novel Block Cipher Technique Using Binary Field Arithmetic Based Substitution (BCTBFABS)" [5]. This is a binary field arithmetic procedure and it consist of five stages. The lengths of input and output block for 4 stages are identical. The last stage length is not fixed and totally different from input. In this case, different operation is performed for encryption and also for decryption also. The large number of binary operation is performed and also the processes of this technique are so lengthy [7,8].

In this novel work, we are proposing a Substitution cipher technique, point reflection based Cryptography method. It is totally a new approach. This work contributes such a motive to improve the overall security of various systems which are based on cryptography system. It is basically an encoded technique where input message is encoded and gives different kinds of text which is totally unrelated with the original text. Here we take the first character of the input text and then generate the random number for security purpose and using these random numbers and also the theta value we able to encoded the input data. In this case, the point is reflected with an imaginary line and then in that line one angel is created. We assume that the angle is theta. Using this angle value, we take the image point from the reflection point and got the encrypted text message. Here we also are using the PRNG technique by which we can get the random number and also use the LFSR technique for robustness of this technique. Here PRNG is used for finding the y co-ordinate value and also for finding the c value that means the straight line constant value. LFSR technique is used for finding the m value that is the slop of the line value. Finally, our main objective is to increases the robustness of the security system and for doing these things our technique helps us to do this job properly [15,16].

2   Point Reflection

Reflection is the innovation in control of a wave front at an interface between two different medium so that the wave front returns into the medium from which it created. Examples of reflection are the reflection of light, sound and water waves. The law of reflection says that for specular reflection the angle at which the wave is incident on the surface equals the angle at which it is reflected. Mirrors exhibit specular reflection. In geometry, a point reflection or inversion in a point is a type of isometry of Euclidean space. An object that is invariant covered by point reflection is said to occupy point symmetry; if it is uniform into point reflection through its center, it is said to possess central symmetry or to be centrally symmetric. A reflection can be considered as flexion or "flipping" an object over the line of reflection. The original object is called the pre-image, and the reflection is called the image. A point reflection subsists when a figure is created around a single point called the center of the figure, or point of reflection. For every point in the figure, there is another point found directly opposite it on another side of the center such that the point of reflection turns the midpoint of the segment joining the point with its image. Under a point reflection process, figures do not alternative the size or shape. While any point in the coordinate plane may be applied as a point of reflection, the mostly used point is the origin point.

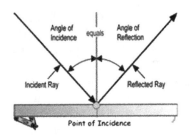

Fig. 1. Point reflection on a plane

From the reflection technique, we know that when a point is reflected in any plane the point is reflected at a certain angle. Here, we take this angle as theta. By using this angle value, we find the encoded data value. In any plane the straight-line equation is:

$$y = m \times x + c \tag{1}$$

The angle is theta where the point is meeting with the line. If two lines are perpendicular to each other then:

$$m_1 \times m_2 = -1 \tag{2}$$

In this case, $m_1 * m_2 = cos(\theta)$. Here the value of θ is 180°. m_1 is the first line slope and m_2 is the second line slope. The equation for second line is:

$$(Y - y)/(X - x) = m_2 \tag{3}$$

And we know that the midpoint formula for any line is:

$$(x_1 + X)/x = 2 \ and \ (y_1 + Y)/y = 2 \tag{4}$$

Here (x_1, y_1) is the image point of that reflected point [4, 15].

3   Background Architecture

3.1   Key Generation Using PRNG

For key generation we use pseudo-random number generator (PRNG) technique which helps us to generate new random number. It is a program written for, and used in, probability and statistics applications when big amount of random digits are needed. Greater portion of these programs generate endless strings of single-digit numbers, usually in base 10, known as the decimal system. When taking large samples of pseudo-random numbers, each of the samples 10 digits in the set 0, 1, 2, 3, 4, 5, 6, 7, 8, 9 occurs with equal frequency, even though they are not evenly distributed in the sequence [12]. Formula for generating random number is:

$$x_{n+1} = p_1 x_n + p_2 (mod \ M) \tag{5}$$

where n = 0, 1, 2 . . . and x_0 is given.

The notation mod M means that the expression on the right of the equation is divided by M, and then replaced with the remainder. Here we take a simple example by which the random number is [6, 13]. Here we take x_0 as 79, M is 100, p_1 is 263, and also p_2 is 71. Then we get:

$$x_1 = 79 \times 263 + 71 (mod \ 100) = 20848 (mod \ 100) = 48$$
$$x_2 = 48 \times 263 + 71 (mod \ 100) = 12695 (mod \ 100) = 95$$
$$x_3 = 95 \times 263 + 71 (mod \ 100) = 25056 (mod \ 100) = 56$$
$$x_4 = 56 \times 263 + 71 (mod \ 100) = 14799 (mod \ 100) = 99$$

Successively the other numbers are: 8, 75, 96, 68, 36, 39, 28, 35, 76, 59, 88, 15, 16, 79, and 48. We are using this technique for finding y co-ordinate value and also for c value which will help us to fill up the imaginary starting point pair and also help us to solve slop value. As we know that the value of x co-ordinate are coming from original text message. Overall this procedure helps us a lot for generating the random number through which we can secure the system properly and also for the attacker it will be quite impossible to decode the text message.

3.2   LFSR Technique

In enumerating, a linear-feedback shift register i.e. LFSR is a shift register whose input bit is a linear function of its preceding state [9]. The most usually used linear function of individual bits is exclusive-or. In this way, an LFSR is most often a shift register whose input bit is transferred by the XOR of some bits of the overall shift register value. The beginning value of the LFSR is called the seed value. Since the operation of the register is deterministic, the stream of values produced by the register is completely composed by its present or preceding state. However, an LFSR with a well-chosen feedback function can generate an order of bits that comes randomly and has also a very long cycle. The equation of LFSR which we are using in this proposed technique is:

$$S_{i+3} = (S_{i+1} + S_i) \, mod \, 2 \tag{6}$$

Here, we assume $S_0 = 1$, $S_1 = 0$, $S_2 = 0$. Here we use this LFSR technique for random number generation which will help us to send the encoded text in a secure way. All the values which we get from this question are all binary values. After getting all the value we convert the value into a decimal value. Then performing addition operation between the value from the text message and LFSR value. At last use these values as a slope values means the m values.

4   Proposed Algorithm

4.1   Encoding Technique

First of all, we take the first character from the input text as the x co-ordinate value then generate the PRNG value for y co-ordinate value. We know the equation of the straight line which is given in Eq. 1.

Here m_1 is the slope of the line and c is the constant value. The value of y and c are also coming from PRNG value and m_1 value is coming from LFSR value. We also know the equation of if any line that is perpendicular to another line which is mentioned as Eq. 2.

In our proposed method we take in place of -1 as a $cos(\theta)$. The value of angle must be varying depending on the value of theta. First value of theta we take as 180°. Again we know from reflection technique that if the point is reflected on the imaginary line the equation for that line is that is also given in the above Eq. 3.

By solving these two Eqs. 1 and 3, we find the value of x and y value which are actually the midpoint value. Now apply the midpoint formula for finding the image of the reflected point. Formula for any midpoint is given in previous Eq. 4. Here x_1 and y_1 are the image point. At last we get the encoded text value which is the value of x_1 and the y_1 value will be the next theta value. The pseudo code for the encryption algorithm is explained in Algorithm 1 and the block diagram of proposed encoding method is shown in the Fig. 2.

4.2   Decoding Technique

It is the inverse of encoding technique. In this technique the encoded text will be decrypted by using the decoding algorithm and the receiver gets the original text which was sent by the sender. In this case the receiver first take the encoded text then apply the reflection procedure, LFSR and PRNG technique for getting the key value. Finally we got the original text message without any interpretation. The pseudo code for the decryption algorithm is explained in Algorithm 2.

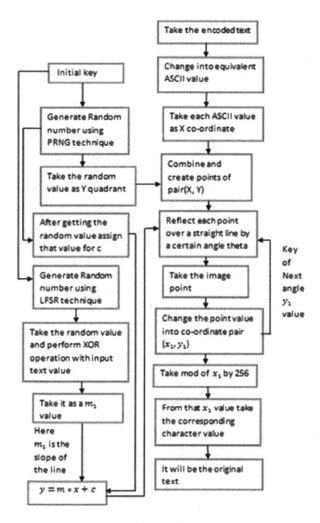

Fig. 2. Block diagram of proposed encoding method

5   Result and Discussions

Suppose two co-ordinates x and y and assume the text is 'WELCOME' then we will take the first text as W. The ASCII value of W is 88; take it as an x value. Now take the y value from key array generated by the PRNG technique. The equation for PRNG is already given in Eq. 5.

Here, $x_1 = 88$, $p_2 = 0$, $M = 2^3 1 - 1$ and $p_1 = 7^5$; The first value for y is 1479016. We know that for any straight line the equation is that is already given in Eq. 1. For the value of m_1 we take the key generator LFSR technique and find the value into the binary form and then add this value into original text value.

Algorithm 1. Pseudo code of the Encryption Algorithm:

Input = text[i]

for i = 1 to N //N is the size of the array **do**

 Convert the text char into ASCII value

 X = ASCII value of (text [i])

end for

Use PRNG technique for finding the value of Y

$Y[k] = p_1 x_n + p_2$ (mod M) // where n = 0, 1, 2, ..., $p_1 = 7^5$, $p_2 = 0$, M = 2^3, x_n given, k = 1 to n (natural number)

Use LFSR $S_{p+3} = (S_{p+1} + S_p)$ mod 2 // where p is the binary number for finding the value of m_1

$M[l] = S[j] + X[i]$ //l is the natural number 1 to n & also j = 1 to n // n is any natural number

$c[o] = Y[k]$ //same as the Y value

$Theta(\Theta) = 180$ //initially

$y = m \times x + c$ //straight line equation, we take m_1 for m

$m_1 \times m_2 = cos(\Theta)$ //take $cos(\Theta)$ is the angle. $m_1 \times m_2$ = -1, if two lines are perpendicular to each other

$(Y - y)/(X - x) = m_2$ //another equation for straight line

Find x and y //these are the midpoint of the line

$(x_1 + X)/x = 2$ //x_1 is the image point co-ordinate

$(y_1 + Y)/y = 2$ //y_1 is the image point co-ordinate

Find x_1 and y_1

$x_2 = mod(x_1; 256)$

$T[f] = char[x_2]$ // The value of T will be the encoded value. f = 1 to n, n means natural number.

Theta $(\theta) = y_1$

Algorithm 2. Steps of the Decryption Algorithm:

Take the encoded text value

Convert the text into ASCII value

Each ASCII value will be the X co-ordinate value

Y co-ordinate value coming from the key array

Take the straight line equation: $y = m \times x + c$ // here $m = m_1$

m_1 value is coming from LFSR and c value is coming from PRNG

Second equation $(Y - y)/(X - x) = m_2$

$m_1 \times m_2 = cos(\Theta)$ // if the Θ value is 180° then $m_1 \times m_2 = -1$

Solve the above equations find x and the y value

Apply midpoint theory $(x_1 + X)/x = 2$ and $(y_1 + Y)/y = 2$ //x_1 and y_1 is the image point

convert x_1 value into the ASCII value and

finally got the original text value

And then finally got the m_1 value. For c value take the PRNG value same as Y value.

Now for theta value we take first value as 180° then the next value will be coming from y_1 value which will be generated later after generating the image point. $m_1 \times m_2 = cos(\Theta); \Theta = 180$; Another equation for straight line that is also given in the above Eq. 3.

From these two equations we find the value of x and value of y. These values are the midpoint value. Now find the image point value by using midpoint formula that is also described in previous Eq. 4.

Now take the mod value of x_1 by 256 and take the integer value so, finally we got the new value of x_1 and the value of x_1 will be $(87, 180, 189, 177, 179, 187)$ for y_1 the value of y_1 will be the very large value. Ultimately we got the final ciphertext for the plaintext string which is shown below: Here we use the coding text operation to the plain text 'WELCOME' and then encoded it which will help the sender to send the encoded text to the receiver in a proper way. Here we see encoded text is totally different with the original text message and for creating this encoding text it takes less time for executing the whole process. It is much easier process than the other encoding process and also it will give us much more security.

In the below figure we see that if we send the plain text after encoding it will give a totally unfamiliar text which will help us to secure the system in a proper manner.

Plaintext   :   WELCOME

Ciphertext   :   ©»′½±³»

Fig. 3. Plaintext and corresponding ciphertext

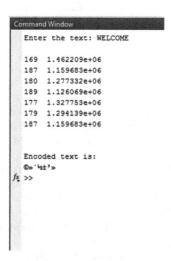

Fig. 4. Implementation of encoding method in Matlab

After receiving the encoded text the receiver also decoded the text and that's why the decoding operation is performed and it is urgent for the receiver to decode text. So here in our novel technique we just give a brief overview. In this case we use the decoding operation technique, here we take the decoding code and apply the reverse procedure of the encoding technique and try to decrypt the text. Here in this case if the sender wants to send the text "WELCOME" first he encoded the text and then send to the receiver. After sending the text the receiver get the encoded text as shown in Fig. 3 and by using the algorithm he decrypt the encoded text and get the original text message in this case it will be "WELCOME". In the below figure we see that the receiver decrypt the encoded text and see the plain text message without any third party attacker [11].

6   Conclusion

In today's world cryptography technique is excessively demand for securing the data system. Here we see several new cryptanalysis techniques also appear as a third party attacker in the networking system. In that case we cannot say that our security system is 100% secure. So in this situation we are proposing a novel technique that can help the sender for sending the data in a very secure way. We proposing here totally a new technique based on point reflection procedure. By using this technique the user can send the data very easily and it does not takes much time that means the time complexity is much less than the other security process. In this novel technique we only focus on security system that's why we are proposing this technique by which the message is to be encrypted. The third party attacker will be unable to understand the message easily if the algorithm is not known to him. Here the total process of encryption is based on point reflection process.

References

1. Agrawal, R., Srivastava, M., Sharma, A.: Data hiding using dictionary based substitution method in DNA sequences. In: 9th International Conference on Industrial and Information Systems (ICIIS), pp. 2164–7011 (2014)
2. Jakobsen, T.: A fast method for the cryptanalysis of substitution ciphers. Cryptologia 19(3), 265–274 (1995)
3. Web link. https://en.wikipedia.org/wiki/Substitution_cipher
4. Web link. https://en.wikipedia.org/wiki/Point_reflection
5. Kumar Pal, J., Mandal, J.K.: A novel block cipher technique using binary field arithmetic based substitution (BCTBFABS). In: Second International Conference on Computing, Communication and Networking Technologies (2010)
6. Gurubilli, P.R.: Random number generation and its better technique. Doctoral dissertation, Thapar University Patiala, June 2010
7. Sgarro, A.: Error probabilities for simple substitution ciphers. IEEE Trans. Inf. Theory 29(2), 190–198 (1983)

8. Garcia-Bosque, M., Sánchez-Azqueta, C., Celma, S.: Secure communication system based on a logistic map and a linear feedback shift register. In: 2016 IEEE International Symposium on Circuits and Systems (ISCAS), pp. 1170–1173. IEEE (2016)

9. Dilip, P.S., Somanathan, G.R., Bhakthavatchalu, R.: Reseeding LFSR for test pattern generation. In: 2019 International Conference on Communication and Signal Processing (ICCSP), pp. 0921–0925. IEEE (2019)

10. Kahate, A.: Cryptography and Network Security, 2nd edn. Tata McGraw Hills (2009)

11. Schneier, B.: Applied Cryptography Protocols, Algorithms And Source Coding, 2nd edn. Wiley (1996)

12. Blum, M., Micali, S.: How to generate cryptographically strong sequences of pseudo random bits. In: Providing Sound Foundations for Cryptography: On the Work of Shafi Goldwasser and Silvio Micali, pp. 227–240 (2019)

13. Ahmad, M., Doja, M.N., Beg, M.M.S.: A new chaotic map based secure and efficient pseudo-random bit sequence generation. In: Thampi, S.M., Madria, S., Wang, G., Rawat, D.B., Alcaraz Calero, J.M. (eds.) SSCC 2018. CCIS, vol. 969, pp. 543–553. Springer, Singapore (2019). https://doi.org/10.1007/978-981-13-5826-5_42

14. Forouzan, B.A.: Cryptography and Network Security. Tata-Mcgraw Hill Book Company

15. Thomas, S.A., Gharge, S.: Review on various visual cryptography schemes. In: 2017 International Conference on Current Trends in Computer, Electrical, Electronics and Communication (CTCEEC), pp. 1164–1167. IEEE (2017)

16. Li, P., Liu, Z.: A novel visual cryptography scheme with different importance of shadows. In: Kraetzer, C., Shi, Y.-Q., Dittmann, J., Kim, H.J. (eds.) IWDW 2017. LNCS, vol. 10431, pp. 365–377. Springer, Cham (2017). https://doi.org/10.1007/978-3-319-64185-0_27

17. Yang, R., Xu, Q., Au, M.H., Yu, Z., Wang, H., Zhou, L.: Position based cryptography with location privacy: a step for fog computing. Future Gener. Comput. Syst. **78**, 799–806 (2018)

Security and Anonymity Aspects in Tails and Windows 10 Operating Systems

Vipul Singh Negi[✉] and Nirmalya Kar[✉]

National Institute of Technology Agartala, Jirania, India
vipulhld001@gmail.com, nirmalya@ieee.org

Abstract. In this technological world, all our devices require an operating system to enable them to function properly. From digital clocks to laptops as a hardware devices, we require various types of operating systems to manages those resources. With so many devices we also need some privacy, and to do that we need good security hardware; software. But along with hardware, we need to rely on software too. Currently, Windows 10 has over 1 billion users worldwide. On the other hand we have chosen Tails that is a Linux based operating system with 25k active users and increasing day by day. Unlike windows which is centered around productivity, Tails is completely centered around anonymity. In this paper, we explore the security and anonymity issues in both the operating systems and the observations are well explained. The paper also include observations related to compatibility with hardware, installation process and various other features to identify the most suitable system in terms of security parameters.

Keywords: Tails · Windows · Security · Anonymity · PLED · Operating system

1 Introduction

Tails [1] and Windows 10 [2] are two different kind of OS, one focuses on anonymity and the other focuses on productivity. We all are aware that this is the age of technology, from self-driving cars to sending those cars into outer space we all need the golden system that joins us and the hardware and that golden system is the heart of any device. Windows Vista was a failure but the new iteration Windows 7 just stole the show, one thing can either make it or break it. Windows 10 is the successor of Windows 7 as it clearly improves the older system. One main reason for Windows 10 success is the updates they have switched to feature updates which was essential and simple. In this paper, both the operating system are judged on some basic points such as device support, network capabilities, memory management, etc. The greatest example is SE Linux [3]. NSA developed SE Linux especially to deal with online content. Security-enhanced Linux (SE-Linux) is a reference implementation of the Flask security architecture [4] for flexible mandatory access control. This Operating System

© Springer Nature Switzerland AG 2020
N. Kar et al. (Eds.): ICCISIoT 2020, CCIS 1358, pp. 188–199, 2020.
https://doi.org/10.1007/978-3-030-66763-4_17

used to be the security benchmark a few years back and now those features exist in normal operating systems.

Tails was released on 16 August 2009, as "intrigeri" announced the first release of amnesia on the tor talk mailing list. The name Tails (The Amnesiac Incognito Live System) was opted in 2011. It is based on Debian [5] and ships with GNOME Desktop [6]. Just like the older versions of Windows it doesn't support feature updates. This paper attempts to find out weather Windows and Tails prevail in providing us the best service possible.

2   Experimental Setup

2.1   Test Bench

For windows bench, we are using 8 GB of memory with a two-core i5 5200U CPU with a hard drive and the network card is 802.11 bgn. For Tails, we have two test benches with same CPU and Networking

1. A Virtual Machine with 4096 MB of memory with 1 CPU core.
2. A Live environment with 8 GB of memory with 2 CPU cores.

For simplicity, we will call Bench W for Windows 10 and Bench 1 and Bench 2 for Tails respectively (Table 1).

Table 1. OS information

Requirements	Windows 10	Tails
Year of Publication	29 July 2015	16 August 2009
License	MSDN Subscription	GNU GPLv3
Source Model	Closed Source	Open Source
Kernel	Hybrid	Monolithic
Version	1909 new is 2004	4.7
Size	3 GB+	1.2 GB

2.2   Installation

Tails is a portable operating system that protects your privacy and helps you avoid censorship. It is open source so one can download a free copy of it anytime. The commitment to the security of the downloaded OS file is so good that they have created an extension to verify the integrity of the file downloaded, we also get an alternative option for verifying using Open PGP [7] (Fig. 1).

Tails is classified as PLED (Privacy Enhancing Live Distribution) it is for the users who want a lot of portability with mainly having the protection from data recovery tools or, privacy on the internet. Edward Snowden (aka The Whistleblower) [8] insists that everyone should use PLED and to be more specific Tails (Fig. 2).

Fig. 1. Tails extension download.

Fig. 2. Verification of Tails package (left) and Edward Snowden's support for Tails (right).

Windows. Windows is closed source and it provides multiple ways to download the operating system.

1. Using the tool by Microsoft to upgrade from previous versions (Windows 7, 8, 8.1).
2. Using the tool and creating installation media.
3. By
   (a) Sign in to the Volume Licensing Service Center to download Enterprise editions.
   (b) Sign in to your subscription on the MSDN Portal for MSDN downloads.
   (c) Visit the Windows Insider site to download Insider Preview builds.
   (d) Visit the Download Academic Products page for Education editions (product key required).

But with all these options available we found out a majority of people download the pirated versions of Windows which leads them into a vulnerable position. In 2018 a study [9] claims that 83% of users use the pirated version in the Asia region alone. With India at a whopping 91%, Indonesia at 90%, Taiwan at 73%, Singapore with 55% and the Philippines at 43%.

2.3   List of Supported Architectures

Table 2 shows the list of popular architectures and according to it, our bench W turns out to be more versatile.

Table 2. List of supported architecture

Architecture	Bench W	Bench 1& 2
IA-32	✓	
x86-64	✓	✓
ARM [10] v7	✓	
ARM64	✓	

2.4   List of Supported Devices

Windows. All hardware devices with the specifications given in Table 3 are supported but with lower memory systems the system might crash sometimes.

Tails All hardware devices with the specifications given in Table 3 are supported but with lower memory systems the system might crash sometimes (Lower than 2 GB of RAM) [11].

Table 3. Minimum requirements for Bench W and Bench 1&2

	Bench W	Bench 1 & 2
Medium	8 GB USB or a DVD recordable	8 GB USB or a DVD recordable
Processor	1 Ghz or faster processor or SoC	64-bit x86-64
RAM	1 gigabyte (GB) for 32-bit or 2 GB for 64-bit	2 gigabyte
Space	16 GB for 32-bit OS 32 GB for 64-bit OS	Uses the Medium
Graphics card	DirectX 9 or later with WDDM 1.0 driver	
Display	800 × 600	Any

3   Features

The basic standards by which an OS is identified is its features. We have taken all sorts of internet-related features because that's where we need a lot of Anonymity.

Table 4. List of features

	Bench W	Bench 1 & 2
Internet	✓	✓
Captive Portals	✓	Using Unsafe Browser
WiFi Cards	✓	Only approved ones
Persistence Storage		✓
Anonymous Internet		✓

3.1   Persistence Storage

The Persistent Storage is an encrypted partition protected by a passphrase on the USB stick. If you start Tails from a USB stick, you can create a Persistent Storage in the free space left on the USB stick. The files and settings stored in the Persistent Storage are saved encrypted and remain available across different working sessions.

You can use this Persistent Storage to store, for example: Personal files, Some settings, Additional software, Encryption keys etc. This storage is not hidden and should be used when you are dealing with large issues. You cannot set up this storage in a VM so our Bench 1 was not able to create it, one more thing to keep in mind is to use Etcher, it is what they recommend us to use to create the USB stick but in our case, this didn't work properly as we did create it with Etcher. So this storage system is a hit or misses some time.

3.2   Boot up Speed

Bench 1 performed uncommonly but bench 2 was acceptable, for some reason bench W was not producing any result because the software's for it was unreliable. But it did provide us with a BIOS time of 3.2 s. Since we are using HDD, the time is high for a system to boot but if an SSD was used the times would have been easy to digest. The detailed comparison is mention in Table 4 (Fig. 3).

3.3   Encryption and Privacy

These are necessary elements since we are talking about security. These features are compatible with windows too, but you have to side load them all. Table 5 shows such tools.

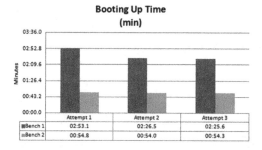

Fig. 3. Booting up speeds (in min).

Table 5. Tools of encryption and privacy

Tools	Bench W	Bench 1 & 2
LUKS [12]		✓
Open PGP		✓
GTKHash [13]		✓
KeyPassXC [14]		✓

3.4 Sharing

However good our benches are if we weren't able to share our work this defeats the point of productivity. In the case of bench W everything related to sharing is possible but in case of bench 1 and 2 we only have a few ways, one of them is Onion Share [15]. Without a good sharing system, the whole operating system is crippled because whatever one is creating one probably wants to share it (Fig. 4).

Onion share is a simple program, you upload your files and the system will provide you a link, this link only works with Tor browser because regular browsers can't access .onion web pages. The thing is very simple yet elegant it shows real-time file downloading by the receiver and it automatically uses zip files to save space and to ease the downloading. The link is automatically copied to the clipboard and you can see how many times the file has been downloaded in the top right corner. Bench W can also do this kind of sharing using Onion share or use Mozilla's Firefox Send. Both options are stunning but sharing is done frequently these days and setting up tor to access the share links is a bit time taking. Due to the existence of Firefox Send, the bench W wins the sharing battle.

3.5 Anonymous Internet

Anonymity is the main focus of this paper. To check the anonymity of the system, we compare our Bench 1 and 2 with Bench W. The results were amazing.

Fig. 4. File Sharing using Onion Share. Sharing URL (left) Link Creation (right).

Speed. The internet speed makes a lot of difference. In case of entertainment stuff like watching clips and playing games we need high speeds on the other hand to browse quickly and effectively one just don't need much speed as we found out when we used our bench 1 and 2. The results of the speed test (Fig. 5) were terrible for bench 1 and 2 but the overall performance was good. All the speed tests were done with a 50 Mbps internet connection. The speed tests paint a difficult picture for us to understand but the high ping values in bench 1 and 2 do make it a bit choppy because of the routing used by Tor circuits, otherwise the essentials work fine. If ones workflow requires high-speed connectivity, we would suggest to choose bench W because bench 1 and 2 will not be able to keep up with it.

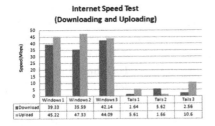

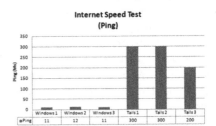

Fig. 5. Speed Test Download and Upload Speeds (on left) Ping (on right).

Anonymity Tests. Anonymity test includes a lot of tests like fingerprinting, DNS leak test, social media login detection, Content Filters and Proxy detection, IP address and much more. Using these test we checked our benches and the results are bit of an eye-opener. The detailed analysis of these tests are presented below.

1. Panopticlick:- Panopticlick [16] is a research project of the Electronic Frontier Foundation. Panopticlick will analyze how well ones browser and add-ons protect one against online tracking techniques. They will also see if one system is uniquely configured–and thus identifiable–even if one is using privacy-protective software. However, they only do so with your explicit consent. The test tries to collect data such as Screen Size, Device Memory, and others using bits of identifying information and exactly showing us how many bits of data are being sent. The results of the test for benches are in Table 6. It is easy to figure out that bench W is sending a lot of background data than the other one and that deduced some valuable information correctly.

   Firstly due to the Time Zone they now know our location, Secondly the screen resolution, Thirdly the series of graphics card one is using, and lastly the Device Memory. With all this data one can easily identify our device just by using google, Bench W failed this test but Bench 2 successfully preserved our identity.

2. WebRTC Leak Test [17]:- Real-time communication is similar to the previous test done using bench W revealing a lot of data than expected. Our IP address and the knowledge about our camera and microphone were also leaked so bench W fails it big time, on the other hand, bench 2 disclosed nothing.

3. SSL/TLS Client Test:- This test is where bench W takes a lead because newer versions of the TLS protocol enable more modern cryptography and are broadly supported across modern browsers but bench 2 still supports the legacy versions, which is not bad for web browsing but providing support for legacy websites may cause some long term problems. Bench W is still capable of using the legacy versions but Chrome is not using it which is a plus point to its security.

   The pandemic is effecting this change a lot because a lot more people are using a few outdated websites right now and it will probably take some time for them to update their systems "Microsoft will wait till the April release and then the option will be gone". The more certificates one browser contains the more websites it can connect to, but the open-source nature of bench 2 requires some legacy features.

4. Social Media Login Detection:- This one is simple, it tells us about the social media platform one is currently logged into let's say we have Gmail, Amazon logged in so this test will tell us how many social accounts we have currently logged in. Bench W failed but bench 2 succeeded.

5. Content Filters and Proxy Detection:- This just detects if the network is connected to a tor relay or not. Bench W is not connected but Bench 2 is connected to the Tor relay which is more secure.

6. IP Address :- The most common test among all these, due to which we expected very little from it but to our surprise, it was so amazing, not only

this test uncovers our IP on the bench W it also shows all the personal information of our service provider which is both hysterical and troublesome at the same time. We may have to warn him, cause this test not only found out his contact information but also traced his home address using the details provided at the time of registration of the connection. See this proves our point further, people are so clumsy and lazy. Instead of using his office address, he selected his home cause it would be more convenient for him to receive mails or packages that way. Another interesting thing happened with bench 2, it showed us our true system bandwidth, it happened because the test knew we were using a Tor Relay. The current Tor network is quite small compared to the number of people who are using Tor. Tor relays are also referred to as "routers" or "nodes." They receive traffic on the Tor network and pass it along.

There are three kinds of relays that you can run in order to help the Tor network: middle relays, exit relays, and bridges. For greater security, all Tor traffic passes through at least three relays before it reaches its destination.

The first two relays are middle relays which receive traffic and pass it along to another relay. The bench 2 also used both IPv4 and IPv6 but bench W only used IPv4 which tells us about the complexity of both the networks, because everyone knows version 6 is way better than version 4, and sooner or later we will have none of the version 4's left to work with.

7. Font Fingerprinting:- Fonts can also be used to fetch information. The best example of this is former Pakistani Prime Minister Nawaz Sharif it all hinged on a document (Fig. 6) that the Sharif family had produced in an attempt to distance the prime minister from questions about who owned four properties in an upscale part of London. The document was supposed to be written in February 2006 but court-appointed investigators concluded that it was forged, noting that it used the Calibri font, a Microsoft licensed typeface that was not commercially available at the time.

   In bench W we got 165 fonts and 147 unique metrics from the list of 512 fonts. In Bench 2 we got 0 fonts and 3 unique metrics from the list of 512 fonts. Other than the former Prime Minister getting caught, this test is neutral in both the cases.

8. Do Not Track:- The name says it all Do Not Track, it usually happens when you leave a website and the former website tracks where you are going. In bench W we manage to get 1 request but on the bench 2 we didn't get any of it. In my opinion, both are pretty safe for this test. But regardless of it, some websites are still able to access this data, but there is no way to identify those because the internet is an ocean of websites.

Table 6. Panopticlick report

Characteristics	Bench W bits	Bench 2 bits	Value of W	Value of 2
User Agents	6.94	3.91	True	True
Browser Plugin	9.8	0.89	·Identified	Undefined
Time Zone	4.49	2.8	True	False
Screen Size	3.69	13.65	True	False
Cookies	0.17	0.17	Yes	Yes
Web GL Vendor	7.44	3.21	True	None
Language	0.85	0.85	en-US	en-US
Platform	1.04	3.38	True	True
Touch Support	0.68	0.68	True	True
Ad Blocker Used	0.43	0.43	False	False
H/W Concurrency	1.84	2.46	True	False
Device Memory	2.08	0.9	True	N/A

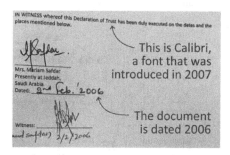

Fig. 6. Fake Document that was caught using font fingerprinting.

4   Observation

Security is always judged using CIA (confidentiality, integrity, and availability). On the availability front Windows is the gold standard but Tails is lacking in the VM department due to the slow loading times. As for confidentiality and integrity, we have to say that Tails is the superior brand because it barely leaked any of our data. Every few months we hear about some new vulnerabilities in the Windows environment which is a huge problem for the billions of people using it. One other important ingredient we need in an OS is Support, Tails doesn't offer much of it but Windows Support is very easy to access (Table 7).

Table 7. Detailed test report

Category	Test	Bench W	Bench 1 and 2
WebRTC Support Detection	RTCPeerConnection	True	False
	RTCDataChannel	True	False
IP Address Detection	Local IP	n/a	n/a
	Public IP	Correct IP Displayed	n/a
	IPv6	n/a	✓
Media Devices	Device Enumeration	True	False
	Has Microphone	True	False
	Has Camera	True	
SSL/TLS Client	TLS 1.3	Enabled	Enabled
	TLS 1.2	Enabled	Enabled
	TLS 1.1	Disabled(Good)	Enabled(Weak)
	TLS 1.0	Disabled(Good)	Enabled(Weak)
Social Media	Social Media Login	✓	No
Content Filter and Proxy	Tor Relay IP	Not Detected	Detected
IP Address	Country	✓	No
	Full Name	✓	Random Name
	Email	✓	Random Email
	Address	✓	Random Address
	Time	✓	Random Time
	Latitude/Longitude	✓	Random
Font Fingerprinting	JS Fonts	✓	None
HTTP Header DNT	DNT	1	Undefined
JavaScript DNT	navigator.doNotTrack	1	Unspecified
	windows.doNotTrack	undefined	Undefined
CSS Media Queries	Screen Resolution	✓	Incorrect
	Color-gamut	✓	No
	Device-aspect-ratio	Out of Range	Incorrect
	Orientation	✓	✓
Navigator Object	Device Memory	✓	No
	Platform	✓	✓
HTML5 Geolocation	Geolocation API	✓	No
HTML5 Canvas Fingerprinting	Canavas Fingerprinting	✓	No
	Image File Size	4653Bytes	166Bytes
	Number of Colors	199	1
	Browser Statistics	Chromium on Windows	n/a
Tor Relay Details	Bandwidth	None	✓
DNS Leak Test	DNS	46 Servers	2 Servers
	DNS ISP	✓	Random
WebGL Browser	Unmasked Vendor	✓	n/a
	Unmasked Renderer	✓	n/a

5   Conclusion

After performing a various amount of tests on our benches we have found out that in terms of pure Anonymity and Security Tails cannot be rivaled. But in terms of productivity it is lacking a lot. Windows (Traditional systems) can be more secure by changing some simple things, but sadly they are not. Things are changing for good right now, the new 2004 version of Windows 10 is bringing some good security features.

References

1. Dawson, M., Antonio Cárdenas-Haro, J.: Tails Linux operating system: remaining anonymous with the assistance of an incognito system in times of high surveillance. Int. J. Hyperconnectivity Internet Things (IJHIoT) **1**(1), 47–55 (2017)
2. Hassan, N.A., Hijazi, R.: Windows security. In: Digital Privacy and Security Using Windows, pp. 103–122. Apress, Berkeley (2017)
3. Ko, J., Lee, S., Lee, C.: Real-time mandatory access control on SELinux for Internet of Things. In: 2019 IEEE International Conference on Consumer Electronics (ICCE), Las Vegas, NV, USA, pp. 1–6 (2019). https://doi.org/10.1109/ICCE.2019. 8662112
4. Gregory, M., Loscocco, P.: Using the flask security architecture to facilitate risk adaptable access controls. SELinux Documentation; Published in the Proceedings of the 2007 SELinux Symposium (2007)
5. González-Barahona, J.M., Perez, M.O., de las Heras Quirós, P., González, J.C., Olivera, V.M.: Counting potatoes: the size of Debian 2.2. Upgrade Mag. **2**(6), 60–66 (2001)
6. German, D.M.: The GNOME project: a case study of open source, global software development. Softw. Process Improv. Pract. **8**(4), 201–215 (2003)
7. Callas, J., Donnerhacke, L., Finney, H., Thayer, R.: OpenPGP message format. RFC 2440, November 1998
8. Carlo, S., Kamphuis, A.: Information security for journalists. The Centre for Investigative Journalism, London (2014)
9. Microsoft tests show 91% new PCs from India loaded with pirated software. https://economictimes.indiatimes.com/tech/software/microsoft-tests-show-91-new-pcs-from-india-loaded-with-pirated-software/articleshow/66475487.cms? from=mdr
10. Jaggar, D.: ARM architecture and systems. IEEE Micro **17**(4), 9–11 (1997)
11. Tails Requirement. https://tails.boum.org/doc/about/requirements/index.en. html
12. Creating and using LUKS encrypted volume. https://tails.boum.org/doc/ encryption_and_privacy/encrypted_volumes/index.en.html
13. Calculating Checksum using GtkHash. https://tails.boum.org/doc/encryption_ and_privacy/checksums/index.en.html
14. Managing passwords using KeePassXC. https://tails.boum.org/doc/encryption_ and_privacy/manage_passwords/index.en.html
15. Onion Share. https://onionshare.org/
16. Panopticlick 3.0. https://panopticlick.eff.org/
17. Browser Leak Tests. https://browserleaks.com/

Exploiting Aspect-Classified Sentiments for Cyber-Crime Analysis and Hack Prediction

Shaurjya Mandal$^{(\boxtimes)}$, Banani Saha, and Rishov Nag

Department of Computer Science and Engineering, University of Calcutta,
Kolkata, India
shaurjyacs@gmail.com, bsaha_29@yahoo.com, rishovnag@gmail.com

Abstract. In today's world both cybercrimes and the huge data on social media have been a subject of study and recent research has shown that there is a strong correlation between the two. The occurrence of cyber threats is hard to predict because of the sporadic nature of such events. Generally the hackers and other cyber criminals tend to conceal their activities. But it is often seen that majority of such activities occur as a response to a social incident involving phenomenal discussions on the social media. Accurate study of the available data can allow us to predict such crimes and thus can be used to generate an alert in appropriate time. This paper has been aimed at considering the different aspects of social events, responses and their relations to further improve the classification of the social sentiment. The proposed method covers not only the response due to major social events but also predicting and generating alert for situations of significant social importance. The approach has made use of Twitter datasets and performed aspect-based sentiment analysis on the obtained text data. It is shown to outperform the state of the art methods.

Keywords: Cyber security · Machine learning · Sentiment analysis · Text mining · Natural Language Processing

1 Introduction

Social Networks are platforms designed to aid exchange of information in real time. These platforms also serve as discussion forums for sensitive social issues. They produce over a billon posts in a month. Twitter alone is reported to generate over 300 million tweets all across the world.

Twitter may reflect biased views from users about general subjects and social events. Few of them come with geographic embedded data (e.g., assisted GPS coordinates). Streams of tweets generate valuable information that can be modelled as a social sentiment detector to capture real-world events. It also aids in prediction of such events by analysis of interconnected topics.

© Springer Nature Switzerland AG 2020
N. Kar et al. (Eds.): ICCISIoT 2020, CCIS 1358, pp. 200–212, 2020.
https://doi.org/10.1007/978-3-030-66763-4_18

Cyber threats are hard to identify and predict as the hackers that conduct these attacks often hide their activity to avoid being detected. They might still use publicly accessible forums to discuss vulnerabilities and responses and look forward to exploit them. The behaviour of a malicious community at such information exchange forums may give useful insight regarding the possible threat in the immediate future.

Users tend to express their opinion on different aspects of a given situation. The proposed approach in the paper iteratively models the influence from the other aspects to generate accurate target aspect representation. In sentences containing multiple aspects, the main challenge an Aspect-Based Sentiment Analysis (ABSA) classifier faces, is to correctly connect an aspect to the relevant phase that enlightens us about the underlying sentiment [8].

The primary raw data obtained from scrapping is unstructured and have to be dealt with before the sentiment analysis methods could be rightfully implemented. After this data is structured that it can be classified by our model for further predictions.

The approach deals with the efficient data gathering from twitter followed by pre-processing which aids in structuring the data before it can be fed for further analysis. Thereafter, the Aspect Aware Sentence Representation has been incorporated on the tweets and the model processes and classifies the tweet by identifying the aspects accordingly. The related work done so far has been discussed in Sect. 2, while Sect. 3 gives details of the work that include data gathering, pre-processing and training. Section 4 discusses the results obtained from our model and also gives the Comparative study of the approach with respect to the other state of the art methods. Finally, Sect. 5 concludes the work and proposes the future work.

2   Related Work

According to a study in [13] cyber-attacks are rising due to global insurgency in political contexts. These attacks pose major concerns due to the data breach caused for a large number of users and application compromise. Thus prevention measures such as forecasting of such hacks are useful in the prospect.

Data from Social Networks are useful for enhancing capabilities of Intrusion Detection and Intrusion Prevention Systems. Sentiment Analysis is an integral part of Natural Language Processing and finds its use in a wide range of Social media useful in these situations [17], stock market prediction [16], fake news detection [18] and so on. A document on strategies has been proposed which can be used to identify and prevent practises like malicious attacks and spamming [14]. A sentiment extractor has been proposed that works in an unsupervised way using emoticon signals for model learning [3].

Predictive analysis can be done in a more reliable way in Twitter due to its various features like re tweets, replies, etc. [15]. These can be categorized together to understand the polarity of the sentiment obtained. L2 Regularization and L1 Regularization have been used earlier to analyse major cyber-attacks [1].

3 Work Details

The proposed approach aims at distinctive identification of the tweets related to the aspects that involve data breach and cyber-crimes. It can be used as an alert generation system as a caution for hacks and cyber-attacks.

This work comprises 3 main modules:

- The first module includes the Data Gathering from Twitter making use of the Scrapy Engine and storing it in an SQL based Database for easy retrieval of the data and efficient structuring.
- The second module comprises the data pre-processing model for our approach. This forms a crucial step as the data is sorted and obtained in the desired form before it can be fed to the Inter-Aspect Relation model [2] for sentiment extraction.
- The third module consists of the main algorithm for building the model for efficient sentiment extraction and classification. The different steps required for the data along with their respective relevance are discussed in this module.

3.1 Data Gathering

Data gathering methods are designed so that we could write queries to collect the Twitter data in a sorted manner. Recent works on sentiment analysis use a public information streaming platform known as Twitter Standard Search API, which is an interface that has capabilities for information retrieval in chronological order. In this paper, the approach proposed for retrieval of data is by querying Twitter search endpoints. The web crawling tasks are done with web spiders' engines designed for automated document scraping. Information is processed by Scrapy, a Python Web Scraping Framework that extracts embedded text in HTML tags and simultaneously uses recursive functions to analyse each link to follow other tweets [9] (Fig. 1).

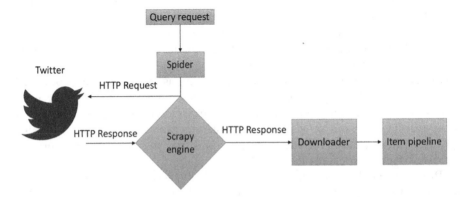

Fig. 1. Data Gathering from Twitter using Scrapy Engine.

Collecting data is performed by querying the Twitter endpoints arranged with respect to days at regular intervals. Queries responses are processed by a web spider towards the endpoint and redirected to a Scrapy download layer [1]. The Scrapy engine takes care of the unprocessed data and removes the hypertext tags to retrieve each tweet in text format. The retrieved text is processed independently in Scrapy pipes that handle data streams into objects to be stored on a relational database. Here MySQL has been used as the relational database.

The collected tweets are added to the corpus X. where Xi (each element of the Corpus) corresponds to the ith tweet in the Corpus, stored as a set of four elements; namely, id, text, date and language. Each tweet in X is assigned a (primary key, Tweetid), which is used to identify unprocessed tweets [5].

3.2 Data Pre-processing

The raw text data that has been collected from users is unstructured and undoubtedly informal owing to the way how the users write in social media. Also it contains different kinds of unwanted noise which makes the data very difficult to interpret. Thus it is very difficult to determine correctly the sentiment of the user from their posts. So here we first perform speech tagging for the tweets and then use noise removal techniques to get structured and clean data on which we can operate. The steps followed during the pre-processing of data include speech tagging, noise removal and sentiment extraction from emoticons (Fig. 2).

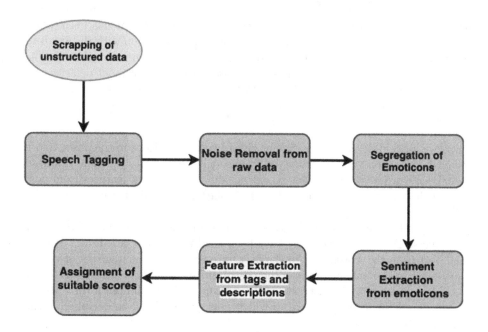

Fig. 2. Flowchart showing various steps of pre-processing.

Speech Tagging. Speech tagging makes provision of each tweet to be divided into parts such as adjectives, names, verbs and nouns. These are then used as suitable indicators to find the expression behind each tweet and the user's sentiment. Emoticons, exclamation marks, etc. are also taken into account to validate our choice of sentiment and also provide further insight into the possible expression of the tweet and their further determine the areas that the user wanted to stress upon.

The set of tags used in our work is an optimized version of the compendium of Peen Treebank [5]. Each collected tweet is then analysed in terms of syntactic annotations, which include emoticons, hashtags as well as syntactic patterns, which are caused due to causal writing, deliberate spelling errors, difference in dialect, and use of creative language.

Noise Removal. Not all text we obtain from the Tweets are relevant for analysis of the sentiment. Some of them hardly have a relation to the intended message or the sentiment of the user. They are mostly the URLs embedded in the text or other shorthand texts which hardly contribute a thing to our analysis. The process of noise removal deletes such occurrences. To retrieve such Tweets, we shall make use of the Primary Key as mentioned in the above section.

Handling of Emoticons. Based on sentiment consistency theory post level emotion indication assumes the strong correlation of sentiment polarity of a post and the corresponding emotion signals [7]. The main purpose of modelling post-level emotion indication is to reduce the margin of error between the sentiment polarity and result obtained from Emoticon Indication. Also it has been found that the overall sentiment of a post shows a positive correlation with the words in that post. By analysing word-level emotion indication, we can utilize the valuable information in the sentiment analysis framework to infer sentiment polarity of a post. To model post-level emoticon indication, we use a classifier

$$y = f(x), \tag{1}$$

where y $\varepsilon[0, 1]$ indicates the sentiment given by the emoticons in the posts, and x (the list of features) can be extracted from social media posts [4]. In addition, to model the word level indication, we extract different types of features from post text, including platform-independent and platform-specific features, on social media.

The platform independent features are n-gram features [6]. Time Frequency and Inverse Document frequency have been used to compute a feature vector of each post from the words used in the post with respect to the main set of vocabulary used in the entire corpus. Whereas platform dependent features attempt to capture the linguistic patterns for the specific social media platform with the use of a predefined set of heuristics which play a crucial role in deciphering the sentiment behind each post.

Feature Description for Twitter:

HASHTAG: The number of hashtag in the post, e.g., #cybersecurity

QUESTIONMARK The number of question marks (?) in the post

EXCLAIMATION The number of exclamation marks (!) in the post

NEGATION The number of negative words in the post, e.g., not.

TEXT_LEN The length of the post by removing irrelevant mentions and URLs.

Data Pre-processing Algorithm. Data pre-processing forms a crucial part of our approach. The data we obtain from Twitter using the Scrapy Engine is unstructured, informal and far from ready to be fed into our model. Speech Tagging is performed on the data to sort the relevant subjects followed by noise removal which gets the data structured and fit for sentiment extraction and testing of relevance. Emoticons form a very important part of the Tweets from which sentiment can be predicted and analysed. In our approach emoticons are not removed as a part of the noise but taken into consideration which gives us a further insight about the person's emotions and the their expression regarding a particular issue or incident. Emoticons are segregated and processed for sentiment extraction as per [12]. Emoticons alone are far from sufficient to give us a complete conclusion regarding the polarity of a post or tweet or its intensity. Furthermore a post might not contain emoticons at all. So in this analysis the sentiment obtained through emoticons has been assigned a score depending on their number, selection and placement. This has been done only for the posts having emoticons and so no special bias has been provided to the posts devoid of emoticons. The score thus obtained here forms a relevant part of the training phase and classification of the samples.

4   Proposed Work

Many social incidents that occur are the cause of an outburst of negative sentiments. Many of these don't directly relate to our problem as they hardly concern the potential cyber criminals and hackers. This demands a sentence representation that reflects the sentiment regarding one of our targeted aspects related to cybercrimes and hacking. This representation can be obtained with the Aspect Aware Sentence Representation [2,8].

In the memory representation for our system, both single and multiple memory hops have been implemented for more accurate results. Both single memory hops and multiple memory hops have been implemented for efficient results [2,10].

IARM Algorithm. The Inter Aspect Relations Modelling (IARM) Algorithm has been used to train our model. The training algorithm follows a series of steps carried for each epoch to successfully train our model. This model is primarily responsible for polarity classification of the Tweets. This combined with the results from the Aspect Aware Sentence Representation (AASR) module, gives

us the tweets concerned with the topic of cyber crimes or hacks. The architecture
adopted by our model is given in Fig. 3.

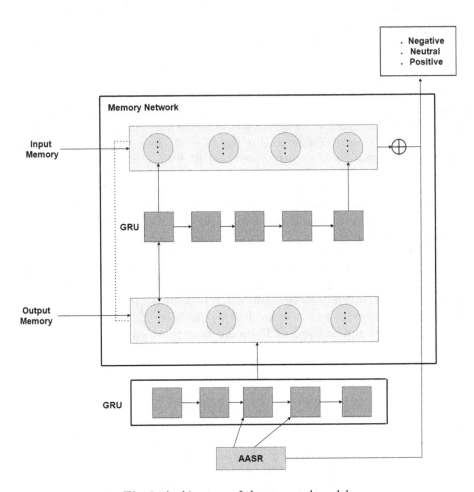

Fig. 3. Architecture of the proposed model.

Two sequential sets of 5 Gated Recurrent Units (GRUs) have been used for
training the model. The output from the GRUs are propagated to the input and
output memories. It took 22 epochs to train the model and SoftMax has been
used as the activation function to classify the text efficiently and a dynamic
threshold value is taken up which is a weighted mean of factors like the population impacted by a certain event or the relative response in comparison to other
issues (determined by the scores initiated during pre-processing).

For optimization, Stochastic Gradient Descent (SGD)-based ADAM algorithm [11], is used with learning-rate 0.01 due to its parameter-wise adaptive
learning scheme. Grid-search has been employed to obtain the best hyper-

parameter values for more accurate results. The steps involved in training in the model has been shown in Fig. 4.

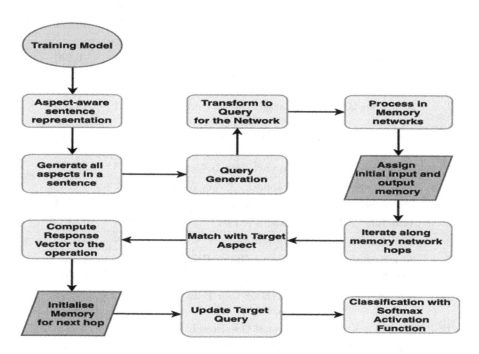

Fig. 4. A flowchart representing the steps involved in training of our model.

After being trained, primary testing of our model is done where the testing set is passed through the trained models to get the required results in classification.

4.1   Computational Results

The study has been performed on 16 major cybercrime and hacking incidents in the last 5 years and the Tweets have been selectively extracted, labelled and determined according to its relevancy to cybercrimes. The proposed model identifies the negative samples from the tweets and highlights the ones with a matching aspect, that is relevant to cyber security and hacks. The results observed are as follows:

The model shows appropriate results with respect to the polarity of the tweets and the ones relating to the aspect of instigating cybercrime and hacking. The results definitely show a positive correlation between the occurrence of the major cyber-attacks and the negativity of posts or agitation of people at a given point of time. The model further takes into consideration multiple aspects of cyber security and labels them as potential threats rather than just ordinary extraction and traditional string matching. This can find its use in predicting major hacks

Table 1. Results from our trained model

Index	Date	News	Negative sample	Security relevant
1	2nd January, 2016	'Anti-IS group' claims BBC website attack	46,810	16,021
2	21st June, 2016	'Russian hackers reportedly Access Clinton Foundation'	33,612	16,840
3	30th June, 2016	'Hackers reveals New Trove of DNC Documents and Answers a Few Personal Questions'	32,514	19,218
4	8th March, 2017	'Equifax Data Breach'	14,615	8,597
5	14th March, 2017	'WannaCry Cyber Attack'	14,532	9,622
6	18th February, 2018	'Under Armour'	20,614	12,331
7	14th June, 2018	'Exactis Attack'	16,228	7,813
8	26th June, 2018	'MyHeritage'	16,789	11,765
9	30th August, 2018	'Newegg Online Hack'	8,239	5,152
10	12th December, 2018	'Major Quora Hack'	12,511	6,992
11	6th February, 2019	'Facebook User Data Leaks'	15,893	11,291
12	22nd March, 2019	'Capital One Breach'	9,231	5,322
13	24th May, 2019	'The Canva Hack'	11,167	6,348
14	1st August, 2019	'The Quest Diagnostics Breach'	8,955	4,875
15	4th May, 2019	'The DoorDash Hack'	10,613	6,985
16	14th January, 2020	'The Peekaboo Moment'	8,236	3,826

and cybercrimes which are usually concealed till the point the hackers reveals the data. This can be done by studying the trends of the relevant data or a sudden saturation of tweets that hold true regarding the problem. Moreover as we are able to obtain the location stamp in the tweets, the model is suitable for prediction for small scale hack incidents as well as those arising from more impactful and well spread experiments. Also accurate results for incidents like the "Equifax Data Breach" and "Facebook Data Leak" have been observed. Such events involve major breach in privacy and enable a third party to handle the data of millions of users thus causing major distress among the data owners. An early alert for these incidents is always better as sometimes this breach or leakage of data occurs through months before it is detected and steps are taken to counter it.

A Comparative Study Has Been Performed Between the Methods Involving L1 Regularization, L2 Regularization and the Proposed Methodology. In L1 normally we shrink the parameters to zero. When input features have weights closer to zero that leads to sparse L1 norm. In Sparse solution majority of the input features have zero weights and very few features have non zero weights. L1 regularization does feature selection. It does this by assigning insignificant input features with zero weight and useful features with a non-zero weight. In L1 regularization we penalize the absolute value of the weights. Lasso produces a model that is simple, interpretable and contains a subset of input features.

L2 regularization forces the weights to be small but does not make them zero and does non sparse solution. L2 is not robust to outliers as square terms blows up the error differences of the outliers and the regularization term tries to fix it by penalizing the weights. Ridge regression performs better when all the input features influence the output and all with weights are of roughly equal size.

Prediction of cyber hacks and crimes had been done earlier using L2 and L1 regularization techniques. The present model has been compared with the above methods for the 16 situations of our result that included major data breaches and hacking incidents.

Table 2. Count of detected cyber security based negative tweets for all 16 events using three different approaches (κ)

Event number	κ using L1 regularization	κ using L2 regularization	κ using proposed model
1	12,186	15,380	16,021
2	10,401	13,372	16,840
3	17,021	19,767	19,218
4	7,259	5,349	8,597
5	7,275	9,152	9,622
6	12,331	11,945	12,331
7	5,149	6,214	7,813
8	13,036	6,995	11,765
9	3,830	4,095	5,152
10	5,244	7,166	6,992
11	10,070	10,680	11,291
12	4,789	3,894	5,322
13	3,476	5,390	6,348
14	4,133	4,345	4,875
15	6,486	6,985	6,985
16	4,072	4,566	3,826

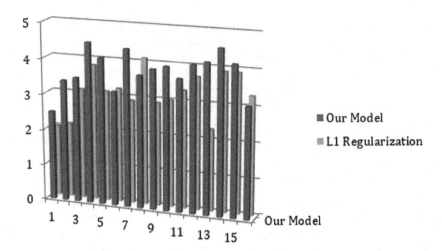

Fig. 5. Performance of the proposed model vs L1 regularization. **X-Axis:** Event ID **Y-Axis:** measure of security relevant threats in a scale of 5

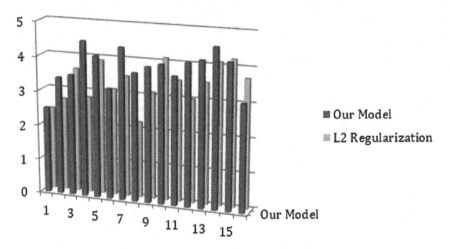

Fig. 6. Performance of the proposed model vs L2 regularization. **X-Axis:** Event ID **Y-Axis:** measure of Security Relevant Threats in a scale of 5

In Table 2 we make an observation regarding the count of the negative tweets based on the aspect of cybersecurity and hacking (κ) for the 16 incidents considered in Table 1. We have compared the results of our proposed model with the existing L1 and L2 approaches when applied for the same 16 incidents (Figs. 5 and 6).

The ratio of the detection obtained by the 3 methods have been computed and mapped in a scale of 5. The proposed model shows a better promise with regard to most of the situations and thus can be referred to as a more reliable method for alert generation and forecasting of hacks occurring at different levels.

Also the proposed model has outperformed the existing methods in case of the events of comparatively less social importance which is a remarkable trait when it comes to predicting hacks.

5   Conclusion

This paper proposes a method that uses Inter-Aspect Relation Modelling to achieve results in sentiment analysis and to predict cyber crimes and hacks. The approach uses data from Twitter and focus has been laid on setting up proper tags and aspects related to cyber security issues. It further involves efficient detection which in turn can generate alert through the use of structured response vectors. The emoticons which form a particularly large part of social posts today have been exploited to ensure higher veracity. In today's world where we see the phenomenal rise of data each day, strengthening the security of the information is a crucial task. Our approach gives accurate insight regarding the risks of hacks and data breaches when observations are carried out over a period. But the performance is limited to the cases where the tweet data could be structured conveniently. Data scrapped from Twitter, although easy to structure, is a comparatively limited source for obtaining solid evidence for future hacks. The future work regarding this approach may aim at achieving better accuracy in hack predictions taking into consideration more complex linguistic structures including informal comments and relevant discussion forums.

References

1. Hernandez-Suarez, A.: Social sentiment sensor in Twitter for predicting cyber-attacks using L1 regularization. Sensors (2016)
2. Majumder, N., Poria, S., Gelbukh, A., Shad Akhtar, Md., Cambria, E., Ekbal, A.: IARM: inter-aspect relation modeling with memory networks in aspect-based sentiment analysis. In: Proceedings of the Conference on Empirical Methods in Natural Language Processing (2018)
3. Deb, A., Lerman, K., Ferrara, E.: Predicting cyber events by leveraging hacker sentiment. Information (Switzerland) (2018)
4. Shu, K., Sliva, A., Sampson, J., Liu, H.: Understanding cyber attack behaviors with sentiment information on social media. In: Thomson, R., Dancy, C., Hyder, A., Bisgin, H. (eds.) SBP-BRiMS 2018. LNCS, vol. 10899, pp. 377–388. Springer, Cham (2018). https://doi.org/10.1007/978-3-319-93372-6_41
5. Hernández, A., et al.: Security attack prediction based on user sentiment analysis of Twitter data. In: IEEE International Conference on Industrial Technology (ICIT) (2016)
6. Fürnkranz, J.: A study using n-gram features for text categorization. In: Proceedings of the Third Annual Symposium on Document Analysis and Information Retrieval (2001)
7. Sabottke, C., Suciu, O., Dumitras: Modeling inter-aspect dependencies for aspect-based sentiment analysis. In: Proceedings of the 2018 Conference of the North American Chapter of the Association for Computational Linguistics: Human Language Technologies, vol. 2 (2018)

8. Hazarika, D., Poria, S., Vij, P., Krishnamurthy, G., Cambria, E., Zimmermann, R.: Vulnerability disclosure in the age of social media: exploiting Twitter for predicting real-world exploits. In: Proceedings of the 24th USENIX Security Symposium (2015)

9. Hernandez-Suarez, A., Sanchez-Perez, G., Toscano-Medina, K., Martinez-Hernandez, V., Sanchez, V., Perez-Meana, H.: A web scraping methodology for bypassing Twitter API restrictions (2018)

10. Shalyminov, I., Eshghi, A., Lemon, O.J.: Challenging neural dialogue models with natural data: memory networks fail on incremental phenomena. In: Proceedings of the 21st Workshop on the Semantics and Pragmatics of Dialogue, Saarbrucken, Germany, pp. 125–133 (2017). ISSN 2308-2275

11. Kingma, D.P., Ba, J.: Adam: a method for stochastic optimization. In: 3rd International Conference for Learning Representations, San Diego (2015)

12. Hogenboom, A., Bal, D., Frasincar, F., Bal, M.: Exploiting emoticons in sentiment analysis. In: Proceedings of the 28th Annual ACM Symposium on Applied Computing (2013)

13. Kirichenko, L., Radivilova, T., Carlsson, A.: Detecting cyber threats through social network analysis: short survey. SocioEconomic Challenges, Sumy, Ukraine (2017)

14. Gharibi, W., Shaabi, M.: Cyber threats in social networking websites. arXiv 2012, arXiv:1202.2420. [CrossRef] (2012)

15. Gayo-Avello, D.: A meta-analysis of state-of-the-art electoral prediction from Twitter data. Soc. Sci. Comput. Rev. **31**, 649–679 (2013). [CrossRef]

16. Bollen, J., Mao, H., Zeng, X.: Twitter mood predicts the stock market. J. Comput. Sci. **2**, 1–8 (2011)

17. O'Connor, B., Balasubramanyan, R., Routledge, B.R., Smith, N.A.: From tweets to polls: linking text sentiment to public opinion time series. In: ICWSM (2010)

18. Shu, K., Sliva, A., Wang, S., Tang, J., Liu, H.: Fake news detection on social media: a data mining perspective. ACM SIGKDD Explor. Newsl. **19**(1), 22–36 (2017)

Internet of Things (IoT)

Application of IoT and Weather Prediction for Enhancement of Agricultural Productivity

Basudeba Behera(✉) (iD), Smita Kumari, Alisha Kumari, and Ajay Kumar

Department of Electronics and Communication Engineering,
National Institute of Technology, Jamshedpur, Jamshedpur, India
basudeb.ece@nitjsr.ac.in

Abstract. This paper will help in monitoring the various parameters such as temperature, humidity, soil moisture, etc. required for the favorable growth of any particular crop. The proposed system makes use of technologies such as Wireless Sensor Networks (WSN) and Internet of Things (IoT) for solving the major challenges faced in agricultural fields. The WSN includes the various sensors interfaced with Raspberry pi whereas with the help of IoT we will be able to obtain the acquired data globally. The acquired data about various parameters will be sent over to the cloud platform where it will be analyzed and processed against the required climatic conditions and the further processed data can be used for weather prediction using Machine Learning (ML) and Application Programming Interfaces (APIs) and further, the farmers can be informed about the same so that they can aim for increased agricultural productivity. It will also help in using the limited amount of resources available in a more effective manner.

Keywords: Raspberry pi · Sensors · IoT · Agricultural productivity · Machine learning · Weather prediction · ThingSpeak

1 Introduction

India is a country which has its economy majorly dependent upon the agricultural sector. Not only does it provide a livelihood to the farmers but also contributes to the overall GDP of the country. The harsh and unpredictable climatic conditions prove to be a boon in the productivity of the agricultural sector. However, the modern technologies can be used in such a way so that not only is the irrigation supply made automatic but also, we can predict the favourable factors or conditions for the growth or productivity of any particular crop. Wireless Sensor Networks (WSN) along with the Internet of Things can help us in regular monitoring of the different parameters required for the crop growth. WSN is considered to be a realizable and a quite economic solution in

Supported by NIT Jamshedpur, India.

terms of the various challenges faced in the agricultural sector [1, 2]. Being a subset of IoT, it includes the connection of various sensors and actuators and also their interfacing with a microcontroller unit. By integrating the various modules of the wireless sensor network with the cloud, we obtain the data and use the same developed real-life solutions for the problems faced by the farmers in day to day life. In this work, we propose solutions to some of the problems faced in the agricultural fields such as [3]:

- Effect of adverse climatic conditions on the crops
- Shortage of water resources
- Deterioration of the soil quality due to lack of necessary minerals

Thus, with the help of the proposed system, we have an idea about the limited amount of resources available in the field of agriculture. Therefore, the automation achieved using smart technologies will help us in conserving resources as well as utilize the available resources in a much more effective and efficient manner. The proposed system attempts to serve the following objectives related to the agricultural sector.

- Reduce the amount of water consumed for irrigation
- Lead to a modernized approach of agriculture
- Effective usage of the rainwater
- Provide idea about climatic conditions to save crops from a crisis situation

2   Literature Survey

There has been some major research work done previously in the process of increasing agricultural productivity with the help of advanced technologies. Kasim et al. studied Precision Agriculture and gave a solution based on wireless sensor networks for intelligent greenhouse management systems [1]. The solution was reliable but obsolete as the GSM technology was used which has now been replaced by better options such as the internet. A model for smart agriculture using IoT was proposed by two professors of MET BKC in Maharashtra where they used the idea of cloud storage instead of gsm [5]. The system dealt with obtaining data from sensors and sending them to the cloud but no specific data manipulation was done in order to obtain favourable results. Later there were works done which were based on IoT and were supported by Cloud Computing where the data obtained was manipulated and alerts or notifications were sent as and when required [7]. Roselin et al. studied the concept of smart agriculture using a wireless sensor network using Atmega controllers and GSM [8]. Elia et al. got her work published which was based on Weather Prediction and the algorithm that she used was Decision Tree [9]. Salman et al. studied Weather forecasting using deep learning techniques and data from a weather station [9]. They employed algorithms such as Recursive Neural Network and Convolutional Neural Network. Unlike them, we have gone through the process of data collection as well as data processing. Parmar et al. deployed an Artificial Neural Network Model for the prediction of rainfall [10].

Kumar et al. made a comparative study among three different Machine Learning algorithms K-nearest neighbours, Support Vector Machine, Least Squares Support Vector Machines in order to predict the efficient crop yield which varies due to the climate change [11]. Aftab et al. in 2018 published their research work which consisted of the detailed study of research works done until then in the field of rainfall prediction [12]. They went through some important research questions and tried to answer them in their paper. Varghese et al. gave the idea of affordable smart farming. Their work was based on IoT to collect data and ML to predict future growth of the crops using the collected data [13]. Parashar et al. collected data using various sensor and used the same data to predict the weather using Machine Learning [14]. Parmar et al. depicted how the agricultural sector in India is majorly affected by the climatic changes [15].

3   Technology Stack Used

3.1   Internet of Things

Internet of Things (IoT) is basically a system that connects the different devices(which are already connected with each other) globally with the help of the internet. In other words, we can say that the wireless sensor network is the subset of the Internet of Things and IoT is the superset of WSN. The different sensor nodes in the wireless sensor system sense the data and send the same to the main base station. IoT then plays its role where the data from the base station or gateway is sent to a cloud platform with the help of the internet. Further, the data can be studied and manipulated from the user's end. IoT provides an easy interface between the user and the wireless sensor network globally. Today IoT finds a large number of applications in the fields of health monitoring, agriculture, industrial sector and also in our day to day lives.

3.2   Machine Learning

Machine Learning is the field of study that gives the computer the ability to compute and learn without being explicitly programmed. It is said that a computer program will with experience E in relation to some class of task T and performance measure P if the performance of Task T increases with experience [6]. Machine Learning is further classified into two categories Supervised and Unsupervised Learning based on the output we are trying to predict.

4   Algorithms Used

4.1   Deep Neural Networks

Deep neural network (also known as a convolutional network) is a type of artificial neural network having a large number of hidden layers to improve the efficiency of the model. This algorithm is inspired by the human brain to help computers to become intelligent without any explicit programming.

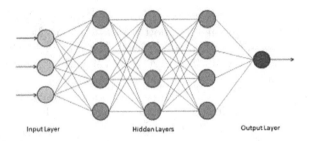

Fig. 1. Structure of deep neural network. (Source: Google)

Figure 1 depicts the structure of neural networks as well as the difference between simple and deep neural networks on the basis of hidden layers. The formula of output of a layer of neural networks is given as Y:

$$Y = f(b + \sum_{i=1}^{n} x_i w_i) \tag{1}$$

Where f can be any function like sigmoid, relu, etc. Y = output b = bias x = input data w = weight of different parameters

4.2 Random Forest Algorithm

Random Forest Algorithm is a supervised learning algorithm which comes under the classification of bagging type ensemble learning algorithm. An ensemble learning algorithm is an algorithm that combines several algorithms into one model to enhance the working of model by reducing the variance and bias. Figure 2 depicts the random forest algorithm. A decision tree is a model which predicts the output based on the various input parameters. In random forest algorithm, large number of decision trees are used in which every tree works on different subsets of data, in which data are chosen randomly and repetitively. The output is determined by taking the aggregate of the results of all the decision trees. This helps enhancing the result by training same set of data multiple times to increase accuracy.

5   System Architecture

Figure 3 shows the hardware circuitry that has been used in developing the prototype. It shows the raspberry pi and the different sensors that have interfaced with it in order to gather data. The system proposed has the central microcontroller unit as the Raspberry pi along with the sensors and actuators interfaced with it. The prototype of the system is shown below where the DHT11 sensor gives the temperature and humidity values. The soil moisture sensor measures

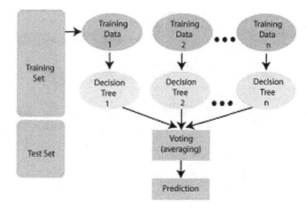

Fig. 2. Random forest algorithm. (Source: Google)

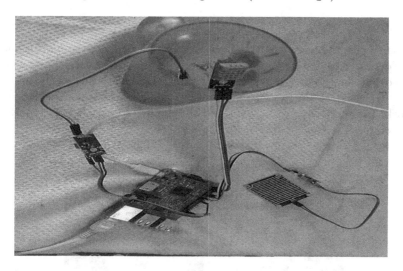

Fig. 3. Prototype for the proposed system

the adequate amount of moisture required by the crop and also instructs the pump to be switched on or off through the pi and relay. Further, we have used a rain sensor in order to detect the rainfall which will detect rainfall and will be beneficial in automated irrigation. Figure 4 shows the block diagram of the system proposed. The raspberry pi acting as the main central unit interfaced with the various sensors whose data is read and sent to the cloud platform for further processing.

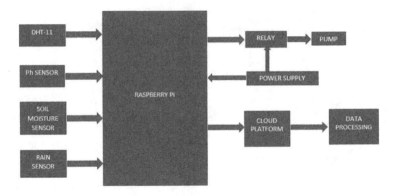

Fig. 4. Block diagram of proposed system

5.1 Raspberry Pi 3

Raspberry pi is the main central unit of the entire proposed system. It is a small microcomputer having its own central processing unit and own memory which is plugged into another computer or TV. Its GPIO pins are used to communicate with the sensors while they read data from the environment. The Raspberry pi works in an open source system and the main software which supports the microcomputer is Raspbian (Fig. 5).

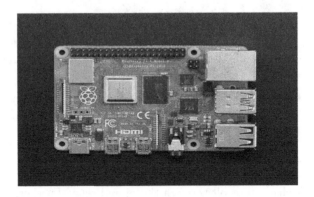

Fig. 5. Raspberry pi (Source: Google)

5.2 DHT 11 Sensor Module

The DHT11 sensor is one of the most commonly used temperature and humidity sensor and is generally responsible for giving analog and digital outputs. The DHT11 sensor shown in Fig. 6 is a compact sensor and also consumes less power. Also its range of operation is a wide one extending to up to 20 m.

Fig. 6. DHT11 sensor

5.3 Soil Moisture Sensor

The volumetric water content of the soil is obtained by the soil moisture sensor. It is easy to use and gives both analog and digital output. In digital output gives high (5 v) output moisture content is higher than a particular threshold value and low (0 v) otherwise. The threshold value can be adjusted by the potentiometer attaches on the sensor. The analog output is connected to ADC of the microcontroller to get the exact amount of volumetric water content of the soil. It is used to detect the moisture content of the soil for predicting whether the soil is too wet or too dry for the particular crop or plant. Figure 7 shows the soil moisture sensor.

5.4 Rain Sensor

Rain sensor which is shown below in Fig. 8 is a kind of switching device which is used to detect rain. When rain is detected switch goes from normally open to normally closed position thereby generating an alarm. It gives both digital and analog pin. This sensor works on a principle similar to that of resistive dipole, in which the resistance varies in accordance with moisture.

5.5 BMP-180

BMP-180 sensor is a high precision sensor used to measure specific atmospheric pressure. The pressure value measured by it is controlled and sent towards the microcontroller by using a I2C interface. Figure 9 depicts the sensor module used to monitor the atmospheric pressure.

5.6 Raspbian (Raspberry Pi)

Raspbian is the operating system software that is completely free of cost and is commonly used in all raspberry pi applications. It can be easily installed on any pc and a user can go through its documentation in case he or she faces any problem. The Raspbian software is based on Debian and there are a large number of packages that are already installed in it and can be used in the different projects that include Raspberry pi [16].

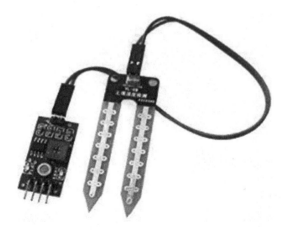

Fig. 7. Soil moisture sensor

Fig. 8. Rain sensor

Fig. 9. BMP-180

5.7   ThingSpeak

ThingSpeak is the open source cloud platform that is used for uploading data through any IoT device. It can be accessed by the user anytime and anywhere. Also if the user wants to customize his or her data as private or public, even that feature is available in this cloud platform. Here we are sending the various sensor readings to the cloud platform where we can obtain graphical representation of the data which can be regularly monitored. The data can also be stored for future use and can be retrieved as and when required.

5.8   Jupyter Notebook

The Jupyter Notebook is basically an app which consists of notebook documents and a notebook kernel. It is mainly a server-client based application that has the feature which allows us to edit and run the notebook documents through a web browser.

6   Weather Prediction

After we have collected the data from the various sensors and uploaded the same on a cloud platform, our next step is to predict the actual weather conditions which will be prevailing in the coming days and then accordingly inform the end-user to take effective measures in order to save the resources as well plan the effective the growth of the crops. Using the machine learning model we will be predicting the temperature and rainfall. We have extracted the dataset from kaggle. The dataset which we are using contains the weather data of regions of Australia collected from numerous weather stations. It contains the data collected on a daily basis for over 10 years dated from 1Nov2007 to 1Jun2017. The dataset contains 24 columns. The dataset contains the following parameters:

- Date
- Area
- MinTemp
- MaxTemp
- Rainfall
- Evaporation
- Sunshine
- WindGustDir
- WindGustSpeed
- WindDir9am
- WindDir3pm
- WindSpeed9am

- WindSpeed3pm
- Humidity9am
- Humidity3pm
- Pressure9am
- Pressure3pm
- Cloud9am
- Cloud3pm
- RainToday
- RISK_MM
- RainTomorrow

We first perform the data cleaning process then use different sets of parameters for predicting rainfall and temperature. Figure 10 depicts the various plots obtained on the cloud showing the variations in weather and soil moisture (Figs. 11 and 12).

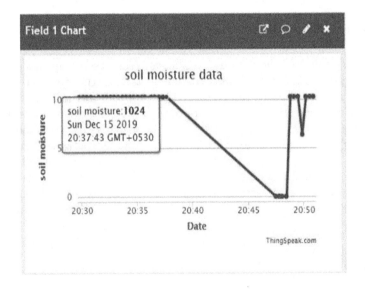

Fig. 10. Plots obtained on ThinkSpeak (a) Soil moisture

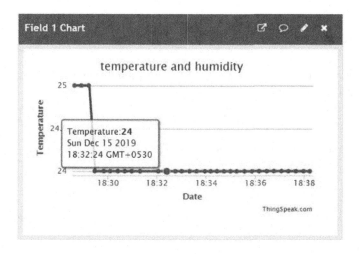

Fig. 11. Plots obtained on ThinkSpeak (b) Temperature

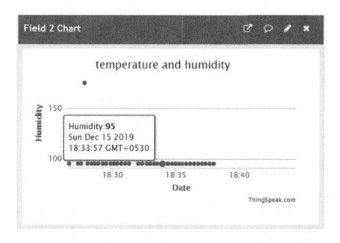

Fig. 12. Plots obtained on ThinkSpeak (c) Humidity

6.1 Predicting Temperature

We are using a Deep Neural Network regression model for predicting temperature. The main advantage of using the deep neural network regression model is that the model learns from itself. i.e. it predicts the weights and bias of the various parameters at various layers independently. The equation used to compute the output layer has been depicted in Eq. 1. We are using the ReLu activation function for the hidden layers. Figure 13 shows the Relu curve. ReLu or Rectified Linear Unit is the most commonly used activation function in neural networks. The loss function used to calculate the loss of our model for temperature prediction is mean squared error. The mean squared (MSE) is given as:

$$MSE = \frac{1}{n}\sum_{i=1}^{n}(y_i - y_i')^2 \qquad (2)$$

Where y is the actual value and $y^{\hat{}}$ is the predicted value. The mathematical representation of ReLu is:

$$ReLu(x) = max(x,0) \qquad (3)$$

Where x depicts the input parameter.

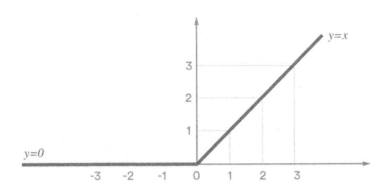

Fig. 13. Curve of ReLu function

6.2   Predicting Rainfall

We are using a binary classifier model for prediction. In this model we would be predicting 'rainTomorrow' column of the dataset using other parameters. The output column will have 1 if it would rain and 0 if it would not. We are using Random Forest Algorithm for the binary classification. This algorithm is a supervised algorithm. The training data is divided into various groups and it then averages the results of all the decision trees. Hence it has less chance of overfitting. The model has been trained in such a way that once we enter the different atmospheric parameters for the current day. it predicts the rainfall probability for the next day. The working of the algorithm is depicted in the Fig. 14.

7   Methodology

The proposed system is supposed to obtain the various parameters related to the environmental conditions which affect the growth of a crop. The raspberry pi acting as the main control unit having all the sensors connected to it serves as the central node. The DHT11 sensor reads the temperature and humidity

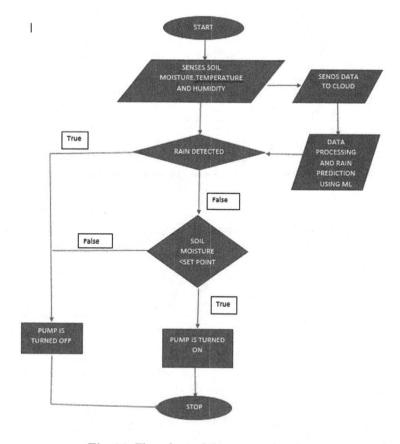

Fig. 14. Flow-chart of the proposed system

values from the surroundings and sends it to the pi. BMP 180 predicts the atmospheric pressure. The soil moisture sensor checks the moisture level. Once the moisture value crosses the threshold value the pi indicates the pump to be off with the help of a relay. Also, the system is provided with a rain sensor which detects rainfall and thus indicating the same to the pump. In case of rainfall and in case the adequate amount of moisture in the soil is attained, the pump is made automatically off so as to prevent the wastage of irrigation water. The data that is read by the raspberry pi is uploaded on a cloud platform and can be regularly monitored from anywhere. Here, we have used the uploaded sensor data to predict the weather parameters mainly the temperature and precipitation. We have deployed a machine learning model to predicting the temperature and rainfall. We have tried to achieve the maximum accuracy through ML models. After we have predicted the weather conditions, we alert the end user/farmer about the same so that he can take the necessary steps to save his resources as well as to increase his agricultural productivity. The flow of the system is shown in Figs. 14, 15 and 16.

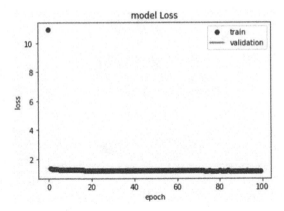

Fig. 15. Performance the DNN for predicting temperature (a) Represents the loss of model

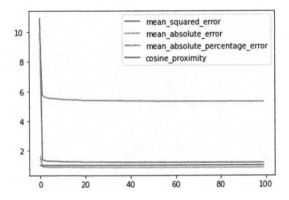

Fig. 16. Performance the DNN for predicting temperature (b) Represents the curves of various errors

8   Results

After carrying out proper experimentation and implementation of the hardware circuit the results were obtained. The data that was read by the sensors was transmitted to pi and same was obtained on the cloud platform ThingSpeak using IoT. The data was used to predict the weather conditions using the Machine Learning model. The performance of the machine learning model has been shown in Fig. ??. The performance of the random forest algorithm is determined by the confusion matrix which shows the different combination of predicted and true values as shown in Fig. 17. In this confusion matrix the number of cases of true positive is 17414, number of cases of false positive is 236, number of cases of false negative is 0 and the number of cases of true negative is 4935. The accuracy is approximately 98.9%. The useful information which is also sent to the concerned person through SMS shown in Fig. 18.

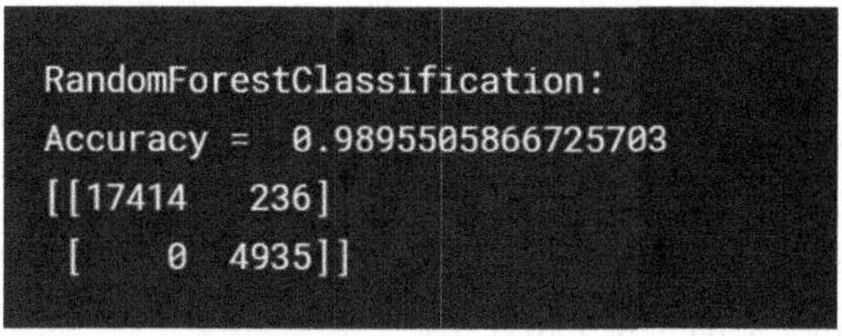

```
RandomForestClassification:
Accuracy =  0.9895505866725703
[[17414    236]
 [    0  4935]]
```

Fig. 17. Performance of random forest algorithm

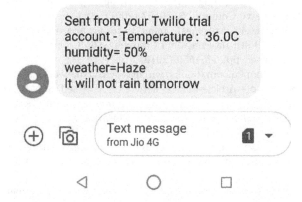

Fig. 18. Message received on user's phone

9   Conclusion

The major objective of obtaining the data about various environmental factors affecting crop growth was achieved using IoT. The data on the cloud platform was retrieved and used to predict the weather conditions using appropriate Machine Learning models. The wastage of the water required for irrigation was minimized by using the rain sensor and the automated pump operation. The graphs showing the gradual change in the weather conditions and the moisture level was plotted. The predicted weather conditions were further used to alert the farmers so that they can take the required steps. We have used the data recorded over a short period but a larger dataset would be more beneficial for the prediction. Also, the different types of crops can be categorised and a detailed study about the favourable climatic growth of these crops can be done. Different crops flourish in different weather and after the study is done the same machine learning model can be used to predict the type of crop suitable for the upcoming weather.

References

1. Gondchawar, N., Kawitkar, P.R.S.: Smart agriculture using IoT and WSN. Int. J. Innov. Res. Comput. Commun. Eng. 4(6), 12070–12076 (2016). https://doi.org/10.15680/IJIRCCE.2016.0406285

2. Manjunatha, S., Sivakumar, B.: Development of smart network using WSN and IoT for precision agriculture monitoring system on cloud. Int. Res. Jo. Eng. Technol. (IRJET) 04(05), 1502–1505 (2017)

3. Kiani, F., Seyyedabbasi, A.: Wireless sensor network and internet of things in precision agriculture. Int. J. Adv. Comput. Sci. Appl. 9(6), 99–103 (2018)

4. Wark, T., et al.: Transforming agriculture through pervasive wireless sensor networks. IEEE Pervasive Comput. 6, 50–57 (2007)

5. Kumar, J., Kumari, A.: Automatic plant watering and monitoring system using NodeMCU. In: 2019 9th International Conference on Cloud Computing, Data Science and Engineering, pp. 545–550 (2019)

6. https://www.intechopen.com/books/wireless-sensor-networks-technology-and-protocols/overview-of-wireless-sensor-network . Accessed 10 Nov 2020

7. Ruby Roselin, A., Jawahar, A.: Smart agro system using wireless sensor networks. In: International Conference on Intelligent Computing and Control Systems ICICCS 2017, pp. 400–403 (2017). 978-1-5386-2745-7/17

8. Elia, G.P.: A decision tree for weather prediction, Universitatea Petrol-Gaze din Ploiesti, Bd. Bucuresti 39 Ploiesti Catedra de Informatică, vol. LXI, no. 1, (2009). 6

9. Salman, A., Kanigoro, B., Heriyadi, Y.: Weather forecasting using deep learning techniques. In: ICACSIS 2015, pp. 281–285 (2015). https://doi.org/10.1109/ICACSIS.2015.7415154

10. Parmar, A., Mistree, K., Sompura, M.: Machine learning techniques for rainfall prediction: a review. In: 2017 International Conference on Innovations in information Embedded and Communication Systems (ICIIECS), pp. 1–6 (2017)

11. Kumar, A., Kumar, N.: Efficient crop yield prediction using machine learning algorithms. Int. Res. J. Eng. Technol. 05(06), 56–72 (2018)

12. Aftab, S., Ahmad, M.: Rainfall prediction using data mining techniques: a systematic literature review. Int. J. Adv. Comput. Sci. Appl. 9(5), 143–150 (2018)

13. Varghese, R., Sharma, S.: Affordable smart farming using IoT and machine learning. In: 2018 Second International Conference on Intelligent Computing and Control Systems (ICICCS), pp. 645–650 (2018). https://doi.org/10.1109/ICCONS.2018.8663044

14. Parashar, A.: IoT based automated weather report generation and prediction using machine learning. In: 2019 2nd International Conference on Intelligent Communication and Computational Techniques (ICCT), Jaipur, India, pp. 339–344 (2019)

15. Parmar, B., Verma, D.: Climate Smart Agriculture, August 2019

16. https://www.raspbian.org/ . Accessed 10 Nov 2020

Enhancing Data Privacy in the Internet of Things (IoT) Using Edge Computing

Kazi Masum Sadique$^{(\boxtimes)}$ ⓘ, Rahim Rahmani ⓘ, and Paul Johannesson ⓘ

Department of Computer and Systems Sciences, Stockholm University,
Borgarfjordsgatan 8, SE-164 07 Kista, Sweden
{sadique,rahim,pajo}@dsv.su.se
https://dsv.su.se/en/

Abstract. The vast deployment of the Internet of Things (IoT) is improving human life standards every day. These IoT applications are producing a massive amount of data from the environment where it is deployed. The collected data are mostly including end-user private data or industrial data, which are transmitted over the internet to the cloud devices for storing, processing, and sharing with the connected applications. Recent IoT data privacy-related researches are mostly focused on data privacy within a particular location of the network or at a specific device, but as per our knowledge, none has pointed and listed all the places where the end-user or industrial data privacy risks exist. In this work, we have addressed both technical and management aspects to enhance the privacy of IoT data. We have identified and listed the places where IoT data privacy risks exist, followed by our proposed model for data privacy enhancement in the internet of things (IoT). A list of ten suggestions for avoiding data privacy leakage to enhance IoT data privacy enhancement is presented. The results of this work should be useful for both academic researchers and stakeholders from the industry while designing and implementing new IoT solutions for the enhancement of human society.

Keywords: Internet of Things (IoT) · Edge computing · Identity privacy · Location privacy · Cloud computing · IoT data privacy

1 Introduction

Internet of things (IoT) applications are involved in data collection and analysis from society to enhance our daily life [15]. Vast amounts of data are produced from the IoT applications, as most of these are data-driven solutions. Some of the widespread use cases of IoT are smart home, smart city, smart grid, smart office, smart healthcare, industrial internet of things, etc. [13]. All these applications are involved in handling user's private data. The process includes data collected from the end devices, data transmission over the internet, data processing at cloud environment, and representation of results in the related user interface or as input to another IoT system for further results or for adjustment of the

N. Kar et al. (Eds.): ICCISIoT 2020, CCIS 1358, pp. 231–243, 2020.
https://doi.org/10.1007/978-3-030-66763-4_20

environments where the data are produced [10,17]. IoT data privacy can be categorized as context-oriented data privacy and content-oriented data privacy [13]. The user/device location [10,17] and identity [13] are the two main components of context-oriented data privacy. The content-oriented data privacy is focused on the actual data [13]. Both context and content-oriented data privacy are essential. But based on the current use cases, content-oriented data can be accessed by third-party applications for research and development. An example use case can be access to the patient's sensitive data by a third-party research institute without proper concern from the patient. Whenever data (content or context) are shared with a third party, the data owner must get informed. There is confusion about the owner of the data. If the person/organization producing the data is the owner or the organization handling the information, is the data owner? The organization storing the data owns the right to store or share the data only after getting concerns from the person or organization producing it. Sometimes data are stored at the device (sensors, actuators, user's mobile devices), sometimes stored at IoT gateways, and at the last stage at cloud storage. As the IoT data transferred over the internet via different network devices and stored at different locations within the network, the traditional data security and privacy rules are not enough for the protection of IoT data. Motivated by the above, we have performed our research on IoT data privacy risks and possible measurements that need to be taken for any organization to protect sensitive user data at different layers of the IoT paradigm. Our research questions and contributions are described below.

1.1 Research Questions

In this paper, the following research questions are answered:

1. What are the IoT data privacy risk domains?
2. How can we solve the IoT data privacy problem using edge computing?

1.2 Our Contributions

The main contributions of this paper are as follows:

- In this paper, we have discussed the different data privacy risk domains of IoT solutions.
- We have proposed a new model based on service localization and intelligent edge gateway for the enhancement of data privacy in the internet of things (IoT).
- We have identified and listed ten suggestions for IoT data privacy enhancement, which can be used as a checklist to avoid data privacy leakages.

1.3 Road Map for Readers

The rest of the paper is organized as follows: in Sect. 2, we have the related works for IoT data privacy. Section 3 describes the IoT privacy risks and proposed solution, consisting of three subsections: in Sect. 3.1, we have discussed IoT data privacy risks. In Sect. 3.2, we have presented our proposed edge computing-based privacy enhancement model. In Sect. 3.3, we have listed ten suggestions for IoT privacy enhancement, followed by Sect. 4, which is the conclusion and future works.

2   Related Works

Recently, many researchers have discussed IoT data privacy. In [6], authors have presented a context-aware software-defined model for IoT data privacy enhancement. The authors have proposed a cloud-centric solution model for smart cities. Cloud-centric models are more vulnerable to IoT security and privacy because of more user data at the cloud layer with access by different entities. An edge centric privacy enhancement model for smart cities is proposed in [5]. The authors have presented the ontological representation of different components of a typical smart city environment with flow charts for their proposed model. They have also discussed performance evolution, but the detail about the tools used is missing. In [3], IoT risks and different IoT privacy research challenges are discussed. The proposed suggestions in this work are mostly focused on access control.

Decentralized identifier-based privacy enhancement is proposed in [9]. This work is also focused on identity and access control for privacy enhancement. But only the access control is not enough for IoT privacy improvement. Another recent research has discussed edge computing-based solutions for smart cities [16]. The authors have presented their intelligent offloading method with simulation results applied for a collaborative smart city. In [4], a detailed survey on the privacy of data at the cloud computing platform is performed. The authors have discussed different privacy challenges, applied methods for data privacy, and existing data privacy-related products. In [2], authors have extensively discussed the European Commission's data privacy rules and regulations, namely the General Data Protection Regulation (GDPR). They have also discussed in detail their Snap4City smart city solution. In [8], authors have presented their work on local monitoring and evolution of network traffic from IoT devices and connected mobile devices. This work is focused on the localization of data for privacy enhancement. As per our knowledge, none of the recent research has addressed the points we have discussed in detail in this paper.

3   IoT Privacy Risk Domains and Proposed Solution

In this section, we have discussed different IoT privacy risks at different layers of the IoT paradigm, followed by our proposed edge-centric location-based IoT privacy enhancement model. At the end of the section, we have briefly described our identified ten privacy enhancement measurements.

3.1 Identified IoT Privacy Risk Domains

IoT data privacy risks exist at different stages of data collection, data analysis, and storing processes. For enhancement of IoT data privacy, it is essential to identify each of the individual domains where there are possibilities of the potential risk of data privacy leakage. In our option, a domain can be anything like a software application, hardware, a network device, an activity performed by the user, an automated activity conducted by a network device, or a server. Based on our above definition, we have identified the following domains where IoT privacy risks need proper attention:

IoT End Devices: Third parties can possess IoT end devices, and they can exact data. The end devices are mostly unmanaged and unmonitored, allowing adversaries to take control of those devices and extract data from them. For example, if a door sensor at a personal property is hijacked, hackers can extract data from it and perform harmful activities when the proprietor is not present at the location. The same applies to medical sensors. If bad guys get control of end devices, they can extract data from it. As a result, IoT end devices have a risk of privacy leakage.

IoT Gateways: Adversaries can possess an insecure IoT gateway. IoT gateways can have similar privacy risks as the IoT end devices. But the IoT gateway holds more data than an IoT end device, so it is more vulnerable. A hijacker of an IoT gateway can extract more data about any person or organization if he/she gets access to an IoT gateway. Besides the risks of data extraction, possession of an IoT gateway has more risks if the intruder gets write access to the device and can perform many dirty activities, which may lead to loss of assets and even loss of life if it is related to healthcare.

Cloud Devices: Cloud computing is famous for storing and analyzing IoT data as it has enough storage, memory, and computational power to perform many complex tasks. Besides scalability, security, storage, and analytics, cloud computing facilitates inter-organizational communication. The cloud application programming interface (API) allows organizations to collaborate and share data. While sharing data with other organizations, it is a risk factor for the company to lose its or employee's private data due to wrong configuration and lack of proper authorization in the back-end system.

Mobile Devices: The user's mobile devices are enhanced with many capabilities to track different activities performed by the user. For example, a step count application keeps track of walking; many location-enabled applications keep track of the user's location, and so on. A mobile device has privacy risks because if it is lost or possessed by a third party, the user's data can be extracted from the device. Also, mobile devices may have few applications installed by the user, collecting and sending personal data to a server without taking concern from the user. A mobile device is also at risk when used as a data collection or analysis tool because access to insecure data sources can make the device vulnerable.

Automatic Data Upload: One of the features of recent mobile applications is the auto-upload of user data to the service providers' cloud storage. Though it is a useful facility and users don't need to worry about the details, it introduces data leakage risks. For example, a user's data can be sent to cloud storage and accessed by the employees within the application developer's organization, which is not acceptable if the user does not approve it on that device.

Insecure Communication Channel: Many IoT applications communicate between each other's, with the gateways, with the cloud storage over insecure communication channels, allowing man-in-middle attackers to collect data from the network and further perform harmful and malicious activities.

Databases: There are privacy risks at the backend databases. IoT data stored in databases can be extracted due to insecure configurations. For example, a web application's front end can have more data sent from the server, which is not shown at the front end of the application but can be extracted from the data variable of the source code of that front end. Also, SQL injection can be performed to extract data from poorly configured databases.

Unauthorized Access: There exist vast risks of unauthorized access to IoT data. In many cases, IoT devices and related storage devices are configured with authentication mechanisms only. While at a big organization, it is crucial to have a proper authorization mechanism over the authorization processes. For example, in a healthcare application, a nurse may not have accessed part of the patient data, and even a general physician may not be allowed to access part of the patient data without proper concern. But a poorly configured system may lead to privacy risk.

People's Awareness: People's awareness is very crucial. IoT privacy risks exist due to a lack of understanding and knowledge. An example scenario can be a mobile device user using mobile devices without a password or pin code. In this scenario, if the mobile is lost, an unauthorized person will access the user's data. Another example could be a Wi-Fi password. Without enough knowledge, general users may use Wi-Fi devices without changing the default passwords. Intruders can easily monitor the network traffic by connecting the Wi-Fi using the default pin code/password. They may access the user's private data.

3.2 Proposed Model

As discussed in the previous section, there are several IoT data privacy risks at different IoT paradigm layers. To solve the issue mentioned above, we have designed a new model (see Fig. 1). In our model, IoT services and applications are localized at the edge devices and within the cloud computing layer. IoT devices within a specific location transfer data to the nearest edge gateway(s). The intelligent edge gateway only shares part of the collected data with the cloud devices. The spatiality of the edge devices is data filtering before transferring data to the cloud. The edge IoT devices are responsible for data aggregation and processing and data storage as well. In our proposed model, the end-user IoT applications communicate to the cloud servers to access data or information processed at the cloud devices. In specific scenarios, the IoT end-user applications can directly access the edge gateways. This model enhances the IoT data security and privacy by localizing services and reducing data transfer between the IoT gateways and the cloud devices.

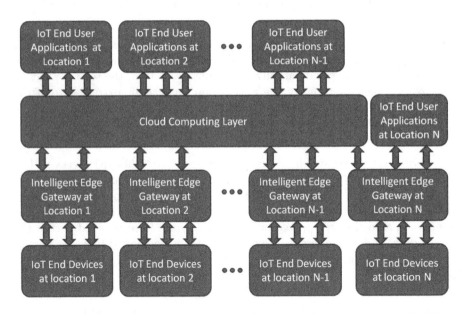

Fig. 1. Proposed IoT privacy enhancement model using edge intelligence and localization of services.

To understand our proposed model, we can consider an example scenario: a user may have access to data collected from different locations. IoT devices are connected to the IoT gateways at different locations. Access to the data is only allowed after the data filter at the intelligent edge gateway. The gateways collect the data and share part of the data with cloud storage. In some use cases, user end-device applications access the data from the edge gateways. For proper privacy implementation, an intelligent edge gateway verifies users' identity and authorization before allowing access to any data source.

It could happen that intruders got access to the IoT gateways. So, it is essential to have private data filtered before the intruder gains access. The intelligent IoT gateways need to identify sensitive personal information so that the private data can categorize. In such cases, intelligent gateways will use machine learning algorithms to categorize data and sources. As machine learning algorithms required more resources and the edge gateways may have limitations, so we propose Support Vector Machine (SVM) [7,14] or Naive Bayes [14] as the machine learning algorithm. But at the initial stage, the machine learning algorithm will not have enough data to predict user activity. As a result, a rule-based classifier [1,11] can be used for data and source/user categorization at the initial stage. Rule based classification can be performed with very few stages/steps [1]. Figure 2 represents different steps for rule based categorization.

Fig. 2. Steps for rule based categorization.

The intelligent edge gateways will also include trusted storage modules to protect unauthorized access to users' private data. A trusted storage module can be build based on the concept of trusted execution environment [TEE] [12]. To restrict access to trusted storage area, source categorization can be implemented. We propose the following simple algorithm for source filtering:

Algorithm 1: Source Categorization

Result: Access or denial to trusted storage
Read incoming source information;
if *authorizedSource* **then**
| Allow access to trusted storage;
else
| Deny access request;
end

It is also important to categorize data before it is stored in the data storage. An intelligent gateway will categorize the data based on the data type. Demographic data should be stored in the storage with extra padding, and the padding values should be secret. We propose the following simple algorithm for data categorization:

Algorithm 2: Data Categorization

Result: Categorize data with or without padding
Read data from the buffer;
if *demographicData* **then**
| Add padding to data;
| Save modified value in database;
else
| Save original value in database;

3.3 Suggestions for Improvement of IoT Data Privacy

We have identified ten main points for the enchantment of IoT. Our identified points are valid for any IoT applications and give research directions for academics and industrial bodies. Detailed descriptions of our identified points are below:

Ensure Security at Devices to Enhance Privacy: IoT devices are mostly unmonitored and remotely mounted for data collection from the environment it is applied. The physical security of the device is essential for the enhancement of the privacy of the IoT data. The communication between the device and the nearest IoT device must be secure and needs to be tempered resistance. Remote connections to the IoT devices need to be restricted. In case the device allows remote connection, it should always have a strong password to protect it from hackers. For example, cameras mounted at smart buildings and assets monitoring are mounted at different locations and are mostly not physically monitored by the authorities. In case an intruder gets access to the data generated by these cameras can perform analysis of activities of any authorized person within that area and make harmful activities to him or on the property itself based on his intention.

Ensure Security During Communication to Keep Data Privacy: As the data collected from the IoT devices are mostly transferred to the cloud, secure communication between the IoT end devices and the cloud servers is worthy. Due to the heterogeneous distribution of IoT devices, traditional network security cannot completely secure the IoT data during communication.

The communication security for the enhancement of IoT data privacy needs at three different stages:

- At the communication between the IoT devices and the IoT gateways
- At the communication between the IoT gateways and the cloud storage
- At the communication between the cloud servers and end-user IoT applications

Any eavesdropping on data at these three stages of communication is against the privacy of IoT data. Due to the difference in communication media and communication protocols, security implementations should be different at these three stages. For example, an end device can connect to the IoT gateway using wireless communication like Bluetooth, or Zigbee or Wi-Fi or mobile network (3G, 4G, and 5G), etc. An IoT gateway may have a wired connection to the cloud servers. And the cloud servers may share results to the end-user applications using wired or wireless communication based on the end-user devices.

IoT Data Privacy at IoT Gateways: IoT data is collected, aggregated from the raw sensor devices, and processed at the IoT gateways before sending it to the cloud server. Implementation of appropriate security rules at IoT gateways is significant for the privacy of data. The IoT gateways should have proper authentication and authorization mechanisms for the protection of data. The IoT gateway itself is vulnerable to security attacks. The remote communication to the IoT gateways needs to be secure and restricted. For example, a secure shell (SSH) connectivity should be allowed only from a trusted entity. Private tunnels between the IoT gateway and the service provider's devices can improve security and privacy. Here the service providers are the entities who are the owner or the maintainer of the IoT gateway. Access to the IoT gateway data needs to be restricted even for the employees within the service provider organization.

Enforcement of Cloud Layer Data Privacy: The Cloud layer provides scalability, flexibility, robustness, reliability, and more secure data storage and processing than any other layer where the IoT data is stored and processed. Besides the benefits, cloud layer data processing can increase data privacy risk because IoT data becomes more visible and accessible to the third party at the cloud layer. For example, application programming interface (API) connectivity to the cloud data is a prevalent tradition for integrating organization and the increase of productivity at different organizations. API based data access is mostly performed using authentication tokens. Sometimes the same token is used for all the communications between the requester (client device) and a cloud server, but accessing different endpoints and resources using the same access token increases the data privacy risks. There could be scenarios where the authentication tokens have to be changed periodically with the increased number of requests from the clients. In such a case, A rule based classifier model (see Fig. 2) can be used. The users get notified, and the token should be revoked so that the same token cannot be used again in further request. An unauthorized person within the service provider organization can read and modify the private data of end-users using the token. It is hard to track the data modifier if several persons within the organization use the same authentication token. Another privacy issue at the cloud layer is the implementation of data access policies for the users and organizations accessing the data. It is prevalent at the current age that IoT device users use his/her username and password for authenticating third-party applications to access his/her data from the cloud. But if the authorization processes at the cloud servers are not strict, the third party can get access to sensitive private data of the user, while the users didn't get informed at all of this.

Proper Enforcement of Access Rules on Data Storage: IoT data can be stored at many different devices and accessed by various applications. The most common data storages are IoT devices, where the data is stored for a tiny amount of time before transferring to the IoT gateways. The following data storing devices are IoT gateways, at the cloud devices, and at the end-user mobile application and/or computers from where the results are accessed. Based on scenarios, databases are accessed by the IoT user's application, cloud applications for data analysis, third party applications via APIs, and IoT applications that are used for adjustment to the environment (machine to machine communications). Implementation of access rules with proper authentication is crucial for the privacy of IoT data. API access is implemented for external access to the databases from the third-party application, needs more attention. The same rules applied for the IoT gateway storage. Also, for the privacy of IoT data at gateway devices, it is necessary to monitor access to the devices. While considering data privacy at the end-user devices, it is important to store the data in a manner that other applications cannot access the data and if the device is stolen, access to the data is not possible by the thief. For example, the users may have the option to erase their personal data by login into his application from another device, which will increase user data privacy. Another important point is logging of access to the data. It is not easy to log all the activities, but the unwanted and abnormal movements need to be logged in the databases.

Role-Based Authentication and Authorization Model: It is crucial to ensure proper authentication and authorization to IoT data in the cloud as the cloud data is more visible to different users, organizations, and applications. Role-based authentication and authorization can improve data privacy. In a role-based model, users or applications get access only to the part of the data; it should need access, and other parts of the data have restricted access. The same rule is applicable for API based access to the database. The APIs should be designed very carefully with proper authentication and authorization rules to enhance data privacy.

Limited Data Sharing with the Cloud: As the cloud layer is more visible from the world, it is better to store only relevant data to the storage and limit storing private data, which is not related to the specific IoT application for which the data is collected. This increases data privacy and reduces the risk of access to the user sensitive data by third parties. For example, a user's full name, address, personal social security number, age, weight cannot be relevant for some applications, and it could be useful for other applications. In these scenarios, the data storage in the cloud should be designed so that only relevant data should be stored and accessed from the IoT gateways. Limited data sharing also reduces the risk of eavesdropping on private data while transferring via the internet.

Implementation of Edge Intelligence to Enhance Data Privacy: We have proposed a model in which the IoT data processed at the edge IoT gateway and transferred to the cloud for further analysis and storage if required. Intelligent edge gateways will enforce rules on IoT data as closely as to the data source. It will filter the data before transferring it to the cloud. If required, the edge devices will make necessary changes to the data fields (e.g., a dummy value assigned to the private data) before transferring to the cloud layer. The intelligent edge devices will also quickly make decisions near the data source and share it with the related IoT applications. Real-time data processing is crucial, and less interaction with the cloud is needed. Intelligent edge gateways can also log unauthorized and abnormal activities attempted by different applications and generate alarms if any data privacy violation has occurred.

User Awareness and Awareness of Peoples Working with Data: People's awareness of data privacy is crucial. The IoT application users should get accurate information about the data they share and generate using their applications. Sometimes in different user applications, the legal agreements are so long and hard to understand by the end users that users lose interest in reading the details and press the agree on buttons before reading it. The legal documentation on any application needs to be easily understandable for the end-users and should be as short as possible. While preparing a legal document, it is essential to consider that the legal authorities' level of legal knowledge and the end-users are not the same.

Law Enforcement and Law Awareness for the Peoples Working with Data: There are laws related to data privacy that needs proper enforcement all over the world. As the data on the internet can travel the world, the laws for data privacy leakage should be at the same level worldwide, and people's awareness about it is worthy. Any employee joining an organization where personal data is processed should get proper training on the data privacy requirement and know his right to access data at different systems.

4   Conclusion and Future Works

In this paper, we have discussed IoT data privacy risks at different stages of an IoT paradigm. We have proposed an edge centric privacy solution for the IoT paradigm. We have also identified ten main points that need to be considered while implementing an IoT application scenario. The identified ten points can be considered as a checklist for the privacy enhancement of any IoT solutions. Our proposed model will reduce the leakage of sensitive user data during transmission and due to loosely configured cloud access. It will also protect from the entry of intruders who may have access to user data but are dishonest. We have suggested a rule-based classifier at the early stage of deployment. After a specific time, the system will have enough data for SVM or Naive Bayes machine learning algorithms to predict unauthorized malicious activities. We will extend our work on the intelligent edge gateway model for the IoT data privacy enhancement with validation in our future work.

References

1. Arefi, H., Alizadeh, A., Ghafouri, A.: Building extraction using surface model classification (2013)
2. Badii, C., Bellini, P., Difino, A., Nesi, P.: Smart city iot platform respecting gdpr privacy and security aspects. IEEE Access **8**, 23601–23623 (2020)
3. Bertino, E.: Data privacy for iot systems: concepts, approaches, and research directions. In: 2016 IEEE International Conference on Big Data (Big Data), pp. 3645–3647. IEEE (2016)
4. Domingo-Ferrer, J., Farràs, O., Ribes-González, J., Sánchez, D.: Privacy-preserving cloud computing on sensitive data: a survey of methods, products and challenges. Comput. Commun. **140**, 38–60 (2019)
5. Gheisari, M., Wang, G., Chen, S.: An edge computing-enhanced internet of things framework for privacy-preserving in smart city. Comput. Electr. Eng. **81**, 106504 (2020)
6. Gheisari, M., Wang, G., Khan, W.Z., Fernández-Campusano, C.: A context-aware privacy-preserving method for iot-based smart city using software defined networking. Comput. Secur. **87**, 101470 (2019)
7. Huang, J., Lu, J., Ling, C.X.: Comparing naive bayes, decision trees, and svm with auc and accuracy. In: Third IEEE International Conference on Data Mining, pp. 553–556. IEEE (2003)
8. Klement, F., Pöhls, H.C., Spielvogel, K.: Towards privacy-preserving local monitoring and evaluation of network traffic from iot devices and corresponding mobile phone applications. In: 2020 Global Internet of Things Summit (GIoTS), pp. 1–6. IEEE (2020)
9. Kortesniemi, Y., Lagutin, D., Elo, T., Fotiou, N.: Improving the privacy of iot with decentralised identifiers (dids). Journal of Computer Networks and Communications **2019** (2019)
10. Malina, L., Srivastava, G., Dzurenda, P., Hajny, J., Ricci, S.: A privacy-enhancing framework for internet of things services. In: Liu, J.K., Huang, X. (eds.) NSS 2019. LNCS, vol. 11928, pp. 77–97. Springer, Cham (2019). https://doi.org/10.1007/978-3-030-36938-5_5
11. Qin, B., Xia, Y., Prabhakar, S., Tu, Y.: A rule-based classification algorithm for uncertain data. In: 2009 IEEE 25th International Conference on Data Engineering, pp. 1633–1640. IEEE (2009)
12. Sabt, M., Achemlal, M., Bouabdallah, A.: Trusted execution environment: what it is, and what it is not. In: 2015 IEEE Trustcom/BigDataSE/ISPA, vol. 1, pp. 57–64. IEEE (2015)
13. Sarwar, K., Yongchareon, S., Yu, J.: A brief survey on IoT privacy: taxonomy, issues and future trends. In: Liu, X., et al. (eds.) ICSOC 2018. LNCS, vol. 11434, pp. 208–219. Springer, Cham (2019). https://doi.org/10.1007/978-3-030-17642-6_18
14. Williams, N., Zander, S., Armitage, G.: A preliminary performance comparison of five machine learning algorithms for practical ip traffic flow classification. ACM SIGCOMM Comput. Commun. Rev. **36**(5), 5–16 (2006)

15. Wong, K.S., Kim, M.H.: Towards self-awareness privacy protection for internet of things data collection. Journal of Applied Mathematics **2014** (2014)
16. Xu, X., Huang, Q., Yin, X., Abbasi, M., Khosravi, M.R., Qi, L.: Intelligent offloading for collaborative smart city services in edge computing. IEEE Internet Things J. **7**(9), 7919–7927 (2020)
17. Zhou, X., Yang, L., Kang, Y.: A research on the IOT perception environment security and privacy protection technology. In: Hung, J.C., Yen, N.Y., Hui, L. (eds.) FC 2017. LNEE, vol. 464, pp. 104–115. Springer, Singapore (2018). https:// doi.org/10.1007/978-981-10-7398-4_11

Priority Based GTS Allocation in Zigbee Wireless Sensor Network

Soumik Ghosh[1]([✉]), Ekata Ghosh[2]([✉]), Indrajit Banerje[1]([✉]),
Debajyoti Kundu[3]([✉]), and Biswajit Mandal[4]([✉])

[1] Indian Institute of Engineering Science & Technology, Howrah, India
soumik.iiest@gmail.com, ibanerjee@it.iiests.ac.in
[2] Accenture, Dublin, Ireland
ekata369@gmail.com
[3] JPMorgan Chase and Co, New York City, USA
debajyoti.kundu.1987@gmail.com
[4] Indian Statistical Institute, Kolkata, India
biswajit.mandal@aol.com

Abstract. IEEE 802.15.4 protocol has been a milestone in the Wireless Sensor Network (WSN) and eventually has become a standard in internet of Things (IoT). In IEEE 802.15.4 GTS (Granted Time Slot) is allocated in FCFS (First Come First Serve) basis. Due to the use of FCFS strategy, some shortcomings have been observed in GST based IEEE 802.15.4 protocol. This research proposes a solution to overcome some the shortcomings in the GTS allocation of the node based on the data prioritization for reliable transfer of high priority data using FCFS. This can be overcome by using a priority-based GTS allocation mechanism in IEEE 802.15.4 /Zigbee in beacon enable mode. The proposed approach shows promising outcome, as it able to reduce transmission delay for high priority data in a Zigbee network.

Keywords: Guaranteed time slot · IoT · Zigbee

1 Introduction

There has been a revolution in IoT domain which resulted a significant increase in use of IEEE 802.15.4 which in turn became a standard for Wireless Sensor Network (WSN) [1,2].The IEEE 802.15.4 protocol provides a communication solution for low-rate frequency wireless technologies which are used in different applications by sufficiently setting its considerations [3]. In order to reduce associated cost and power consumption, IEEE 802.15.4 has been upgraded [4]. ZigBee provides data security via encryption, data routing and can work on mesh networking with better and wider transmission thereby taking IEEE 802.15.4 one notch up.

In Zigbee protocol network is divided in four layers as describe in Fig. 1. There are four MAC frame formats defined by IEEE 802.15.4. These are beacon

© Springer Nature Switzerland AG 2020
N. Kar et al. (Eds.): ICCISIoT 2020, CCIS 1358, pp. 244–255, 2020.
https://doi.org/10.1007/978-3-030-66763-4_21

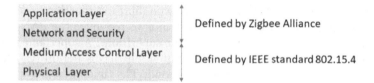

Fig. 1. Protocol Stack of ZigBee

packet, data packet, acknowledgment packet and MAC command packet [5]. Reduced Function Device (RFD) and Full Function Device (FFD) are the two types of nodes that work in a ZigBee network (see Fig. 1) [5]. While RFD has slow processing power, smaller memory and computation abilities facilitate in implementation of only a subset of functions, FFD can either act as a coordinator for a group of RFD or can be Personal Area Network Coordinator (PANc). The PANc creates and manages a network (see Fig. 2) [6].

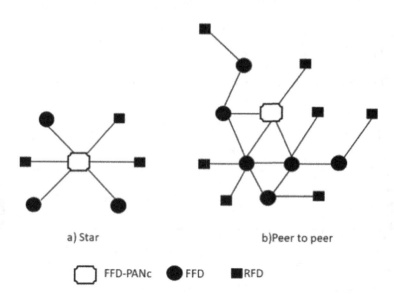

Fig. 2. Network topology supported by the IEEE 802.15.4 MAC layer

There are two communication mechanisms of Zigbee namely: beacon enable mode and non-beacon enable mode [7]. These modes facilitate in movement of data packets. The beacon enable mode facilitates in transmission within two beacons. Time period between two beacons is also divided in three-time frame [8]. A beacon enabled network is formed via creation of synchronization between all devices. On the other hand, non-beacon enable mode does not require any synchronization to among devices [8].

There are three basic functions of a beacon [5]. First function is device synchronization in the network. Second function is to recognize the PANc and the third function is to define the structure of the superframe. A superfame is divided in three time slots (see Fig. 3) namely Contention Access Period (CAP), Contention Free Period (CFP) and Inactive Period. The time interval between two successive beacon frames is called a Beacon Interval (BI) which is the summation of CAP, CFP, Inactive Period. Active time within a BI is called Superfame Duration (SD). Beacon Order (BO) and Superfame Order (SO) are the two features which are used to determine BI and SD [9].

BI can be represented as following (see Fig. 3) [9].

$$BI = aBaseSuperframeDuration \times 2^{BO} \tag{1}$$

$$for\ 0 <= BO <= 14$$

The SD can be stated as [10]

$$SD = aBaseSuperframeDuration \times 2^{SO} \tag{2}$$

$$for\ 0 <= SO <= BO <= 14$$

For both Eq. (1) and Eq. (2),

$$aBaseSuperframeDuration = minimumdurationofthesuperframe$$

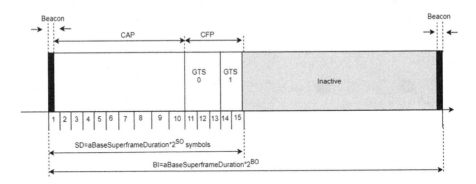

Fig. 3. Structure of Superframe in the beacon enabled mode

Using Garneted Time Slot (GTS), IEEE 802.15.4 protocol/ ZigBee facilitates in real-time data transfer under CFP. Maximum of seven GTS can be allocated in each superframe [9]. First Come First Serve (FCFS) strategy is used for allocating GTS and due to usage of FCFS some shortcomings have been observed. Many a times, some nodes do not get GTS as the nodes requesting first get the slot. In a situation wherein a selfish node, which always gets GTS, arrives in the network; the other nodes caring critical data might fail to book a slot in subsequent super-frame. In such scenarios, the node will not able to transfer data which might lead to delay or loss of data packet [10]. Therefore, data prioritization is one of the most significant requirements in WSN.

The present research focuses to solve the issue of node prioritization in GTS al-location, reliable transfer of high priority data packets and to minimize network delay in IEEE 802.15.4/ ZigBee for high priority data packets. Current paper is partitioned into the following sections: Review of literature is explains the prior works. Next part is proposed method section which has been elaborated the proposed approach. Remaining section shows the simulation methods and analyzing the result of the simulation. Last section defines the conclusion.

2 Review of Literature

Many researchers have conducted different researches associated with IEEE 802.15.4/ ZigBee and the issue of GTS allocation. In a study conducted by Koubaa, Alves and Tovar (2006) [10], the mechanism of allocation of GTS in IEEE 802.15.4 was analysed in the aspects related to throughput, delay and power efficiency. The study further suggested a methodology using Network Calculus Formalism for analysing GTS for IEEE 802.15.4 protocol. Zheng and Lee (2006) [11] conducted a performance analysis of IEEE 802.15.4 protocol through a sim-ulator called NS2 and conducted five experiments to study different associated parameters. The study concluded IEEE 802.15.4 protocol to be favourable for the applications requiring low energy consumption and low data rate.

Lei et al. (2012) [12], proposed a solution to the problem associated with allocation of GTS in case of critical data in WAPN namely Emergency Data GTS (EDG). The study proposed a method for GTS allocation of the nodes with criti-cal data so that such nodes can have access to time slots as per their request and critically of the data. The results of simulation showed the proposed system to provide allocation of GTS to nodes with critical data thereby improving the throughput. In 2012, Lee, Lee and Shin [12] proposed an improvement of reliability of transmission of data associated with GTS allocation. The study proposed an GTS allocation scheme using cluster-tree. Here emergency data slot was used to reduce the delay in transmission and improve the throughput of data packets. This scheme was found to increase the efficiency of critical data transmission.

Another performance analysis was conducted by Patil and Kazi (2013) [2] who analysed IEEE 802.15.4 protocol and suggested a technique which can improve performance of the protocol. The study analysed performance parameters which are loss rate, throughput and average delay. The study used AODV protocol for analysis and compared the results obtained from the simulation model with the existing model. An alternate GTS scheduling method was proposed by Thuy and Phuong (2019) [13] which improves the performance of GTS allocation.

In a recent work conducted by Fatima, Baig and Uddin (2018) [14], a system was proposed to deal with the inefficiencies of ZigBee including the issue of data prioritization in GTS allocation. The proposed system was found to improve the throughput and increased the ratio of packet delivery while a significant reduc-tion was observed in the loss of data packet. It was concluded that proposed sys-tem improved the performance of the considered parameters. Sarkar, D., et al. (2019) has proposed a model to represent the flow of data in different time stamps [15]. Roy. S et al. (2018) has proposed a model for alternate ranking find-ing in cricket [16].

3   Proposed Method

3.1   Methodology and Implementation

To address the issue of prioritization in GTS allocation, this paper proposes a priority-based GTS allocation scheme. Under this scheme, one sensor is attached with one zigbee device which is considered as an individual node. In this study, the priority of the nodes is decided as per research conducted by Cao et al. 2009 [17]. The prioritization is divided into four categories namely Highest Priority, Very High Priority, High Priority and Low Priority.

As per the existing methodology, the nodes that which requires GTS, send a GTS request to the PANc. Figure 4 describes the structure of a GTS request frame. Under GTS characteristics, GTS length indicates the number of GTS requested for allocation, GTS direction indicates the direction of flow of data (transmission of data from PANc to requesting node or vice versa) The charac-teristic type field holds the value 0 or 1 wherein 0 denotes GTS allocation and 1 denotes GTS deal-location. MHR field represents the MAC header.

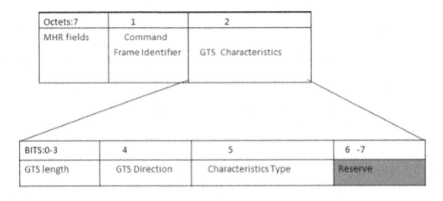

Fig. 4. Structure of GTS Request Frame

The proposed system uses the Reserved field as a "Priority" field (see Fig. 5). The Priority field can contain 2 bit of data thus it can contain a numerical value ranging from 0 to 3 where 0(00 in binary) indicates highest priority data, 1(01

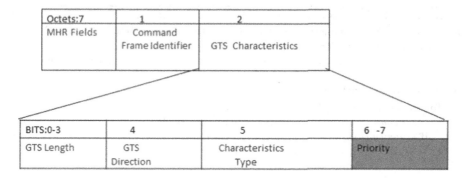

Octets:7	1	2
MHR Fields	Command Frame Identifier	GTS Characteristics

BITS:0-3	4	5	6 -7
GTS Length	GTS Direction	Characteristics Type	Priority

Fig. 5. Proposed Structure of GTS Request Frame

in binary) is very high priority data, 2(10 in binary) is high priority data, 3(11 in binary) is low priority data.

Here, during CAP, when a GTS request comes to the coordinator, the coordinator will check the priority field. In the frame header, PANc will have the information about the source node. By looking at the short address of the node, the PANc can identify the sensor node from which the request has come. Thus, the node with the highest priority will be assigned the GTS first followed by the nodes with lower priority.

In proposed method PANc maintaining a stack of size 7 and store the GTS request packet as per the priority in the stack. If some node request for multiple GTS then PANc insert same packet multiple time in the stack. Nodes who get the acknowledgement packet of GTS request are eligible for sending data in GTS.

The Algorithm 1 starts with all the GTS request packets which are come to PANc within a CAP. The algorithm initialize an empty stack, S of size 7, to store selected GTS request packets by the algorithm. The algorithm also initialise a variable with the lowest priority, i.e., $priority\_thresold$, to indicate highest priority of all requests with in the stack. The algorithm process all the GTS request packets with in CAP one after another.

At the beginning, Algorithm 1 check the current GTS requests packet and calculate for how many GTS allocation it has requested for and store it in the variable GTS_count (step 2). Then Algorithm 1 compare the priority filed value from the GTS request packet with the $priority\_thresold$ (step 3). If the value of the GTS request packet priority is lower or equal to the $priority\_thresold$, then push GTS request packet R_i into the stack S until either stack is full or no more GTS requests (step 4–7). After inserting the GTS request packet into the stack update $priority\_thresold$ value with GTS request packet priority value (step 8).

If priority of the data packet is higher then $priority\_thresold$ then the algorithm go with following steps. The algorithm keep removing packets one by one from the stack S and push these requests on a temporary stack T until the $priority\_thresold$ is less than priority of R_i (step 10–13). In the steps 14–17, the algorithm keep pushing the current GTS requests, R_i, again and again into

Algorithm 1. A method to assign GTS based on the priority of GTS requests

Input: A set of GTS request from nodes within the a ZigBee network
Output: Allocate GTS for most crucial GTS request(s)
Initialization: An empty stack of size 7, S, to hold GTS request packets along with it's priority and set *priority_thresold* $\leftarrow$ minimum priority value,
Steps of the algorithm:

1: **for** each GTS request R_i within a CAP **do**
2:     $GTS\_count \leftarrow$ Number of GTS slot requested by R_i
3:     **if** *priority_thresold* $\geq$ priority of R_i **then**
4:         **while** S is not full $\wedge$ GTS_count **do**
5:             PUSH R_i into S
6:             $GTS\_count -= 1$
7:         **end while**
8:         *priority_thresold* $\leftarrow$ priority of R_i
9:     **else**
10:         **while** S is not empty $\wedge$ *priority_thresold* $<$ priority of R_i **do**
11:             POP top element from S and PUSH into T
12:             *priority_threshold* $\leftarrow$ priority of top request in T
13:         **end while**
14:         **while** S is not full $\wedge$ GTS_count **do**
15:             PUSH R_i into S
16:             $GTS\_count -= 1$
17:         **end while**
18:         *priority_thresold* $\leftarrow$ priority of R_i
19:         **while** S is not full $\wedge$ T is not empty **do**
20:             POP R_i from T and PUSH into S
21:         **end while**
22:         *priority_threshold* $\leftarrow$ priority of top request in S
23:         Clear the stack T
24:     **end if**
25: **end for**

the stack S until either stack is not full or count of the requested GTS in the R_i is 0. Update the *priority_thresold* value with the priority of R_i (step 18). Now get the elements from stack T and push it into stack S one by one until stack S is not full or temporary stack T is not empty (step 19–21). Update the *priority_thresold* with the priority value of the top packet element of the stack S (step 22). Now clearer the temporary stack T.

This paper proposes, allocation of GTS based on priority of GTS request packet. For that we are using the out put stack from the propose algorithem Algorithm 1. In the proposed method acknowledgement frame of GTS request packet will be send at the end on CAP. When a node receives an acknowledgement frame, it extracts all GTS related information which is set by PANc and transmits data in GTS accordingly.

3.2 Simulation

For the analysis of the performance of the proposed mechanism we have used NS2 simulator. Figure 6 shows simulation image.

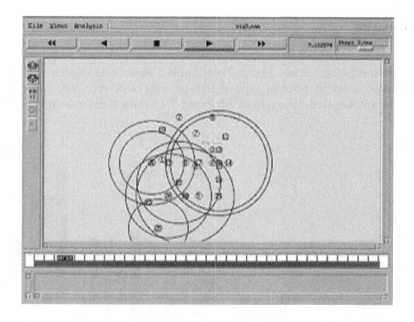

Fig. 6. Simulation model for NS2 simulation

The simulation is performed on a IoT based patient monitoring system where each patient is attached with different type of sensors which are used to monitor the health condition of the patient and each one of the sensor is attached with one ZigBee. So different sensor has its own priority based on the type of the sensor. Table 1 shows the priority of the sensors. For simulation we have taken 27 nodes with one PANc.

Table 1. Node priority and corresponding sensors for simulation.

Node Type	Sensor	Priority
Respiratory	Wireless respiration measurement	0
Chest	Fiber optic	1
Cardiovascular	Blood pressure sensor	2
Lower genitourinary Tract	Bladder pressure sensor and volume sensor	3

With the help of NS2 simulation, an artificial environment is created, and data has been gathered. The results indicate a reduction in the delay for high priority data in the simulated environment using the proposed scheme. The delay calculation is performed as suggested by Koubaa et al. 2006 [18]. A significant reduction in delay for high priority data was observed after implementing proposed priority scheme in NS2 simulation.

4   Results

In this section discusses the results of simulation of the proposed model and compare it with existing models. Figure 7 and Table 2 shows comparative analysis of transmission delay of different type of high priority data in priority based GTS data transmission technique and FCFS based GTS data transmission technique.

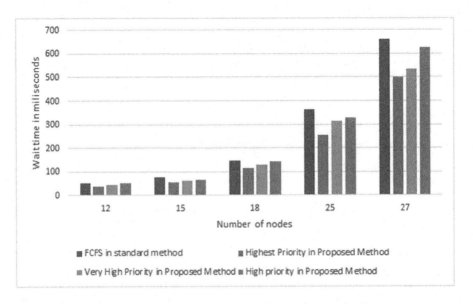

Fig. 7. Graphical representation for change in waiting time for GTS according to the priority level

Table 2. Transmission delay based on Node Count.

Node Count	12	15	18	25	27
FCFS in standard method	53	76	148	365	659
Highest Priority in Proposed Method	39	57	116	256	498
Very High Priority in Proposed Method	46	62	128	316	536
High priority in Proposed Method	51	68	142	327	624

The result shows increase in number of nodes results in increase in delay of the high priority data transfer. The delay incurred in standard FCFS technique is much more than proposed method. There is a 25% improvement for delay reduction for the Highest Priority (priority 0) of data packet. For High Priority (priority 1) of data packet data packet delay average 6.4% reduced wait time.

4.1   Comparing Proposed Solution and EDG Algorithm

Comparing the transmission delay with the increasing number of hop count is discus in this section. It can be observed in Fig. 8 and Table 3 that transmission delay in the EDG technique is more than proposed priority-based method for priority 0 and priority 1 data packet.

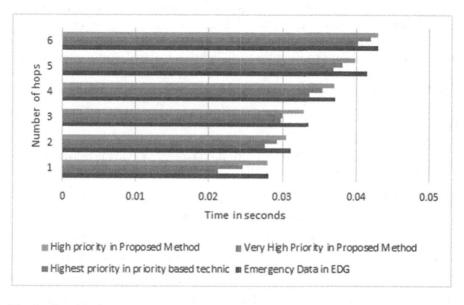

Fig. 8. Graphical representation compression with EDG and proposed method for change in waiting time depending on hop count

Table 3. Transmission delay based on Hop Count.

Hop count	1	2	3	4	5	6
Emergency Data in EDG	0.0281	0.0311	0.0335	0.0371	0.0415	0.043
Highest priority in priority based technique	0.0213	0.0276	0.0297	0.0336	0.0369	0.0402
Very High Priority in Proposed Method	0.0246	0.0293	0.03	0.0354	0.0381	0.042
High priority in Proposed Method	0.028	0.0305	0.0329	0.037	0.0398	0.043

A cluster tree network has been created to check the performance of proposed method and EDG in NS2 simulator. It can be observed from the result that with the increase of hop count there is an increase in delay for the high priority data transfer in EDG technique than proposed method. The result indicates that, the proposed technique offers 12% improvement in delay reduction for priority 0 data packet.

5   Conclusions

The present research has been conducted to propose a solution to reduce the shortcomings associated with GTS allocation in Zigbee wireless sensor network. These issues include node prioritization in GTS allocation, reliable transfer and low network latency in IEEE 802.15.4/ ZigBee for high priority data packets.

This proposed method can be used in any IoT based solutions where efficient priority-based data transfer through Zigbee is required. Automated patient moni-toring system, IoT based fire alarm etc. are few domains where the proposed method can offer more efficient solution.

References

1. Gutierrez, J.A., Callaway, E.H., Barrett, R.L.: Low-rate wireless personal area networks: enabling wireless sensors with IEEE 802.15. 4. IEEE Standards Association (2004)
2. Katiyar, A., Kumar, J., Khilar, P.M.: Adaptive MAC protocol in wireless sensor networks for disaster detection. In: Pattnaik, P.K., Rautaray, S.S., Das, H., Nayak, J. (eds.) Progress in Computing, Analytics and Networking. AISC, vol. 710, pp. 95–103. Springer, Singapore (2018). https://doi.org/10.1007/978-981-10-7871-2_10
3. Lei, X., Choi, Y.-H., Park, S., Rhee, S.H.: GTS allocation for emergency data in low-rate WPAN. In: 2012 18th Asia-Pacific Conference on Communications (APCC), pp. 792–793. IEEE (2012)
4. Tennina, S., et al.: IEEE 802.15. 4 and ZigBee as enabling technologies for low-power wireless systems with quality-of-service constraints. Springer Science & Business Media (2013)
5. Muthukumaran, P., de Paz, R., Spinar, R., Pesch, D.: MeshMAC: enabling mesh networking over IEEE 802.15.4 through distributed beacon scheduling. In: Zheng, J., Mao, S., Midkiff, S.F., Zhu, H. (eds.) ADHOCNETS 2009. LNICST, vol. 28, pp. 561–575. Springer, Heidelberg (2010). https://doi.org/10.1007/978-3-642-11723-7_38
6. Baronti, P., Pillai, P., Chook, V.W.C., Chessa, S., Gotta, A., Hu, Y.F.: Wireless sensor networks: a survey on the state of the art and the 802.15. 4 and ZigBee standards. Comput. Commun. **30**(7), 1655–1695 (2007)
7. Buratti, C.: Performance analysis of IEEE 802.15. 4 beacon-enabled mode. IEEE Trans. Veh. Technol. **59**(4), 2031–2045 (2010)
8. Benakila, M.I., George, L., Femmam, S.: A beacon-aware device for the interconnection of ZigBee networks. IFAC Proc. Volumes **42**(3), 123–130 (2009)
9. Semprebom, T., Montez, C., Moraes, R., Vasques, F., Portugal, P.: Dynamic GTS scheduling of periodic skippable slots in IEEE 802.15. 4 wireless sensor networks. IFAC Proc. Volumes **42**(3), 110–117 (2009)

10. Koubaa, A., Alves, M., Tovar, E.: GTS allocation analysis in IEEE 802.15. 4 for real-time wireless sensor networks. In: Proceedings 20th IEEE International Parallel & Distributed Processing Symposium, p. 8 IEEE (2006)
11. Zheng, J., Lee, M.J.: A comprehensive performance study of IEEE 802.15. 4. Sens. Netw. Oper. **4**, 218–237 (2006)
12. Lee, H., Lee, K., Shin, Y.: A GTS allocation scheme for emergency data transmission in cluster-tree WSNS. In: 2012 14th International Conference on Advanced Communication Technology (ICACT), pp. 675–678. IEEE (2012)
13. Dinh, T.N., Ha, P.H.: Advanced GTS scheduling in IEEE 802.15. 4 networks for industrial application. In: 2019 16th IEEE Annual Consumer Communications & Networking Conference (CCNC), pp. 1–4. IEEE (2019)
14. Fatima, M., Baig, A., Uddin, I.: Reliable and energy efficient mac mechanism for patient monitoring in hospitals. Int. J. Adv. Comput. Sci. Appl. **9**(10), 10–14569 (2018)
15. Sarkar, D., Roy, S., Giri, C., Kole, D.K.: A statistical model to determine the behavior adoption in different timestamps on online social network. Int. J. Knowl. Syst. Sci. (IJKSS) **10**(4), 1–17 (2019)
16. Roy, S., Dey, P., Kundu, D.: Social network analysis of cricket community using a composite distributed framework: from implementation viewpoint. IEEE Trans. Comput. Soc. Syst. **5**(1), 64–81 (2017)
17. Cao, H., Leung, V., Chow, C., Chan, H.: Enabling technologies for wireless body area networks: a survey and outlook. IEEE Commun. Mag. **47**(12), 84–93 (2009)
18. Koubaa, A., Alves, M., Tovar, E.: i-GAME: an implicit GTS allocation mechanism in IEEE 802.15. 4 for time-sensitive wireless sensor networks. In: 18th Euromicro Conference on Real-Time Systems (ECRTS'06), p. 10. IEEE (2006)

MITM Intrusion Analysis for Advanced Metering Infrastructure Communication in a Smart Grid Environment

Shreyas Kulkarni, R. K. Rahul, R. Shreyas, S. Nagasundari[✉],
and Prasad B. Honnavalli

Center for Information Security, Forensics and Cyber Resilience,
PES University, Bengaluru, India
skulkarni.sk.18@gmail.com, rahulravi.kadam@gmail.com,
rshreyas32@gmail.com, nagasundarisuresh@gmail.com,
prasad.honnavalli@gmail.com

Abstract. As the technology evolves rapidly, its necessary to update the traditional system. A smart grid is a modern and digitally updated version of a traditional electrical grid that makes two-way communication between its customers and the utility possible. Advanced Metering Infrastructure (AMI) plays a major role in a smart grid by automatically reporting the power consumption readings to the utility through communication channels. However, there is always a trade-off. Security of AMI communications is a serious concern that needs to be monitored in order to take full advantage of this technology. This paper analyzes the possible security threats of MITM attack on AMI systems and then focuses on the vulnerabilities in the Modbus TCP/IP protocol used by AMI for communications.

Keywords: Smart grid · AMI · Advanced Metering Infrastructure · Smart grid security · SCADA system · MITM attack

1 Introduction

Electricity is a basic need for every human being. We cannot imagine life on Earth without electricity. Every occupation in the modern world is dependent on it. As demand increases, the price also increases. Therefore, to cut down the cost and to evolve in terms of electricity generation, one must come up with ideas on how to actively participate in the production of it. Consumers receive electricity from the generation end through Electric grids. The current existing Electric grid was conceived and designed over a hundred years ago, when electricity needs were simple, power generation was localised and energy demands were less. The main function of the traditional grid was to deliver electricity to consumers' homes and to record the overall power being used. A person from the billing company has to physically go to every house in the locality and generate the bill every month. This one-way interaction makes it difficult for the grid to meet the changing and rising energy demands of the 21st century. Due to the increasing demand for electricity, it is essential that these producers are distributed throughout to provide an uninterrupted power supply to all the consumers. When the power generation is centralised, distribution of power to several consumers would include the usage of large power lines and grids. Consumers are passive in the present electric field where they do not actively participate in power generation and distribution. Using a Smart Grid is a great way of integrating power generation through modern techniques. The Smart Grid replaces many flaws that the conventional method has. Both the consumer and producer can contribute to the power generation. Several private business sectors could pitch in finance for power generation and distribution. This would result in an uninterrupted power supply for all consumers. Present Electric grids consist of an analogue or digital power meter which actively monitors the power consumption of the consumer. The billing routine takes up more human resource. All these issues mentioned earlier can be solved using Smart Grids. Smart Grids employ smart meters called Advanced Metering Infrastructure. AMIs are an integral part of Smart grids. They also monitor smart homes where the power consumption of each device can be calculated. AMIs communicate with the head-end system periodically to report the power consumption values and receives several commands from the head-end system. This communication is based on certain standard protocols. It is of utmost importance to secure these communications. Attacks on this communication will result in a huge disruption of the whole Smart Grid System.

Few major security factors of AMI are confidentiality, integrity, availability and accountability [2]. Simulation of these security concerns makes way for analyzing and designing mitigation approach for such threats. LabVIEW and Real-Time Digital Simulator (RTDS) are used to simulate SCADA system and Intelligent Electronic Devices and a mitigation approach for the same has also been proposed in [3]. A MITM attack is a major and one of the most commonly used attacks on the cyber-physical system. [4] discusses the MITM attack and certain prevention mechanisms. Mitigation approaches are essential to avoid security breaches. X. Li [7] proposed a two-step mutual authentication method. A real-time implementation of the PLC and Smart Grid is discussed in addition to using Arduino is explained and Modbus RTU has been used in [9]. Understanding the impact of Cyber-attack on AMI becomes important, [11] discusses the practical approach of using ping based Cyber-attack which also shows the experimental results of ICMP flood attacks on the smart meter. Security attacks may also occur in wired communication. An approach for wired communication between the PLC and RTU using power line communication helps to solve some security issues [12]. L. Wei illustrated that the application of Machine Learning plays a significant role in theft and attack detection in smart meter [14]. This paper includes simulation of AMI and implementation of an attack on a standard protocol known as Modbus TCP/IP. MITM attack on the SCADA system and the head-end system is also analysed in this paper. In this paper, Sect. 2 explains several components of a Smart Grid System. Section 3 discusses the security issues of a Smart Grid. Further sections focus on simulation of an AMI and a practical approach of a MITM attack on its communication. Section 5 discusses the results obtained after the simulation.

2 Smart Grid System

A smart grid is as an integrated connection of smart devices, grid technologies, and control systems that provides and makes use of digital information, communications, and controls to optimize the reliability, efficiency, and security of electric power delivery. In this paper, our main focus is on the AMI systems, which play a significant role in a Smart Grid.

2.1 Advanced Metering Infrastructure

An AMI enables two-way communication between the consumer and the head-end system. Installing this device helps in monitoring and recording the power consumption and also in generating an automated periodic bill. AMI uses WiFi, Zig-Bee or Wi-SUN for its communication. It consists of a Smart Meter, Communication Network, Data Acquisition System, and Data Management System.

AMI can calculate the amount of power being used by the consumer accurately. This makes the data error-free. It uses partial load curtailment in place of load shedding. This helps in adapting to the loss of generation capacity reducing the necessity of using excess energy during peak hours. AMI's communication infrastructure consists of a HAN (Home Area Network), NAN (Neighbourhood Area Network) and WAN (Wide Area Network) as discussed in [1]. It uses the Modbus protocol for communications in the HAN and the NAN as it involves Intelligent Electronic Devices (IED). With all these advantages, AMI also has its drawbacks [2]. The device might lose its confidentiality when there is unauthorized access to the stored information.

2.2 SCADA System

Supervisory Control and Data Acquisition (SCADA) is a computer system which consists of software and hardware components which can supervise, analyse data and control various activities of large scale process. SCADA system essentially comprises of Programmable Logic Devices (PLC), Human Machine Interface (HMI), Communication Interface and Remote Terminal Unit (RTU). This system is majorly used in industries due to its remote monitoring and controlling feature. It makes a system more autonomous and greatly reducing human interference in hazardous environments. PLCs and RTUs communicate using certain protocols. They exchange data regarding various process values and commands. The communication data is regularly updated to the SCADA system. In this way, the operator has remote and organised access to all the activities in the system. Similarly, Smart Grids consists of several sectors like Generation, Distribution, Transmission and Consumers. These sectors can independently have a SCADA system to monitor the activities. These SCADA systems can also inter-communicate to increase the working efficiency of the Smart Grid with less human intervention. In this way, the SCADA system plays a major role in a modernized Smart Grid System.

2.3   Modbus Protocol

The Modbus protocol is used to connect a Remote Terminal Unit (RTU) with a plant or system supervisory computer in SCADA systems in the electric power industry. It is more widely in use than the DNP3 and IEC protocols. DNP3 uses lower bandwidth and if it is converted into ethernet DNP3, then bandwidth must be increased in parallel. If not then it will have a slower link. The newer IEC protocols are not yet standardized and vary from vendor to vendor.

Modbus is now a standard communication protocol and a commonly available means of connecting industrial electronic devices. This protocol establishes a master-slave method where the server requests the data and the client responds. The slave acts as a server and master is the client. AMIs generally use the Modbus TCP/IP or Modbus RTU version. Modbus TCP/IP uses the ethernet physical layer. This protocol enables reliable data transfer. RS485 produces wire termination issues as well as network termination issues. Modbus RTU uses serial communication which makes it slower. These are some of the reasons why Modbus TCP/IP is preferred. One of the advantages of using a TCP/IP version is that it does not require a checksum calculation. The objective types in Modbus word is a request and response method. A request is made to specify the starting point of the coil or register and the quantities of coils or registers that are to be read. A response is made such that the LSB of the first data byte has the coil addressed in the request. And for each register, the first byte has the higher order bits and the second contains lower order bits.

- **Coil:** Used to read the binary status of the discrete coils in slave. There is one coil per bit in a data field.
- **Discrete input:** It reads the binary status of the input in slave. There is one input per bit in a data field.
- **Input registers:** Reads the binary contents of the input registers in slave. It has 2 bytes per register.
- **Holding register:** Reads the binary contents of the holding registers in slave. It has 2 bytes per register as well.

With all the advantages the Modbus has, there are a few disadvantages that must be taken care of. A master can only have 254 slave devices connected to it. If there are excess devices, then a repeater is needed. Modbus does not have an option to raise an exception. Every time the master must check each data field to confirm whether there is a change in data or not. This requires more bandwidth which results in a lower bit rate. One of the main drawbacks is that Modbus is known to be vulnerable to unauthorized commands.

3   Security Issues of Smart Grid

A smart grid consists of many smart devices that manage the electricity supply and supervise network demand. These devices can be used as attack entry points into the network. Furthermore, the enormousness of the smart grid network makes network monitoring and management extremely difficult. A major advantage of using TCP/IP standards in smart grids is that they provide compatibility between the various components. However, devices using TCP/IP i.e. AMIs and RTUs are inherently vulnerable to a number of network attacks such as Denial of Service, IP spoofing, Teardrop, and others. Smart meters collect large amounts of data autonomously and sends it to the utility company, customers and service providers. The collected data includes private information about the consumers' activities, and when the house is vacant. Therefore, Cyber-attacks on Smart Grid can compromise customer security.

3.1   Man in the Middle Attack

MITM refers to stealing or altering the data i.e. intercepting messages or injecting new messages when the two parties communicate. Active eavesdropping can be an example of this attack. To provide protection against these attacks, it is necessary to detect them at the earliest. One of the methods for tamper detection is Latency examination. The detection depends upon the response time of the victims. An attack is detected if there is a delay in the response time. This helps in finding the abnormalities in the response time. Another way to defend a MITM attack is by using a Transport Security Layer with Certification Authority. Here a stable connection is established once the certificates on both server and client sides are verified [4]. But there exists a possibility of threat even though the victims have a legitimate certificate. Public Key Infrastructure can be one of the solutions for the above mentioned threat. The attacks are detected whenever there is a change in certificates or public keys. [4] explains all the major possibilities of MITM threats (Fig. 1).

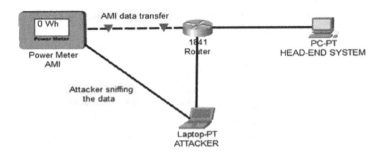

Fig. 1. MITM attack

3.2   ARP Spoofing

Every device consists of an ARP table which translates the IP address to MAC address. A hacker can change the IP to the MAC pairings in the ARP tables by sending a spoofed ARP message onto the LAN. This leads to the linking of an attacker's MAC address with the IP address of an authorized computer/gateway router/server on the network. ARP table consists of mapping of IP addresses to MAC addresses of various system. To successfully conduct ARP spoofing, the attacker changes the contents of the ARP table so that all the packets can be sniffed. Once the attacker system's MAC address is linked to an authentic IP address, it starts receiving any data that is meant for that IP address. ARP poisoning, Ettercap, and Seringe are some of the variations of ARP spoofing. Multiple IP addresses mapped to a single MAC address indicates ARP spoofing. The reply packets in this protocol are not authenticated, it becomes easier to gain illegal access to it. To avoid this attack, [5] suggests a method using the ICMP protocol. Using cryptographic methods to produce digital signatures and locate the origin of ARP packets. It also discusses the algorithm to detect an ARP spoofing attack.

4   Design and Implementation

Extensive simulations have been performed to demonstrate the MITM attack on the Smart Home. The working of the Smart Home is simulated on automation and SCADA software called Interactive Graphical SCADA System (IGSS). IGSS is a full-featured software consisting of several functionalities which allow a complete system to be implemented and to establish communications with the head-end systems. The simulated Smart Homes consists of a Smart Meter, priority devices and control switches. Each Smart Meter or AMI has a Programmable Logic Device (PLC) and a display unit. The Smart Home consists of all sorts of smart devices. These devices are categorised into 3 groups based on the importance and requirement of the device. Priority 1 devices consist of the most essential requirements like lighting and fans and these devices can remain on even after crossing critical power consumption of 90kW. Priority 2 consists of devices like Refrigerators and Washing Machines while priority 3 consists of devices like Television and Air Conditioners. All these devices are virtually connected to the Smart Meter. Smart Meters monitor the power consumption and the incoming Line Voltage from the grids. The power consumption of the Smart Home is calculated as

$$Total = P_1 + P_2 + P_3 \qquad (1)$$

where Total is the total power consumed by Smart Home in kW and P_1, P_2, P_3 corresponds to the power consumed by Priority-1, Priority-2 and Priority-3 devices respectively.

Based on these values, Smart Meters efficiently conserve power by switching on and off different priority devices based on certain conditions. For simulation purposes, these values are considered arbitrarily and almost similar to real-time scenarios. The priority devices work based on the below equations

$$P_1 = \begin{cases} Power_1 & Voltage > 10V \\ 0 & \text{otherwise} \end{cases} \tag{2}$$

$$P_2 = \begin{cases} Power_2 & \text{if } Voltage > 150V \text{ and } Total < 90kW \\ 0 & \text{otherwise} \end{cases} \tag{3}$$

$$P_3 = \begin{cases} Power_3 & \text{if } Voltage > 200V \text{ and } Total < 80kW \\ 0 & \text{otherwise} \end{cases} \tag{4}$$

where Voltage is the Line Voltage in Volts(V) and $Power_1$, $Power_2$, $Power_3$ is the summation of power consumption by all devices in a Priority-1, Priority-2 and Priority-3 respectively (Fig. 2).

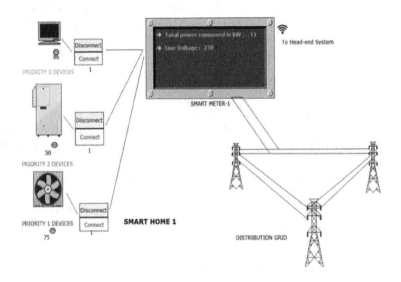

Fig. 2. Smart meter

The basic simulation structure consists of Smart Homes' AMIs communicating with the head end system or the Remote Terminal Unit (RTU) through the Modbus TCP/IP protocol (Fig. 3). A Modbus Slave Software is used to simulate a PLC and Modbus TCP/IP communication with the SCADA at the head-end system. This acts as the server and the SCADA system as a client in the IP configuration. A python script is used to conduct a MITM attack between the AMIs and the head-end system, and to intercept the Modbus packets. Further, Wireshark was used to capture and analyse the communication packets (Fig. 5).

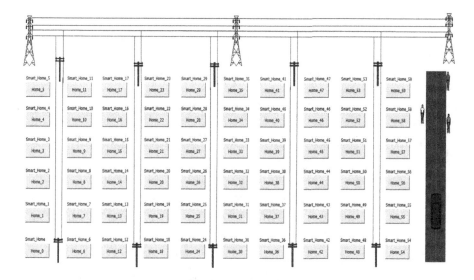

Fig. 3. A locality with 60 smart homes

The simulation of the locality area consists of the homes being monitored at one place. Modbus protocol uses port number 502 to communicate. Therefore, the head end system is the server that accepts connections from the clients or smart homes. These smart homes have random port numbers assigned by the IGSS Software. IGSS also has a feature to raise Alarms. In the simulation, certain alarms or events alert the Operator or the owner of a Smart Home so that required action can be taken to rectify the error. IGSS has a feature in which a daily report can be generated with all the power consumption readings of various devices.

Table 1. Power consumption of few homes at a given instant of time

Smart home	Line voltage (V)	Power consumption (kW)
Home-1	230	27.5
Home-2	180	27.4
Home-3	230	28.1
Home-4	0	27

5   Results

A locality with 60 Smart Homes is successfully simulated using the IGSS software. Modbus protocol was used for communication between each Smart Home's AMI and the head-end system. Automated periodic billing is done for every

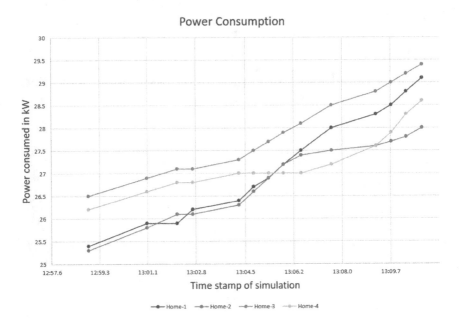

Fig. 4. Power consumption of a few homes with respect to time

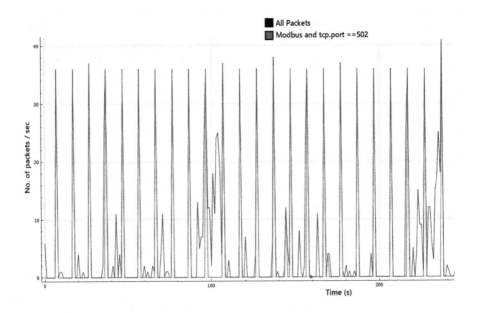

Fig. 5. I/O traffic graph as seen by the attacker

home. To depict the vulnerabilities of Modbus communication, Man-In-The-Middle attack through ARP Spoofing was implemented. Power consumption values of few homes have been plotted over time in the Fig. 4. Table 1 depicts the line voltage and power consumption values of the homes considered in the graph at a given instant of time. The slope of the graph implies the rate of power consumption which is affected by the line voltage received by the homes. When the slope of a line becomes zero it implies that Line Voltage is 0 V. Therefore, the slope of a line is directly proportional to power consumption. The Modbus I/O traffic graph as seen by the Man-in-the-Middle system is shown in Fig. 5. The black line in Fig. 5 corresponds to normal traffic in the attacker's system and the red line corresponds to the traffic due to Modbus packets routed through the attacker's system. It can also be inferred that the communication between the SCADA system and the head-end system happens periodically. Figure 6 depicts the Modbus packets captured on the attacker system.

```
502; ----> ;14900; Modbus Packet captured: ;b'\x00\x00\x00\x00\x00\x06)\x10\x01\xa2\x00\x01'
502; ----> ;14897; Modbus Packet captured: ;b'\x00\x00\x00\x00\x00\x06&\x10\x01\x84\x00\x01'
502; ----> ;14901; Modbus Packet captured: ;b'\x00\x00\x00\x00\x00\x06*\x10\x01\xac\x00\x01'
14902; ----> ;502; Modbus Packet captured: ;b'\x00\x00\x00\x00\x00\t+\x10\x01\xb6\x00\x01\x02\x00\n'
14898; ----> ;502; Modbus Packet captured: ;b"\x00\x00\x00\x00\x00\t'\x10\x01\x8e\x00\x01\x02\x00\x06"
14903; ----> ;502; Modbus Packet captured: ;b'\x00\x00\x00\x00\x00\t,\x10\x01\xc0\x00\x01\x02\x00\x06'
14899; ----> ;502; Modbus Packet captured: ;b'\x00\x00\x00\x00\x00\t(\x10\x01\x98\x00\x01\x02\x00\x06'
14900; ----> ;502; Modbus Packet captured: ;b'\x00\x00\x00\x00\x00\t)\x10\x01\xa2\x00\x01\x02\x00\x06'
14901; ----> ;502; Modbus Packet captured: ;b'\x00\x00\x00\x00\x00\t*\x10\x01\xac\x00\x01\x02\x00\x06'
502; ----> ;14902; Modbus Packet captured: ;b'\x00\x00\x00\x00\x00\x06+\x10\x01\xb6\x00\x01'
14902; ----> ;502; Modbus Packet captured: ;b'\x00\x00\x00\x00\x00\t+\x10\x01\xb6\x00\x01\x02\x00\n'
502; ----> ;14898; Modbus Packet captured: ;b"\x00\x00\x00\x00\x00\x06'\x10\x01\x8e\x00\x01"
502; ----> ;14899; Modbus Packet captured: ;b'\x00\x00\x00\x00\x00\x06(\x10\x01\x98\x00\x01'
502; ----> ;14900; Modbus Packet captured: ;b'\x00\x00\x00\x00\x00\x06)\x10\x01\xa2\x00\x01'
502; ----> ;14901; Modbus Packet captured: ;b'\x00\x00\x00\x00\x00\x06*\x10\x01\xac\x00\x01'
502; ----> ;14902; Modbus Packet captured: ;b'\x00\x00\x00\x00\x00\x06+\x10\x01\xb6\x00\x01'
502; ----> ;14903; Modbus Packet captured: ;b'\x00\x00\x00\x00\x00\x06,\x10\x01\xc0\x00\x01'
14899; ----> ;502; Modbus Packet captured: ;b'\x00\x00\x00\x00\x00\t(\x10\x01\x98\x00\x01\x02\x00\x06'
14900; ----> ;502; Modbus Packet captured: ;b'\x00\x00\x00\x00\x00\t)\x10\x01\xa2\x00\x01\x02\x00\x06'
14904; ----> ;502; Modbus Packet captured: ;b'\x00\x00\x00\x00\x00\t-\x10\x01\xca\x00\x01\x02\x00\t'
```

Fig. 6. Modbus packets captured

6 Conclusion

The Modbus TCP/IP protocol used in AMI communications is not very secure and is vulnerable to MITM, DOS and other such attacks. It can be made secure by adding security measures like Authentication and Encryption of the data being communicated. The IEC protocol is more secure and can be used as an alternative to the Modbus protocol, but it has not been standardized yet. As a continuation of this research project, hardware implementation of this project can be done using PLCs as well as the implementation of a novel countermeasure for such attacks to make the communication secure and reliable.

References

1. Lighari, S.N., Jensen, B.B., Hussain, D.M.A., Shaikh, A.A.: Attacks and their defenses for advanced metering infrastructure. In: 6th International Congress on Ultra Modern Telecommunications and Control Systems and Workshops (ICUMT 2014), St. Petersburg, pp. 148–151 (2014). https://doi.org/10.1109/ICUMT.2014.7002094

2. Cleveland, F.M.: Cybersecurity issues for advanced metering infrastructure (AMI). In: 2008 IEEE Power and Energy Society General Meeting - Conversion and Delivery of Electrical Energy in the 21st Century, Pittsburgh, pp. 1–5 (2008). https://doi.org/10.1109/PES.2008.4596535

3. Chen, B., Pattanaik, N., Goulart, A., Butler-Purry, K.L., Kundur, D.: Implementing attacks for Modbus, TCP protocol in a real-time cyber physical system testbed. In: 2015 IEEE International Workshop Technical Committee on Communications Quality and Reliability (CQR), Charleston, SC, pp. 1–6 (2015). https://doi.org/10.1109/CQR.2015.7129084

4. Conti, M., Dragoni, N., Lesyk, V.: A survey of man in the middle attacks. IEEE Commun. Surv. Tutorials **18**(3), 2027–2051 (2016). https://doi.org/10.1109/COMST.2016.2548426

5. Jinhua, G., Kejian, X.: ARP spoofing detection algorithm using ICMP protocol. In: 2013 International Conference on Computer Communication and Informatics, Coimbatore, pp. 1–6 (2013). https://doi.org/10.1109/ICCCI.2013.6466290

6. McDaniel, P., McLaughlin, S.: Security and privacy challenges in the smart grid. IEEE Secur. Priv. **7**(3), 75–77, May–June 2009. https://doi.org/10.1109/MSP.2009.76

7. Li, X., Liang, X., Lu, R., Shen, X., Lin, X., Zhu, H.: Securing smart grid: cyber attacks, countermeasures, and challenges. IEEE Commun. Mag. **50**(8), 38–45 (2012). https://doi.org/10.1109/MCOM.2012.6257525

8. Yang, Y., Littler, T., Sezer, S., McLaughlin, K., Wang, H.F.: Impact of cybersecurity issues on smart grid. In: 2nd IEEE PES International Conference and Exhibition on Innovative Smart Grid Technologies, Manchester **2011**, 1–7 (2011). https://doi.org/10.1109/ISGTEurope.2011.6162722

9. Kuang, Y.: Communication between PLC and Arduino based on modbus protocol. In: 2014 Fourth International Conference on Instrumentation and Measurement, Computer, Communication and Control, Harbin, pp. 370–373 (2014). https://doi.org/10.1109/IMCCC.2014.83

10. Shu, F., Lu, H., Ding, Y.: Novel modbus adaptation method for IoT gateway. In: 2019 IEEE 3rd Information Technology, Networking, Electronic and Automation Control Conference (ITNEC), Chengdu, China, pp. 632–637 (2019). https://doi.org/10.1109/ITNEC.2019.8729209

11. Kumar, S., Kumar, H., Gunnam, G.R.: Security integrity of data collection from smart electric meter under a cyber attack. In: 2019 2nd International Conference on Data Intelligence and Security (ICDIS), South Padre Island, TX, USA, pp. 9–13 (2019). https://doi.org/10.1109/ICDIS.2019.00009

12. Liu, J., Zhao, B., Wang, J., Zhu, Y., Hu, J.: Application of power line communication in smart power Consumption. In: ISPLC2010, Rio de Janeiro, pp. 303–307 (2010). https://doi.org/10.1109/ISPLC.2010.5479945

13. Thomas, M.S., Ali, I., Gupta, N.: Integration and security analysis of metering infrastructure. In: 2012 IEEE Fifth Power India Conference, pp. 1–6 (2012)

14. Wei, L., Rondon, L.P., Moghadasi, A., Sarwat, A.I.: Review of cyber-physical attacks and counter defense mechanisms for advanced metering infrastructure in smart grid. In: 2018 IEEE/PES Transmission and Distribution Conference and Exposition (T and D), Denver, CO, pp. 1–9 (2018). https://doi.org/10.1109/TDC. 2018.8440552

15. Annaswamy, A.: IEEE Vision for Smart Grid Control: 2030 and Beyond Roadmap. In: IEEE Vision for Smart Grid Control: 2030 and Beyond Roadmap, pp. 1–12, 24 October 2013. https://doi.org/10.1109/IEEESTD.2013.6648362

Smart Border Security System Using Internet of Things

Madhurima Bhattacharya and Alak Roy[✉]

Department of Information Technology, Tripura University, Tripura, India
madhusherlock10894@gmail.com, alakroy@tripurauniv.in

Abstract. National security and defence is incredibly important for a country and its people. For increasing tension in the border areas due to unresolved conflicts, currently national security systems emphasize more on border security to protect the country from terrorist attacks, illegal border crossing and infiltration from the neighbouring countries. To make security system more efficient, a real time border security system is needed which can provide 24 h surveillance in the border areas with high accuracy and that can minimize the need of human involvement by utilizing the most advanced sensors and actuators. Indian Border Guarding forces are already installing and adopting newer technologies in terms of cameras, night vision devices, radars etc. But for the efficient and intelligent use of collected data, involvement of modern and innovative technology like Internet of Things (IoT) is very necessary, which already has been adopted but in very small scale and in limited areas. Whereas, it is the reliable source of accurate data and renowned for smart and fast decision making as it is one of the major fields of implementing Big Data and Analytics. So, a smart IoT based solution has been introduced for securing hazardous border areas with extreme climatic conditions, diverse land forms, river terrains, inaccessible dense forest areas which is very tough to monitor for the individual. This paper "Smart Border Security System using Internet of Things" proposes a low-cost system that uses various sensors like Passive Infrared (PIR) sensor and OV7670 camera module to sense movement of any object within a range and capture images of intruder respectively. The system can upload the sensed data into a cloud server which can be retrieved in a base station by using web and desktop application as well. The system can also send alert to the base station by processing the sensed data. Also, it allows user i.e. the trained security personnel to control the camera and retrieve data from it from a distant. Through the proposed system it is possible to detect the intruder crossing the border area instantly.

Keywords: Internet of things · Border security system · Passive infrared sensor

1 Introduction

Border security is incredibly important to guard vulnerable and valuable assets like an individual, dwelling, community and nation from any harmful activities

© Springer Nature Switzerland AG 2020
N. Kar et al. (Eds.): ICCISIoT 2020, CCIS 1358, pp. 268–279, 2020.
https://doi.org/10.1007/978-3-030-66763-4_23

of an intruder. Universal security issues are imperative, particularly border and coast security to any nation. Border zones are commonly considered as spots where massive brutality, interruption and dispute between several forces occurs. Topography like mountains, cold regions, deserts, unforgiving climate and water bodies frequently lead to troublesome access and observing of outskirt zones [1]. Smart border security system using Internet of Things is an innovative idea to secure our border areas smartly and efficiently with minimal deployment of military in hostile zones.

According to a report of Federation of Indian Chambers of Commerce & Industry (FICCI), forces of the Indian territory is focusing mostly on implementing advance technology like IoT to improve the efficiency and effectiveness of border operations These systems comprises of a sensor layer, which is applied in a planned manner to allow a layered defence mechanism; network backbone, which allows real time data transmission from the field locations to the relevant stakeholders, base command centre, where all decisions are taken. Stakeholders can observe and analyse the incident and launch the response process for event management and control based on predefined Standard Operating Procedures (SOPs) [9]. The combination of traditional methods with current technologies like Internet of Things (IoT) and Wireless Sensor Networks(WSN) can lead to advancement of security system.

The concept of connected device was first introduced since the 70s but the actual term Internet of Things was established by Kevin Ashton [2]. It may be depicted as an group of interconnected computing devices consisting of mechanical and digital devices, any items or any living beings. The Internet of Things objects consist of sensors, software, network connections and necessary electronics and it empowers them to gather and exchange data and make them responsive. On the other hand, Wireless Sensor Network (WSN) can be described as a distributed network of some devices feature capable of local processing and wireless communication [12]. Sensors are used to collect information from a physical environment. For Implementation of wireless communication, industrial areas are necessary because of inaccessibility to remote location, to transmit the information gathered by the sensors and controlling them is not possible every time from a remote location.

In this paper, a smart border monitoring system using Internet of Things is proposed. The main objective of the proposed system is to design a device that can automatically detect the intruder crossing the border areas. The system will help the border security forces to protect the border areas smartly and efficiently with minimal deployment of forces in hostile zones.

The rest of this paper is organized as follows. Section 2 presents recent literature review related to border security systems. Section 3 presents the architecture of the proposed system, module design and working principle of the system. Section 4 discuss the experimental results. The paper concludes with future research direction in Sect. 5.

2   Literature Survey

Being one of the largest country, India has a very large border of around 15,106.7 km along the side of China, Nepal, Bangladesh, Pakistan, Bhutan and Myanmar. Due to unsafe and compel border structure, it gets to be troublesome to oversee and secure the boarder [3]. Many research works done by the students, Professors and research scholars on this field of Internet of Things (IoT), have been inspired as well as helped to do this project in field of IoT. Also the online resources, surveys, blogs and research papers gave light to the way of work, and helped to progress. Hopefully this project will meet all the support, functional and performance expectations of the user. As a reference we can take the following research paper and architecture of the developed system. As a reference we can take the following research paper and architecture of the developed system.

In [1], a system based on WSN (Wireless Sensor Network) and IoT, has been developed by using Raspberry pi, ESP8266, PIR and sound sensors, a 180° controlling motor, two types of Camera (FLIR and night camera), laser pistol and a buzzer. A control station have been set up to establish a communication link within the borders using 2 routers. On movement detection by the sensors, the electric shocker is activated by raspberry pi, also alert is sent to the control station by ESP8266 WiFi module. Horizontal and vertical movement of intruder can also be detected by electric motor. Electric shock can be controlled by control station. The use of both wireless and wired communication increases the reliability of the system. More usage of hardware and their collaboration has made the system very efficient irrespective of season and geographical location.

G. S. Nagaraja and Shreyas Srinath have been introduced an IoT based security architecture implemented in a small scale area in [4]. Proposed IoT based smart home system is designed and implemented to make home or private property more secure which is user friendly also. Sensors used in this proposed scenario are Infrared Rays (IR) sensor, PIR sensor, water flow sensor, temperature and humidity (DHT11) and current sensors, used for turn on or off lights and automatic control of gates, detect human being's presence, to water the garden accordingly with moisture level, to monitor electrical components like light bulb, fan, AC etc. respectively. Wireless sensor network has been implemented by Zigbee technology and Raspberry Pi, running on MQTT protocol, has been used as controller. Mobile application is there for controlling the appliances remotely by the user.

In [7] H Salman ET Al have been developed a low cost real time IoT based solution for home security which includes IR camera, controlled by Raspberry Pi 3B for capturing image, Haar cascade algorithm and LBPH algorithm for face recognition, and also notification system in case of unknown face detection. SQlite along with my SQL has been used to update the database to the web server. The proposed embedded system using Raspberry Pi 3 connected with PIP camera, using the camera, computer vision is utilised to process the taken image by image processing algorithm to recognise the face. LBPH face recognizer has been used for training the data. The trained data was saved as XML or YML format. For testing the data Haar cascade algorithm taken from OpenCV library has been used and implemented in python programming. In the wake of recognizing the picture, it contrasts and the pictures of the client's database. 87% face recognition accuracy has been mate. If different image is detected from the user's database the system subsequently send SMS and email, along with the unknown image, to the user's smartphone. This system uses SMTP protocol for sending email to the user. An IoT based application Twilio sms python api has been used in this system for sms service.

[5] have introduced an IoT based Frontier security and tracking system encompassing with a threshold based algorithm for the effective tracking of boats in the sea. Proposed system encompasses Raspberry Pi 2 as IoT kit and different components such as GPS tracker module, weather forecasting sensors, relay circuit, LCD display and Android application that facilitate effective monitoring and forecasting of unfortunate events in the sea frontiers. This application consists of integrated water alarm which helps the fisherman in an efficient way. Threshold value sets at 5 km from the border line. System triggers an alarm as well as sends an alert message when the fishing boat is near the threshold limit of 5 km. Due to unforeseen circumstances if the boat crosses the nautical border relay circuit will be turned off which is start and shutdown the system. The proposed system helps the fishermen to easily identify the sea frontiers of the countries and they are prevented by entering into other country frontiers by adaptive algorithms.

On contrast to the above cited papers, the proposed framework is considerably a low-cost solution as number of hardware and sensors used are less. Unlike [1], we are not taking automatic action against intruder, but providing real time data to the security personnel for better decision making, also the proposed system is lightweight compared to the systems introduced in [1] and [4], that makes it fit to be used in complex land forms. Although the systems introduced in [4] and [7] are mainly built for small scale area like house, building and private property, and the real time IoT framework introduced in [7] using IR camera, is built to take action by detecting face, but our proposed work combines both the methodology more or less, to introduce a new system that is more compatible and easy to use for the security person who might not be well trained or irrelevant with technology. As the proposed system is a low cost IoT based solution, it can be deployed in a large number. Unlike [5], the introduced system can be suitable to use not only in the coast line, but in any hardly accessible areas like swampy marshes, snow-covered peaks and tropical evergreen jungles, difficult and varied terrain etc.

3   Proposed System

This section presents the architecture, module design, system methodology and working principle of the proposed system "Smart Border Security System using Internet of Things". The proposed system uses sensors, micro-controller board and wireless network to develop an effective device that can automatically detect the intruder crossing the border areas. The system has the ability to notify user by analysing the data collected from the intended border area. The data is uploaded in a cloud server that can be used to analyse the sensory information in order to activate the camera module to capture images of the intruder. The proposed system is more beneficiary than the traditional security system.

3.1 Architecture

The system has been developed with the combination of hardware and software components. The hardware part consists of passive infrared (PIR) motion detection sensor, OV7670 camera sensor, Ardiuno micro-controller board, resistors, connectors and printed circuit board. The software part consists of Arduino IDE, Thingspeak web server, serial port reader. Programming language used are Java, C++. For building up an insightful security gadget dependent on IoT - M2M framework, sensor network and database management are the foundations. Architecture of the system has been shown through block diagram in Fig. 1 where all the hardware is connected with the arduino micro-controller board. The flow of data is shown with arrow mark. Arduino is going to switch on PIR sensor as soon as power supply turns on. Data collected from PIR sensor will be sent to cloud server through ESP8266. Also Arduino will send alert to the control room. On the other hand user can turn on camera module by sending signal to the Arduino board via USB cabel.

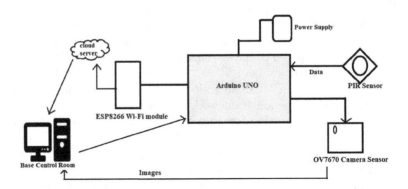

Fig. 1. Architecture of the proposed system

3.2 Module Design

In this section, we are going to discuss about design of different modules that combines to make the whole system. As mentioned earlier, we have divided the whole system in two modules. The given Fig. 2 shows the first module, hardware connection of Arduino board, ESP8266 Wi-Fi module, PIR motion Detector sensor [11] and alarm.

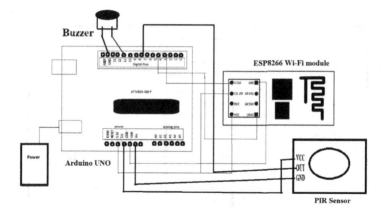

Fig. 2. Circuit diagram of module 1 (i.e. connection of Arduino with ESP8266, PIR sensor and alarm)

In the second part of the module, according to user input Arduino is going to turn on and turn off OV7670 camera module. User can control the camera module via Arduino microcontroller, like selecting port, start clicking photos and also can stop taking photos. User can save images in the system if required. Circuit diagram of this module is shown in Fig. 3 which describes connections between OV7670 Camera module and Arduino board. User can control the camera module through Serial Port Reader Software made for OV7670 camera module [6] which is shown in Fig. 4.

3.3   System Methodology

In the first part described in Fig. 5, PIR motion detector sensor is connected to the Arduino board with connectors. It has 3 pins - VCC, GND, and analog out pin. Among the pins A0, GND and VCC pins are connected to the Arduino Board. The Arduino board is receiving the sensor data through A0 pin that is connected to the sensor. The Arduino UNO microcontroller board based on ATmega328p has 14 digital input output pins and 6 analog inputs with a USB connection and a Power Jack on it. ESP8266 Wi-Fi module consists of 8 pins with patch antenna and a processor.

RX and TX pin is used for data transmission and reception purpose. The data received by the sensor is uploaded in cloud server with the help of Wi-Fi module. Wi-Fi module uses wireless connection to upload the data into the server. In the proposed system ThingSpeak IoT platform [8] has been used as cloud server as they are providing free cloud storage. A buzzer connected with the Arduino board act as output device to send alert in the base station. However, this proposed model is quite small model, to implement it in a bigger area user can use more strong and reliable buzzer or alert system also. In the second part of the system described in Fig. 6, OV7670 Camera module is interfaced with Arduino board. It works on 3.3 V, but Arduino GPIO pin provides 5.5 V power.

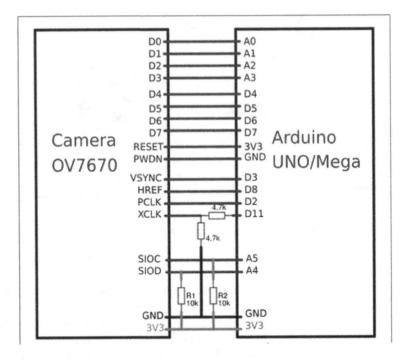

Fig. 3. Circuit diagram of module 2 (i.e. connection of Arduino and camera module)

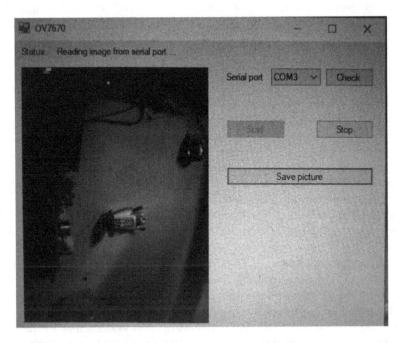

Fig. 4. Serial port reader interface

Fig. 5. Hardware connection of module 1

So we have to use resistors to connect these two hardware. We have used 10 k and 4.7 k resistors. This image sensor is controlled using Serial Camera Control Bus (SCCB) having a maximum clock frequency of 400 KHz. SCCB, which an I2C interface uses SIOC and SIOD pins to connect with the analog pins of Arduino. Handshaking pins like VSYNC(Vertical Sync Output), PCLK(Pixel Clock Output), HREF(Horizontal Reference), XCLK(System Clock) are connected with the digital output pins of Arduino board. Rest of the digital pins are connected with the digital pins of OV7670 to get 8-bit YUV/RGB Video Component Digital Output.

3.4 Working Principle

The system is developed using Arduino board and coding is done using Arduino IDE [10]. Firstly, the PIR sensor is turned on to check motion detection. Along with this, according to the program on Arduino output signal is generated and alert is sent to the base station. The analyzed data is farther stored in the SQL database provided by the ThingSpeak IoT platform using URL command line tool and library through HTTP protocol. On the other hand, for controlling the OV7670 camera module, there should be Serial Port Reader software installed in the system which reads image sensor data through USB cabel. Code uploaded into Arduino captures images as per user request, user can fetch data via the Serial Port Reader interface. The workflow of the system is represented in the following flowchart in Fig. 7.

Fig. 6. Hardware connection of module 2

4   Experimental Result

The system is tested in room temperature and in low light area to understand
the feasibility of the camera. Our experiment has been conducted separately for
both the module as mentioned earlier in Sect. 3. Experimental output, briefly
described in the Table 1 and Table 2 to show the automated working of PIR sensor and Image sensor respectively. Each experiment returned success full result
as desired.

Table 1. Experimental result obtained : part 1

Sl No.	Test Case Description	Desired Output	Actual Output	Status
01	Test the working of PIR sensor by connecting it's 3 pins to the Arduino. It should detect motion .	If motion is detected the PIR sensor will return 1.Data can be seen in serial port.	PIR sensor returning 1 if motion detected, otherwise sends 0. Data is showing in Serial Port	Successful
02	ESP8266 should upload sensor data into cloud server	Graphical representation of data need to show in Thingspeak website.	Graphical representation of data showed in Thingspeak website.	Successful
03	Arduino should send alert through output pin	Buzzer should ring if motion detected	Buzzer rang when motion detected	Successful

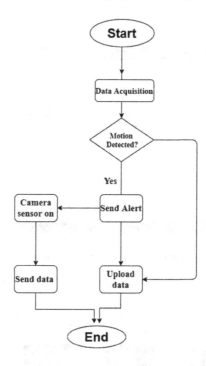

Fig. 7. Flowchart of the proposed system

Table 2. Experimental Result Obtained : part 2

Sl No	Test case Description	Desired Output	Actual Output	Status
01	Serial Port Reader check the port number if OV7670 is connected successfully	Port number will be shown in window	port number showed	Successful
02	Camera data will be shown in the window when user will click start button .	Camera data is viewed in the window	Images displayed	Successful
03	Last updated image will be shown when stop button clicked	camera will stop working and window showed last updated image	Camera Stopped	Successful
04	User can save Picture by clicking on save picture button	User save picture with desired file name and file extension.	Image saved in the system	Successful

Also user interface in Thingspeak web application has been shown in Fig. 8 where user can frequently monitor the status of the sensor by observing the graphical representation. The analysed data is stored in the SQL database provided by the ThingSpeak IoT platform using URL command line tool and library through HTTP protocol. In Fig. 9, snapshot of the folder containing collected data by the Serial Port Reader software have been shown. However, user obtains

Fig. 8. Snapshot of graphical representation of Sensor data in Thingspeak Web Application

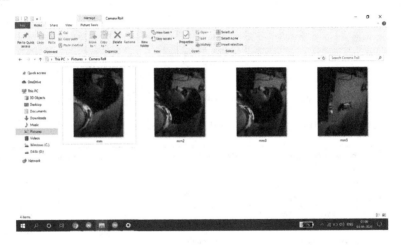

Fig. 9. Snapshot of collected data by OV7670 Image Sensor

live data on the software, also save images in the system if required by simply clicking on the save button of the software interface as shown in Fig. 4.

5   Conclusion and Future Direction

The paper proposed a cost effective smart border security system using Internet of Things. The system can detect the intruder crossing the border areas, thereby helping the border security forces to monitor hostile zones of border areas efficiently with less manpower. The system utilizes the passive infrared sensor which is cheaper as compared to others sensors for intruder detection. The use of such sensor with camera module makes the system more reliable. Presently, the system is developed for small scale area. To implement the system in larger area in near future, a central base station will be required to control the substations in that area. Then, periodical status transmission to the central base station will be possible. Moreover, more attention will be given on improving the user visualization to improve data retrieving performance. Further research can be done to improve the functioning and features of the system.

References

1. ALshukri, D., Sumesh, E.P., Krishnan, P.: Intelligent border security intrusion detection using IoT and embedded systems. In: 2019 4th MEC International Conference on Big Data and Smart City (ICBDSC), pp. 1–3. IEEE (2019)
2. da Costa, K.A., Papa, J.P., Lisboa, C.O., Munoz, R., de Albuquerque, V.H.C.: Internet of things: a survey on machine learning-based intrusion detection approaches. Comput. Netw. **151**, 147–157 (2019)
3. International Land Border. https://www.mha.gov.in/sites/default/files/BMIntro-1011.pdf. Accessed 05 June 2020
4. Nagaraja, G.S., Srinath, S.: Security architecture for IoT-based home automation. In: Satapathy, S.C., Bhateja, V., Mohanty, J.R., Udgata, S.K. (eds.) Smart Intelligent Computing and Applications. SIST, vol. 159, pp. 57–65. Springer, Singapore (2020). https://doi.org/10.1007/978-981-13-9282-5_6
5. Krishnan, R.S., Julie, E.G., Robinson, Y.H., Kumar, R., Tuan, T.A., Long, H.V.: Modified zone based intrusion detection system for security enhancement in mobile ad hoc networks. Wireless Netw. **26**(2), 1275–1289 (2020)
6. How to Use OV7670 Camera Module with Arduino. https://circuitdigest. com/microcontroller-projects/how-to-use-ov7670-camera-module-with-arduino. Accessed 06 Jan 2020
7. Salman, H., Nayeem, M.A.R., Mohammad, A., Bai, X., Mamun, M.R., Ali, M.M., Peol, A.: A low-cost internet of things-based home security system using computer vision. In: Satapathy, S.C., Bhateja, V., Nguyen, B.L., Nguyen, N.G., Le, D.-N. (eds.) Frontiers in Intelligent Computing: Theory and Applications. Salman, H., et al: A low-cost internet of things-based home security system using computer vision. In Frontiers in Intelligent Computing: Theory and Applications, pages 163–170. Springer, 2020, vol. 1014, pp. 163–170. Springer, Singapore (2020). https://doi.org/10.1007/978-981-13-9920-6_17
8. De Nardis, L., Caso, G., Di Benedetto, M.G.: ThingsLocate: a ThingSpeak-based indoor positioning platform for academic research on location-aware internet of things. Technologies **7**(3), 50 (2019)
9. Smart Border Management. http://ficci.in/spdocument/23030/Smart-Border-Management-Report-ficci.pdf. Accessed 05 June 2020
10. Arduino IDE. https://www.arduino.cc/en/Main/Software. Accessed 06 June 2020
11. Interface PIR sensor to Arduino, motion sensor or detector. http://www. circuitstoday.com/interface-pir-sensor-to-arduino. Accessed 06 July 2020
12. Bhasin, V., Kumar, S., Saxena, P.C., Katti, C.P.: Security architectures in wireless sensor network. Int. J. Inf. Technol. **12**(1), 261–272 (2018). https://doi.org/10. 1007/s41870-018-0103-6

Cluster Based Redundancy Elimination Algorithm for Data Aggregation Scheduling Scheme in Wireless Sensor Networks

Komal$^{(\boxtimes)}$ and Amandeep Kaur Sohal

Department of Computer Science and Engineering, Guru Nanak Dev Engineering College, Ludhiana, Punjab, India
LDH.komal@gmail.com, Amandeepkaursohal@rediffmail.com

Abstract. Wireless Sensor Networks (WSNs) is composed of several tiny Sensor Nodes (SNs) ingenious to identify any variation in the environmental situations by using its sensor units. SNs are deployed covering vast regions in a distributed scheme to predict the fluctuation in physical and environmental considerations like sound, pressure, humidity, temperature, etc. SNs communicate with each other to transmit data packets from SN to Base Station (BS). In WSNs, loss of data packets, data latency, energy balance are main challenges in clustering based data aggregation scheme. Many algorithms are designed for data aggregation and data transmission time slots based on time period to sense data and rate of data transmission. Cluster based Data Aggregation Scheme (CDAS) effectively solves the issue of data latency and packet losing. This scheme is based on prioritizing the sensed data. But transmitting huge amount of sensed data to distant BS location causes more depletion of energy of SNs. In this paper, we proposed a Cluster based Redundancy Elimination Algorithm for Data Aggregation Scheme (CREADAS) to eliminate redundancy from sensed data in WSNs. The proposed scheme is the improvement of Cluster based Data Aggregation Scheme (CDAS). Simulation results shows that proposed scheme removes the redundancy issue caused by short time data sensed by SNs and improves the energy efficiency of network and ratio of data delivery.

Keywords: Wireless Sensor Networks · Clustering · Cluster-head · Sensor Node · Redundancy removal · Data aggregation · Minimum spanning tree · Slot scheduling

1 Introduction

Wireless Sensor Networks (WSNs) cover many areas like home security, military, video surveillance, pollution monitoring, water pollution detection, disasters prevention such as earthquake, floods, etc. The WSNs comprised of tiny power units called SNs. The Sensor Nodes (SNs) have the ability to do processing of data

© Springer Nature Switzerland AG 2020
N. Kar et al. (Eds.): ICCISIoT 2020, CCIS 1358, pp. 280–291, 2020.
https://doi.org/10.1007/978-3-030-66763-4_24

and communication. WSNs are more reliable as compared to wired networks deployed in unpredictable environment. The SNs are deployed over large areas in different places like volcano, where humans can't go. The SNs are powered with tiny sized batteries having limited energy. So it is important to make sure that usage of energy is limited. To maintain self-organizing nature, SNs have to communicate with each other. More communication also causes more depletion of energy that affects the lifetime of network. In WSNs, SNs aggregates the sensed data and send it to Base Station (BS) or sink. Sending redundant and unimportant data to distant BS again and again reduces the network lifetime and energy efficiency. Redundancy in WSNs caused by short time data sensed by SN and neighboring SN at the same time. Then sending that data without considering redundancy issue causes transmission of more data packets and it depletes more energy of SNs. Data aggregation is a process to reduce number of transmissions required to transmit data. It is a systematic mechanism for transmission of data gathered from various nodes and sends it in single packet [1]. Many algorithms are proposed based on data aggregation scheme. The algorithm is selected based on network of application and usage of energy. The main data aggregation scheme used in WSNs is cluster based and tree based. In cluster based scheme, network is divided into clusters and every cluster has one cluster head (CH) that responsible for aggregation of data transmitted by other member nodes. Then CH transmits that data to BS or sink. In tree based scheme, the BS acted as root node and other SNs of network acted as leaves. In this data is transmitted from leaves to root node and data aggregation is done at parent nodes [2]. The main issues of cluster based scheme are data latency and balance of energy consumption.

1.1   Problem Formulation

Cluster based Data Aggregation Scheme (CDAS) effectively solves the issue of data latency and packet losing. But it still have some deficiencies.

- Transmitting huge amount of sensed data to distant BS location causes more depletion of energy of SNs.
- More communication between SNs and BS station lowers the life of the network.

1.2   Objectives

- In initial stage, redundancy elimination algorithm is implemented using Mean Averaging method. SNs eliminate redundancy from sensed data using redundancy elimination algorithm and then send sensed data to cluster head (CH).
- Each CH used data compressive aggregation technique on data received from cluster members. Minimum Spanning Tree (MST) based data aggregation tree is generated by BS.
- In final stage, different time slots are assigned for data aggregation to SNs to reduce loss of data packets and data latency.

In this paper, Cluster based Redundancy Elimination Algorithm for Data Aggregation Scheme (CREADAS) is proposed to eliminate redundancy issue, reduce end-to-end data latency and minimize data packet loss rate. To eliminate redundant data, Euclidean based mid averaging mean method is implemented on SNs. Then, MST is generated for data aggregation. After this, scheduling algorithm for timeslots is implemented. This paper is divided into 5 sections. Literature review of related works explained in Sect. 2. The proposed scheme is presented in Sect. 3. Section 4 presents the simulation results and comparison of proposed work. Section 5 concluded the paper.

2   Related Works

Cuicui et al. [2] proposed a cluster based data aggregation scheduling scheme (CDAS), which resolves latency and data packet loss issue. This scheme is divided into two phases. In first, Spanning tree based mechanism is used to aggregate data at CH. In second phase scheduling algorithm is implemented to resolve data latency issue. This scheme helps to reduce average waiting time to arrive data packets at BS.

Mantri et al. [3] proposed a MA-Greedy Algorithm. Which is known as mobile agent based data gathering. This method used binary matrix for compression scheme (CS). To achieve balance level coefficient of variation based matrix is implemented.

Sain and Arshad [4] designed a bandwidth based data aggregation algorithm (BECDA). This proposed work implemented on heterogeneous network based on residual energy and dynamic nature of sink node. The intra-inter-cluster data aggregation technique is used on SNs. Scheduling algorithm for data aggregation also implemented in this work.

Khariji et al. [5] proposed a distributed nature based data aggregation scheduling (DAS) scheme. There are two BS involved in this scheme. In this scheme, at first stage a tree is generated with root nodes acted as virtual sinks or BS. Numbers of children or leaf nodes are counted on individual levels. After this constructed tree taken into account with DAS algorithm that works on timeslots to minimize energy depletion. This scheme designed a unequal clustering based algorithm.

Srinivas [6] proposed an algorithm to eliminate redundancy from aggregated data (REDA). This algorithm generates different patterns to clusters. This aggregation technique used data deferentially method at SNs and iterations method. After generating different patterns to all SNs then that patterns compared with others to select which SN have to transmit data. This algorithm reduces the transmission of redundant data [7].

3 Cluster Based Redundancy Elimination Algorithm for Data Aggregation Scheme (CREADAS)

In this paper, we propose a cluster based data aggregation scheme to reduce data latency and loss of packet delivery issue. In this, whole network is divided into clusters and one SN from every cluster elected as CH based on residual energy. The proposed scheme (CREADAS) works in two phases and first phase is divided into parts:

1. First Phase: Step one, Data redundancy removal algorithm is implemented on SNs. Step two, Data aggregation tree constructed by BS.
2. Second Phase: Scheduling algorithm implemented.

In first phase, Euclidean based minimum distance and averaging algorithm is used to remove redundancy issue caused by data sensed in short duration by SNs and neighboring SNs at the same time. SNs sensed the real-time data. The quality of the data is influenced by external conditions like temperature, moist, humidity, etc. That means that data contains noise in it. To check whether its noise in data or not, threshold value for sensed data is generated and if threshold value of data sensed by SN lies between original threshold range. Then it considered as data without noise. After removing redundancy from data, SNs sends their data to CH. CH aggregates all the data and applies compression function to reduce the size of the data packet. When cluster formed and CHs are elected, then CH sends advertisement (ADV), CHN ID, cluster ID, size of cluster, and energy. Based on position of CHN, BS generates a minimum spanning tree (MST). Then broadcast the information of MST to all CHNs. In second phase, time-slots are scheduled based on data packet loss ratio (PLR) and maximum delay (DM) time estimation, for SNs having real-time data and for rest of the SNs, time-slots scheduled based on rate of data transmission. Because SNs having real-time data faces the issues like data latency and data loss. PLR is estimated at BS and DM is estimated at each SNs (Fig. 1).

3.1 Data Redundancy Elimination Algorithm

In proposed work, Euclidean based Minimum distance (MD) method and Averaging based Mean method are implemented to eliminate redundancy from sensed data by SNs. Data sensed in short duration and at same time by individual SNs causes redundancy issue. Sending unimportant redundant data to distant BS depletes energy of SNs and decreases the lifespan of network. SNs sensed the real-time data. The quality of the data is influenced by external conditions like temperature, moist, humidity, etc. That means that data contains noise in it. To check whether its noise in data or not, threshold value for sensed data is generated and if threshold value of data sensed by SN lies between original threshold range. Then it considered as data without noise. The averaging based method used to calculate arithmetic mean value of all data sensed by SN. Then the Euclidean based MD method used to calculate the lowest distance of valid data.

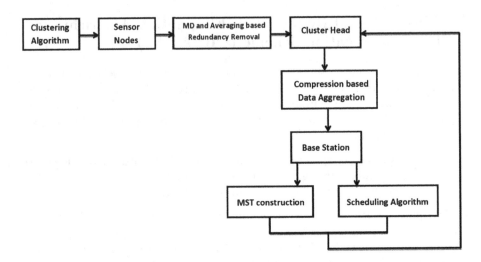

Fig. 1. Architectural view of proposed scheme

$$E_t = \sum_{i=1}^{d} T_i \times \Delta_i \tag{1}$$

Where,

$$\Delta_i = \begin{cases} 1, & T_{min} < T_i < T_{max} \\ 0, & \text{otherwise} \end{cases}$$

In Eq. 1, E_t indicates value based on characteristics of data sensed by SNs in time t, d is the data sensed by SN in time t, Δ_i is the threshold value of sensed data used to check if data is valid or not. If value of T_i ranges between T_{min} and T_{max}, then that data considered as valid. Formula used to find lowest order distance using MD method defines below:

$$E_t = \sum_{i=1}^{d} (T_i \times \Delta_i \times D^2) \tag{2}$$

In Eq. 2, D represents the value for data based on characteristics of data value and that lies between minimum E_t value.

3.2 Aggregation Based Tree Generation

In this phase, CHN aggregates the data transmitted by cluster member nodes (CM) by using compressive data aggregation.

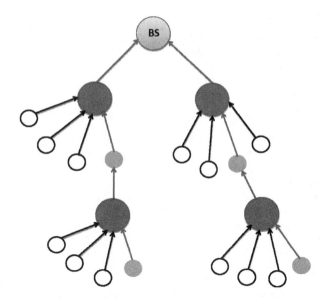

Fig. 2. Cluster based data aggregation tree using shortest distance

Figure 2 shows that in this manner the tree will be generated for aggregation of data. For generation of tree, all SNs will aware of their locations. All CHNs have their cluster information. Then CHN of one cluster will send a message to nearest CHN of other cluster. Then tree will be generated using location and residual energy information of all SNs.

Firstly, CHN broadcast a message containing details of cluster such as ID of CHN (CHN_{ID}), location of CHN (CHN_{loc}), ID of cluster (C_{ID}), size of cluster (C_{size}) and residual energy of CHN and CM (E_{res}), to nearest CHN. After this all CM sends their data to their CHN. CHN calculates the rate of data received from CM. Then CHN aggregates the data received from CM by using compressive aggregation. CHN sends their cluster details and CHN_{loc} to sink. Using CHN_{loc}, BS generates a MST by selecting shortest distance in one tree to other. The MST generates between CHN of one cluster to other.

3.3   Time–Slot Scheduling

In this phase, BS schedules the time-slots for transmitting data based on priority value. This process is defined in first algorithm below. The CHN prioritize the data based on real-time data and non real-time data. If the data is real-time with high deadlines then that data is prioritized and data transmits to BS under reliability based restrains. On the other hand if the data is no real-time data then that data is low prioritized and transmits to BS under lesser restrains. For transmission of low priority data, time-slots are scheduled using data sensing duration and rate of transmission. For transmission of high priority data, time-slots are scheduled after considering rate of data loss and maximum time delay.

Notations:

CHN_j : Cluster Head Node;

CHN_{j+1}: Neighbor cluster head node;

CHN_{id} : Identity of cluster head node;

CHN_{loc} : Cluster Head Node location;

C_{id} : ID of Cluster;

CM : Cluster Members;

ER: error rate;

n: total number of nodes;

b: total bits of data in a packet;

MST : minimum spanning tree;

$V1$: vertex of tree $T1$;

$V2$: vertex of tree $T2$;

$D_{min}(V1,V2)$: Distance between vertex $V1$ and vertex $V2$.

PLR: rate of data packet loss;

D: end-to-end delay;

$P_{priority}$: Priority;

TR_{txn}: Rate of transmission data.

Algorithm 1:

1. For each CHN_j (where j=1,2,3,4,....,n)

   $CHN_j \text{information} \overrightarrow{CHN_{j+1}}, CM$

   CHN_j sends information containing CHN_{id}, C_{id}, CHN_{loc}, C_{size}, E_{res} to neigh--boring CHN and CM.

2. $CM_j \overrightarrow{(DataPackets)} CHN_j$

   Cluster Member (CM) nodes send their data to CHN_j

3. $DR_{rxt} = \prod_{j=1}^{2f}(1 - ER(j))$

   Using DR_{rxt} CHN_j calculates the rate at which packets are generated.

4. $f(l_{CHN}) = \sum_{l=1}^{k} X_i + \frac{1}{N} \sum_{j=1}^{N} Y_i$

   Using $f(I_C HN)$, CHN_j uses compressive data aggregation.

5. $CHN_j \rightarrow CHN_{location} \rightarrow BS$

   CHN_j sends its location to BS.

6. Start if (BS receives $CHN_{location}$),

   then, Stores location information and generates MST based on $CHN_{location}$.

7. End If

8. BS used $D_{min}(V1,V2)$ for MST generation.

9. BS schedules the transmission of data.

10.BS sends MST information and schedule to CHN_j.

Algorithm 2:

1. For each CHN_j (where j=1,2,3,4,....,n)

2. Start IF (Data=Real-time)
   then, $P_{priority} = $ High

3. Else
   $P_{priority} = $ Low

4. End If

5. D $= \sum_{j=1}^{i-1} d_j + \sum_{j=j+1}^{n} d_j$
   Using above equation, CHN_j calculates the delay time (D) w.r.t transmission of data.

6. CHN_j calculates TR_{txn}.

7. CHN_j sends aggregated data by using D, TR_{txn} and $P_{priority}$, to BS.

8. BS used $D_{min}(V1, V2)$ for MST generation.

9. For all aggregated data received from CHN_j, BS checks $P_{priority}$

10. Start IF ($P_{priority} = High$) then,
    BS calculates PLR
    BS schedules time-slots to CHN_j w.r.t $D > delay$, $PLR_{minimum} = PLR$

11. Else
    BS schedules time-slots to CHN_j w.r.t sensing duration and TR_{txn}.

12. End If

13. BS sends the scheduled time-slots to CHN_j.

14. End For

4   Simulation Results

The proposed Cluster based Redundancy Elimination Algorithm for Data Aggregation Scheme (CREADAS) is simulated in MATLAB (Matrix LABoratory) and compared it with Cluster based Data aggregation Scheme (CDAS) and Bandwidth Efficient Cluster based Data Aggregation Scheme (BECDA). The proposed approach (CREADAS) is compared with other data aggregation based techniques such as CDAS and BECDA in terms of density of SNs and network size. The CDAS approach works in the same manner as CREADAS approach. But it does not resolve the redundancy issue in sensing data. CREADAS approach is the improvement of CDAS. Apart from CDAS, BECDA approach also used for comparison. BECDA algorithm effectively solves the issue of data gathering by using inter- intra cluster aggregation. BECDA approach is based on data aggregation scheduling algorithm. Redundancy removal method is used to evaluate the comparison between CDAS, BECDA and CREADAS.

4.1   Simulation Parameters

See (Table 1).

Table 1. Simulation parameters

Parameter	Value
Total number of SNs	200
Size of Network	1000 m × 1000 m
Initial energy of SNs	14.0 j
Transmission Power	0.660 W
Receiving Power	0.4 W
Size of packet	512 bytes
Data transmission rate	50–250 kb/s

4.2   Results and Comparison

The simulation results shows that CREADAS enhances the lifetime of network. Total number of SNs are fixed to 200 and data flows across every cluster is varying between 4–10 to analyze the flow of data. The simulation results shows that CREADAS approach resolves the issues of CDAS and improves the network life.

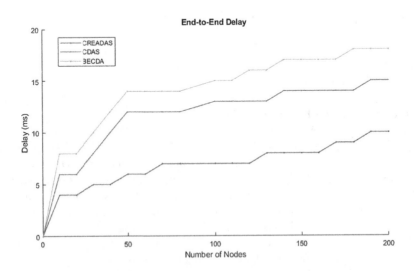

Fig. 3. End-to-end delay comparison

Figure 3 Shows the result of delay comparison of CREADAS with other two schemes. Increase in number of SNs results in increase of routing path length that will cause the increase in end-to-end delay. In CREADAS, delay time increases to 7.5 ms to 14.5 ms. CREADAS decreases the time delay than other two schemes. After removing redundancy from sensed data CREADAS decreases the longer delay in data transmission.

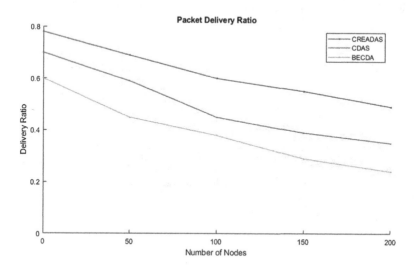

Fig. 4. Packet delivery ratio comparison

Figure 4 Shows the result of packet delivery ratio comparison of CREADAS with other two schemes. Drop rate of data packets increases at leaf SNs with increase in number of SNs. Ratio of delivery at CREADAS decreases from 0.75 to 0.53 that shows delivery ratio is more than other two schemes.

$$Packet\ Delivery\ ratio = \frac{Number\ of\ Packets\ Received}{Total\ Number\ of\ Packets\ Generated} \qquad (3)$$

Figure 5 shows the comparison of average packet drop between CREADAS, CDAS and BECDA. Packet drop at intermediate SNs increases with increase in number of SNs. Drop rate at CREADAS increases from 72.2 to 1998, which is lower than other two schemes.

$$Packet\ Drop\ Rate\ (PDR) = \frac{Number\ of\ Packets\ not\ Received}{Total\ Number\ of\ Packets\ Sent} \qquad (4)$$

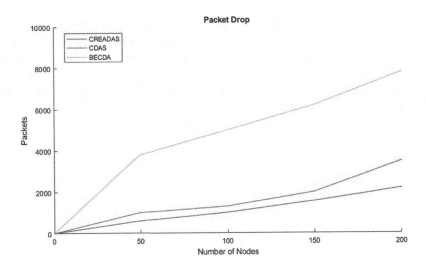

Fig. 5. Average packet drop comparison

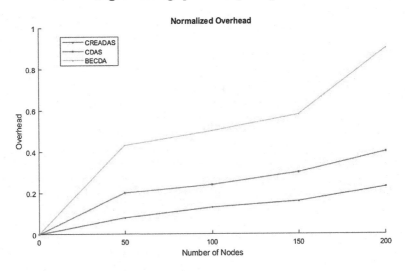

Fig. 6. Overhead comparison

Figure 6 shows the comparison of overhead normalize comparison between CREADAS, CDAS and BECDA. With increase of SNs, aggregation also increases. The overhead of CREADAS lies in 0.14 to 0.27, which is lesser than other schemes.

$$Normalized\ Overhead = \frac{Number\ of\ Packets\ Sent(or forwarded)}{Total\ Number\ of\ Packets\ Received} \quad (5)$$

5 Conclusion

In this paper, Cluster based Redundancy Elimination Algorithm for Data Aggregation Scheme (CREADAS) is proposed. In this scheme redundancy removal algorithm is designed for data aggregation, which effectively reduces the redundancy in data sensed by SNs and use effective data aggregation method to deliver it to BS. The proposed scheme efficiently resolves the time delay and packet loss issue of cluster based data aggregation scheme. Redundancy removal algorithm helps to identify the redundancy in short time data and same data sensed by adjacent SNs at same time. The proposed scheme effectively reduces the energy consumption by SNs. This scheme eliminates redundancy from sensed data and avoids waiting for data transmission which improves the performance of network.

References

1. Devi, V.S., Ravi, T., Bhagavathi, P.: Cluster based data aggregation scheme for latency and packet loss reduction in WSN. In: Computer Communications (2020)
2. Cuicui, Lv., Weipeng, Y.S.: Energy-balanced compressive data gathering in Wireless Sensor Networks. In: JNCA (2016)
3. Mantri, D.S., Prasad, N.R., Prasad, R.: Bandwidth efficient cluster-based data aggregation for Wireless Sensor Network. In: Computer Elec. Eng. (2014)
4. Sain, S., Arshad, J.: Many-to-many data aggregation scheduling in wireless sensor networks with two sinks. In: Computer Networks (2017)
5. Khariji, S., Raventos, G. V., Kammoun, I., Kanoun, O.: Redundancy elimination for data aggregation in wireless sensor networks. In: IEEE (2018)
6. Srinivas, M.B.: Energy efficiency in load balancing of nodes using soft computing approach in WBAN. In: Yadav N., Yadav A., Bansal J., Deep, K., Kim, J. (eds) Harmony Search and Nature Inspired Optimization Algorithms. Advances in Intelligent Systems and Computing, vol, 741. Springer, Singapore. https://doi.org/10.1007/978-981-13-0761-4_41
7. Zhang, C., Haddadi, H.: Deep learning in mobile and wireless networking: survey. In: IEEE Communications Surveys & Tutorials (2019)
8. Heinzelman, W.R., Chandrakasan, A., Balakrishnan, H.: Energy-Efficient Communication Protocol, Wireless Microsensor Networks. In: IEEE (2000)

Integrated Internet of Things and Analysis Framework for Industrial Applications Using a Multi Tiered Analysis Architecture

Ishaan Lodha$^{(\boxtimes)}$, Maroli Karthik Rao, Chinta Subhash Chandra, and Abhimanyu Roy

PES University, Bangalore, India
ishaanlodha@gmail.com

Abstract. As the internet revolution brought the world closer, the internet of things revolution aims to connect everything to one entity. This will lead to a world of connected devices actively sensing stimuli, collectively processing data and making intelligent decisions. Such an approach has massive applications in heavy and high risk industries for reducing risk to life, and for fault tolerance and continuity. A smart and connected factory can achieve greater results with a lower chance of accidents along with support for real time decision making. We propose a smart factory setup with connected machinery and peripherals and a back end with remote controlling of every aspect. A multi tiered analysis tool for premise analysis and insights as well as big-data market analysis has also been proposed. The system allows for a computing architecture with data store and local processing at the on premise edge device. This allows for greater security and complete data ownership but requires more hardware resource. Thus users can opt for a completely cloud based model as well. The system provides complete control on all aspects of the premise and big-data analysis and provides security over the public internet by making using of virtual private networks and tunnelling. The system can lead to the creation of a large source of data across an industry and allow for industry wide demand and supply analysis.

Keywords: Internet of Things · Big data · Hadoop · Spark · Fog computing · Industrial IoT · Sensors · Kafka · Stream processing · Cloud computing

1 Introduction

The smart revolution which aims to connect everything to the internet such that anything can be accessed or controlled from anywhere is based on the concepts of Internet of Things (IoT). IoT refers to the connection of quotidian and mundane devices to the internet creating a collective network for remote sensing and control as well as real time intelligent decision making [1]. IoT applications are data

© Springer Nature Switzerland AG 2020
N. Kar et al. (Eds.): ICCISIoT 2020, CCIS 1358, pp. 292–303, 2020.
https://doi.org/10.1007/978-3-030-66763-4_25

intensive and IoT devices are sources for massive amounts of data, especially sensor data which play a vital role in informed decision making. It is estimated that IoT devices will have been responsible for generating over 500 ZB of data by the end of 2020 [2]. IoT has the potential to convert almost everything into a network connected smart thing, this leads to massive networks with an enormous number of nodes. The extent of scale in IoT can be estimate from the fact that over a trillion smart IoT devices will be connected to the internet by 2022 [3] while by the end of 2021 only 0.06% of all devices that could potentially be connected to the internet would actually be connected [4].

Industry refers to part of the economy that deals with production and manufacture, and processing and manufacture of goods for end users or for consumption by other businesses. IoT has immense disruptive potential in all industries, especially in heavy slow moving industries such as iron and steel. Industry 4.0 refers to the rapidly automating industries leveraging IoT and creating truly connected factories, hailing it as the fourth industrial revolution [5]. Connected industries can have several advantages over conventional approaches such lower risk to employees working with heavy machinery, and data driven decision making process [6]. Several governments have taken special steps to promote IoT in industry with long term goals for adoption and sustainability. China and Germany are leading the adoption of connected industry and using it to push for sustainable industry standards and practises [7].

There has been extensive research on cyber-physical system (CPS) for industrial applications which combine the physical factory floor to the cyber space using a network of devices and computers. These systems aim to completely automate the production line and make industry technology focused. They make use of several custom sensors and actuators, microcontrollers and servers connected together in a large setup. Though there have been great developments in the field of industry related CPS, the overall domain of industry is massive and there room for further development. CPSs are custom built for certain machinery and applications and any changes require further development. This development intensive automation has been a major hindrance in a more rapid adaption of IoT in industry [8–10].

The massive amounts of data generated by IoT devices need specialised systems for processing, thus big data [11] systems have been gaining traction as the back end of IoT applications for data processing [12]. Due to the large scale of the data, cloud [13] based architecture has been followed allowing for processing industrial IoT data. This allows for a lower capital investment reducing the initial cost of adapting IoT onto the factory floor. It also provides elasticity for easy scaling and thus makes the system robust and fault tolerant [14]. Moving all data processing to the cloud posed new sets of problems including latency and data ownership. The problem of data ownership has been attacked by using detailed and well defines service level agreements (SLAs) which clearly delineate component ownership, responsibilities and demarcate jurisdiction [15,16]. Latency is an issue for on cloud based models as network limitations and bottlenecks plague the internet infrastructure causing severe delay in uploading such massive amounts of data to the cloud. Adding heavy security algorithms to IoT devices with minimal processing power further slows down the pipe line dealing a severe blow to real time analysis of data [17].

Fog computing [18], a new dimension in distributed computing has shown promising results in eliminating the shortcomings of the cloud computing model. It aims to bring the processing closer to the edge and thus reduce latency and reduce security gaps. Fog based architecture can increase the capital investment on edge devices with greater compute power but fog computing has been shown to have lower latency due to lesser amount of data being transferred and these computationally strong edge devices can provide proper security for communication with the cloud [19]. A major advantage of fog computing is that allows usage of extant big data software and systems with minimal or no changes; it extends the common principle of distributed computing outside the data centre right to the edge of the network [20]. Big data analysis makes use of specially designed frameworks to enable distributed storage and analysis. Hadoop Distributed File System (HDFS) allows distributed storage of contiguous data over multiple physically discrete datanodes with a central regulating and controlling namenodes. Hadoop MapReduce (MR) is a analysis tool that runs over data across multiple nodes and provides consistent results. Spark is a tool for distributed in memory processing and is generally used for high speed data processing. It has a central master node and distributed worker nodes. Both Spark and Hadoop have been designed for batch analysis and are not directly suitable for real time analysis of streams of data. Streaming Spark is used to collect streamed data and make small batches of them for processing by Spark to provide almost real time processing. Kafka and Flume are tools for receiving data from a streaming source and providing blocks of data to a sink such as HDFS. Thus there are a plethora of big data analysis tools that can be applied for analysis of the massive amount of data generated by smart factories.

We propose an integrated IoT and analysis system with a flexible fog-cloud hybrid back end. The system can have varying degrees of edge and cloud computing as chosen by the user on basis of budget and application. The system connects micro-controllers such as Arduino Uno and NodeMCU directly to the edge node and real time analysis and insights. It provides a web application with a dashboard for viewing insights and remotely controlling all aspects of the factory over the public internet connected using Virtual Private Network (VPN).

2 Related Work

There is extensive literature detailing the use of cloud computing along with IoT for data analysis. Research shows the efficacy and veracity of state of the art IoT systems in smart cities, healthcare and agricultural applications using cloud based back end. The literature also discusses the shortcomings of the system and develops on the promising technological paradigm of fog computing. In [21] an IoT connected cloud based big data system has been proposed for smart buildings. The system makes use of Cloudera's data platform and uses Python scripts for transferring data to the cloud. On the cloud Apache Flume receives the stream and writes it a HDFS cluster deployed on the cloud and uses a Spark cluster for processing the data. This system is not real time and thus does not consider latency issues. A specialised CPS has been proposed for industry applications of IoT in [22]. This system provides for a novel communication protocol stack and algorithms for big data analysis and pattern recognition. It uses a combination of NoSQL databases and HDFS for storage of data and a fuzzy c-means clustering algorithm has been applied on the data.

A novel conceptual design has been proposed for a IoT, big data and semantic web application in [23]. The system has a distinct layered architecture and raw data from the sensors are converted to semantic data after being acquired. Features and samples are extracted from the semantic data and these are sent to the learning model which decides on any action necessary. The system focuses on being open and inter-operable to allow multiple protocols and services to work simultaneously. A greater level of abstraction between the IoT components and the big data components has been introduced in [24]. It proposes a big data as a service framework for IoT data analysis; the IoT system uses defined APIs for communication with the multi-purpose framework while MongoDB clusters are used as datastore and analysis tool on the service side. In [25] and [26] alternate approaches to real time processing of sensor generated big data in the context of traffic management have been discussed.

Fog computing architecture have shown promising results in real time analysis and there has been extensive research on it. Though several typical big data frameworks can be directly applied to fog-cloud architectures, a focus of a lot of the literature is the optimisation of fog computing architectures for the state of the art big data frameworks. A specialised fog architecture for running Spark has been proposed in [27] which uses a multi-tiered setup with master node controlling sub master nodes which in turn control worker nodes. HDFS is used to store data across these worker nodes and the master and sub master nodes are used for time independent compute intensive tasks while the lower worker nodes are used for time aware tasks as they are closer to the network edge. A distributed data flow has been proposed in [28] which attempts to limit data flow using a step wise processing approach. The devices in the network are ordered according to compute power with compute increasing from IoT side to the cloud. A schematic is developed for decision making at the closest possible device with the required compute power and all data needed for the analysis. This reduces latency and network usage as the data does not flow any further than absolutely needed and processing can be real time. Such a setup does not allow for real time availability of all data to administrator and also limits logging without transfer overhead. It also suffers fault tolerance issues as low level hardware is not redundant and failure of any node can bring the entire system down.

Literature has also proposed a system for interaction between dedicated fogs. This allows faster information sharing and collaboration but lacks geographical optimisation and resource sharing optimisation [29]. Fog based systems specifically for Supervisory control and Data acquisition have also been proposed which aim to reduce latency and use a novel authentication process. The system focuses on setting up and deploying fog architectures for IoT networks [30]. The work in [31] concentrates on using the fog layer as a cache for data and supports some extent of processing. It can manage network bandwidth limitations and optimise compute power between log shipping and processing. In [32] a fog system specifically for medical usage has been proposed. It divides the processing across the different levels of compute and even provides abstraction for training and using machine learning models over multiple nodes and tiers. The literature has also focused on sharing tasks and resources amongst the tiers of computation. In [33] a scheduler and optimiser has been proposed which schedules tasks across the tiers of compute. It allocates tasks and schedules tasks according to priority queues, and resource and data required.

3   Our Approach

We propose a fault tolerant, highly available, flexible multi-tiered fog-cloud based framework for IoT sourced big data real time analysis for industrial applications; we also build a smart factory network for proof of concept application of the proposed framework. The system is flexible as it does not have a specific set architecture with respect to amount of compute available at the edge device and the system can be configured to be a almost completely cloud system or an almost complete edge processing system. The choice is based on cost considerations and depends on capital investment available from the user; the lowest initial cost system can even have no edge computing with only a edge gateway to connect to the server but would have greater latency compared to higher edge compute systems. The system also provides a cost model allowing sharing of edge devices across multiple users with geospatial optimisation. The edge and gateway are

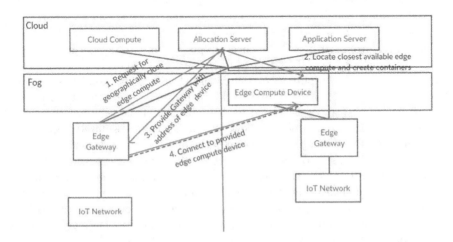

Fig. 1. Different combinations of edge and cloud compute provision

connected to the cloud or other edge devices using VPNs to leverage tunnelling protocols for secure communication over the public internet [34] (Fig. 1).

The flexibility aspect of the system allows greater freedom of cost while deploying the system, it allows the user to choose the extent of money spent on the edge compute device and thus decide the amount of compute power available at the edge. Edge devices and the cloud are compute machines that receive data from the IoT network and send commands and control signals to the IoT network. The amount of compute power available at the edge will have an impact on the latency and performance of the system. It has been observed that factories are located geographically close with demarcated industrial areas and the issue of latency could be mitigated by creating small cloud data centres in these areas or allowing sharing of edge devices. A user whose edge device is not being utilised completely can choose to allow the system to allocate processing tasks from users whose edge devices need more power. This allows the user renting out compute to earn money in lieu of their initial investment while the used using the rented compute gets lower latency than the cloud. This allocation of cross user edge compute happens is geospatially and temporally optimised for users to get the least possible latency by allocating the closest available edge device. Data ownership is ensured using suitable SLAs. The edge device is completely secure and under the control of the system, not directly of the user, this allows security along with placement of encryption and tamper proof physical systems. Thus the system is flexible about amount of edge compute and its allocation making it a truly fog computing model as it allows compute at all placed between IoT device and the cloud.

The system makes use of HDFS for the distributed store and Spark for distributed processing and analysis with an allocation server behind a dedicated VPN server. All processing and storage units are in the form of Docker containers running on a Ubuntu environment; containerisation allows greater utilisation of resources on a system and quick requisition and release of resources. The cloud has the namenode of the HDFS installation with datanode containers distributed all over the cloud and the edge. The system has custom BlockDistributionPolicy for the HDFS installation and allows for custom data allocation to datanodes, the actual allocation of containers for storage is controlled by the proposed system's allocation server which receives the write request from the edge and raises a request with the HDFS namenode while defining which container to be allocated for the write. The allocation server is also responsible for the choosing nodes for data replication and checking the health of edge devices; it has admin control of edge compute and can run diagnostics in case of heath check failure. The node closest to the edge gateway also runs a command container which receives commands, either from users or as a result of set rules from a processing nodes, and invokes necessary routines. Apache Atlas is used to achieve multi tenancy on the HDFS enabling storage of data of all multiple users on the same cluster. The allocation server is itself a distributed fault tolerant service with a master-slave architecture. All requests to the allocation server are routed to one of the slaves by the master, who also performs health check on slaves using a heartbeat. Zookeeper is used for continuity in case the master fails and for leader election. The master also has an orchestration script that enables round robin based load balancing and automatically scales the system according to the load: spawning and bringing down slaves dynamically (Fig. 2).

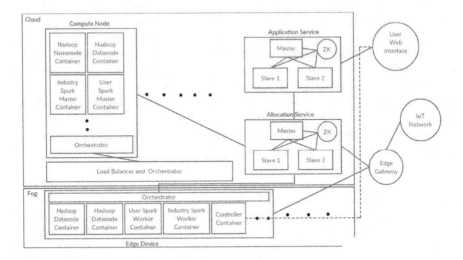

Fig. 2. The overall architecture of the system

The system also has a web application built using reactJS with a dedicated application service providing a data dashboard, the application service has an architecture similar to that of the allocation service with distributed service, fault tolerance and auto scaling. The application service indirectly supports the APIs for providing real time data and insights to users over the internet. To provide data to the user web application, the application service makes a request to the allocation server to know the location of the required data and then sends a request to that location asking for the data to be sent directly to the user, this reduces latency in providing data. On receiving a remote control command, the application server locates the destination location from the allocation server and forwards the command to its destination. The user can also change the set rules for processing of the data and make new rules and routines for the IoT network, which will be updated in real time, through the application server and control container.

Spark is used for data processing and each user has their own dedicated software defined Spark cluster with master node container on the cloud and worker container at all datanodes the user has their data on. Spark analyses data according to a set of rules defined for a particular IoT network. If the analysis yields that any action needs to be taken, Spark sends a request to the control container of that IoT network specifying which routine is to be run. The system also has an optional industry analysis tool that uses insights aggregated from all volunteering users of a given industry and provides these users industry wide insights. This is for ease of doing business users and it is ensured that their raw data never leaves their individual stores but rather inferences and insights from each user's data are aggregate to create industry wide insights. This tool is not real time, instead running a batch analysis on a daily frequency. This is achieved by deploying a larger Spark cluster incorporating all users, containers used are for this purpose as they are easy to deploy and delete. The global Spark cluster reads the data of each user in specific dedicated workers and runs transformation operations to derive insights from the data. Thereafter action operations are allowed so that raw data of any user is not shared on this cluster.

4   Evaluation and Results

We developed a proof of concept IoT network of a chemical factory with several sensors and actions. A plethora of sensors are used in chemical factories creating several combinations of scenarios and equal number of routines to handle them. We used gas, density, flow, motion and smoke sensors connected to NodeMCUs which was connected to a router, acting as the edge gateway, and continuously feeding sensor data to server. A Core 2 Duo machine with 4 GB of DDR3 RAM was used as the edge device and the cloud was deployed on AWS EC2 instances. 24 possible routines were programmed and 46 case based rules with over 3 conditions each were designed to test the system. Additionally, instructions were sent from the user web application. The system was also tested and found fault tolerant against unexpected shutdown of servers, containers and edge compute. Arena simulation software was used to simulate the deployment and working of the system for larger networks and for several users simultaneously. The simulation showed an average latency of 147.83 ms for the proposed system while completely cloud based systems achieved an average latency of 419.52 ms. Thus the system provides a considerable reduction in network latency. As shown in (Fig. 3) (L), the option of sharing edge compute across users has had a considerable impact on latency; the levels of edge compute refers to: 1 - no dedicated edge compute, 2 - minimal dedicated edge compute: not enough for average workload of the system, 3 - enough compute power for average and above workload of the system, 4 - exactly enough compute power for handling peak loads, 5 - excess compute is available even during peak workload. Figure 3 (R) shows CPU utilisation of edge devices under different conditions and proves that sharing of edge compute has allowed optimal usage of available resources.

The built network was also tested with mission critical and emergency events to test response time and latency. Fire system was activated within 370 ms of smoke sensor reporting presence of smoke to NodeMCU, thus the total turn around time of a message from micro controller to analysis tool and command back was less than 370 ms. In comparison a completely cloud based system took 610 ms for the same task.

Security is a matter of great concern in such shared resource frameworks and thus the model was tested for all known exploits in a multi user environment.

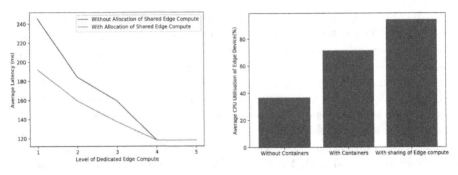

Fig. 3. Comparison of latency with level of edge computing (L); CPU Utilisation of edge devices in different setups (R)

A 4 user environment was setup with scripted continuous logging of data to mimic IoT networks and analysis rules and routines were defined. BurpSuite was used from a user account to test the security and robustness of the system and to try to gain access to the information of other users or cause the IoT network of other users to behave unexpectedly but all such attempts failed. Tamper proof cases for edge devices will ensure that shared edge compute is not physically exploited (Fig. 4).

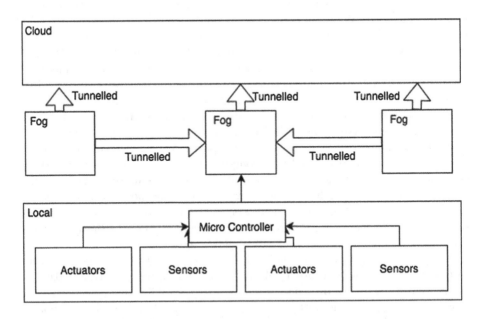

Fig. 4. Experimental system architecture with tunnelling

5 Conclusion

We have proposed a system which provide a flexible, robust and real time IoT analysis tool using extant technologies. The system has highly available and fault tolerant nodes, and uses a fog computing based model to reduce network latency compared to cloud based models. A user web interface allows users to access data and control their factories from anywhere in the world in real time. The system has been implemented using extant conventional technologies and thus allows interoperability and integration into present hardware setups. It requires minor changes in present system architectures ans thus would be cheap to adopt. It even provides a flexible deployment option to accommodate all ranges of capital investment. Thus, it is a cost effective, robust, and fast IoT analysis framework.

References

1. Lee, I., Lee, K.: The internet of things (IoT): applications, investments, and challenges for enterprises. Bus. Horizons **58**(4), 431–440 (2015)
2. Cisco Visual Networking: Cisco global cloud index: forecast and methodology, 2015–2020. white paper. Cisco Public, San Jose (2016)
3. Gendreau, A.A., Moorman, M.: Survey of intrusion detection systems towards an end to end secure internet of things. In: IEEE 4th International Conference on Future Internet of Things and Cloud (FiCloud), pp. 84–90. IEEE (2016)
4. Cisco Global Cloud Index. Forecast and methodology, 2016–2021 white paper. Updated 1 Feb 2018
5. Lasi, H., Fettke, P., Kemper, H.-G., Feld, T., Hoffmann, M.: Industry 4.0. Bus. Inf. Syst. Eng. **6**(4), 239–242 (2014)
6. Vaidya, S., Ambad, P., Bhosle, S.: Industry 4.0-a glimpse. Procedia Manuf. **20**, 233–238 (2018)
7. Xu, L.D., Xu, E.L., Li, L.: Industry 4.0: state of the art and future trends. Int. J. Prod. Res. **56**(8), 2941–2962 (2018)
8. Schütze, A., Helwig, N., Schneider, T.: Sensors 4.0-smart sensors and measurement technology enable industry 4.0. J. Sens. Sens. Syst. **7**(1), 359–371 (2018)
9. Zhong, R.Y., Xu, X., Klotz, E., Newman, S.T.: Intelligent manufacturing in the context of industry 4.0: a review. Engineering **3**(5), 616–630 (2017)
10. Jazdi, N.: Cyber physical systems in the context of industry 4.0. In: 2014 IEEE International Conference on Automation, Quality and Testing, Robotics, pp. 1–4. IEEE (2014)
11. Chen, M., Mao, S., Liu, Y.: Big data: a survey. Mobile Netw. Appl. **19**(2), 171–209 (2014)
12. Xu, L.D., Duan, L.: Big data for cyber physical systems in industry 4.0: a survey. Enterp. Inf. Syst. **13**(2), 148–169 (2019)
13. Velte, T., Velte, A., Elsenpeter, R.: Cloud Computing, A Practical Approach. McGraw-Hill, New York (2009)
14. Li, X., Li, Y., Liu, T., Qiu, J., Wang, F.: The method and tool of cost analysis for cloud computing. In: 2009 IEEE International Conference on Cloud Computing, pp. 93–100. IEEE (2009)
15. Zhang, Z.-K., et al.: IoT security: ongoing challenges and research opportunities. In: 2014 IEEE 7th International Conference on Service-oriented Computing and Applications, pp. 230–234. IEEE (2014)

16. Yang, Y., Longfei, W., Yin, G., Li, L., Zhao, H.: A survey on security and privacy issues in internet-of-things. IEEE Internet Things J. **4**(5), 1250–1258 (2017)

17. Chen, Y., Kunz, T.: Performance evaluation of IoT protocols under a constrained wireless access network. In: 2016 International Conference on Selected Topics in Mobile & Wireless Networking (MoWNeT), pp. 1–7. IEEE (2016)

18. Bonomi, F., Milito, R., Zhu, J., Addepalli, S.: Fog computing and its role in the internet of things. In: Proceedings of the First Edition of the MCC Workshop on Mobile Cloud Computing, pp. 13–16 (2012)

19. Yi, S., Li, C., Li, Q.: A survey of fog computing: concepts, applications and issues. In: Proceedings of the 2015 Workshop on Mobile Big Data, pp. 37–42 (2015)

20. Singh, S.P., Nayyar, A., Kumar, R., Sharma, A.: Fog computing: from architecture to edge computing and big data processing. J. Supercomput. **75**(4), 2070–2105 (2018). https://doi.org/10.1007/s11227-018-2701-2

21. Bashir, M.R., Gill, A.Q.: Towards an IoT big data analytics framework: smart buildings systems. In: 2016 IEEE 18th International Conference on High Performance Computing and Communications; IEEE 14th International Conference on Smart City; IEEE 2nd International Conference on Data Science and Systems (HPCC/SmartCity/DSS), pp. 1325–1332 (2016)

22. Lee, C.K.M., Yeung, C.L., Cheng, M.N.: Research on IoT based cyber physical system for industrial big data analytics. In: 2015 IEEE International Conference on Industrial Engineering and Engineering Management (IEEM), pp. 1855–1859 (2015)

23. Berat Sezer, O., Dogdu, E., Ozbayoglu, M., Onal, A.: An extended IoT framework with semantics, big data, and analytics. In: 2016 IEEE International Conference on Big Data (Big Data), pp. 1849–1856 (2016)

24. Marini, A., Bianchini, D.: Big data as a service for monitoring cyber-physical production systems. In: ECMS, pp. 579–586 (2016)

25. Shi, Q., Abdel-Aty, M.: Big data applications in real-time traffic operation and safety monitoring and improvement on urban expressways. Transp. Res. Part C Emerg. Technol. **58**, 380–394 (2015)

26. Wang, X., et al.: Optimizing content dissemination for real-time traffic management in large-scale internet of vehicle systems. IEEE Trans. Veh. Technol. **68**(2), 1093–1105 (2019)

27. Maleki, N., Loni, M., Daneshtalab, M., Conti, M., Fotouhi, H.: Sofa: a spark-oriented fog architecture. In: IECON 2019–45th Annual Conference of the IEEE Industrial Electronics Society, vol. 1, pp. 2792–2799. IEEE (2019)

28. Giang, N.K., Blackstock, M., Lea, R., Leung, V.C.: Developing IoT applications in the fog: a distributed dataflow approach. In: 2015 5th International Conference on the Internet of Things (IOT), pp. 155–162. IEEE (2015)

29. Al Ridhawi, I., Kotb, Y., Aloqaily, M., Jararweh, Y., Baker, T.: A profitable and energy-efficient cooperative fog solution for IoT services. IEEE Trans. Ind. Inf. **16**(5), 3578–3586 (2019)

30. Baker, T., et al.: A secure fog-based platform for SCADA-based IoT critical infrastructure. Softw. Pract. Exp. **50**(5), 503–518 (2020)

31. Zahmatkesh, H., Al-Turjman, F.: Fog computing for sustainable smart cities in the IoT era: caching techniques and enabling technologies-an overview. Sustain. Cities Soc. **31**, 102139 (2020)

32. Farahani, B., Barzegari, M., Aliee, F.S., Shaik, K.A.: Towards collaborative intelligent IoT ehealth: from device to fog, and cloud. Microprocess. Microsyst. **72**, 102938 (2020)

33. Sun, H., Huiqun, Yu., Fan, G., Chen, L.: Energy and time efficient task offloading and resource allocation on the generic IoT-fog-cloud architecture. Peer-to-Peer Network. Appl. **13**(2), 548–563 (2020)
34. Lodha, I., Kolur, L., Hari, K.S., Honnavalli, P.: Secure wireless internet of things communication using virtual private networks. In: Bindhu, V., Chen, J., Tavares, J.M.R.S. (eds.) International Conference on Communication, Computing and Electronics Systems. LNEE, vol. 637, pp. 735–742. Springer, Singapore (2020). https://doi.org/10.1007/978-981-15-2612-1_70

IoT Sensor Network Based Implementation for Rainfall Induced Landslide Monitoring

Joyeeta Goswami[✉] and Ashim Saha

National Institute of Technology Agartala, Jirania, India
joyeeta@yahoo.com, ashim.nita@gmail.com

Abstract. Nature is the most important part of creating this world. All the living things either humans or animals or decomposers, all are dependent on this nature. With the positive side of this nature some time we also experience the worst face of this nature with some disastrous natural phenomena. Of those phenomena one of the most threatening is Landslide. Every year due to small or large landslide events death troll reaches in thousands on average. Behind this disastrous event to happen, rainfall has a very crucial part with some other causes like earthquakes, floods, forest-fire, mining, etc. In recent days with technological development researchers can predict or identify those natural calamities before their occurrence and try to avoid the losses. In this process, many technologies were used by the developers and till now the R & D is going on with the latest technologies. And from those technologies, the latest and most adaptable is the IoT(Internet of Things). With the help of IoT, we can get information about those would be disasters well before they happen. IoT can connect nature with human beings. In this paper, we have designed a Landslide early warning and detection system using multiple sensor arrays in the IoT stack. With which we can get the landslide related information a bit earlier and can avoid the fatalities.

Keywords: IoT · Landslide detecting system · WSN

1 Introduction

Landslide or Mudslide is one of the most disastrous natural events. This event not only happens in the hilly environment but can happen in coastal cliffs, even under the water level also where it is named as submarine landslide. Landslides are promoted by various factors, they could be natural or be a manned activity. The major natural promoters of landslide are Water, seismic activity, and volcanic activity, but mostly it can be seen that rainfall becomes the main reason for promoting landslide. Other than rainfall these major promoters are related to flood, tsunami, snow-melt, Earthquake, erosion, Sub-marine landslide, etc. And the manned activities are mining, road construction, building construction on hilly areas, etc. More than 30,000 casualties across the world occurred due

© Springer Nature Switzerland AG 2020
N. Kar et al. (Eds.): ICCISIoT 2020, CCIS 1358, pp. 304–316, 2020.
https://doi.org/10.1007/978-3-030-66763-4_26

to rain-induced landslides in the last few years. There is a study conducted by researchers at UK's Sheffield University that was published in the European Geo-sciences Union journal, Natural Hazards and Earth System Sciences. As per the study, around 56,000 people died due to landslide events in the world during 2004–2016 [1]. According to United States Geological Survey(USGS) Department, the average life cost by landslides each year in the United States is 25–50 people [2]. In June 2013, the Kedarnath landslide in Uttarakhand, India in June caused by flash floods that resulted in over 5,000 deaths, was identified as the most tragic such disaster [3]. It was the worst and deadliest natural disaster of the country after the tsunami 2004. In August 2014 a series of landslides had happened in the Hiroshima area in Japan due to heavy rainfall, which came up with a lot of casualties and killed about 74 lives [4]. Another horrible rain promoted landslide occurred in the city of Mocoa, Putumayo, Colombia in April 2017. Colombia National Risk Management Unit declared 9 deaths, 70 missing, and 3 injuries [5]. The biggest landslide in Bangladesh's history happened in June 2017, stated by the head of Bangladesh's Disaster Management Department. This was also caused by heavy monsoon rain in Bangladesh, which took about 152 lives as per the official statements [6]. One of the most shocking Landslides of the year 2017, occurred in the capital city of Freetown in Sierra Leone which took about 1141 lives and left more than 3000 people homeless [7]. In the year 2020 with the pandemic situation of COVID-19, the world witnessed some major natural disasters also such as flood, volcanic eruption, forest-fire which all are the promoters of landslide and this cause a great loss of the human race.

Multiple pieces of research are done to make landslide predict and alert system using different technologies such as Analytics, Satellite Remote Sensing or RADAR, Satellite Aperture RADAR(SAR) system, LiDAR, GIS(Geographic Information System), Image Processing, ANN or CNN, IoT, etc., from which WSN, Image processing, RADAR and IoT are the main basic technologies based on which the variation of techniques are made. Among those basic technologies, IoT or Internet of Things is one of the most widely used technology for landslide detection and early warning system. IoT also combines several technologies under a common umbrella. It combines the hardware sensor data with the cloud. Through several sensor data related to environmental parameters are captured and based on the data gathered, proper measures are taken. There are several advantages of IoT technology so it can be deployed in almost all conditions ubiquitously. A comparison is made in Table 1. between those above mentioned basic technologies other than IoT that is mostly used in Landslide detection and early warning systems.

In the paper, we have presented an IoT based implementation of landslide early warning and alert system. Primarily we have used multiple sensor arrays to get information about different physical parameters. These data are then stored and processed in the cloud for warning signals. Lastly, we have discussed our future plans on how we can leverage data to make the system more efficient.

Table 1. Comparison between the Basic technologies of Landslide detection and early warning system

Technologies	Advantages	Disadvantages
WSN	Reliable system, Less power Consumption, Ability to connect in different networking protocols	Actual Deployment in remote locations is challenging, different sensors have different electrical and environmental characteristics, False trigger may also happen, as sensing are localized, multiple sensors needs to be deployed
RADAR	Deployment is easier and can be deployed to cover large area. Can be used for multiple purpose. Can provide information even if the area is covered.	RADAR systems require antenna, which requires huge power to operate. RADAR systems can not be used for specific targeting sue to wider beam range
Image Processing	Real time monitoring is more efficient. Can be used for multiple parameter detection	Deployment in remote place is challenging. Sometimes reducing the noise in the image is tough. Using high definition camera for low light imaging is costly

2 IoT Communication Protocol

As an enormous and continuously advancing network, IoT has its range of protocols also transcend. From those protocols, some are not well known but some are very usual and used extensively in every field. These protocols establish communication between devices to exchange information with each other in a secure manner. There are multiple communication channels available for both Near Field and Far Field Application. For devices that are in near proximity to each other, Bluetooth, Zigbee, and NFC is dominantly used for communication. And for far-field communication, technologies like Wi-Fi, Cellular are being used. Recently Narrowband-IoT-based communication channels are also becoming very popular due to their low bandwidth requirements. Some of the technologies used are LoRAWAN, Sigfox, Zwave, etc. Presently this LoRa gas gained a huge demand due to its use in various smart city projects. Researches show that [12] for Smart Cities, using LoRa the scalability of the network can be significantly improved to get around 95% of packet success rate for serving more than 15000 nodes. The most popular communication technologies or protocols are described in the following table in Table.2.

3 Literature Survey

As nature plays a big role in human life, people always need to stay concerned about it. The geologist as well as other scientists and researchers are always

Table 2. IoT Communication mediums comparison.

Technology	Data rate	Range	Power use	Application
GPRS/HSDPA [8,9]	*Upto 10 Mbps*	Long Range	High	Cellular/Remote Sensing
LTE [8,9]	*Upto 20 Mbps*	Long Range	High	Cellular/Remote Sensing
Wi-Fi [9,10]	*Upto 54 Mbps*	300ft	High	Home Automation/Remote Device Control
BLE(Blutooth Low Energy) [8]	*Upto 3 Mbps*	300ft	Low	Home Automation/Wearables Smartphone Control/Automotive
ZigBee [8,11]	*Upto 250 kbps*	Upto 2kms Los	Low	Home Automation/Mesh Network/Manufacturing/Traffic Control systems
Sigfox [8–10]	Upto 1 Kbps	Long Range	Moderate	Remote Sensing/Smart City
LoRA [9,12]	Upto 50 Kbps	Upto 4 Kms LoS	Moderate	Remote Sensing/Smart City/Industrial

trying to analyze or predict natural calamities like landslides, as early as possible, and to reduce the losses caused by them. Different people are trying their way, by finding different problems behind landslides and floods. In the survey done by G.Mei et al. [13], it has been shown that geo-hazards like landslide, debris-flow, rockfall is mostly monitored by real-time video monitoring systems. But the use of this technology has some limitations like insufficient area and data coverage, inadequate automation, problematic data transmission, maintenance, etc. On the other hand, IoT can solve those mentioned problems without being affected by the weather, coverage area, etc., even can automation is also very easy-going. IoT used the sensors to collect the data which are of very low cost and less vulnerable to weather, easily transmit the data using the cloud, and also use AI to predict the upcoming landslide events. The authors [13] also describe different types of IoT based systems like monitoring of ground displacement, rainfall, wireless accelerometer for debris flow, Micro Electro Mechanical Systems (MEMS) based systems, WSN based systems, and many more. After experiencing the dark side of landslide locally, the researchers of a university in the southern part of India has made a landslide warning system analyzing heavy rainfall and other soil features using wireless sensor network(WSN) and signal processing [14–16]. They experimented and deployed their model in a practical field. In this model, they have implemented the hardware model using geophones, strain gauges, transducers, and other various sensors. After collecting the data of these sensors using WSN they analyzed them with the help of some algorithms [16] based on the time delay inherent in the transmission of waves via the surface of the earth and was able to issue a warning about landslide from them [14,15]. A big part of researchers thinking by means of image processing with their unique techniques. Some researchers take the satellite images to identify the landslide-prone area by measuring the soil sedimentation [17], some made probabilistic topic model (MedLDA-maximum entropy discrimination latent Dirichlet allocation), for landslide detection with satellite images [18], some studied rainfall promoted landslide by satellite images [19]. Z.Y.Lv et al. [20] taken the bi-temporal images to apply some analytical methods for finding the error, ground-truth making, etc. then applied some image differencing method, multi-thresholds method, and made the final binary change image to detect the landslide. All these Image processing based processes mainly require the real-time images of the affected or suspected area either using high-definition cameras or with the help of satellite images both of which have a huge number of complications. Favorably IoT makes it easier, presently Image processing has been updated with IoT by using video cameras. Real-time pictures have been taken from the cameras by virtue of IoT and after applying some algorithm the warning of the landslide can be produced and the message can be transferred through the internet to the android users or to any other source [21]. Some IoT based works are there where authors used multiple sensors for data collection. C.D.Femandez et al. [22] rain gauge and accelerometer are used for data collection and GSM is used for data transmission. With the real-time collected data, a threshold is set which gives a warning about the upcoming disaster. Another similar energy-efficient IoT-based Early Landslide Detection model is proposed by R. Dhanagopal et al. [23] where a combination of vibration and rain sensor is used to collect the data, then those data are transmitted and stored using the cloud and an early warning alert is produced. The various types of Radar-based monitoring systems using IoT stack [24–26] are also used in the landslide detection process. Some researchers thought to make a detecting system of landslide-prone areas and to produce an early warning system by using Google API [27]. Some Telemetry-based landslide detecting systems are also there which included Network System, Host System, Cloud System, and together they provide the landslide detection system [28]. Some researchers are thinking about the residual networks based on Convolutional Neural Networks(CNN), using some spectral data and topographical variables [29]. Though different researchers are using different technologies but at some point, those are being coupled with IoT and making the process more effortless.

4   System Design

The total system comprises a sensor network, a host microcontroller, and a cloud server. The sensor network is used to get information regarding the different physical parameters repeatedly. The information is then sent to the Host microcontroller to process and then sent to the cloud. The cloud is used to process all information and store data. The cloud server is also to generate trigger periodically if something is out of the threshold level. In the future, we will add some AI capabilities to make some automated decisions based on real-time data. The cloud server curates data from distributed nodes and saves in a common database. A proper mechanism is used to avoid data redundancy in the cloud.

4.1 Sensor Network

The system comprises multiple sensors and microcontrollers. To minimize the chances of false triggers Different sensors were used to measure different physical parameters like Water level, Rain Fall, Soil Moisture, and Soil displacement. To measure the water level we have used Water Level Depth Detection Sensor, for rainfall we have used Raindrops Detection Sensor Module, for soil moisture we have used Capacitive Soil Moisture Sensor V2.0, and for displacement we have used the MMA7361 sensor. The sensor network is connected to an Arduino based host microcontroller to process the data in runtime. All the sensors are synced to send real-time data information to the host microcontroller. The host microcontroller is connected to the cloud server to send the data to the server where the server processes the information and generates the trigger.

Typically, rainfall is the most common reason for the landslide. That is why it is very crucial to sense the rainfall and volume of rainfall. We have used two different sensors for this issue. One sensor is used to detect the rainfall and the other is used to measure the increased water level. Typically, the water level sensor is based on a parallel-plate capacitor submerged in water. When the water level changes the capacitance of the plate also changes which leads to different readings of the sensor. The water level sensor is used to check the rainfall quantity and intensity and to check if the level is increased beyond a set threshold level. Any abrupt change or a sudden increase in the water level is a crucial parameter in the landslide early detection system. The water level sensor is used to measure the water level of a particular place and based on that a trigger is sent to the cloud.

Although rainfall is the main cause of most of the landslides, it can also occur due to other reasons like earthquakes, stream erosion, changes in groundwater level, etc. In such scenarios, early prediction of landslides is not possible in most cases. Using a water level sensor constant monitoring of the water level is possible but in most cases, the change is so slow-going process that it is not prudent to generate a trigger mechanism for this. For such cases we have only opted for constant monitoring of the parameter and the data is sent to the server via the host microcontroller.

The soil moisture is also an important parameter to monitor. Any abrupt change in soil moisture levels is often an early warning of the landslide. But the chances of a false trigger are also possible in these cases. So instead of relying on only one moisture sensor, we have used an array of sensors placed over a particular area. All the sensor data is fed to the host microcontroller which then processes the sensor information and sends it to the cloud. At the time of setup, multiple experimentations were carried out to calculate the threshold level of the moisture level. If the threshold level is crossed, then a trigger mechanism is raised. To raise the trigger mechanism few of the sensor values are compared in the location to avoid the chance of false triggers. The sensors are connected to the Host Microcontroller via I/O pins. These sensors are analog, so they are connected to Analog to Digital Converter (ADC). The ADC converts the analog sensor value to digital levels, and it is fed to the host microcontroller for further processing.

The displacement sensor is an important sensor for landslide detection. Any sudden movement in the field can be detected using a displacement sensor. This sensor can calculate the displacement in 3 coordinates. This sensor is also an analog sensor and the sensors are extremely sensitive to change in parameters. These sensor data are first converted to digital then mapped to a standard range to be able to handle the data more prudently. Multiple sensors are placed in a place to get real-time information about the location. The value from the sensor array is also used to eliminate the chance of a false trigger.

This array of the sensor network is used to get information regarding multiple parameters in the location. The multi-sensor system is very prudent to give more information about the situations compared to the single sensor arrangements. Also, this system is useful to minimize the chance of false triggers along with constant monitoring. Multi-sensor data is also especially useful to determine or predict the chances of the landslide in real-time.

This sensor network is connected to a Host microcontroller via I/O Lines. All the sensors are analog sensors, so they are connected to the microcontroller via ADC. The Host microcontroller just receives the information from the sensor network and passes them to the cloud server.

4.2 Microcontroller Board

For the experimentation, Raspberry Pi was used. Unlike Arduino, which is a microcontroller board, Raspberry Pi is a Single Board Computer. Raspberry Pi was selected over Arduino for Two major reasons. First, Raspberry Pi runs 32-bit Linux while most Arduino has an 8-bit controller only. Second, using Raspberry Pi, we can store data locally and see them easily just by connecting a monitor. In Arduino storing and retrieving data is a cumbersome process. Lastly, we can directly connect the Internet dongle and ethernet on Raspberry Pi and use the internet, wherein Arduino we must connect every sensor manually and configure them. This process is helpful for Rapid prototyping and deployment in remote nodes.

We have used Raspberry Pi model 3 for our testing and development. Using I/O Headers all sensors are connected to the Raspberry Pi. Internet Modem is connected via the USB Port to connect the Pi with the cloud server. There are no other arrangements than that for the microcontroller. All the sensors are interfaced using external ADC.

4.3 Cloud Server

The cloud server is used to aggregate and store the data received from the different sensor networks. The back-end server is based on Amazon Web Services (AWS) IoT Hub. AWS IoT Hub provides inbuilt capabilities to manage thousands of IoT Nodes on a scale. The cloud server also provides an inbuilt database to store the sensor information. AWS IoT Core provides End to End encryption to securely transfer data between the sensor data and cloud server. In a typical web-server, all tools and security need to be manually set up and configure. Although AWS IoT Code provides self-security policies, a manual setup can also be done. AWS IoT Core is also designed to handle low bandwidth and intermittent connections. AWS also provides inbuilt MQTT capabilities. Using MQTT small amount of data is securely transferred to the server without any loss of data. We have used AWS IoT Core as the base and integrated a few other services also. As the AWS IoT Core works only on secured channels, we have used a Public-Private Key authentication mechanism to connect with the AWS IoT Core. AWS also provides a Software Development Kit (SDK) for python. The Python SDK is installed in the Raspberry Pi for seamless communication with AWS IoT Core. The connection also requires a Device certificate, certificate private key, and CA certificate to securely connect to the cloud service. This ensures end to end encryption between the sensor nodes and the cloud. Using different registry it is very simple to manage a large number of devices at scale.

The received sensor data are stored in AWS Dynamo DB NoSQL Database as a Key-Value pair with a timestamp. This Data is then analyzed in real-time to check for any anomaly. To generate an automated trigger in case of an anomaly, the AWS Lambda function is used. Using serverless computing infrastructure, we rapidly reduced the time and infrastructure cost without compromising on scalability and security issues. NoSQL databases are easily scalable. The data from the sensor nodes will be huge in quantity. To easily store the sensor data as key-value JSON pair NoSQL database is chosen. Sensor values coming to the AWS server is showing in Fig. 1.

4.4   Algorithm

For the alarm trigger, all the sensor information is simultaneously used. Based on the different sensor values the algorithm is made. All sensors are assigned some priority levels. Displacement Sensor has the highest priority. If there is an abrupt change in the displacement sensor the highest alarming trigger is generated. To eliminate the chance of false trigger value of multiple sensors are checked. Any abrupt changes are checked for an anomaly. The value of other sensors is also checked parallelly. If the water level sensor is showing higher water levels, then a Warning trigger is generated. If the water level is continuously getting increased or there is any other anomaly such as high-water moisture levels or displacement sensors etc. a high alert trigger is generated. In all cases, multiple sensor arrays are used to avoid the chances of a false trigger. The flowchart of the algorithm is given below. The displacement sensor is denoted as dispSens, the soil moisture sensor is denoted as soilSens and the water level sensor is denoted as waterSens. The whole flow diagram is shown in the Fig. 2.

4.5   Communication

In remote places, internet connectivity is not at all reliable. Issues of frequent loss of network are predominant. If internet connectivity is not there, chances of

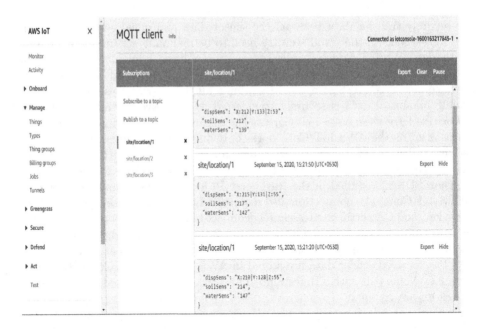

Fig. 1. Sensor values coming to AWS MQTT.

data loss is a significant issue. To handle this issue, message queuing techniques are often used in IoT related applications. For this scope of work, we have used Message Queuing Telemetry Transport widely known as MQTT. MQTT is a very lightweight but efficient standard for messaging. MQTT is very much efficient in low bandwidth conditions. MQTT is based on the publish/subscribe protocol and encrypts all messages using TLS.

All host microcontrollers are connected to different MQTT Channels on the AWS IoT Core. All nodes publish the sensor data on different pre-set Topics. This topic is based on the registry of the host microcontroller. The alert generation system is subscribed to different channels of different microcontrollers. Using the MQTT topics the system identifies the different microcontrollers in a different locality. All the sensor data are sent in JSON format from the raspberry pi devices and stored in Key-Value Pair in the NoSQL database. The whole communication process is shown in Fig. 3.

5   Future Work

This implementation is just a proof of concept testing for IoT based landslide monitoring. This system will be used for getting data from the actual field. For this implementation, we have taken a fixed threshold value for the sensor anomaly detection. However, in real-time, these threshold values will be different for different locations. With the data generated from the different locations, we will analyze and incorporate variable threshold limits for different locations. Also,

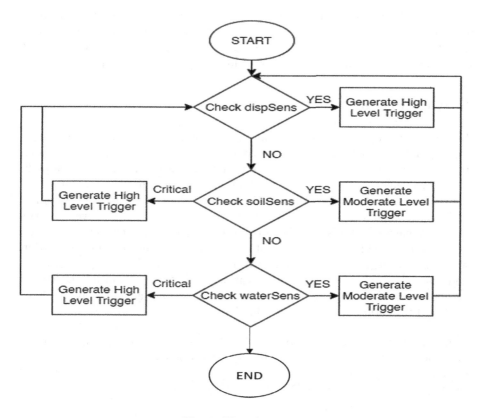

Fig. 2. Flow diagram.

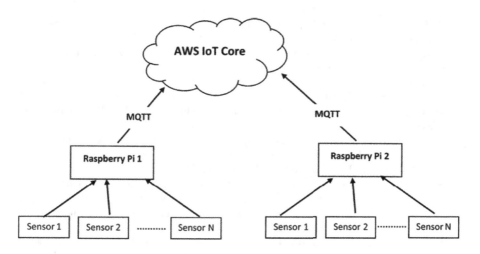

Fig. 3. Communication process.

currently, all the processing happens on the cloud. If the network failure happens for a long time, then the system will not be reliable. In our future developments, we will incorporate local offline processing of the data. To do this the data that is being generated from the current system will be extremely helpful.

6   Conclusion

In this paper, we have implemented an IoT sensor network-based landslide monitoring and detection system promoted by rainfall for hilly regions. The system includes a wireless sensor network that continuously monitors the rainfall, ground movement, soil moisture, etc., and data collected by those sensor arrays are then stored in the cloud server. Based on those data the ultimate decision has been taken using a novel algorithm about the upcoming landslide event. In the Paper we have briefly discussed various basic technologies used in the landslide detection system and the communication mediums used in IoT Implementation with their comparative study. Then we reviewed some of the implementation and researches performed on the application of IoT in the Landslide Detection system. Then the whole system design is described in detail. Lastly, we have discussed the future objective of the implemented idea.

Acknowledgement. This research work has been carried out in National Institute of Technology, Agartala, India sponsored by Department of Science & Technology (DST), Govt. of India under Interdisciplinary Cyber Physical System (ICPS) Program (Ref No: DST/ICPS/Cluster/IoT/2018/General Dated: 26.02.2019).

References

1. Froude, M.J., Petley, D.N.: Global fatal landslide occurrence from 2004 to 2016. https://www.nat-hazards-earth-syst-sci.net/18/2161/2018/nhess-18-2161-2018.pdf. Accessed 23 Aug 2018
2. https://www.usgs.gov/faqs/how-many-deaths-result-landslides-each-year?qt-newssscienceproducts=0#qt-newsscienceproducts
3. Remembering 2013 Uttarakhand Floods. https://www.downtoearth.org.in/coverage/natural-disasters/heavens-rage-41497. Accessed 22 June 2016
4. 2014 Hiroshima Landslides. https://en.wikipedia.org/wiki/2014Hiroshimalandslides
5. 2017 Mocoa landslide. https://en.wikipedia.org/wiki/2017Mocoalandslide
6. Bangladesh landslide toll reaches 152. https://www.financialexpress.com/world-news/bangladesh-landslide-toll-reaches-152/718595/
7. Sierra Leone mudslides. https://en.wikipedia.org/wiki/2017SierraLeonemudslides
8. 11 Internet of Things (IoT) Protocols You Need to Know About. https://www.rs-online.com/designspark/eleven-internet-of-things-iot-protocols-you-need-to-know-about. Accessed 20 Apr 2015
9. Hasan, M.: Top 15 Standard IoT Protocols That You Must Know About. https://www.ubuntupit.com/top-15-standard-iot-protocols-that-you-must-know-about/

10. Sakovich, N.: Internet of Things (IoT) Protocols and Connectivity Options: An Overview. https://www.sam-solutions.com/blog/internet-of-things-iot-protocols-and-connectivity-options-an-overview/. Accessed 22 Aug 2018
11. Rouse, M.: Zigbee. https://internetofthingsagenda.techtarget.com/defin-ition/ZigBee. Accessed June 2017
12. Magrin, D., Centenaro, M., Vangelista, L.: Performance evaluation of LoRa networks in a smart city scenario. In 2017 IEEE International Conference on Communications (ICC), pp. 1–7. IEEE, May 2017
13. Mei, G., Xu, N., Qin, J., Wang, B., Qi, P.: A survey of Internet of Things (IoT) for geo-hazards prevention: applications, technologies, and challenges. IEEE Internet Things J. **00**(0) (2020)
14. Kunnath, A.T., Ramesh, M.V., Selvan, V.: Signal processing for wireless geophone network to detect landslides. In: 2010 International Conference on Computer Applications and Industrial Electronics (ICCAIE 2010), 5–7 December 2010, Kuala Lumpur, Malaysia. https://doi.org/10.1109/ICCAIE.2010.5735049
15. Ramesh, M.V.: Real-time wireless sensor network for landslide detection. In: 2009 Third International Conference on Sensor Technologies and Applications (2009). https://doi.org/10.1109/SENSORCOMM.2009.67
16. Kunnath, A.T., Ramesh, M.V.: Wireless Geophone Network for remote monitoring and detection of landslides. In: 2011 International Conference on Communications and Signal Processing (2011. https://doi.org/10.1109/ICCSP.2011.5739283
17. Lira, C., et al.: Automatic detection of landslide features with remote sensing techniques: application to Madeira island. In: 2011 IEEE International Geoscience and Remote Sensing Symposium (2011). https://doi.org/10.1109/IGARSS.2011.6049520
18. He, S., Tang, H., Li, J., Tang, Z., Li, S.: Landslide detection with two satellite images of different spatial resolutions in a probabilistic topic model. In: 2015 IEEE International Geoscience and Remote Sensing Symposium (IGARSS) (2015). https://doi.org/10.1109/IGARSS.2015.7325787
19. Beyene, F., Busch, W., Knospe, S., Ayalew, L.: Heavy rainfall-induced landslide detection from very high resolution multi-aspect TerraSAR-X images in Dessie, Ethiopia. In: 2012 IEEE International Geoscience and Remote Sensing Symposium (2012). https://doi.org/10.1109/IGARSS.2012.6350791
20. Lv, Z.Y., Shi, W., Zhang, X., Benediktsson, J.A.: Landslide inventory mapping from bitemporal high-resolution remote sensing images using change detection and multiscale segmentation. IEEE J. Sel. Top. Appl. Earth Obser. Remote Sens. **11**(5) (2018). https://doi.org/10.1109/JS-TARS.2018.2803784
21. Aggarwal, S., Sumakar, K.V.S., Mishra, P.K., Chaturvedi, P.: Landslide monitoring system implementing IOT using video camera. In: 2018 3rd International Conference for Convergence in Technology (I2CT) (2018). https://doi.org/10.1109/IC3IoT.2018.8668131
22. Femandez, C.D., Mendoza, K.J.A., Tiongson, A.J.S., Mendoza, M.B.: Development of microcontroller based landslide early warning system. In: 2016 IEEE Region 10 Conference (TENCON) – Proceedings of the International Conference (2016)
23. Dhanagopal, R., Muthukumar, B.: A model for low power, high speed and energy efficient early landslide detection system using IoT. Wireless Person. Commun. (2019), https://doi.org/10.1007/s11277-019-06933-7
24. Dabbiru, L.A., Aanstoos, J.V., Hasan, K., Younan, N.H., Li, W.: Landslide detection on earthen levees with X-band and L-band radar data. In: 2013 IEEE Applied Imagery Pattern Recognition Workshop (AIPR) (2013). https://doi.org/10.1109/AIPR.2013.6749306

25. Melo, S., et al.: Photonics-based dual-band radar for landslides monitoring in presence of multiple scatterers. J. Lightwave Technol. **36**(12), 2337–2343 (2018)
26. Setiadi, B., Chan, Y.K., Koo, V.C.: A ground-based synthetic aperture radar system using portable VNA for landslide monitoring. In: 2017 International Symposium on Antennas and Propagation (ISAP) (2017). https://doi.org/10.1109/ISANP.2017.8228785
27. Hartomo, K.D., Yulianto, S., Maruf, J.: Spatial model design of landslide vulnerability early detection with exponential smoothing method using Google API. In: 2017 International Conference on Soft Computing, Intelligent System and Information Technology (ICSIIT) (2017). https://doi.org/10.1109/ICSIIT.2017.37
28. Khoa, V.V., Nakano, T., Masanori, H., Takayama, S.: Detection of Landslide disaster by telemetric sensing node network system. In: 2017 11th Asian Control Conference (ASCC) Gold Coast Convention Centre, Australia 17–20 December 2017
29. Sameen, M.I., Pradhan, B.: Landslide detection using residual networks and the fusion of spectral and topographic information. IEEE Access (Early Access). https://doi.org/10.1109/ACCESS.2019.2935761

Multi Agent Based Resource Provisioning in Fog Computing

Ashish Virendra Chandak[1(✉)] and Niranjan Kumar Ray[2]

[1] Department of Information Technology,
Shri Ramdeobaba College of Engineering and Management,
Nagpur, Maharashtra, India
achandak.nitrkl@gmail.com
[2] School of Computer Engineering, Kalinga Institute of Industrial Technology,
Bhubaneswar, Odisha, India

Abstract. A number of IoT devices are continuously increasing day by day and these devices are delay-sensitive and require a quick response. These devices are connect-ed to a cloud environment for processing but there is latency in computation. To overcome this situation, the fog environment is kept at the edge of the IoT device layer to perform the quick computation for delay-sensitive applications. For quick computation, adequate number of resource should be available for processing of request. Resource provisioning is big challenge in fog computing and hence intelligent technique for resource provisioning is required. Here in this paper, we pro-posed an multi agent based algorithm for resource provisioning which allocate re-sources according to load. This paper consider three types of agents for resource provisioning e.g. task agent, fog agent and node agent. To evaluate the performance of proposed agent based resource provisioning we have compared it with already proposed technique of resource provisioning and simulation results demonstrates that proposed strategy minimizes makespan, average execution time and flowtime as compared to existing resource provisioning technique by Meera et al. [1].

Keywords: Fog computing · Agent · Resource provisioning

1 Introduction

Use of IoT devices in smart home, smart factory, internet of vehicles, smart office, healthcare system, military system are continuously increasing and these entities are connected to internet through IoT devices for communication. These devices contains sensors which sense the data and generating tremendous amount of data. This generated data is passed to cloud for storage and processing which is geographically distributed. This model is not useful in future and if there are billions of IoT devices generating data then it will likely to increase communication latency which may result in degradation of QoS and QoE [2]. To tackle this

© Springer Nature Switzerland AG 2020
N. Kar et al. (Eds.): ICCISIoT 2020, CCIS 1358, pp. 317–327, 2020.
https://doi.org/10.1007/978-3-030-66763-4_27

problem, an alternative solution is to bring computing resource closer to IoT devices for faster processing. This will reduce amount of data pass to cloud and consequently reduce delay of processing data. These computing resource reside between IoT devices and cloud layer. It emerges the concept of fog computing in which computing resource reside at the edge of IoT devices [3].

Resource provisioning is one of the big challenge in fog computing. Resource provisioning refers to effective management of resources for optimal usage and allocation and it determines the amount of resources required for processing of request. It influence the quality of service and quality of experience in IoT environment. Improper resource provisioning will lead to degradation of QoS and QoE. Hence an intelligent resource provisioning technique is required to improve quality of service and quality of experience in fog computing. To cope with this issue, a multi agent based resource provisioning technique is proposed for management of resources which identify load on fog nodes and allocation of resource is done according to load. with the help of various agents viz. fog agent, task agent and node agent. The proposed strategy list of overloaded, underloaded and balance node list based on load of fog node and it is compared with existing technique of resource provisioning by Meera et al. [1] on the basis of makespan, flowtime and average execution time.

The principle contribution of this paper are as follows:

- We proposed an architecture for agent based resource provisioning which uses multiple agent managing resource allocation.
- We proposed an algorithm in which fog nodes are categorize as overloaded, underloaded and balance according to CPU utilization.
- We compared proposed resource provisioning with existing technique on the basis of makespan, flowtime and average execution time.

The rest of the paper is organized as follows.

Related work is describe in Sect. 2 while architecture for fog computing proposed in Sect. 3. Agent based Model proposed in Sect. 4. Section 5 describe proposed algorithm while performance analysis of proposed algorithm carried out in Sect. 6. Section 7 conclude the paper.

2   Related Work

Numerous articles has been published related to resource provisioning in different contexts. They are as follows.

[1] proposed dynamic resource provisioning using agent based strategy in which tasks are divided into two categories viz. prime tasks (high cost function) and normal tasks. Prime tasks are assigned to fog nodes while normal tasks are assigned to cloud using mobile agent. [5] proposed agent based resource provisioning in which agent uses machine learning technique. When multiple agents are used for resource provisioning then there may be synchronization problem but to overcome this situation centralized scheduling technique is used. [6,7] proposed a multi agent resource allocation technique in cloud computing. [1] an

agent based resource monitoring in cloud computing in which agent continuously monitor the performance of virtual machine using CPU and memory utilization parameters. Resources are allocated based on CPU and memory utilization. [8] proposed resource allocation technique for fog computing which uses Lyapunov optimization technique for resource allocation to minimize latency.

[9] proposed resource provisioning for IoT devices in fog computing environment using the concept of fog colonies. Fog colonies are made up to micro data centers which consist of fog cells. Fog colonies cooperatively does task execution. The proposed approach minimize delay and maximizes resource utilization. Santos et al. [10] proposed resource discovery method for IoT services. For resource it uses discovery a Distributed Hash Table (DHT) in which nodes are not arranged in any hierarchy. DHTs provide a important information for resource provisioning such as availability of RAM and disk.

Singh et al. [11] proposed a QoS aware resource provisioning in cloud computing in which workload on resources categorize according to common pattern and resource provisioning is done for cloud workload. Proposed technique reduces queuing time, over and under utilization of resources. Proposed technique reduces execution time and execution cost of cloud workloads thus lead to effective resource scheduling.

3   Proposed Fog Computing Architecture

In this section, agent based fog computing architecture has been presented which is suitable to run proposed algorithm and it is divided into three layer IoT layer, fog layer and cloud layer (Fig. 1).

- IoT Layer (Layer 1): This layer contains IoT devices viz. PDA, mobile, laptops etc. These devices contains sensor and data is generated by these sensor by sensing environment. This data has been pass to upper layer i.e. at fog layer for processing. Data generated from this layer has been passed to upper layer for processing to get the strategic information. Detailed analysis of generated data is done at cloud layer. This generate data can contain time sensitive information and thus it need to be process at the fog layer for immediate action. It contains task agent which collect incoming task and forward it fog agent for processing.
- Fog Layer (Layer 2): Data generated from IoT devices is processed in this layer. It contains fog nodes which processed incoming data and less important data can be skipped. This layer contains fog agent and node for processing of tasks. Task agent from IoT layer forward collected tasks to fog agent. Every fog node has node agent is associated with it. Node agent collect CPU and memory utilization of fog node and forward it to fog agent. Fog agent collect CPU and memory utilization from node agent and prepare list of overloaded, underloaded and balance node list. Fog agent forward tasks according to load on fog nodes. Following conditions can change load on fog nodes.

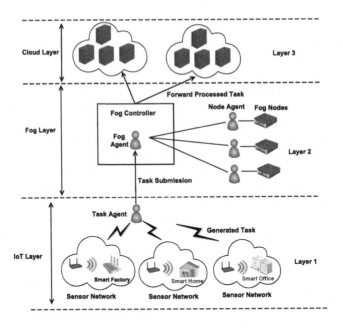

Fig. 1. Fog Computing Architecture

- New task is arrived
- Task execution is completed.
- Existing fog node is removed.
- Failure of fog node
- The node become overloaded
- Cloud Layer (Layer 3): This layer contains storage and computation server and data from fog layer has been further processed and stored in this layer. Detail analysis of data done in this layer. It store data permanently and periodically.

3.1   Notations and Definitions

In this section, we presented notations and definitions use throughout the paper.

Definition 1. Completion Time: It is defined as sum of start time and execution time of task (Table 1).

$$CT_i = S_i + E_i \tag{1}$$

Definition 2. Flowtime: Flow time is sum of completion time of task [12].

$$Flowtime = \sum_{n=1}^{n} CT_i \tag{2}$$

Table 1. Notations

Notation	Meaning
T	Set of Task
C_i	Completion time of ith task
f_i	i^{th} fog node
ST_i	Starting time of ith task
ET_i	Expected execution time of ith task
T	Total number of task
H(CPU)	Highest threshold value of CPU utilization
L(CPU)	Lowest threshold value of CPU utilization

Definition 3. Average Execution Time: It is described as completion time of all tasks divided by number of task [13].

$$AvgExecutionTime = \sum_{i=1}^{n} CT_i/T \tag{3}$$

Definition 4. Makespan: It is computed as the maximum of completion time(CT) [14].

$$Makespan = max(CT_i) \tag{4}$$

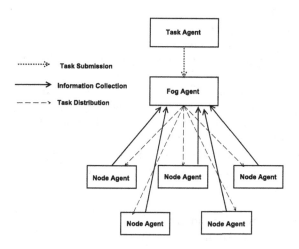

Fig. 2. Agent Based Model in Fog Computing

4   Proposed Agent Based Model

this study, we designed three types of agents viz. task agent, node agent and fog agent. They cooperate with each other for effective resource provisioning and they have their own rules. The proposed agent based resource provisioning algorithm is intended to take advantage of the agent characteristic to create a self-adaptive and self-sustaining load balancing system. It consists of three types of agents, task agent, fog agent and node agent. Task agent collect tasks and forward it to fog agent. Fog agent collect load information of each fog node through node agent and create overloaded, underloaded and balance node list based upon load information and to forward task according to load. Interaction between three agent shown in Fig. 2 and detail function of each agent is as follows.

Level 0: Task Agent. Task agent is located at the top of hierarchy. It perform following functions.

- To collect tasks which are generated by IoT devices.
- To forward tasks to fog agent for further processing.

Level 1:Fog Agent. Fog agent is located at level 1. It perform following functions.

- To receive tasks from task agent.
- Sending tasks to node agents.
- To collect and maintain CPU and memory utilization of each fog node from each node agent.
- To dispatch tasks to fog nodes.
- To take task dispatch decisions.
- To maintain overloaded, underloaded and balance node lists. These list are created under following criteria.
    - Overloaded Node List: The fog node will be added in this list if CPU utilization value is above H(CPU) or memory utilization is above 80
    - Underloaded Node List: The fog node will be added in this list if CPU utilization value is below L(CPU).
    - Balance Node List: If the fog node is not in overloaded list or not in underloaded state. These node have more load as compare to underloaded node and less loaded than overloaded node.

Level 2: Node Agent: Each fog node have node agent associated with it and which is located at bottom of hierarchy. The functions of node agent is as follows.

- To maintain CPU and memory utilization of fog node.
- To receive task from fog node.
- To provide continuous updates about CPU and memory utilization of fog node.
- Send result of task execution to fog agent.

5   Proposed Algorithm

In this section, we present a novel agent based solutions for resource provisioning. The proposed solution contains two pseudo codes. The algorithm for fog agent is presented in Algorithm 1. Fog agent assign tasks to fog nodes which are collected at instant δt. Line 1–4 represents fog agent collect task which is to be executed, line 6–7 represents CPU and memory utilization which is collected from fog nodes. Line 10–19 classifies fog nodes into overload, underload and balance node category. Line 21–22 sort the nodes in overload and underload category by CPU utilization. Lin 27–28 represents logic for forwarding task to cloud if task execution in not possible on fog nodes. Logic for updating overloaded, underloaded and balance node list written on line 31. All described steps are repeated in lines 3–32 until all tasks are allocated to fog nodes.

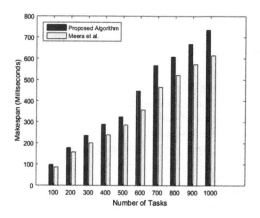

Fig. 3. Makespan comparison

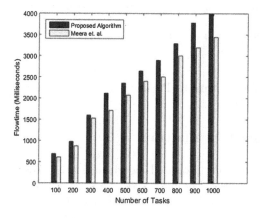

Fig. 4. Flowtime comparison

Input: A set of tasks and Nodes
Output: Completion Time of Tasks
1. allocated = FALSE
2. Task agent collect all tasks T up to time δt
3. Submit collected tasks to fog agent.
4. **For** all submitted task T in the queue **do**
5. **While** there are no unscheduled task
6. Send load information from each node agent to fog agent.
7. Calculate CPU Utilization of each fog node
8. Categorize the node into Overloaded, underloaded and balance node.
9. over-node-list=0; under-node-list=0;balan-node-list=0;
10. **For** every fog node N do
11. **If** (Node(CPU-U) $\geq$ H(CPU)) then
12. add node in over-node-list.
13. **Else If** (Node(CPU-U) $\leq$ L(CPU)) then
14. add node in under-node-list.
15. **Else**
16. add node in balan-node-list
17. **End If**
18. **End If**
19. **End For**
20. **while**(under-node-list $\neq \phi$)
21. Sort over-node-list in descending order according to CPU utilization
22. Sort under-node-list in ascending order according to CPU utilization
23. **If** node accommodate task then
24. Assign the tasks to the node of under-node-list by FCFS Algorithm
25. allocated = TRUE
26. Update load on node
27. **Else If** allocated == FALSE
28. Forward task to cloud for computation
29. **End If**
30. **End If**
31. Update under-node-list, over-load-list and balan-node-list
32. **End While**
33. repeat steps 2) to 32) until all task are mapped
34. **End While**
35. **End For**

Algorithm 1: Pseudo code for Fog Agent

6   Experimental Evaluation

We have implemented our proposed algorithm in the iFogSim environment to analyze the effectiveness of the proposed algorithm which is configured on Intel Machine. The experimental setting consists of ten fog nodes for existing and proposed algorithms. To analyze the effectiveness, we have to change the number of tasks from 100 to 500. The parameters used for simulation are given in Table 2. It demonstrates the evaluation set up to quantify the performance of our model.

Table 2. Simulation parameters

Model	Intel PC
Processor	2.oo GHz Intel(R) Core(TM) i3-5005U
Operating System	Windows 10
RAM	4 GB
Number of Fog Nodes	10
Task ETC	1 to 10 (Random Distribution)
Task Arrival	Poisson Distribution
RAM	512 MB
MIPS	1000
Simulation starts at	100 tasks
Simulation end at	500 tasks

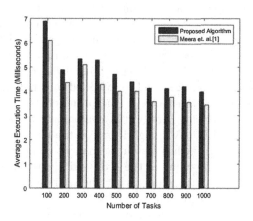

Fig. 5. Average execution time comparison

Makespan Comparison: The Makespan of tasks is calculated by the formula (4). In our simulation, makespan has been calculated for a different set of tasks after execution on fog nodes which is shown in Fig. 3. As the number of tasks increases, the makespan value also increases. The incremental value of makespan in the proposed agent based provisioning is less than existing algorithm.

Flowtime Comparison: Flowtime is defined as the sum of completion time of all tasks and it is calculated by the formula (2). Through simulation, flowtime is calculated for a different set of tasks after execution on virtual machines. As the number of tasks increases, flowtime also gets increases. From Fig. 4, by comparing the performance of algorithms, it is concluded that the proposed agent based provisioning gives less flowtime as compared to existing technique of resource provisioning by Meera et al. [1].

Average Execution Time Comparison: Here, the average execution time of the proposed agent based resource provisioning is compared with Min-Min, FCFS, and Random algorithm. This is calculated by the formula (3). Smaller the value of average execution time, better the system efficiency. We have calculated average execution time by changing a number of tasks as shown in Fig. 5. With the increase in a number of tasks, average execution time gradually increases. From the simulation, it is observed that the proposed algorithm gives lesser average execution time as compared to existing technique of resource provisioning by Meera et al. [1].

7   Conclusion

Quality of service and quality of experience is very important in fog computing environment and to improve QoS and QoE intelligent technique is required for managing resources. In this paper, a multi agent based resource provisioning technique is proposed for resource provisioning the fog computing environment. It uses three types of agent viz. fog agent, node agent and task. Task agent collect tasks, node agent collect fog node utilization and fog node collects CPU utilization of all fog nodes. This strategy, first of all, collect tasks and then categorize fog nodes into underloaded, overloaded and balance node category. In order to evaluate the performance of the proposed technique, performance analysis has been carried out. Firstly, the comparison of proposed algorithm and Random, FCFS, and Min-Min algorithms on the basis of makespan carried out. The proposed algorithm has less makespan as compared to the existing algorithm. Secondly, the flowtime of the proposed algorithm is compared with existing algorithm and it is concluded that the proposed algorithm has lesser flowtime as compared to algorithm proposed by Meera et al. [1]. Comparison on the basis of average execution time has been carried out and simulation results show that the proposed algorithm gives better average execution time as compared to existing algorithms. From the simulation experiment, it is concluded that the proposed algorithm gives better performance as compared to existing technique of resource provisioning by Meera et al. [1].

References

1. Meera, A., Swamynathan, S.: Agent based resource monitoring system in IaaS cloud environment. Procedia Technol. **10**, 200–207 (2013). First International Conference on Computational Intelligence: Modeling Techniques and Applications (CIMTA) 2013
2. Hong, C., Lee, K., Kang, M., Yoo, H.: qCon: QoS-aware network resource management for fog computing. Sensors (Switzerland) **18**(10), 3444 (2018)
3. Bonomi, F., Milito, R., Zhu, J., Addepalli, S.: Fog computing and its role in the internet of things. In: Proceedings of the First Edition of the MCC Workshop on Mobile Cloud Computing, ser. MCC 2012, pp. 13–16. Association for Computing Machinery, New York (2012)

4. Singh, S., Chana, I.: QRSF: QoS-aware resource scheduling framework in cloud computing. J. Supercomput. **71**(1), 241–292 (2014). https://doi.org/10.1007/s11227-014-1295-6

5. Prashant Sangulagi, A.S.: Agent based dynamic resource allocation in sensor cloud using fog computing. Int. J. Emerg. Technol. **34**(12), 122–128 (2019)

6. Fareh, M., Kazar, O., Femmam, M., Bourekkache, S.: An agent-based approach for resource allocation in the cloud computing environment, November 2015

7. Venticinque, S., Tasquier, L., Di Martino, B.: Agents based cloud computing interface for resource provisioning and management. In: 2012 Sixth International Conference on Complex, Intelligent, and Software Intensive Systems, pp. 249–256 (2012)

8. Abouaomar, A., Cherkaoui, S., Kobbane, A., Dambri, O.A.: A resources representation for resource allocation in fog computing networks. In: IEEE Global Communications Conference (GLOBECOM) 2019, pp. 1–6 (2019)

9. Skarlat, O., Schulte, S., Borkowski, M., Leitner, P.: Resource provisioning for IoT services in the fog, November 2016

10. Santos, J., Wauters, T., Volckaert, B., Turck, F.D.: Towards dynamic fog resource provisioning for smart city applications. In: 2018 14th International Conference on Network and Service Management (CNSM), pp. 290–294 (2018)

11. Singh, S., Chana, I.: Q-aware: quality of service based cloud resource provisioning. Comput. Electr. Eng. **47**, 138–160 (2015)

12. Chekuri, C., Goel, A., Khanna, S., Kumar, A.: Multi-processor scheduling to minimize flow time with resource augmentation. In: Proceedings of the Thirty-Sixth Annual ACM Symposium on Theory of Computing, ser. STOC 2004, pp. 363–372 (2004)

13. Mao, Y., Zhang, J., Letaief, K.B.: Dynamic computation offloading for mobile-edge computing with energy harvesting devices. IEEE J. Sel. Areas Commun. **34**(12), 3590–3605 (2016)

14. Raju, R., Babukarthik, R.G., Chandramohan, D., Dhavachelvan, P., Vengattaraman, T.: Minimizing the makespan using hybrid algorithm for cloud computing. In: 2013 3rd IEEE International Advance Computing Conference (IACC), pp. 957–962, February 2013

Author Index

Printed in the United States
By Bookmasters